MW01225033

K

DATE DUE

Brodart Co.   Cat. # 55 137 001   Printed in USA

Experiencing Environment and Place through Children's Literature

Nature, places and ecological themes are not simply backdrops or plot devices for the development of characters and action in children's literature. In storybooks, mythic tales and image-based texts, authors and illustrators use children's literature to represent a wide range of understandings and experiences of environments and places, including the people and other 'presences' that may be found therein.

This edited collection brings together a set of original research-based papers exploring how such literature contributes to experiences and understandings of environment and place. Drawing on a wide range of critical and international perspectives, contributors explore the specific and general ways in which children's literature provides what are arguably some of the most formative engagements that children may have with 'nature'. Chapters examine how children's literature affords a range of openings for dialogue both with and against dominant cultural texts, images, narratives and figurations of eco-cultural relations, as these relate to place, nature, identity and injustice. The collection also addresses key questions about children's literature and children's and adults' conceptions and constructions of an eco-identity, -citizenship or -responsibility, and critically discusses the various roles and challenges for an environmental education in school, at home and in the field that engages these themes.

This book was originally published as a special issue of *Environmental Education Research*.

Amy Cutter-Mackenzie is a Senior Lecturer in the Faculty of Education at Monash University, Australia. She is the Founder and Leader of the Sustainability, Environment and Education (SEE) Research Group in the Faculty. Her research interests focus on children's and teachers' thinking and experiences in environmental education. Amy is also the Editor of the *Australian Journal of Environmental Education*.

Phillip G. Payne is Associate Professor in the Faculty of Education at Monash University, Australia. He joined Monash in early 2006 as the Course Director of Sport and Outdoor Recreation and Research Leader of the Movement, Environment and Community (MEC) group. He is an international editorial board member for *Environmental Education Research, Journal of Environmental Education,* and *Australian Journal of Environmental Education.*

Alan Reid is Senior Lecturer in Education and member of the Centre for Research in Education and the Environment at the University of Bath, UK. He is the editor of *Environmental Education Research*. His research interests focus on teachers' thinking and practice in environmental education, and policy-related, methodological and philosophical issues in environmental education theory, research and practice.

Experiencing Environment and Place through Children's Literature

Edited by
**Amy Cutter-Mackenzie, Phillip G. Payne
and Alan Reid**

Routledge
Taylor & Francis Group

LONDON AND NEW YORK

First published 2011
by Routledge
2 Park Square, Milton Park, Abingdon, Oxon, OX14 4RN

Simultaneously published in the USA and Canada
by Routledge
711 Third Avenue, New York, NY 10017

Routledge is an imprint of the Taylor & Francis Group, an informa business

British Library Cataloguing in Publication Data
A catalogue record for this book is available from the British Library

ISBN13: 978-0-415-67286-3

Typeset in Times
by Taylor & Francis Books

Disclaimer
The publisher would like to make readers aware that the chapters in this book are referred to as articles as they had been in the special issue. The publisher accepts responsibility for any inconsistencies that may have arisen in the course of preparing this volume for print.

Printed and bound in Great Britain by the MPG Books Group

Contents

Notes on Contributors   vii

Foreword: Experiencing environment and place through children's literature
Amy Cutter-Mackenzie, Phillip G. Payne and Alan Reid   1

1. Through green eyes: complex visual culture and post-literacy
Sidney I. Dobrin   13

2. Re-searching and re-storying the complex and complicated relationship of
biophilia and *bibliophilia*
Heesoon Bai, Daniela Elza, Peter Kovacs and Serenna Romanycia   27

3. Remarkable-tracking, experiential education of the ecological imagination
Phillip G. Payne   43

4. Children's literature as a springboard to place-based embodied learning
Linda Wason-Ellam   59

5. The stories are the people and the land: three educators respond to
environmental teachings in Indigenous children's literature
Lisa Korteweg, Ismel Gonzalez and Jojo Guillet   75

6. What's there, what if, what then, and what can we do? An immersive and
embodied experience of environment and place through children's literature
Geraldine Burke and Amy Cutter-Mackenzie   95

7. Exploring instructional strategies to develop prospective elementary
teachers' children's literature book evaluation skills for science,
ecology and environmental education
J. William Hug   115

8. Developing environmental agency and engagement through
young people's fiction
Stephen Bigger and Jean Webb   131

9. *The Lord of the Rings* – a *mythos* applicable in unsustainable times?
Alun Morgan   145

10. Reading *The Lorax*, orienting in potentiality
Amy Sloane   163

Afterword: Openings for researching environment and place in children's
literature: ecologies, potentials, realities and challenges
Alan Reid, Phillip G. Payne and Amy Cutter-Mackenzie   177

Index   211

Notes on Contributors

Heesoon Bai is Professor in Philosophy of Education in the Faculty of Education at Simon Fraser University, Canada. Her research focuses on the contemplative approaches to education, including environmental education.

Stephen Bigger researches educational issues relating to values, race, motivation and achievement including an interest in people's sustainable relationship with the environment. He has a particular interest in twentieth century young people's literature, especially that relating to war and reconstruction, and writes stories for children for use in school.

Geraldine Burke is a Studio Art/Art Education Lecturer at the Monash University. Her PhD studies and recent journal articles explore the role of immersive pedagogy within art practice and pedagogy. She has an abiding interest in the way that local knowledge and immersive art practices can be developed by schools and community groups to create learning experiences that connect people to place, space, and each other. Recent work as an artistic coordinator for the *Creative Junction* community art and environment project, along with her lecturing work, informs her emerging views on creativity, pedagogy, sense of place/space, and artistic practice.

Amy Cutter-Mackenzie is a Senior Lecturer in the Faculty of Education at Monash University, Australia. She is the Founder and Leader of the Sustainability, Environment and Education (SEE) Research Group in the Faculty. Her research interests focus on children's and teachers' thinking and experiences in environmental education in a range of contexts and spaces (including schools, teacher education, higher education, research, community and early years settings). Amy is also the Editor of the *Australian Journal of Environmental Education* and serves as a Consulting Editor for the *Journal of Environmental Education*.

Sidney I. Dobrin is Associate Professor of English at the University of Florida. He has written and edited more than a dozen books about writing, environment, and ecology, including *Wild things: Children's culture and ecocriticism* (co-edited with Kenneth B. Kidd) and *Ecosee: Image, rhetoric, nature* (co-edited with Sean Morey). He is currently completing a monograph about visual rhetoric and nature called *Cracks in the mirror*.

Daniela Elza is a doctoral candidate in philosophy of education at Simon Fraser University. Daniela is defending her thesis in April 2011. Her poetry has won numerous prizes, and has been published in academic journals, literary magazines and anthologies.

Ismel Gonzalez is a PhD candidate in the Faculty of Education, Lakehead University, Thunder Bay, Canada. Current research interests include critical modern language studies in education, including Indigenous languages, language and cultural revitalization, and decolonizing language pedagogy.

Jojo Guillet is a sessional instructor at Lakehead University. She is an Aboriginal curriculum specialist in Thunder Bay, Canada. Current research interests include professional development of teachers in Aboriginal education, Indigenous arts integration in schools and community–urban transitions for Indigenous students. She is currently working on assessment and program development for First Nation Students moving to urban centres.

J. William Hug serves as an Assistant Professor in the Elementary/Early Childhood Education Department and Director of the Excellence in Elementary Science and Math Education Center at California University of Pennsylvania. His research and teaching focuses on elementary school science teacher education, environmental education and place-based education.

Lisa Korteweg is Associate Professor in the Faculty of Education, Lakehead University, Thunder Bay, Canada. Current research interests include Indigenous and non-Indigenous (environmental) alliances, decolonizing non-Indigenous teachers and curriculum, and urban Aboriginal education.

Peter Kovacs is also a doctoral candidate in philosophy of education at Simon Fraser University. A serious bibliophile, he is highly regarded for his linguistic abilities.

Alun Morgan taught Geography in Secondary schools in England and Wales for ten years before becoming the Education for Sustainable Development Officer for Worcestershire County Council, a teacher advisory role. From 2002 he worked as a Lecturer in Geography Education at the Institute of Education, London. He moved to London South Bank University in January 2009 to take up the post of Director of the Education for Sustainability Program. Currently he is a Research Fellow at the Graduate School of Education, University of Exeter. He has a long standing interest in the educational importance of 'place' as an holistic concept which formed the focus of both his Master's and Doctoral research.

Phillip G. Payne is Associate Professor in the Faculty of Education at Monash University, Victoria, Australia. He is the Faculty's Research Group leader of the Movement, Environment, Community (MEC) collective. Phil was recently a visiting Research Fellow at the University of Bath's Centre for Research in Environmental Education (CREE).

Alan Reid is Senior Lecturer in Education and member of the Centre for Research in Education and the Environment at the University of Bath, UK. He is the editor of Environmental Education Research. He contributes to a range of undergraduate and graduate teaching programmes on social science research. His research interests focus on teachers' thinking and practice in environmental education, and policy-related, methodological and philosophical issues in environmental education theory, research and practice.

Serenna Romanycia majors in Anthropology, and her research interests lie in education and cultural-economic globalization. When she is not tutoring children how to achieve a deeper educational experience, she is attempting to deepen her own.

Amy Sloane is a Faculty Associate with the Undergraduate Research Scholars program at the University of Wisconsin-Madison. She teaches environmental education and philosophy of education at UW-Madison, and has worked with nonprofits in Wisconsin, Costa Rica and Nicaragua to help K-12 teachers integrate outdoor environmental learning into math and English curricula. She studies history and philosophy of environmental thought and is completing her joint PhD in Curriculum and Instruction, and Forest and Wildlife Ecology.

Linda Wason-Ellam is Professor in the College of Education, at the University of Saskatchewan, Canada where she teaches courses in reading, children's literature and crosscultural literacy and does research in the inner-city schools.

Jean Webb is Professor of International Children's Literature and Director of the International Forum for Research in Children's Literature at the University of Worcester, UK. She is widely published including: Cogan Thacker, D., and Webb, J. (2002) *Introducing Children's Literature: Romanticism to Postmodernism*, London, Routledge; and Webb, J ed. (2007) *"A Noble Unrest": contemporary essays on the work of George MacDonald*, Cambridge Scholars Press. She is on the editorial board of a number of journals including: *The Journal of Children's Literature Studies*; *ChLA India*; and *Children's Literature in Education*.

FOREWORD

Experiencing environment and place through children's literature

Once upon a time ...

> Not so long ago, a well overdue clean out of the garage and its accumulated 20 years of family life stored in an array of deteriorating boxes led Phil, one of the co-editors of this special issue, to reflect on the glorious story that might be told by those forgotten artefacts. But, it was time for this bloke to reclaim the garage as his 'shed.'[1]

> However, what my partner and I had expected to be only a few short hours of sorting donations for a local charity shop and recycling depot was soon capsized: we had stumbled our way into something far more absorbing. The boxes held many story books and, thus, parenting memories of what we had read and showed to our child as a baby, a toddler, a young child and the ones she read later as she became textually and visually literate. As we opened successive boxes with a *I wonder what's in this one?* on our silent lips, we found ourselves re-inspecting each book with much shared 'memory work' about the stories we had read, time and time again, to our then child. Shifting gear, a morning's labour became a nostalgic engagement with things past and with fondly remembered 'once upon a times'. We were re-imagining what we valued most in our parenting. And what we thought about the future. Needless to say, many of the boxes of books were returned to the rapidly diminishing prospect of an uncluttered shed. For we now thought that many of those story books could be read once more, even time and time again, to an imaginary child of our daughter should she one day become a parent.

Recent scholarship on children's literature displays a wide variety of analytical interests in exploring key classic and contemporary children's books.[2] As yet though, the bulk of this work has not engaged the significance of either an ecological imagination or socio-ecological experiences to both the authors and (younger or older) readers of these texts. So-called 'ecocriticism' has begun to make some inroads into illuminating these particular blind spots in the context of literary theory and criticism in general as well as in relation to environmental education (see, for example, Garrard 2004, 2010). This special issue of *Environmental Education Research* also sets out to address these concerns but offers a different route through some of the challenges this contested terrain presents.

Bringing together a set of original research-based papers, the special issue explores the role of children's literature in environmental education and its research through a particular focus on how children's literature contributes to an experiencing of environment and place. To this end, it critically explores the value and relevance of children's literature in providing what are arguably some of the first and possibly most formative engagements that some children may have with 'nature'. It examines how children's literature variously represents, mediates and informs experiences and understandings of diverse environments and places as well as the people and other 'presences' (that may be, are no longer, or never are) found therein, be these imaginatively construed or firmly rooted in a diversity of realities. The collection is framed by the assumption that engaging with children's literature, in the form of storybooks, mythic tales, and image-based and/or written texts, can be deeply pleasurable as well as troubling, on aesthetic and ecopolitical as well as affective and connective levels. Such literature can afford openings for dialogue both with and against dominant cultural texts, images, narratives and figurations of eco-cultural relations, and may offer incompatible as well as compelling understandings of childhood, adulthood, place and nature. It may also encourage a 'comparing and contrasting' of these alongside questions of the ecologies and cultures depicted in children's literature, including children's and adults' conceptions and constructions of environment that might be experienced with or through them, their senses of an eco-identity, -citizenship or -responsibility related to such places and nature, and the significance that immersive pedagogies might play in engaging these themes and their challenges.

'Alan, you are an ecocosmopolitan.' A warm-hearted remark in a colleague's email that emerged after our recent 'hanging out together' at an international conference, the possibility that it wasn't meant as a compliment is not my immediate concern here. Rather, it is how it has undone some of my assumptions. My prior understanding of 'cosmopolitan' had been that it spoke of a comparative disposition: towards experiences of the processes of cultural uniformity and divergence, the scope and limits of our understanding and truth in the face of otherness, the responsibility of recognizing subjectivity as not objectifiable, and so forth. Yet since this ascription, I notice I have regarded the eco-inflection as suggesting a need to consider this again and other dimensions, such as some of the conditions and challenges faced by contemporary 'types' of ecologically minded, self-regulating, self-validating 'citizen-consumers'. Perhaps most likely a postmodern-ish (sub-)urbanite, not probably living in the 'countryside' let alone 'bush', he or she may still likely have an interest or maybe even a wild hope that the 'nature', 'places' and 'environments' that surround the 'urbs will yet have some bearing on matters 'professional, domestic and recreational'. Liberally sprinkled with accounts of our various shortcomings and delights amid the everyday and exceptional of our conditions, expectations and life histories, these had, of course, been some of the things my colleague and I had been idly discussing. That is, until we embarked on a more portentous narrowing in on some of the circumstances and choices we lived by or with and to which we were about to re-engage once more and more fully, following our imminent returns home.[3]

A few months later, with this editorial now firmly in view, I found myself pondering our conversations and their ramifications once more. One thing I began to question with 'critical friends' was whether the notion of an 'ecocosmopolitan' really had any legs, so to speak. Might such a category hold some potential for making sense of the conscious features of a life most often lived in and around Bath? Did it even have something to say about the books we selected, read, gave, borrowed or shared as a family and with friends? Digging a little further, I noted that Ulrich Beck (2002, 37) had recently claimed, 'Cosmopolitanism presupposes individualization.' My gut response was to interpret this as challenging some of the naivety and provincialism of my 'lifeworld'. Yet having an empirical bent too, I wanted a second crack at this. I should test my reaction as well as some of my wonderings further in relation to matters 'eco' and children's literature-wise, before (perhaps) bringing this to the attention of a wider audience.

Tentatively at first [… would I need to secure ethics clearance on this with the university?], but soon overtaken by the sure knowledge that something always seemed to emerge (even if not as originally envisaged) whenever I proceeded this way, I continued my inquiries. With my family hat firmly on, I got to work, seeking out someone close to me who might offer an alternative view, albeit in a register and framing quite different from Beck, my colleagues and me.

'Lucy, do you mind if we have a look at some of your books together please …'

Our call for papers for this special issue invited environmentally oriented educators and researchers to submit manuscripts that were informed by research and that focused on experiencing environment and place through children's literature in environmental education. We sought contributors who would write in scholarly, creative and insightful ways about the key arguments and features of a socio-environmentally conscious experiencing of children's literature, and who would draw on research and scholarly literature that might add to current discussions of key examples, themes, trends, issues and tensions in this field.

We also encouraged authors to consider the value of adopting an auto-ethnographic approach in presenting and discussing pedagogical uses of children's literature that would engage different types of experiences and dialogue about the meanings and values of environment and place. We envisaged the collection would include diverse pedagogical and theoretical frameworks and examples, such as social ecology, socio-cultural theory and a/r/tography. And alongside original research and critical commentaries, the call solicited contributions that reviewed, synthesized and critiqued policy and practice in using children's literature in teaching and learning about the environment and place, as well as constructing/writing/creating that literature.

… Lucy, aged 6 at the time, took her dad, approaching 40, up to her bedroom to do some reading. Choosing some picture books, she took the lead and exclaimed 'Charlie and Lola' were 'great' and 'very funny', and we should read some of those first. Lucy immediately drew out similarities between Lola's life with her older sibling Charlie, and those of her own interactions with her *two* slightly older brothers, Tom and Jonathan; but I just had to interject: couldn't we read something else this time, as I was now quite familiar with Lola's escapades. Lucy paused. *Hmm. Something else by Lauren Child, dad?* Okay then, yes. *No!* For Lucy, Child's tales about Clarice Bean (her 'slightly sassy' and 'spunky young heroine') were probably what dad had had in mind but these were just a bit too serious and not as amusing as those with her beloved Lola in. She took *What planet are you from, Clarice Bean?* (2001) from her bookshelf and sat me down on her bed. With 'Dad's iPhone' on mute, it was time for our lesson to begin …

Child's books are award winning and highly regarded for their mixed-media artwork, illustrative styling and witty text – a heady mix of collage, textiles, photographs, drawings, paintings and creative fonts on each page, coupled with an arresting line in smart banter, casual sarcasm, and engaging characterizations and plotlines to boot. Or, at least that's what Lucy's dad had been led to believe. Lucy gave me a forgiving smile that nearly managed to mask her exasperation at my blindness to a larger truth. She turned to the first page.

So, Clarice Bean's Planet. We are immediately confronted with a fast-paced tale that starts with Clarice arriving just a little bit late for school. In the first few pages, we learn that gravity is an amazing force to Clarice, as is the fact that the sea doesn't spill over at its edges. Her teacher, Mrs Wilberton, assigns the class a report to write on 'the Environment'. As usual, Clarice's creative mind sparkles at the possibilities: *Can it be more than simply all that nature in the backyard? Or how about holes in the sky caused by her sister's hairspray? Or should it be about the self-styled nature safari right there in her older brother's bedroom?* Except back in classroom realities [slightly different from Lucy's, she observes ex tempore], it's just Clarice's luck that she's been paired with annoying Robert Granger once again to complete her project. (This is Clarice's third outing in the series, and Robert, the pesky next door neighbour, is her nemesis, appearing in many of the tales.)

Robert insists on doing the report on 'who can walk faster, a snail or a worm?' Clarice protests that this isn't important, but Mrs Wilberton overrules in Robert's favour [prompting an (intertextually aware? or … ?) 'again!' that Lucy and I sigh together]. Outside of school now, brother Kurt (not a Charlie but representative of the typically silent and moody teenage boy type) has learnt that the local council plans to cut down an old tree on their street. In fact, the whole family, including grandfather and parents, become upset about what might happen. The normally lazy Kurt is spurred into action to become an 'ecowarrior'. He ends up camping in the branches so it can't be cut down, waving a sign that says, 'Free the Tree' ('because it rhymes'). In the end, Clarice's entire family joins Kurt, and as the story reaches its climax, they even find time to enjoy a pasta supper between the leaves. A local reporter takes their picture – Robert, who Clarice just can't seem to get rid of, manages to muscles in on this, much to her annoyance – but that's not to distract from the positive note sounded in the final pages: the Beans have saved the tree, leaving Clarice in the much better position of being able to complete her report on being an ecoguardian instead. *The End …*

Okay, … so you don't really like Clarice and her adventures, is that it?

Clarice is okay, she's quite cool and the story's kind of interesting – well, sort of – … and Robert is so like Harley at school. But can't you see, it just isn't as good as Lola! And Dad, why is it you always want us to talk about the book afterwards …?

Lucy, you know that's not quite true, or fair … but before we start on the next one, for just a moment, perhaps we look this book up online and see what some other people have said about it … Okay – here, let me read you this; it's from Amazon. It's about the book, mainly to get people to read it, and buy it, at home, in libraries, at schools:

> *What planet are you from, Clarice Bean?* is perfect for children ages four to eight. It handles the important topic of the environment in a lighthearted way, so that even though several things are explained (such as the hole in the ozone layer, pollution, and grassroots protest action) readers won't even realize they've learned something.

And here's someone else, not a reviewer this time but from the publishers:

> In a new installment in the Clarice Bean escapades, Lauren Child makes a clear case for ecoaction – and gives the cause of saving the planet a hilarious new spin.

And look at this link, there's even some activity sheets you can get online too. This one, *What can I do to help the environment?* is a writing and colouring sheet. It says it invites children your age to 'put down all the things that you and your family are doing (or would like to do) to protect the environment'; while, *Clarice Bean's 5 favorite [sic] ways to save the planet* combines extracts and illustrations from the book, so that children, their parents and family can see the different ways they might: '(1) recycle; (2) keep it clean; (3) save energy; (4) respect wildlife; (5) protect growing things …'

Dad, dad, stop! I'm bored now. This isn't school! Can we all go out now please, with mum? Or can I play on your phone, please! Can I ring Ruby? I want to talk to my friends.

Lucy shuts the book and the internet browser. And I'm left wondering whether such observations, possibilities or indeed (mis)handlings of events say anything: to the 'ecocosmopolitan', to how we understand or approach children's literature within or as an environmental education, and to how any of this deserves a closer reading, interpretation and analysis in other parts of a life, be that at 'work' or at 'play' …

It is easy to say stories matter, and clearly some have come to matter more than others and most profoundly to our various ways of living, experiencing and evaluating the world. Our senses of life and death and the horizons for all that lies between and beyond are the very stuff of culture and its expression, exploration and contestation in and through literary forms. Be they the stories we can and do tell one another and ourselves, or those we are no longer able to or won't give voice to, stories also matter to our individual and collective sense of experience, nature, environment and place, as crafted and (re)told across a range of times, places, realities and worldviews. Obfuscate a central aspect of a character or setting, a plotline or convention, a twist or discovery, and a story can fail in its imaginary as much as in its telling. Continue to tell stories that no longer hold true to current times, and we risk condemning them to the realm of historical curiosity and nostalgia. Create new ones, grounded in close attention and exploration of experience and imagination, and we may yet reinvigorate what Rushdie (1990) terms the 'Sea of Stories' on which we navigate, narrate and name our lives.

The environmental philosopher, Arran Gare, drawing on Ricoeur (1990, para. 11), notes how 'learning how to live through stories is at the same time learning who one is. It is through stories that people define themselves and establish their identities'. In the face of so many 'Processes too Complicated to Explain' (Rushdie), be it in our relations to one another and the world, who we are and what we might be, we often ground our experience and reality in narrativizations to give an account of ourselves. Hence, it is through stories, their telling, contestation, reception and rejection, that relationships and identities are 'established, stabilized and defined and redefined' (Gare 2001, para. 11) between diverse and evolving situations: communally, culturally, socially, institutionally, politically, ecologically, personally and so on. Analysing the transformative power of stories to the ethics and politics of environmentalism, Gare also writes:

> People are 'caught up' ... by stories and the world is experienced as having a claim on them ... Understanding such a story situates the recipient as a potential participant in the story, as someone who could play an active part in shaping the future projected by the story. This is associated with the appreciation of the corporeality of human existence, that people (including ourselves) are not detached consciousnesses but as actors bodily engaged in the world. [para 25]

Turning to MacIntyre's (1984, 216) *After virtue*, Gare quotes the following much-cited passage:

> I can only answer the question, 'What am I to do?' if I can answer the prior question 'Of what story or stories do I find myself a part?' We enter human society, that is, with one or more imputed characters – roles into which we have been drafted – and we have to learn what they are in order to be able to understand how others respond to us and how our responses to them are apt to be construed.

MacIntyre (1984, 216) continues – tellingly for this collection – as follows:

> Deprive children of stories and you leave them unscripted, anxious stutterers in their actions as in their words. Hence there is no way to give us an understanding of any society, including our own, except through the stock of stories which constitute its initial dramatic resources.

The papers brought together under the auspices of this collection tackle a wide range of aspects to the call and its thematics. Our first paper, by Dobrin (University of

Florida), is titled 'Through green eyes: complex visual culture and post-literacy'. Dobrin seeks to unsettle our understandings of the green metaphors and visual rhetorics that educators and researchers expect in and from children's eco-related literatures and environmental criticism. Whether this necessarily requires embracing film, television, graphic novels or Web 2.0-type open texts and interactions as the focus of inquiry in environmental education remains an open question. Dobrin though offers a map for prospective travellers of this increasingly virtual terrain; his contribution suggests a complex set of debates and traces some of the key problems and challenges within contemporary scholarship on children's literature, culture and subject formation. Arguably, key tensions emerge when scholarship and pedagogies are brought face-to-face with various technological shifts (as represented by the features and modes of the 'network society'), with new priorities being argued for in ecocriticism by the likes of Lawrence Buell and those drawing on systems ecology, and by those noting the increasing importance of visual texts (given the rise of screen-based cultures and their constitutive forms of interaction and exchange) to children's lived experiences and interpretations of environments and place. Taken together, Dobrin insists, also requires us to consider whether a shift is required in scholarship: away from a focus on narratalogical and interpretational expectations in inquiries towards directly addressing matters of the production, circulation and networking of children's subjectivities, literatures and engagements with environment and place.

Wason-Ellam's contribution (University of Saskatchewan) follows and offers a provocative twist on some of the themes outlined by Dobrin. In the context of globalization, her paper considers how those westernized children living as 'social cyborgs' in 'technospace', 'estranged' and 'de-placed' from their locales may have these effects countered by place-based education approaches to education that engage children and environmental educators in textual and visual activities for 'embodied learning'. 'Children's literature as a springboard to place-based embodied learning' autoethnographically describes her studies with a third grade class in a school that is variously understood to be marked by scarcities in resource, equity and opportunity. Her illustrations of the 'learning in the making' that is engendered in children's activities in the field along a local Saskatoon river valley, coupled with preparation and extension work with picture books and arts-based learning in the classroom, communicate the need for educators to be mindful of how feelings of attachment, respect and responsibility are afforded within and through socially and ecologically critical place-based pedagogies. Her particular interest is in approaches that set out to challenge those 'pedagogies of poverty' that are often the default mode of schooling in such settings and for these particular 'learning communities'. In such circumstances, Wason-Ellam asks us to consider if learners are better understood to be 'active risk takers who accept challenges and understand how and why to learn'? Indeed, does a critical place-based pedagogy or an environmental education more widely provide children with 'opportunities to restructure information in ways that make meaning personal' when working with children's literature?

The next two partially autoethnographic contributions come from authors who were and are variously teachers, teacher educators, scholars and researchers at Monash University. First, Payne's 'Remarkable-tracking, experiential education of the ecological imagination' draws on his longstanding interest in telling stories about 'hairy Peruvian' gnomes as an experientially driven way of playfully considering the openings they present for engendering an 'ecocentric sense of self'. Payne's paper illustrates how ecoaesthetically aware imaginative encounters with the ecological otherness of nature's places, and a slower paced embodied and experiential education in story's places, might provide a counter narrative to the 'fast, literate, urban, technologically saturated and consumptive postmodern world'. This storied counter critique is also set against Australia's colonial past and our collective forgetting of its still inhabited place in the everyday lives of many of today's young children, beginning teachers and old researchers. Payne achieves this by drawing eclectically on the texts of Robert Ingpen's *Voyage of the poppykettle* and David Abram's *Spell of the sensuous* and his leading over many years and in different places of gnome-tracking expeditions, poetry and song. All are part of a deeper, richer and longer quest to connect experience, literature and art in the ongoing puzzle and challenge to develop those 'artful' pedagogies and pedagogues that are necessary for nurturing the 'still elusive reconciliation of human, social and more-than-human natures'. And in this case, as Payne notes, given Australia can be rendered the 'unchosen land' as much as it is the 'fatal shore' (Robert Hughes), such an ecopedagogical reconciliation allegorically aims to (re)incorporate the Indigenous ones into whose culture–nature relations the mischievous hairy Peruvians gnomes sailed over 400 years ago.

Burke and Cutter-Mackenzie's contribution 'What's there, what if, what then, and what can we do? An immersive and embodied experience of environment and place through children's literature' offers a series of questions drawing on arts-based methods to unsettle some of the usual answers to visual and ecological literacy approaches and curricula. As with Wason-Ellam and Payne, the assumptions and valuing of 'embodied learning' (as opposed to decontextualized and abstracted conditions and priorities) both inside and outside the classroom underpin their deliberations. Their paper discusses how immersive investigations of children's picture books can help learners and educators (re)examine concepts and experiences of environment and place, and describes an immersive process informed by 'a/r/tography'. This is extended to introduce a working model of 'a/r/t-*e*-ography' to foreground the dispositions and roles of 'the environmentalist' (established or nascent) as a vehicle for promoting environmental awareness and action. The paper is illustrated throughout with autoethnographic encounters and ruminations about Baker's (1991) picture book *Window*, and the windows that the children, pre-service teachers and the authors craft during the process. Burke and Cutter-Mackenzie invite readers to consider the qualities of experience afforded by such an approach to interacting with children's literature – in terms of interest, involvement, imagination, and interaction – alongside the 'ways of knowing' that are championed and silenced in this and other work with children's literature. Finally, the paper reflects on the 'ethics of being' *with* and *for* the other (human and more than or other than human) afforded by an environmental education that draws on experiences with children's literature and whether this is indeed efficacious in fostering a critical form of ecoliteracy.

The next two papers return us to Canada. The first, by Korteweg, Gonzalez and Guillet (Lakehead University), focuses on how Indigenous children's literature might challenge adult and child readers to consider different meanings and worldviews of the environment as a land-based value system. In 'The stories are the people and the land: three educators respond to environmental teachings in Indigenous children's literature', they use reader-response theory 'to explore a collection of rich alternative narratives of Indigenous land-based knowledge systems available in the work of Indigenous authors and illustrators of children's literature' (2010, 331). Referring once more to recent theorizings of and debates about critical pedagogies of place (most notably in the work of David Greenwood [Gruenewald] and Greg Smith), their study considers how Indigenous picture books might serve to 'decolonize environmental consciousness through offering accessible and immersive Indigenous stories of the land' (331) Their paper illustrates their own responses to and analyses of Indigenous children's literature, and works from a prior commitment to the process of decolonization as a 'critical self-reflexive political process in which one's colonized beliefs are explicitly pinpointed, challenged and countered by Indigenous worldviews and perspectives' (2010, 331).

Another multiculturally authored work that draws on autobiographical, collective and reflective approaches to engaging some of the themes of the collection can be found in the next paper: 'Re-searching and re-storying the complex and complicated relationship of *biophilia* and *bibliophilia*'. Bai et al. (Simon Fraser University) offer a 'collaborative bricolage of poetry, autobiographical fragments, essay pieces, and images' to portray their 'ongoing existential, psychological, and epistemological struggles as educators and learners, parents and children' (2010, 351). They identify *biophilia* (love of life/nature) as a key learning in environmental education, and use their own life histories to explore how biophilia relates to *bibliophilia* (love of books). As with Wason-Ellam, Payne, and Burke and Cutter-Mackenzie, Bai and her co-authors identify an 'indwelling experience' of children's literature as a key to an environmental education that contributes to the experiencing of environment and place, but given their particular interests, in ways that seek to broaden this out to advocating poetry-making and story-telling as methods for fostering such indwelling, biophilia and bibliophilia.

Children's literature tends to be used with preschool and primary audiences rather than in secondary- or tertiary-level contexts, and this can speak to some of the limits rather than strengths in contemporary theory and practice in this field. In 'Exploring instructional strategies to develop prospective elementary teacher children's literature book evaluation skills for science, ecology and environmental education', Hug, currently a science teacher educator at California University of Pennsylvania, uses a vignette to start his reflections on his work to those ends. Hug dwells on two recurring themes that have emerged in his autoethnographically based inquiries: questions of *scientific accuracy* and *anthropomorphism* in the prospective teachers' thinking and evaluations. He suggests that cultural, instructor and student expectations merit close attention in the framings of practice and research in environmental education, notwithstanding a critical disposition to our self-narratives, career trajectories and positionings, and the opportunities and constraints on using children's literature for science, nature and environment work in schools and teacher preparation across a range of sectors.

Morgan's (Exeter University) contribution illustrates the ways some texts may come to overshadow others in these ecocritical times. While Amy Sloane (below) takes this in another direction, Morgan appreciates that it can be hard to break away from being funnelled towards a received reading of a familiar text. Indeed, while finding a space to strike new ground in an analysis of a well-known mythos and its reception is not impossible, it may involve a long and arduous journey. It goes without saying that there are still many stories yet to be told, be they the stories we might tell or about those we are told. With this in mind, in '*The Lord of the Rings* – a *mythos* applicable in unsustainable times?' Morgan considers the relevance of Tolkien's Middle Earth saga to environmental education and contemporary concerns about social and environmental injustices. Drawing on his own recent reacquaintance with the text, in both written and movie formats, he probes the author's environmental biography and those aspects of the story that highlight the connection between, on the one hand, Tolkien's personal experiential *informal* environmental education learning journey in the real world and, on the other, that of his imaginative 'sub-creation'. Morgan considers the saga 'a work of "fantasy" or "speculative fiction" that holds the potential to re-enchant the world by engaging the *mythopoetic* imagination' (2010, 383).[4] He dwells on its treatment of place, character, journey and environmental ethics and how 'the story implicitly promotes, and is grounded in, a "creation-centred" ethic of stewardship' (383). As with many of the authors in this collection, Morgan concludes his contribution with a discussion of the pedagogical considerations that his observations and arguments foment, in this case, focussing on the saga's status as 'an inspirational work of literature, and its potential and limits as a source of inspiration for those engaged in challenging social and environmental injustices' (2010, 383).

The next contribution also emanates from the British Isles. 'Developing environmental agency and engagement through young people's fiction', by Bigger and Webb (University of Worcester), draws on a wide range of ideas and theorists, including Paul Ricoeur (on hermeneutics and narrative), John Dewey (on primacy of experience) and John Macmurray (on personal agency in society). Bigger and Webb understand reading fiction about places as 'hermeneutical, that is, interpreting understanding by combining what is read with what is experienced' (2010, 401). They explore this line of reasoning through examples and contrasts of four children's writers, Ernest Thompson Seton, Kenneth Grahame, Michelle Paver and Philip Pullman. The second part of their paper focuses on questions of critical dialogue and active democratic citizenship that experiences of children's literature might foster. Their paper concludes by considering whether 'the concept of *heroic resister* might encourage young people to overcome peer pressure and peer cultures that marginalize environmental activism' (2010, 401).

For Amy Sloane (University of Wisconsin-Madison), such a concept must arguably be tested against our assumptions about the human, humanity's potentiality and, in particular, the potential of a text to transmit and violate natural life. In 'Reading *The Lorax*, orienting in potentiality', Sloane uses Theodor Seuss Geisel's popular children's book to encourage a step change in our thinking: the strong environmental message it transmits has been discussed extensively, but what of the 'activity of transmission itself'? Sloane's work brings that of Agamben and Foucault into conversation with this well-known tale from Dr Seuss about the Once-ler, the child and their Thneeds. Amid the ravaging of Truffula trees, Swomee-Swans, Bar-ba-loots and Humming-Fish, Sloane's 'post-anthropocentric' elaborations (for want of a better provocation) in this collection set out to offer a reorientation to environmental education theory and practice and a different way of conceiving the child, reading and critique. We no longer need to engage in either a first- or second-order 'dividing and abandoning' of the grounds of the field's pedagogical premises, because these are always already inherently problematic and confounding. Rather, what remains, Sloane avers, is to take up the challenge of offering 'a mode of teaching without transmitting' (2010, 423), realizing the potential in environmental education 'not to transmit'. She concludes, 'perhaps environmental education can save the past by realizing that the child's task, if it can be called one, is not to receive a message but to play without it' (427).

And they all lived happily ever after …? Or did they?

Lily was born at 3:45 pm, 14 August 2008, in 'Bays Hospital', Mornington. Chris (Amy's partner) and I had spent the last nine months talking and reading to her in utero. We started off with some of our favourites, including *Where the rainforest meets the sea,*

Hidden forest, and *Possum magic.* When we read to her, she became animated, lightly kicking and moving about. When she was born, to our amazement she didn't cry or fuss. It was like we already knew each other, and just a couple hours later we read to her. Yet when a maternity nurse witnessed this, she affronted us with, 'She can't understand. It's too early for that.' Not wanting to deny our previous activities, I countered quickly and somewhat wistfully, 'This isn't the first time we've read to her, we're just picking up where we left off.'

I really saw the first six weeks of Lily's life as a fourth trimester where we were continuing our getting to know each other. Children's literature provided an opening to nature and wild things, all the while opening up a beautiful and imaginative world to us both. Lily is now 19 months and we still read together each day, be that at home, in the car, under a tree, in the garden, at childcare … She now turns the pages, points and talks to the pictures, revealing an immense wonderment and fascination with this 'world', and Chris and I are fascinated by where this might lead.

It is little more than a cliché to observe this can never be the end of the story for how we might address the themes and challenges broached by such a collection. And being mindful that we can but look forward to seeing this work and its framings engaged and contested in the field, in the final contribution (Reid, Payne and Cutter-Mackenzie) to this special issue, we try to offer some modest possibilities and potential lines of inquiry toward that end. Our final paper sketches the ecologies of fear, risk and of hope that lurk within, between and around the papers published herein. It also aims to encourage a wider development of the discourse of environmental education research that, in this instance, clearly engages how children's literature also has a pedagogical place in the positive social construction of intergenerational ethics told through story and illustration and associated means, and which grapples with the elusive ends of encouraging consideration and engagement with questions of social and ecological justice. That is, as illustrated in the vignettes throughout this editorial, we ask not just about the hows and the whats, but the whys and what ways textual and visual messages are passed on to the next generation, and how and what they might take up in ways that are more positive and generative than ill-thought through or stymied. Finally, given the scope of this special issue, we engage a series of possible research issues that we hope will broadly nurture the development of scholarship on children's ecoliterature, arguing that it is still a nascent field of inquiry that works with limited evidence to justify its purposes or elaborate its values and usefulness, all of which warrant further development.

In conclusion, our expectations for this collection remain twofold. First, that this special issue offers readers a wide range of possibilities and provocations for further scholarly debate and engaged research development as it relates to environmental education. Second, that it might help achieve two broader and related intentions: that this research community and interested persons continue research-based conversations and build credible bodies of knowledge while, at the same time, reflexively forge a more comprehensive theorizing of an aesthetics as well as ethics and politics of environmental education and its research, that is informed by and informs plentiful 'ecos' – be they pedagogical, curricular, imaginary, literary, experiential, interpretational, constitutive, or otherwise.

Notes

1. Sheds, like gardens, are often a somewhat secretive place that might no longer be all that real to which an individual, or parent and child, can temporarily escape from the hurly

burly of the everyday, do odd jobs, fossick around in or, more earnestly, pursue or pass down a long forgotten but meaningful craft.

2. Recent Anglophone examples include *Children's literature: Classic texts and contemporary trends*, edited by Montgomery and Watson (2009). Essays therein examine, among others, *Little women, Treasure island, Peter Pan, Swallows and amazons, Tom's midnight garden, Northern lights, Harry Potter and the Philosopher's Stone, Junk* and *Mortal engines*. We note *Children's literature: Approaches and territories*, edited by Maybin and Watson (2009), has contributions in *Part V: Words and pictures*, on 'Texts and Pictures', 'Picturebook Codes' and 'Postmodern Experiments'. Tatar's (2009) academic-popular hybrid, *Enchanted hunters: The power of stories in childhood*, is noteworthy for this special issue too, given its exploration of the power of children's literature to take hold of their imaginations, how classic and contemporary tales of beauty, terrors, death and horror stimulate their curiosity, and how transportation and transformations may evoke wonder and engage emotions in ways adult readers may not expect. But despite its scope, it does not offer a significant analysis of place, nature and environment. Similarly with Gubar's (2009) *Artful Dodgers: Reconceiving the golden age of children's literature*. Even though it critiques the power and focus of children's literature studies, and in particular, both 'the cult of the child' and Rose's (1984) analysis of it in *Peter Pan and the impossibility of children's Literature* (arguing that, for example, 'Golden Age' authors were centrally concerned with the complexities of children's agency), Gubar frames this anthropocentrically rather than with ecological or socio-ecological considerations in mind. Also, in focusing on recent texts on children's literature, this is not to forget that young adult/juvenile/ adolescent literatures have also received similar treatments; while some texts, such as *Where the wild things are* and *Alice's adventures in Wonderland* have continued to attract new generations of young readers in the decades since their initial publication, and this has often been triggered by film versions – see Morgan (2010) too.

3. Our wider conversations had included sharing a mutual cherishing of Leopold's (1948/ 1987) *Sand County Almanac, and sketches here and there*. This too would suggest another dimension to ecocosmopolitanism to consider: on the importance of having embodied selves not always turned citywards, but landward, at least once in a good while.

4. The MacIntyre (1984) quotation noted on p. 261 continues, 'Mythology, in its original sense, is at the heart of things.' Arguably Leopold's *Almanac* is littered with mythologies. It exemplifies a form of nature writing whose register, structuring and foci both celebrate natural history, processes and rhythms, and lament the narrowing and diminution of the West's 'ecology of values' to utilitarianism, expediency, conquest and self-interest, in this case, through careful observation and illumination of the local and wider effects of Abrahamic, evolutionary and ecological community conceptions of land. Leopold's meditation on the geese returning in March to Sand County rhetorically asks, 'Is education possibly a process of trading awareness for things of lesser worth?', concluding that the mid-twentieth-century consciousness of the well- and 'overeducated' risks the same end as that of the goose 'who trades his': she or he is equally soon 'a pile of feathers' (1948/1987, 18). The question is also raised by Cooper's (2002) recent philosophical and historical meditations on humanism, humility and mystery. We return to some of Cooper's themes in our endpiece in remarks on how literature-based ecopedagogies might engage aspects of the (ir)real, but note here that Cooper's essay is a fine examination of the history and consequences of a lack of humility in humanism and absolutism in the face of the mystery inhering in nature and 'the Other'. It also offers an account of how this 'virtue' for our beliefs and conduct might overturn the default 'hubris' of modern-day encounters with realities independent of the 'human contribution', albeit striving via quite different means for something approximating to a 'harmony with land' among a people who 'have forgotten there is any such thing as land, among whom education and culture have become almost synonymous with landlessness' (Leopold 1948/ 1987, 210).

References

Bai, H., D. Elza, P. Kovacs, and S. Romanycia. 2010. Re-searching and re-storying the complex and complicated relationship of *biophilia* and *bibliophilia*. *Environmental Education Research* 16, nos. 3–4: 351–65.

Baker. J. 1991. *Window*. London: Walker Books.

Beck, U. 2002. The cosmopolitan society and its enemies. *Theory, Culture and Society* 19, nos. 1–2: 17–44.

Bigger, S., and J. Webb. 2010. Developing environmental agency and engagement through young people's fiction. *Environmental Education Research* 16, nos. 3–4: 401–14.

Burke, G., and A. Cutter-Mackenzie. 2010. What's there, what if, what then, and what can we do? An immersive and embodied experience of environment and place through children's literature. *Environmental Education Research* 16, nos. 3–4: 311–30.

Cooper, D. 2002. *The measure of things: Humanism, humility, and mystery*. Oxford: Oxford University Press.

Dobrin, S. 2010. Through green eyes: Complex visual culture and post-literacy. *Environmental Education Research* 16, nos. 3–4: 265–78.

Garrard. G. 2004. *Ecocriticism*. New York: Routledge.

Garrard, G. 2010. Problems and prospects in ecocritical pedagogy. *Environmental Education Research* 16, no. 2: 235–45.

Gubar, M. 2009. *Artful dodgers: Reconceiving the golden age of children's literature,* Oxford: Oxford University Press.

Hug, J.W. 2010. Exploring instructional strategies to develop prospective elementary teachers' children's literature book evaluation skills for science, ecology and environmental education. *Environmental Education Research* 16, nos. 3–4: 367–82.

Korteweg, L., I. Gonzalez, and J. Guillet. 2010. The stories are the people and the land: Three educators respond to environmental teachings in Indigenous children's literature. *Environmental Education Research* 16, nos. 3–4: 331–50.

Leopold, A. 1948/1987. *A Sand County Almanac, and sketches here and there*. New York: Oxford University Press.

MacIntyre, A. 1984. *After virtue*. 2nd ed. Notre Dame, IN: Notre Dame University Press.

Maybin, J., and N.J. Watson, eds. 2009. *Children's literature: Approaches and territories*. London: Open University Press/Palgrave Macmillan.

Montgomery, H., and N.J. Watson, eds. 2009. *Children's literature: Classic texts and contemporary trends*. London: Open University Press/Palgrave Macmillan.

Morgan, A. 2010. The *Lord of the Rings* – a *mythos* applicable in unsustainable times? *Environmental Education Research* 16, nos. 3–4: 383–99.

Payne, P.G. 2010. Remarkable-tracking, experiential education of the ecological imagination. *Environmental Education Research* 16, nos. 3–4: 295–310.

Reid, A., P.G. Payne, and A. Cutter-Mackenzie. 2010. Openings for researching environment and place in children's literature: Ecologies, potentials, realities, and challenges. *Environmental Education Research* 16, nos. 3–4: 429–69.

Ricoeur, P. 1990. The self and narrative identity. In *Oneself as another*, trans. K. Blamey, 140–68. Chicago: University of Chicago Press.

Rushdie, S. 1990. *Haroun and the sea of stories*. New York: Viking.

Sloane, A. 2010. Reading *The Lorax,* orienting in potentiality. *Environmental Education Research* 16, nos. 3–4: 415–28.

Tatar, M. 2009. *Enchanted hunters: The power of stories in childhood*. New York: WW Norton.

Wason-Ellam, L. 2010. Children's literature as a springboard to place-based embodied learning. *Environmental Education Research* 16, nos. 3–4: 279–94.

Amy Cutter-Mackenzie, Phillip G. Payne and Alan Reid

Through green eyes: complex visual culture and post-literacy

Sidney I. Dobrin

Department of English, University of Florida, Gainesville, USA

By way of reclamation of the metaphor 'green,' this paper contends that research regarding the relationships between children's literatures and cultures and environmental experience requires a reinvigorated consideration of the role of the visual. The heightened importance of visual texts is made evident via three primary, contemporary conditions of textual dissemination: hyper-circulation, shifts from page to screen as the dominant method of textual transmission, and increases in visuals as the primary mode of information conveyance. The conditions of textual distribution also call to question the status quo understanding of children's subject formation. This paper contends that by examining new media technologies in conjunction with methodologies borrowed from studies of complex ecology and systems theories, research might be able to better theorize how and why children's texts influence children's lived experiences with environments and place. Ultimately, this paper proposes not just that a greater attention to the visual rhetoric of children's texts is crucial, but that researchers also consider how current contexts encourage child subjects to produce texts as active agents within complex networks, not only interpret them.

'Green'

The metaphor 'green' has been adopted as a way of indicating environmentally conscious political positions. To 'go green' implies active participation in environmentally or ecologically sound practices. To 'be green' is to advocate environmental protection, to be attuned to nature. To manufacture 'green products' is to make goods in ecologically friendly ways. Etymologically, green is derived from *gréne* and *growan* verbs, indicating *to grow plants* and, in turn, *growth*. The metaphor is derived from a sense of the visual, a metaphor adopted as representing the color of photosynthesizing organisms, a foundational level of complex ecological energy exchanges. *Green* is seeing the color of plants. It also has roots in representations of the sea, the color of Neptune's realm. Green combines the foundational attributes of ecological life on earth: water and light/photosynthesis. Green has been naturalized as a metaphoric representation of nature and environment, a metaphor in need of reclamation. We must, for instance, also take into consideration that 'green' can serve other metaphoric purposes, including the understanding that to be green is to be new growth, to be new. In this way, to be *green* might also suggest both innocence and inexperience. To 'be green' is to be fresh, just grown, but it also implies being unripe or immature. To 'be green' is to be a novice, one lacking experience (e.g., a greenhorn). *Lack of experience* can suggest being unaware, something to be taken advantage of, a simpleton. To 'be green' is to exhibit the condition of ignorance and inexperience. In some cases, this greenness is pejorative, suggesting feeblemindedness; in others, green suggests the possibility of growth and the shedding of innocence with the acquisition of experience.

Green, of course, is a visual metaphor, one reliant upon at least a tacit understanding of light and color. Falling between yellow and blue within the spectrum, green is how we see light of wavelengths between 520 and 570 nanometers. The metaphor of green is grounded in light, a foundational element of both life and vision. While the relation between light and life intrigues me as an avenue of research not often taken up outside of the sciences, I am curious about the role light plays as a central characteristic of the ability for visual texts to convey meaning. From a visual rhetorical standpoint, the intersections of children's literature and environmental criticism provide interesting opportunities to consider not just the role of children's literatures in environmental education and experience, but to greatly expand the inquiries of intellectual endeavors that undertake these intersections. In the spirit of this collection, in its forward thinking to push at the boundaries of how we understand the relevance of children's literatures and texts to environmental education and experience, I propose a re-situation of ecological literary criticism (ecocriticism) and studies in children's literatures/cultures focusing on the role of the visual and the ways in which 'green' subjects engage visual information. This focus, however, should not be heard as a simple need to become more attentive to the role visual texts play either in children's literatures or in ecocriticisms, or to the need to extend analytical or interpretive methodologies to texts that might be labeled as falling within the aegis of either (or both) areas of study. Arguably, each has already developed traditions of 'reading' or 'seeing' visual texts as artifacts, as representational technologies, as contributors to the cultural milieu in which such texts function (see Bigger and Webb 2010; Korteweg, Gonzalez, and Guillet 2010; Sloane 2010). Instead, I want to consider the role of the visual in relation to the construction of the child subject and as part of networked culture, as part of a more complex ecology than either children's literature or ecological literary criticisms have taken up before. Ultimately, what I hope to initiate is a conversation that (re)invigorates a critical investment in the role of the visual in light of complex ecology and network theory. Given the complexity of network societies and the (hyper)circulation and velocity of information and text in the network, a more complex notion of ecology should begin to fuel our investigations and research. Where this argument leads (I hope) is to a recognition that the limited ecology of ecological literary criticism hampers what we can know, teach, and learn about children and children's texts and their deeply complex ecological relationships to the systems in which they function, natural and otherwise.

Lawrence Buell, in the concluding section of his manifesto *The future of environmental criticism: Environmental crisis and literary imagination* (2005), prophesizes the future of environmental criticism by way of four challenges: 'the challenge of organization, the challenge of professional legitimation, the challenge of defining distinctive models of inquiry, and the challenge of establishing their significance beyond the academy' (128). The subtext of Buell's prophecy, however, is an open call for the development of critical methodologies that are not hamstrung by the very methodologies that have propelled environmental criticism over the past 10 years. My intent in this opening contribution to the collection is less a representation of a specific body of research or methodologies than it is an answer to Buell's call in the form of a suggestion that appears – at least to me – to begin to address Buell's challenge. In order to accomplish this, and in light of the green metaphor, I contend that future avenues of research regarding the relevance of children's literature – and by extension children's texts, all literature, and all text – demand greater attention to visual components, particularly given the rapidly increasing consequence of visual media in contemporary information exchange (see Kress 2003). To this end, I first consider the development of the child subject as connected with technological development and the growing importance of the visual in children's subject formation. I contend that cultural moves from page to screen as the dominant medium of information exchange open doors for reconsideration not just of the relationship between literature and children's environmental education and experience, but the very idea of the child subject. I introduce concepts of complex ecology as possibly providing one methodological basis for examining the relationship between children's texts and the formation of child subjectivity. I call for not just a reinvigorated consideration of the visual for the sake of interpreting visual information, but toward the inclusion of textual *production* alongside textual interpretation as central to examining how literatures contribute to both child subject formation and the relationship between child subjects and environment/place.

Since the introduction of more contemporary concepts of the construction of the child subject, children have been cast as green figures in both senses of the metaphor, both tied to nature and environment as well as considered innocent, ignorant, and inexperienced (Stables 2009). If children are understood to be inexperienced – and simultaneously innocent – their greenness has also been understood to provide a connection to nature that is lost as one loses innocence and gains experience. Loss of youth and innocence distances one from nature and environment, a trope profoundly evident throughout children's literatures (e.g., see Burnett 1983; Hiaasen 2006; Kingsley 2007; Porter 2006; Bigger and Webb 2010; Morgan 2010; Wason-Ellam 2010). This duality between greens, flanked by inexperience and environmental attachment, situates children in the problematic realm between their greenness of inexperience, denying the child subject any experience for understanding what a connection to nature might mean, and an attachment to nature that can only be fleeting. Understanding these dubious constructions as central to the construction of children, children's texts, and the representation of children in children's texts (and the acknowledgment that these three distinctions are often blurred and inseparable) motivates the affiliation between studies in children's literatures/cultures and environmental criticism, studies central to any research regarding the relationship between children's literatures and environmental education.

Children's literatures and visual rhetorics

Childhood in the West, we might say, is increasingly a function of technology, specifically, information technologies. Scholars of children's literatures and cultures have proposed that the subjectivity of the child dramatically shifted from that of miniature/ amateur adult who was expected to participate in daily life, sharing the burden of economic labor, to a transitional position between infancy and adulthood (Aries 1962). It has also been widely understood that much of this shift can be attributed to the spread of literacy (Morgenstern 2002; O'Malley 2003). As European culture shifted from primarily feudal systems of social organization to systems with greater dispersions of class division and greater focus on commerce and urban life, the rise of a middle class that displaced the aristocracy as the primary producers of 'authorized' culture evolved hand in hand with the rise of the spread of commerce. We now recognize much of this class shift as influenced by technological advances, many of which have also been linked to the rise of environmental/ecological 'crisis' (think industrialization and its effects). Within this class configuration, children of the new middle class were less likely to enter into the family business immediately because the family business now required forms of (literate) experience (education, training, acculturation) that extended beyond that required to engage in physical labor. Children of the labor classes experienced vastly different childhoods than did children of the middle or upper classes, as they were expected to contribute labor at an earlier age (globally, such divisions remain). The children of the new middle classes were afforded a period between infancy and adulthood with little, if any, expectations of economic contribution.

Between the fourteenth and seventeenth centuries, as the use of Guttenberg's moveable-type printing press technologies spread throughout Europe, so too did the ease and velocity of information dissemination increase dramatically. The middle class rose hand in hand with the spread of information technologies. I do not mean to argue that childhood was a result of new information technologies in the same way that many have argued that the very idea of childhood as we now conceive it resulted from the rise of the middle class; I do mean to suggest that the very idea of childhood – and in turn the ideas that there can be something codified as children's literature, and in turn the study of childhood and children's literatures – cannot be separated from understanding developments in information technologies, and that, in fact, as Western culture now shifts from an era of information technologies grounded in the page to one dominated by the screen (Kress 2003), studies of children and children's literatures should make disciplinary accommodations to again rethink not just children's texts, but the very idea of the child subject (see also Stables 2009). Thus, as contemporary technologies engulf the child subject and subsume it within larger networks of information exchange, the child subject becomes more akin to other subjects, no longer separated from culture in transitional forms. Instead, the child subject is now cast as another node within the hyper-circulatory networks of contemporary information exchange. The child subject is provided greater access and maneuverability within the network, able to access not only children's texts, but all texts, granting the child authority to experience the world much more rapidly and wide-ranging than were children of the past. And, as I address later, the child subject is authorized to participate in the network, contributing to the flow and velocity of information circulation, no longer only a consumer of culture, but an active node producing, remixing, and circulating information within the network.

Certainly, some have noted that such shifts have direct implication upon the development of the child subject, forcing the 'immature' subject into spaces that require experience and maturity for effective (and healthy) engagement. For instance, Baroness Susan Greenfield (2009) has argued that contemporary 'screen culture,' characterized by heightened audio and visual sensations, is 'primarily a world of a small child' in which immediacy dominates over long-term result and consequence. In March 2009, Greenfield reported to the UK Government's House of Lords that the rise of screen culture over the past decade may, in fact, be changing how human brains develop and how those changes might be measured against other identifiable changes, such as a threefold increase in Attention Deficit Disorder pharmaceuticals prescribed for children over the same time frame. Greenfield's claims about brain research, to be clear, are not those of cause and effect or even of direct linkage between these two conditions, but one of caution and a need to explore such links.[1] For my purposes here, there are two key points that must be elicited immediately from Greenfield's claims. First, that the Westernized child subject is becoming more and more immersed in the technologies of screen culture to the degree that in such immersion it becomes difficult, if not impossible, to differentiate the child subject from any other subject form within the network (whether such immersions are or are not negative is insignificant in this inquiry). Second, that the relationship of the subject – child or otherwise – with information technologies is an ecological relationship, grounded in how an organism (subject/agent) interacts within an environment and establishes its niches.[2] In Greenfield's construction, the image is a predominant characteristic of the new environment.

Within the networks of contemporary information and cultural circulation then, we are witnessing a (re)turn to the image as the dominant means of information conveyance. As literacy theorists, including Gunther Kress (2003), have noted, while 'language-as-speech' is likely to remain the primary mode of human communication, 'language-as-writing' is rapidly being displaced by image in public communication (1). This shift, Kress argues, has profound effects on how we engage the world: '*The world told* is a different world to *the world shown*' (1, original emphasis). While these 'profound changes' might affect how we think of literacy, information, and communication (and I believe they do), for scholars of children's literatures and cultures – or more accurately, scholars of children's subjectivities – such changes offer a unique opportunity to step to the fore and provide a well-established history of inquiry into the value of image as mechanism for information exchange and acculturation. As modes of information exchange shift from page to screen and new media and literacy theorists turn a fresh lens to image, childhood studies and children's literature scholars already understand that technology and image are at the center of the function of literature, literacy, information, acculturation, and subjectivity (Jenkins 1998).

Like children themselves, visual texts have (until very recently) been considered green texts, texts thought to be immature, undeveloped, or designed for inexperienced readers. Conventional wisdom suggests that visual texts are pre-literate, designed to convey information to subjects not yet imbued with the experiences necessary to interpret written-textual information. Visual texts[3] are naïve texts intended for green readers. Yet, the turn from page to screen has caused a (re)questioning of this traditional position of the visual. As visuals become a dominant form of information conveyance – or more accurately, as they become a more immediate form of information conveyance – they are cast not as pre-literate forms of communication, but post-literate forms (though some, like Greenfield, take a different approach, claiming that such turns 'infantilize'). Gregory Ulmer (2003) has established that we are witnessing a shift from literacy to 'electracy,' a shift he likens to the shift from orality to literacy that preceded. Electracy is to the digital age what literacy was to the print age. Such shifts do not eliminate the prior modes of communication, but supersede them as primary. Visual texts, forms of which dominated communicative methods of writing early in writing's development (hieroglyphs, pictograms), have again become a dominant mode of textual representation. For studies of children's literatures, attention to visuals has been central. In fact, I would argue that only recently has the field moved toward emphasizing written texts and that such moves were understood as a maturation of the field, a move from the pre-literate to the literate; a disavowal of the visual and move toward the written promoted as a validation of the discipline. While the field has a larger visual history than does studies of 'adult' literatures that history has been shaded by an anxiety of validation, a fear that academic legitimacy is lost because of the predominance of visual texts in the corpus. Recent questions regarding the legitimacy and value of comic studies or graphic novel studies – complicated and interesting forms thought to fall between the pre-literate and literate – stand as exemplary. Similarly, picture books, which hover between the literate and pre-literate, call to question the validity of studying visual texts. This disciplinary neurosis of validation though must now be set aside and, on the one hand, embrace visual texts as pre-literate, literate, and post-literate (electrate) and, on the other, central to the transfer of information in the formation of subjects, which in turn, are critical to investigations regarding the role of children's (visual) literatures in environmental education.

Early texts for children, in addition to relying on the visual, emphasized children's associations with the natural world (bestiaries and *Orbis Pictus* standing here as exemplary). Children's texts have long been identified as instructional or, more specifically, as acculturating, initiating children into an adult world by providing children with guidelines, values, and expectations of that adult world. Children's texts, even those considered to be fantasy or imaginary, were considered to be preparatory, texts designed to move the subject away from greenness through literate experiences. Such enculturation has also been identified as adult colonization of the child subject (Lesnik-Oberstein 1994; McGillis 1996; Rose 1992). For ecocriticism, the role of acculturation of the child subject as green subject has been a critical aspect of inquiry, questioning in what ways children's texts contribute to long-term attitudes toward nature and environment and how the child is represented textually as connected with nature/environment (Dobrin and Kidd 2004). Given that children's texts have traditionally incorporated both of these characteristics – the visual and the natural – it would seem that extended examinations of visual representations of nature in children's literatures/cultures would evolve within studies in children's literature to a greater degree.

The current hyper-circulatory condition of information exchange and the dominance of visuals within such environments demands that more complex understandings of visual ecologies be developed. Networked technologies (and cultures) alter child subjectivity not by way of the content or form circulated, but by the very fact that the child subject is now more directly enmeshed within larger systems of circulation and that within those systems, the velocity of hyper-circulation arranges subjects in more complex ways than previously considered. The child subject's ecological relationship within the network requires more complex understandings not only as to what subjectivity and childhood might mean, but specifically how the relationship between child subject (if there is even such a thing any longer) and visual circulation counter-affect the construction of each. Avenues for examining this degree of complexity might be found within the theories and methodologies of complex ecology.

Environmental criticism and complex ecology

The ecology of ecocriticism has only flirted with the 'systemness' of writing and the complexity of textual systems. Ecocriticism's ecology, for the most part, has been flat, limited to an ecology bound to the 'placeness' of writing and nature, and an over-exerted attention to nature writing and environmental politics instead of any serious attention to the ecologies of writing and texts themselves (and, in turn, the ramifications upon subject formation, or in the case of children's literatures, subject colonization). Perhaps this is the case because ecocriticism embraced a definition of ecology that focused particularly upon the relationships between organisms and their environments as a manner of promoting environmental (green) politics (see Garrard 2010). It is for this reason that part of my call here incorporates a turn to complex ecology and systems ecology as more productive avenues for ecological readings of all texts, particularly those categorized as children's literature – or more to the point those texts which researchers are eager to identify as evidently effecting how children engage nature and environment. Environmental literary criticism, like the science of ecology, requires a more complex notion of ecological methodologies in order to account for the complexity of textual systems, particularly as the current hyper-circulatory condition now demands more complex theories than ecocriticism has previously provided in examining the 'relationship between literature and the physical environment' (Glotfelty and Fromm 1996, xviii), theories that now need to evolve within a context of new rhetorics – like complex ecological, post-human, or visual rhetorics – without being bound to ensconced rhetorics and politics.

In 2004, my colleague Kenneth B. Kidd and I published a collection that began to push past ecocriticism's proto-ecological tendencies. One of the objectives of *Wild things: Children's culture and ecocriticism* was to move beyond traditional concepts of literature and text and toward more complex understandings of what ecocriticism can be. Within this special issue of *Environmental Education Research*, we see similar steps taken by scholars such as Phillip Payne, whose re-imagining of imagination through the combination or intersecting ecology of textual, visual, and embodied/experiential walks hand in hand with Gunther Kress' (2003, 3) formulation that imagination is the very method through which language is used in making meaning. Likewise, Stephen Bigger and Jean Webb's call to activism by way of story enables a reconsideration of the ecological relationships between reader and text, as does Geraldine Burke and Amy Cutter-Mackenzie's work with children and preservice teachers using A/r/t-*e*-ography and immersive pedagogies, and Amy Sloane's examination of the orientations and potentialities of texts such as *The Lorax*. Projects like these – and, in fact, the entire special issue – are efforts to slip the bonds of traditional literary or environmental criticism toward the end of a more rigorous consideration of the complexities of literatures, child subjects, and environmental education. I believe that by turning more direct attention toward visual texts, screen cultures, and complex ecologies, we can step beyond the ecological limits imposed by environmental criticisms.

The science of complex ecology is most often credited to the work of George van Dyne, the first Director of the Natural Resource Ecology Laboratory at Colorado State University (1970–1973), who argued for interdisciplinary methods of ecology and promoted some of the first systems-based approaches to ecology. Complex ecology evolved as a kind of critique of traditional ecological methods which, van Dyne and others argued, could not provide answers about the incalculable complexity of the world's ecologies. Complex ecology, as Bernard C. Patten (1995) pointed out, though, is a transitional ecology designed to move ecology 'from an empirical descriptive science to a powerful systems science of wholes,' but its current phase is 'an alchemic phase … the movement is just beginning' (xiv). A similar thing might be said of environmental criticism (thus, perhaps, the impetus for Buell's call). Ecology, as it was adopted by ecocriticism, was understood to be the study of relationships between organisms and their environments and within such study it is considered legitimate to concentrate on specific organisms – in the case of childhood studies and children's literature and culture, this focus turned to child subjects – or on the environments in which those organisms thrive. Systems ecology, which is closely tied to complex ecology, was first expressed by E.P. Odum in a 1964 issue of *BioScience* as addressing the 'structure and function of levels of organization beyond the individual and species' (1964, 14). What is interesting about this approach is not that it serves to overturn the 'old' ecology, but to work in conjunction with it to provide a more holistic view of systems, bringing together multi-disciplinary approaches that inform the larger picture. Granted, much of systems ecology is founded in the application of mathematics to understanding ecosystems, but its broader approach of attention to systems becomes useful for environmental or ecological criticisms, particularly in its claim that systems approaches require different theoretical and analytical tools than have sufficed in standard ecological methods. I take this as an indication that if scholarship and research on children's literature and environmental criticism are to provide any insight into the functions of children's texts (those for, by, and about the child subject) within the complex networked systems in which they circulate, such investigations cannot rely solely upon the methodologies already in place in either area of study, particularly when the complexity of networks now in place in which children's texts circulate are examined as a primary influential factor in both the dissemination and circulation of children's texts and, ultimately, children's subjectivities.

For ecocriticism, such a move also requires an expansion beyond literary forms to a greater understanding of textual transmission and circulation. As the idea of 'literature' becomes even more problematic amidst the rapid invention and dissemination of texts in networked culture, we must now consider the role visual texts play in transmitting environmental and ecological meaning/knowledge not as literature, but as post-literate text. For example, children's relationships with nature, place, and environment are likely to be as influenced (if not more so) by various new media texts as by what we might consider to be 'literature.' For instance, popular video games like Zoo Tycoon flagrantly call into question the relationship between human management and animal other, while games we might not immediately consider to be *about* environment, in fact, require detailed consideration of a players encounter with imagined places. Likewise, the ubiquity of films – those geared toward children and adult – which depict human–nature interactions contribute greatly to the viewer's environmental education. Consider, for instance, the barrage of American films that were produced leading up to the millennial shift about cataclysmic events: *Twister* (1996), *Volcano* (1997), *The Edge* (1997), *Dante's Peak* (1997), *Armageddon* (1998), *Deep Impact* (1998), to name but a few. Note the overriding themes in these films of nature's hell-bent attempt to destroy humans, and the ultimate outcome that humans will survive. Or, more accurately, note the deeply American attitude of natural conquest that permeates this genre. Note, too, that the period just before 2000 found the USA in an unusual situation of not having a specific named enemy toward which to direct nationalistic antagonism (a situation resolved by the 9/11 attacks and the redirection of antagonism against populations in the Middle East). The convenient emergence of these films allowed (or encouraged) the construction of nature as enemy. Note, too, the radical shift to include global politics in later films like *The Day After Tomorrow* (2004) and the politicizing of natural events (often named natural disasters) as was the case in the 2005 Hurricane Katrina and the 2004 Indian Ocean tsunami. While 2009's *Avatar* has led to a slew of comments about its ecocritical credentials, we must not forget that television, too, contributes to a never-ending, lifelong environmental education, for good and ill. Discovery Channel, National Geographic Channel, The Nature Channel, and other broadcast channels can contribute daily to viewer's attitudes toward environment, nature, and place (consider the role of Discovery Channel's *Shark week* shows). Many television shows now call into question the very reality of environmental depiction, relying on computer-generated graphics to reconstruct life-like visual depictions of extinct animals (consider *Dinosaur planet*, narrated by Christian Slater). Or the performances of *When dinosaurs walked* featuring life-like robotic and animatronic dinosaurs 'live on stage.' Examining the complex ecologies of these kinds of post-page texts becomes as important as understanding *how* they transmit or engage information about physical environments and nature. Ecology, for ecocriticism and environmental criticism – or any study that examines the relationships between agents and their environments – can no longer merely be about 'natural' ecologies; rather, the ecologies of information, network systems, and texts themselves must be central to understanding how ideas, relationships, and information about environments (all environments, not only natural ones) circulate and interact with subjects and their environments. While calls like those made by Richard Louv in his magnificent book *Last child in the woods: Saving our children from nature-deficit disorder* (2008) are right-minded in promoting a greater awareness of 'Nature,' they must be understood as greatly limiting the view of the contemporary child subject. One can no longer conveniently separate the ecological relationships between the child subject and natural environments from the ecological relationships of the child subject *and* the natural environment with the technological/digital environment. They are complex and inseparable.

The technologically driven media boom of the late twentieth and early twenty-first centuries has revealed textual circulation to be ecologically complex in ways not yet accounted for. Complex ecological approaches begin to account for the complexities of textual circulation, complexities that we must admit are so diverse and divergent that we may never be able to fully account for all of facets and functions. Consequently, we can assume that the theoretical methods used to engage children's texts in the past no longer provide the expansive needs of such examinations, thus limiting what we can know about the relevance of literatures to environmental education. Like the science of complex ecology which ventures off the beaten track of traditional scientific methods, children's literature and ecocriticism now hold the potential to provide new approaches to examining systems of circulation that engage visual textual information. In many ways, then, the shift from page to screen, from writing to visual, binds ecocriticism and children's literature in intellectual pursuit, their methodologies and purpose overlapping to the point of inseparability.

What makes this shift of particular interest to scholars of children's literatures and cultures and environmental criticism is an opportunity to redefine the nature–child connection in some rather exciting ways. The child subject historically has been presented as connected with Nature, a connection that is enhanced by the child's inexperience and innocence – green. Innocence lost distances the child from Nature/environment, eroding the connection. In networked culture, Nature/environment and the network are indistinguishable. The network is the environment. The nomos/physis binary unravels as the two become inextricably meshed and indistinguishable. This techno/natural hybrid is the environment to which the child is connected, and given its ever fluctuating state, it remains, at all times, green, connected with natural environments and as new growth. Literary depictions of children as chimera, hybrid, or cyborg not only ask us to consider the role of technology and networked culture as environment, but also begin to hint at the need to consider the child subject in light of post-humanist theory (see Anderson 2004 and Stables 2009). Given the (perhaps total) inescapability of the effects of biotechnical engineering, pharmacology, and information technologies upon nature that directly affect children and the continued hybridization of the two, ecological criticism requires a reframing of its central inquiry to ask not of the relationship between literature and the physical environment without acknowledging the technological reformation of that physical environment, and, in turn, the relationship between (child) subjectivity and those same environments. Such inquiries now require a more complex understanding of ecology and system because the child–nature relationship is more complex than traditionally engaged in scholarship. Shades, hues, variants, and degrees of green have emerged. To be merely green, now, is an oversimplification of both green and the complex subject–nature interaction. Part of this complex relationship is driven by the subject's ability to participate in the network, to stand as not just an interpreter of information, but an active producer of new growth.

From interpretation to production

Environmental criticism, like most other forms of literary criticism, is founded in methods of reading and analysis; that is, it is interpretive. However, given that environmental criticism now faces the challenge of considering how individual subjects interact with environments other than those considered 'natural,' it must also begin to account for the ways in which those same subjects contribute to the construction of those environments by way of the texts they produce, re-mix, and circulate. That is to say, no longer can ecocriticism be limited to inquires of interpretation, but should now also consider the role production plays in the relationship between subjects and their environments. This is of particular interest, I think, for those who work in the areas of children's literatures and ecocriticisms as such inquiries resituate the child subject not as empty vessel to be filled with the experiences of adulthood, not to be acculturated through text or literature into relationships with environment, but as active agents in the production and circulation of literatures, cultures, and identities. The child subject's ecological connection with environment, then, comes not from inexperience and innocence, but specifically from active participation. Connection with the environment is not heightened through ignorance, but empowered as an agent of circulation. Information is not merely cast down to the child subject, but is processed, remixed, and re-circulated between subjects.

Production, for children's literature, has traditionally been relegated to a condition of 'play' and as such devalued as a legitimate form of cultural production. The child-making is not the subject producing, but the subject forming. Yet, children produce: imaginative play, storytelling, building with blocks, and drawing pictures (see Bai et al. 2010; Burke and Cutter-Mackenzie 2010; Korteweg, Gonzalez, and Guillet 2010; Payne 2010), for instance, are all forms of production. Yet, when these forms have been regarded as educational, as methods for novice subjects to gather the experiences necessary to be authenticated as full-formed subjects, conventionally it has not been as authentic or valid forms in and of themselves. Education, in this paradigm, moves from the active (making) to the passive (interpreting) with the creation of interiority and subject formation. This is shaking off the green. Making a child's things – stories, imagined situations, a tower of blocks – is limited in circulation. Frequently, too, the things children make – a tower of blocks, a picture – are visual, pre-literate. Children are encouraged to begin with the visual and move to the verbal, the written, to become literate, thus becoming post-child. Pictures become stories become essays: visual to oral to literate, green subject to subject. Validation and authentication are granted when the visual is all but erased from the subject's production.

This paradigm is now in decay. Children – particularly in the West – are still inundated by visual texts, but the newer forms provide a significant difference from visual texts of the past: circulation. Circulation, here, does not merely imply that children have more rapid access to a wider variety of texts more quickly, but that they themselves can now circulate their own productions within the network in ways not before possible. Or to be more accurate, the child subject now circulates within the network in complex ways not yet considered. Children, like any other active subject within networked culture, operate not as agents outside or adjacent to the network, selecting and extracting information from the network or passively fed information from the network, but as conductors within and indistinguishable from the network, producing, remixing, and circulating information. Understanding the child subject in this way permits us to abandon the fetishization of the child as a green subject and begin to theorize the child subject as active and authentic. Only when the child subject occupies such a position within the network environment, will ecocritical inquiries into children's literatures and cultures be able to theorize the complex relationships those subjects form with all of their environments. If the underlying agenda of ecocriticism is to continue to forward green political positions, then there exists, too, an ethical imperative that those political positions not be constructed as independent of the network environments in which information is circulated, understanding that in screen culture nature/culture or nature/technology divisions can no longer be seen as identifiable binaries, but as integrated wholes. *Nature* and *environment* becoming empty metaphors when not situated in relation to the very networks through which they are defined. In this way, too, subjects – child, adult, learner, teacher, or otherwise – participate in an ongoing process of producing the very environments – natural, imagined, digital, or other – in which they circulate; a form, we might think of as digital photosynthesis, forming the foundation of information exchange within the network environment.

Production then is understood not as a moment of origin, but as a point of circulation, re-mix, and exchange. The child subject contributes to the flow and velocity of information exchange as an active agent not adding new information to the circulation, but by remixing its own version of that which already circulates. This is evident when children engage online texts, specifically (reading online texts, posting images, emailing, contributing to online communities, playing video games, etc.), but the connection extends beyond the evident online apparatus. The integration of digital technologies into everyday children's culture now dominates a child's engagement with text. Toys, like Webkins, provide online environments designed to appear as extensions of the physical play world, functioning more accurately as more expansive marketing mechanisms. Texts like books, films, and television programs now provide direct links to online environments for further, extended engagement. Even television networks devoted to children's programming encourage children to produce texts – art, written comments, images, etc. – for circulation and broadcast, stimulating not only active production of the child subject, but promulgating a culture of visual recognition that invigorates the idea that agency within the network is attained when one's productions are made visible by the network. This is evident in the broadcast and featuring of children's stories, artwork, and other productions on television stations and web pages. Such network mechanisms also contribute to the West's fascination with celebrity and the desire to be 'seen.' Likewise, wearable digital devices like cell phones, digital cameras, and digital video cameras are all signs of a cultural impetus upon making and circulating information – particularly visual information – within the network.

Screen cultures, networked societies, and visual rhetorics are the environments in which texts for the child subject, texts about the child subject, texts about texts-for-the-child-subject, and the child subject now function. Such environments are inextricably bound to the construction of such texts and subjects to the extent that they cannot be separated. Understanding the relationships between text, network, and subject require complex theories (and a complex of theories) and readings beyond what ecocriticism and children's literatures have thus provided. Such inquiries now require greater dedication to the role of the visual as visual elements evolve into a dominant form of information exchange. No longer relegated to pre-literate forms, visuals should take up a more significant position within the exchange between ecocriticism and children's cultures (cf. Hug 2010).

If we are to engage research toward the end of exploring the relevance of children's literature to environmental education, then part of our methodologies must be to see through green eyes, not in the ways that we might assume the inexperienced child subject sees the world, but in complex, rigorous ways that account for the role of the visual in all environmental education. The green subject is a visual subject, operating in a visual culture. Disciplinary anxieties must now be set aside in favor of an embrace of the visual and digital, as any hope there might be of the child subject better understanding the long-term effects of environmental interaction cannot be separated from the networks in which the child subject circulates.

Notes

1. What Greenfield does not claim in her report to the House of Lords is that such changes are inherently negative, but instead that there is a need to better understand the role of screen culture and information technologies and the ways in which humans are adapting to such changes in environmental conditions. The news media following her report, however, accentuated such changes as specifically negative, altering the perception of Greenfield's carefully chosen words to warnings. Greenfield's premises are intriguing, and certainly demand the kinds of research for which she calls.

2. Out of an interest for further explanation into Greenfield's ideas (which, interestingly, she often reports as 'suggestions' rather than more concrete forms of claims), I do want to note that when addressing the role of information technologies and social spaces – that is *MySpace, Facebook, YouTube* – Greenfield's notions of social interaction and technology seems to create a binary between a form of 'reality' and a technological simulacra. I find this kind of separation to be suspect in its authentication of pre-digital technologies as 'reality' and would – in another venue – like to explore the idea that technological spaces are 'less real' than other forms of spaces; I do not believe they are. Greenfield's claims have been criticized (correctly, I believe) as technophobic.

3. I use the term *visual texts* to suggest texts that rely primarily on visual representations other than writing. Writing, of course, is itself a visual text, but I mean here to distinguish between writing and other forms of texts. These terms are, of course, problematic, particularly for those of us interested in image as mechanisms of information conveyance given that the making of a visual is akin to the act of writing, if not identical. Likewise, the term *visual text* is used generically to include many forms of visual representations, including but not limited to images, graphics, animations, video, and so on. *Visual*, then, is intended as an umbrella term. I note these terminological differences because within the study of visual rhetorics the distinction between kinds of visuals is significant in how meaning is conveyed.

References

Anderson, M.T. 2004. *Feed.* Sommerville, MA: Candlewick Press.

Aries, P. 1962. *Centuries of childhood.* New York: Vintage Books.

Bai, H., D. Elza, P. Kovacs, and S. Romanycia. 2010. Re-searching and re-storying the complex and complicated relationship of *biophilia* and *bibliophilia. Environmental Education Research* 16, nos. 3–4: 351–65.

Bigger, S., and J. Webb. 2010. Developing environmental agency and engagement through young people's fiction. *Environmental Education Research* 16, nos. 3–4: 401–14.

Burke, G., and A. Cutter-Mackenzie. 2010. What's there, what if, what then, and what can we do? An immersive and embodied experience of environment and place through children's literature. *Environmental Education Research* 16, nos. 3–4: 311–330.

Burnett, F.H. 1983. *The secret garden.* New York: Signet Classic.

Dobrin, S.I., and K.B. Kidd. 2004. *Wild things: Children's culture and ecocriticism.* Detroit, MI: Wayne State University Press.

Garrard, G. 2010. Problems and prospects in ecocritical pedagogy. *Environmental Education Research* 16, no. 2.

Glotfelty, C., and H. Fromm. 1996. *The ecocriticism reader: Landmarks in literary ecology.* Athens: University of Georgia Press.

Greenfield, S. 2009. *Screen culture may be changing our brains.* http://www.abc.net.au/7.30/content/2009/s2521139.htm.

Hiaasen, C. 2006. *Hoot.* New York: Yearling.

Hug, J.W. 2010. Exploring instructional strategies to develop prospective elementary teachers' children's literature book evaluation skills for science, ecology and environmental education. *Environmental Education Research* 16, nos. 3–4: 367–82.

Jenkins, H. 1998. *The children's culture reader.* New York: New York University Press.

Killingsworth, M.J., and J.S. Palmer. 1992. *Ecospeak: Rhetoric and environmental politics in America.* Carbondale: Southern Illinois University Press.

Kingsley, C. 2007. *The water-babies.* Fairfield, IA: First World Library.

Korteweg, L., I. Gonzalez, and J. Guillet. 2010. The stories are the people and the land: Three educators respond to environmental teachings in Indigenous children's literature. *Environmental Education Research* 16, nos. 3–4: 331–50.

Kress, G. 2003. *Literacy in the new media age.* New York: Routledge.

Lesnik-Oberstein, K. 1994. *Children's literature: Criticism and the fictional child.* Oxford: Clarendon Press.

Louv, R. 2008. *Last child in the woods: Saving our children from nature-deficit disorder.* Chapel Hill, NC: Algonquin Books.

McGillis, R. 1996. *The nimble reader: Literary theory and children's literature.* New York: Twayne.

Morgan, A. 2010. *The Lord of the Rings* – a *mythos* applicable in unsustainable times? *Environmental Education Research* 16, nos. 3–4: 383–99.

Morgenstern, J. 2002. The fall into literacy and the rise of the bourgeois child. *Children's Literature Association Quarterly* 27, no. 3: 136–45.

Odum, E.P. 1964. The new ecology. *BioScience* 14: 14–16.

O'Malley, A. 2003. *The making of the modern child: Children's literature and childhood in the late eighteenth century.* New York/London: Routledge.

Patten, B.C. 1995. Why 'complex' ecology? In *Complex ecology: The whole-part relation in ecosystems,* ed., B.C. Patten and S.E. Jørgensen, xiii–xxiii. Upper Saddle River, NJ: Prentice Hall.

Payne, P.G. 2010. Remarkable-tracking, experiential education of the ecological imagination. *Environmental Education Research* 16, nos. 3–4: 295–310.

Porter, G.S. 2006. *The girl of the limberlost.* Winnetka, CA: Norilana Books.

Rose, J. 1992. *The case of Peter Pan or the impossibility of children's fiction.* Philadelphia: University of Pennsylvania Press.

Sloane, A. 2010. Reading *The Lorax,* orienting in potentiality. *Environmental Education Research* 16, nos. 3–4: 415–28.

Stables, A. 2009. *Childhood and the philosophy of education: An anti-Aristotelian perspective.* London: Continuum.

Ulmer, G.L. 2003. *Internet invention: From literacy to electracy.* New York: Longman.
Wason-Ellam, L. 2010. Children's literature as a springboard to place-based embodied learning. *Environmental Education Research* 16, nos. 3–4: 279–94.

Re-searching and re-storying the complex and complicated relationship of *biophilia* and *bibliophilia*

Heesoon Bai, Daniela Elza, Peter Kovacs and Serenna Romanycia

Faculty of Education, Simon Fraser University, Burnaby, BC, Canada

This article is a collaborative bricolage of poetry, autobiographical fragments, essay pieces, and images assembled together as a portrait of the authors' ongoing existential, psychological and epistemological struggles as educators and learners, parents and children. The article captures a reflective exploration and collective sharing of their own life experiments, seeking to create ripples of provocation as well as resonation in the reader. Identifying *biophilia* (love of life/nature) as a key learning in environmental education, this work looks into the complex and complicated relationship between *biophilia* and *bibliophilia* (love of books). The article ends by identifying indwelling experience as key to *biophilia*, and suggests and advocates poetry-making and story-telling as methods for fostering indwelling.

Our story

> The main battlefield for good is not the open ground of the public arena, but the small clearing of each heart. (Yann Martel 2001, 102)

We, the authors of this article, are teachers, mothers, a father and a young adult daughter. As well, we are poets, visual artists and environmental activists. Since this writing is a piece of narrative inquiry with an autoethnographic component, we place here a brief introduction of ourselves.

Heesoon Bai is a Professor in Education, and started a PhD program in philosophy of education that offers integrative studies in *ecology, consciousness* and *community*, or as she captions it, 'Soil, soul and society'. Prior to entering graduate studies, she spent 10 years homeschooling her two daughters. Serenna Romanycia (age 21), Heesoon's younger daughter, majors in anthropology, focusing on political ecology, and minors in education. Daniela Elza, a multilingual poet with numerous prizes in poetry, is a PhD student of Heesoon Bai in philosophy of education who poeticizes philosophy and philosophizes poetry, and brings them both to bear on school reform and cultural ferment. Her daughter Mina (age 12), whose voice also figures in this work, although not as an author of this article, is already an environmental activist in her own right (see http://cobwebsandseaslugs.com and also http://childrenforna-ture.com) as well as a voracious reader and writer of poetry and novels (see http://www.pandorascollective.com/eternalgarden.html, http://www.pandorascollective.

com/dragonfly.html and http://www.pandorascollective.com/mypetmountain.html).
Peter Kovacs, another polyglot and also a PhD student of Heesoon Bai in philosophy
of education, has an extraordinary sensibility to language and love of books.

All of us are serious *bibliophiles* and *biophiles*. What initially drew the three
parents (Heesoon, Daniela and Peter) together to work on this research project that
resulted in writing this article is the discovery that in our respective lived experiences
of parenting we tried to cultivate in our children *biophilia* through *bibliophilia*, imagining that there was a direct and straightforward connect, almost a causal connection,
between the two. However, reality most often works out differently from our hopes
and expectations. Our own two daughters, whose voices and experiences about their
embodiment of *biophilia* we invited to this project and included in this article,
illustrate complicated connections, as we shall see. Our parenting experience 'taught'
us that the *biophilia–bibliophilia* connection we were seeking is much more complex,
ambiguous, surprising and even tenuous. Especially in the case of Peter, the *bibliophile extraordinaire*, he is facing the devastating irony of his autistic son possibly not
speaking or reading, let alone writing. In our research he represents the silent voice
that has to witness the very absence of any actual evidence of *biophilia–bibliophilia*
connection in his parenting. His contribution to this work has been valuable in terms
of providing insightful ideas and helping with writing.

This article captures a reflective exploration and collective sharing of our own life
experiments, seeking to create ripples of provocation as well as resonance in the reader.
Given this intent, it is fair to declare from the outset that our work blurs
autoethnographic techniques with those of narrative work. Hart states: 'at its best, narrative inquiry has the power to bring together stories and in so doing transform the story
and the participants in the process' (Hart 2003, 9). He further states: 'explanations
appear to settle issues… whereas narratives raise issues, inviting us to rethink what we
thought we knew' (9). Exactly, our own work here confirms Hart's understanding. Our
article does not aim to prove, disprove or even recommend any generalizable pedagogic
thesis, if indeed such research intent is possible today in a postmodernity burdened with
the understanding that 'there can never be a final, accurate representation of what was
meant or said – only different textual representations of different experiences' (Denzin
2003, 5). Our kind of research *re*-searches lived experience to glean insights and further
illuminate and animate personal experience. It is best offered, we believe, as an invitation to the reader to enter into a textual field of resonance and see how the text evokes,
provokes, illuminates and animates their own subjective experience.

Another way of understanding the nature of this work is as a philosophical
rumination, a well-practiced genre in traditional philosophical writing. The matter that
we place before our reader to ruminate with us is what we see as the insufficiency of
biophilia (love of life/nature), which we contend has resulted in environmental
devastation, including accelerated rate of species extinction. As Raimondo Panikkar
says: 'holistic Philosophy… makes us very sensitive to the state of the world today
and constantly brings our philosophical discussion to the vital problems of our
contemporary human predicament' (1992, 237). As authors who attempted to enact
the *biophilia–bibliophilia* relationship in our own parenting and being parented, we
are now ruminating together to compare notes on how our love of words and worlds
came to shape and colour our parenting, teaching and learning over the years at home
and at our respective learning institutions, and how we might better incline *bibliophilia* towards *biophilia*. The result – this article – is a bricolage of our own poetry,
select autobiographical fragments that the four of us authors generated since the fall

of 2008 through emailing each other questions and responses during the preparation of this work, and essay pieces assembled together over time, as a portrait of ongoing struggle 'to know, to love, and to heal – all in one', which is the 'task of Philosophy' (Panikkar 1992, 237).

Looking up, on the lap

Parents are the first teachers of children. Our children learn how to be in the world – what to value or what not to value, how to treat others, how to love and care or exploit, neglect and abuse – from the very first moment of their coming into this world. This learning does not have to be didactic or even discursive. How we touch and caress – or not touch – our babies, how we carry them about, how we look into their eyes, how we sing to them, how we sunbathe them, let the wind play on their faces and hair, how we bring them to flowers and trees to look at and touch, how we call their attention to the birds in the sky and on tree tops. How we attend with them. How we listen to what they have to say, even when they cannot say much. And how we interpret what they say within the context of our experience and theirs. What we read to them, and more importantly, *how* we read to them. All these are subtle but powerful lessons we teach them about the world and their relationship to the world, and our place in the world. Are we 'organs of this world, flesh of its flesh, and… the world is perceiving itself *through* us?' (Abram 1996, 68). Or is this world alien and something we have to fear and work against?

A major part of our own struggle as parents (Heesoon, Daniela and Peter) has been how and to what extent to protect our children from societal values and practices that we perceive as harmful prejudices and influences on the young, impressionable minds, as far as teaching *biophilia* goes. Not everything that goes on under the auspices of education and/or schooling is wholesome and worthy of respect. This is particularly the case in today's world whose dominant ideology is consumer-capitalism and whose dominant value is instrumentalism. *Biophilia* is not too well nurtured and does not grow within instrumentalist ideology and value for the simple and clear reason that what is not human only has the use value to human needs and wants (Bai and Scutt 2009). In many instances, conventional education is none other than the transmission of the prevailing societal value of instrumentalism. This we know articulately now and have the words to describe and explain in the context of our academic studies. As young parents, we (Daniela and Heesoon) intuited the problem of instrumentalism with respect to nature in the context of encountering the depiction of nature as primitive, dangerous, dark and cruel, as portrayed in many traditional fairytales. Such depiction goes hand-in-hand with normalization of actual practices of instrumentalism such as battery farming and clear-cut logging, just to mention two of the better-known examples. We as young mothers struggled with the decision about whether or not to expose our babies to fairytales such as those of the Brothers Grimm (Zipes 1987), because of violent, cruel, sexist, anti-nature notions and imageries:

> I never felt comfortable reading fairytales to my kids. I did not see much value in them or much excitement and opportunities for creativity and play. It is one thing to read them as some oddity from centuries past, like watching a commercial, knowing it is trying to sell you something, but I felt like I would be committing a crime if I took the sell as an entry into the world. I cannot defend Jack in 'Jack and the Beanstalk'. In fact, I thought Jack acted irresponsibly when he robbed the giant, and at the end killed him. Or take the case of the Big Bad Wolf. Wolves were my daughter's favourite animals, so the Big Bad Wolf was a hard sell. Sleeping Beauty was definitely not what I wanted my daughter to emulate. (Daniela)

There was no way that I was going to inflict images of dark scary forests and monstrous beasts on my own babies. I did not want my children to grow up under the psychological conditioning of fear from darkness, forests and animals. Certainly, children need to learn caution and care when it comes to their safety in the world, but the psychological hampering of children by fear-induction is morally reprehensible. I speak from my own experience. I was terrified of darkness as a child because of all the scary stories told to me in association with darkness. When I was growing up, electricity was scarce, and every night, I had to walk to the outhouse in the dark to pee, and I was petrified. Also I was scared of animals (except little insects that were around me aplenty), not because I was exposed to them but, again, because of the psychological condition of fear and disgust injected into me. Animals were portrayed as brutes. So, in my own parenting, I was careful about not transmitting to my children negative perceptions about darkness, animals, and forests. I am happy to know that my daughters do not suffer from such fears. (Heesoon)

The following fragment by Heesoon's younger daughter corroborates Heesoon's decision on the choice of children's literature in terms of *biophilia*:

My love of nature has always had a deep connection to literature. I was a voracious reader; I grew up in my imagination, in a fantasy world full of different spaces and contexts and characters. I loved *Wind in the willows*, Beatrix Potter, the *Narnia* books – these books shaped my perception of the world. The forests of my childhood were sometimes real, sometimes fantasy, and they were both psychologically and literally where I grew up. They were full of safety, full of adventure, full of connectedness and peace. I would retreat into the forests of my imagination whenever I felt like the real world was upsetting or scary. I believe all children retreat into their imagination, but I am glad that in mine there were always woodlands and forests and creatures waiting there for me. As I grew into an adolescent, the transition from imagined forests to real forests was natural – I would seek out nature to find peace and calm, just like I sought out my fantasy nature to find peace and calm as a child. I recall that some of the happiest moments of my childhood were found in reading my favourite books alone (Figure 1). (Serenna)

Children do need stories to have ideas about the world, to find out how they fit in, and to discover what sorts of relationships they could have with the world. We agree with Dehò (2007, 121) who says: 'We know that children love stories, and they need them as a way of putting order into the "things" of this world. And books contain secrets'. But what is the order into which we want to put the 'things' of this world? For a long time now we have been establishing certain orders that we now entitle as 'Modernity'. Increasingly, however, people are becoming disillusioned with the beliefs and values of modernity: anthropocentrism, unlimited human progress through domination and control of the material world (also known as nature), instrumental values of non-human animals and other sentient beings, and the so-called inanimate 'things', and privileging of the rational (that humans are supposed to possess but something that animals lack) over the affective. The list is long and painful to those who have become disillusioned with beliefs and values of modernity. As teachers and parents we need to ask ourselves whether the worldview and values that children's literature or, for that matter, *any* texts, that are assigned to children portray and support *biophilia* or, as David W. Orr (1994, 137) calls it, *biophobia* (fear of life). When we see humanity engaging in activities that directly and massively precipitate species extinction, which is surely necrophilic, we do need to critically and carefully investigate the connections between what we put before our children to read and what actions are taking place in the world (Bonnett 1997; Bowers 1995). Additionally, going a step further, we need to ask: what kinds of children's literature would develop new

Figure 1.   *Unity* by Serenna Romanycia (2008).

sensibilities and sensitivities that support and promote biophilia? We are happy to see that in the field of children's literature, there are now many studies that provide a comprehensive guide to children's books that attempt to restore 'endangered relationship' between the natural world and humans (Trousdale 2008, 43).

Teaching love of nature does not mean we do not need to teach safety and self-protection in nature or around non-human beings. We are not advocating naïve romanticism about nature. Mature love includes respect, care and protection of self and others, and concern for the well-being of all involved. But it is fear, suspicion and, perhaps worse, indifference, towards what is not human, which often implicitly defines what nature is or means, that we are questioning. For instance, in the name of teaching children about the real world full of evils and misfortunes, and the need to overcome obstacles and battle evil, it has been advised that parents expose, in varying degrees, their children to stories of evil – actual or imagined – that are projected onto beings of nature. Bettelheim was one such thinker. In his highly influential book, *The uses of enchantment*, Bettelheim (1977) examines some of the best-known stories told to children in the west. From his Freudian perspective, beloved tales like 'Cinderella',

'Hansel and Gretel', 'Little Red Riding Hood', 'Snow White', 'Jack and the bean-stalk' and 'The Sleeping Beauty' contain invaluable moral lessons. Bettelheim argues that, far from being merely simplistic tales of magic and enchantment, these stories are laden with lessons in moral education, demonstrating the dire consequences of not obeying one's parents and of venturing too far off the beaten track. Bettelheim believes that these fairytales are more than cautionary tales about what happens when someone deviates from the norm; in his opinion they also help children to resolve conflicts they might be experiencing in their lives, showing them the most effective way to deal with certain unpleasant situations or offer explanations that will help children deal with a feeling of resentment or a sense of alienation, for instance. These tales get across to the child the crucial message that a struggle against considerable difficulties in life is inevitable, but if one 'steadfastly meets unexpected and often unjust hardships', one can overcome any and all difficulties (8).

Bettelheim (1977, 8) argues that fairytales present 'existential dilemma[s] briefly and pointedly', and this allows the children 'to come to grips with the problem in its most essential form'. We agree with Bettelheim's reasoning, but question his defence of traditional fairytales with their blatant anthropocentric projections of human cruelty and evil. Serenna, Heesoon's daughter, takes a middle ground on the issue:

> Of course, I also read stories in which animals were cruel and vicious, and forests were dark and threatening – and this is not entirely untrue. Nature is full of pain and suffering – one life form eats another life form, after all. But to me, the most important thing was that literature constantly exposed me to different perceptions of nature, and I grew to be familiar with it and with multiple perceptions of it. It is akin to knowing all sides of a parent – their loving side, their angry side, their forgiving sides, and their stubborn side. I grew to love nature because I am not unfamiliar with it. It does not feel like a stranger to me. It is woven into me through all the stories I have listened to, all the forests I have walked through, all the experiences I have had, both directly and vicariously. It has become so completely integrated into my experience that I cannot help but try to pass the experience on, to tell my own stories, to repeat what I know to others. And I can only hope my love of nature will continue. (Serenna)

Pointing to the moon

Love of nature, *biophilia*, is, like most things in our culture, a language-mediated practice. Humans are conceptual beings. We experience – not only think about, but also perceive and feel – the world through our conceptual assemblages. What nature is like to us is no exception. Teaching our children to respect, revere and be compassionate and nurturing towards nature will have to be, and is, a conceptually mediated practice. Words (both spoken and read) and images (both seen and imagined) are a major vehicle in sharing our own love and appreciation of nature with our children or students and fostering theirs. This is where *bibliophilia* and *biophilia* came together for us, the authors of this article. To wit:

> Literature was definitely a strong influence in my childhood. Books created and fuelled my imagination, and I don't ever remember there being a shortage of books! Every new book I read added on to the world inside my head, and the books that I loved the most were always about animals and nature, so it would make sense to me that literature was perhaps the strongest influence of my childhood. (Serenna)

Here is another account, this time from Serenna's mother, on how words are the midwife who births the relationship of articulated knowing between us humans and the green kingdom:

My girls and I lived in a small forest in the middle a bustling city, Vancouver. This forest, an endowment land to the University of British Columbia, was a significant part of my girls' childhood and their formation of self-identity and (com)passion for the natural world. Walks and other activities in the forest was our daily fare. One time we signed up for a nature walk with a local botanist who was a graduate student. As we walked through the trail, the botanist pointed to all sorts of bushes, shrubs, trees and low-lying plants and told us their names and their growing habits. What happened then was rather magical! Suddenly, after hearing the names of what were previously to me just various clumps of green matter, I saw them as distinct and unique individual beings. It was as though these green masses came into a different sphere of existence: unique individuals with names and faces that I could relate to personally. The power of naming and being named! I had a whole different sense of their existence, and my relationship to them changed… forever. (Heesoon)

Notwithstanding the power of language in its ability to nurture *biophilia*, the power of discursive language also runs the danger of inhibiting *biophilia*, and this concern goes beyond that of the right choice of literature that we discussed in the previous section. Let us explain the basis of our claim: all relationships run the danger of one member overwhelming and colonizing the other. The relationship between *words* and *worlds* runs the same risk. Humans are so deeply languaged that we forget that language is only an act of pointing, like the finger that points to the moon. With this forgetting, we end up only gazing at the finger, mistaking the finger for the moon. This is particularly the case with explicative language, as in our empirical discourses that tell us what the *facts* of the world are. We forget that the nature that lies outside the human conceptualization does not come already classified in the way our language(s) require(s). For example, the habit of dividing nature into two fundamental categories, the animate and the inanimate, is something we learn as members of a modern western culture that speaks certain languages. Yet, the learning is so deeply internalized that we cannot help seeing the world in terms of the animate/inanimate binary. The point we are making is not that we should not see the world in terms of this binary, or that some other truths lie 'out there' that we do not know about. Rather, our concern is that we forget that our language is no more than fingers pointing, and that there are more than one correct finger that can point and more than one way of pointing. And most importantly, we forget to look at the moon beyond the finger. This warning assumes an unprecedented magnitude today as the world becomes almost completely urbanized, and our children, surrounded by every imaginable media devices, are less and less exposed to direct contact with nature. Nature as non-discursive phenomena has never been so far away from humanity as today:

Today, around the world, many children grow up without having set their foot on humus-rich soil in a forest but only on concrete pavements of a city. I remember hearing from one of the students I was teaching in my graduate class, who was a high school teacher, that he observed a strange phenomenon among some of his students: they kept losing their balance and falling down all the time when he took them out on a nature walk. He discovered that these teenagers, many of whom grew up in the dense mega-cities of Asia, never walked in the forest. They had one job in life, which was to study hard day and night and do well in school. Their feet were used to only the smooth and hard surface of pavements, and could not handle the uneven ground full of slippery logs, rocks and cavities. The parents of these urbanized children themselves may have come from rural environments, but for them nature does not have a high value. Nature is everything that is uncivilized, pre-modern and, therefore, not progressive: something they worked incredibly hard to move away from, physically and emotionally. As parents these people would teach their children, explicitly and implicitly, that nature is dirty, dangerous, primitive, has no intrinsic worth other than use value only to humans. Worse, they also teach their children to see nature as something that should be destroyed and replaced by civilization full of written words, media and information technology. (Heesoon)

It makes sense to assume that all children in their embodied totality start out as potential lovers of nature, full of curiosity and wonder. As the painter and writer Bateman (2000, 31) explains:

> Children are naturally enchanted by the world of trees, birds, plants, and rivers, and some take delight in drawing and painting them. Most stay interested until the age of twelve or thirteen, but some, like me, never lose their enthusiasm.

What causes most of them to fall out of love with nature around or before the time they reach puberty? Canadian philosopher Neil Evernden (1985, 14) observes:

> ... our transformation from beings with an interest in a mechanical order did not come easily or quickly, and still does not. Children are prone to assume that the world is, like themselves, alive and sensate. Only age and education can 'correct' their view.

Both Aldo Leopold (1949) and David Orr (1994), separated by nearly half a century, have thought similarly about the egregious role of education focused on discursive, disembodied – the so-called 'bookish' – learning in diminishing our sensibility and *biophilia* towards nature. We may teach children *about* nature through books, films, and online materials, but such learning is not the same as experiential learning through direct contact with nature and through embodied participation. In the terms of Zen, we need to *become one with* nature (Carter 1995) in order to become deeply *biophilic*. But as long as we think that nature is outside us, physically and psychologically, and that humans belong to a superior order of being, true *biophilia* will not be learned, even if mediated by the best and most powerful literature. We will return to this point in the penultimate section in making the distinction between teaching as information transmission and teaching as storytelling.

When we externalize nature, we are prone to separating nature from culture, and then get into an untenable position of trying to protect nature from culture (society and humanity). In our own parenting, we struggled with this issue, especially given that all of us were deeply *bibliophilic*, and book reading and studying was a very strong family culture that permeated our households. We found ourselves unwittingly walking into a conflict between 'being out in nature and playing' and 'staying indoors and studying', and perpetuating the dominant school culture of 'indoorism' (Orr 1994). Neither side wins from such conflict. Both lose. The most viable course of action would be seeing nature and culture as intertwined and working in partnership towards biophilia. However, this viewpoint necessitates, first of all, discarding the exclusionary definition of nature as what human beings are not; and secondly, reconceptualizing nature differently. But how? Mina, our 12-year-old environmental activist who exemplifies youth eco-leadership in school, shares the following observation that we find insightful:

> It is hard to say what actually influenced me, however I was not inhibited from being in nature (and getting 'dirty') and it seems that that connection formed naturally (no pun intended). It is not a matter of being influenced to embrace nature so much as not being influenced not to. (Mina, Daniela's daughter)

Mina's remark reminds us of Bateman's remark, which we quoted previously, that 'Children are *naturally* enchanted by the world of trees, birds, plants, and rivers...' (2000, 31, italics ours). In other words, *biophilia* is inherent in us and teaching biophilia is not so much about introducing something new to and imposing something on our children as it is about not suppressing or killing what is already in them through the process of so-called becoming educated and cultured or civilized. Let us probe a little further this notion of nature as what is already in ourselves.

According to Jan Zwicky (2008, 90), 'Nature is the tendency in things to be what they are, and in that tendency to present themselves as both distinct and connected'. This definition of 'nature', if embraced wholeheartedly, would have a great impact on how we educate children. Nature in the sense of the 'tendency in things to be what they are' is another meaning of 'wild' or 'wilderness'. Our children are 'wild' as long as we do not crush their natural tendencies. Hence teaching *biophilia* is not about teaching them *about* nature, as in a science or environmental class, or even particularly or exclusively about taking them outdoors and to wilderness in experiential learning. To note, there are research and publications that deal with science education as environmental education (Littledyke 2004; Vazquez 2008), and we do not discount their pedagogic value. They have their place in formal learning. However, since our foremost concern in terms of teaching *biophilia* is disembodiment connected to discursive and informational learning, we focus our work on the more philosophical discussions about the word–world relationship and how that plays out in teaching *biophilia*.

Forest of colours

Birds chirp in golden notes
Trees whisper silently
in their silken green kimonos of leaves
A violet butterfly prances to and fro
on the breeze
softly blowing away the swirling white mist
The hot orange sun blazes down
Dancing on blue rippling streams
The yellow of the dandelions
The turquoise of lambs quarters
are what makes this place
this place

Mina Elza (2005)

Becoming the moon

Our own growing conviction as we ruminate and write this article together is that, when it comes down to the essence, teaching biophilia has less to do with using the right literature, or interacting with nature in the outdoors and wilderness; it has more to do with not suppressing but tending to children's absorption and delight in *being* who they are, how they are and where they are. As parents and educators, the hardest lesson we ever learned in parenting and teaching is tending whole-heartedly to our children's and students' absorption in their *being* (Fromm 1996). Our tendency, based on the way we were educated, is to interfere and intervene whatever children and students are doing, 'stealing' their attention from where they belong – to their being, insisting that they pay their attention to always something else more important, educational, productive, that lies outside their subjectivity, rather than what they are already experiencing and paying attention to in the moment. It is in this vein that many parents schedule just about every minute of their children's day with one form of (learning) activity or another, including, probably, earth-saving ecological activities. *Biophilia* as love of life/nature has no chance to take root in a consciousness that is busily and excessively into 'doing' and 'having', however educational. *Biophilia* grows in *being*: *being senses, being bodies, being perceptions, being feelings*. And *being* requires the experiencing subject's attending to and indwelling his or her experience *here and now* (Bai 2001). This is why, we think, the typical pedagogic impulse to continuously siphon out students' attention and draw them away from their selves to external objects of learning, however worthy and useful, does not cohere with our understanding of education for *biophilia*. For love of life/nature to grow in our children and students, we need to return their attention and energy to their being – to themselves. But how do we do this in terms of school learning, especially in language arts, since our interest is the intersecting relationship between *biophilia* and *bibliophilia*? We shall gesture towards two figures on the horizon of being: poetry and storytelling.

Jan Zwicky (2008, 88) states: 'Nature poetry's business is not actually words, it is the practice, the discipline, of wholeness, a coming-home to the unselfed world'. What is this 'unselfed' place? From our own experience of living, playing and learning with our children, we answer: when we are moved deeply, when we resonate with the coherence of the world that surrounds us, we become 'unselfed' and *biophilia* bursts open in our being. When we experience the other as 'a dynamic presence that confronts us and draws us into relation' (Abram 1996, 56) we are unselfed. 'To touch the coarse skin of a tree is thus, at the same time, to experience one's own tactility, to feel oneself touched by the tree' (68). Otherwise, we are always captives of our own ego selves, and the world 'out there' (even if by that we mean 'nature') is just the projections of our ego features. We wish to accent that this learning to enter into interbeing of mutuality (Hanh 1999) or co-emergence with the world (Varela, Thompson, and Rosch 1991) is the real lesson in ecology and environmental education. To the extent that we remain in the egoic consciousness that externalizes nature/life and world, and draws a boundary around the self and sees the world as otherness, to that extent ecology is a failed lesson, even if we are tracking in wilderness and know a million bits of important ecological facts. *Biophilia* only emerges when we can indwell our beingness or be present to the here and now, wherever we are. Not surprisingly, this is the same lesson in poetry-making and moving into a poetic consciousness.

What is most poignant about poetry is that, unlike the explicative language, it is aware that it is pointing and invoking. Explicative language tends to fool us into thinking that it describes the world 'out there', unlike poetry that imagines. Again and again, we are trapped in the binary of reality and imagination. But, says Abram:

> … that which we call imagination is from the first an attribute of the senses themselves; imagination is not a separate mental faculty (as we so often assume) but rather the way the senses themselves have of throwing themselves beyond what is immediately given in order to make tentative contact with the other side of things that we do not sense directly, with the hidden or invisible aspect of the sensible. (Abram 1996, 58)

The pedagogical import of what Abram says here is immense and challenging. Learning and using learning in schooling and elsewhere is far more into the explicative than into the evocative, and this imbalance, as reflected in our education system, is problematic in terms of the openness and connection we seek with/in nature. Note here that we are not saying that the explicative per se is problematic. The explicative has its role and use, and we need it. Rather, we are pointing to its preponderance, and the relative paucity of the evocative, that is, the poetic. The resonant space of indwelling experience,

where the world moves us to exclaim, point to what moves and call each other's attention, is rather rare in our everyday environments of home, school and everywhere else.
We are not easily moved. We rarely resonate with the world around us. But uninhibited
children, especially young ones, do. Poetry gushes out of them and pierces us into the
knowledge that we are also dealing with forces we do not necessarily understand. But
demand for exactitude of explication, required for control and prediction favoured by
science and technology, is what drives much of our learning and working.

Storytelling has much in common with poetry in terms of provoking presencing.
Storytelling is not information transmission but consciousness transformation. It sinks
into our being, and alters who we are. To wit:

> I have come to realize that my love of nature would be quite different had I experienced
> it without the captivating magic of stories. It seems to me that many children today are
> 'taught' to love certain things by being given pleasant and positive information about
> these objects of learning; children are given wonderful facts about nature, asked to
> engage in activities and given texts to read about those things 'to be loved', and are
> expected that this information will instill a love of that subject within them. But the mere
> appreciation that information gives is not equivalent to the deep meaning and values that
> is derived from storytelling. The difference between storytelling and information is well
> described by cultural critic, Walter Benjamin (Benjamin and Jennings 1999, 729): 'the
> value of information does not survive the moment in which it was new'; it is disposable
> and is easily forgotten. Storytelling, on the other hand, is 'the art of repeating stories'
> (729), and it becomes integrated into the listener's life experience. Storytelling 'does not
> aim to convey the pure essence of the thing, like information or report. It [instead] sinks
> the thing into the life of the storyteller, in order to bring it out of him again' (729).
> Stories, then, become engrained in our memories not because they are compilations of
> interesting information that we make a conscious effort to remember, but because we
> simply cannot forget them. Good stories effortlessly work their way into their listeners
> and transform them into storytellers themselves.
>
> Stories are not merely the experience of the individual, but the shared meaning held by
> communities of listeners who repeat the tale amongst themselves and to others. If the
> community of listeners disappears, the story dies as well, which has happened in many
> indigenous communities around the world. In this way, storytelling is fraught with both
> profound meaning and deep love.
>
> My love of nature grew within me through listening to stories, stories that sunk deeply
> into my perception of the world and consequently shaped the stories that I tell, and will
> continue to tell, my entire life. Literature is certainly not the only form of storytelling,
> but it is a powerful one, especially because it is most often an individual experience. In
> the stories I read I forged a deep and intimate connection with nature, and I am sure that
> this has much to do with the reading choices my parents, especially my mother, gave me
> (Figure 2). (Serenna)

Ineonclusion

The research that has culminated in writing the present collaborative article has been
a great opportunity for us the four authors to trace the connection between *bibliophilia*
and *biophilia* as it played out in our respective lives. In lieu of a research conclusion,
we are invoking Hart's idea (2003, 9) of the power of narratives to 'raise issues, inviting us to rethink what we thought we knew' as we continue to navigate the terrain of
environmental education.

A signpost, then, for fellow travelers on the journey called '*human life on earth*'.
Children are constantly striving to intuit the wholeness and its coherence and

Figure 2. *Highnoon* by Serenna Romanycia (2008).

complexity of what is around them, be that the meadow, or the story. It may be hard to accept this Buddha-like quality, but many of us who have lived with and loved children are familiar with it, recognize it, and we secretly cherish it. If we listen care-fully, quite often they pierce us with their perceptions and leave us longing after a wholeness we may have lost sight of. The heart of ecological perception and understanding is precisely this intuiting of wholeness. The ecological consciousness is therefore nascent in young children. *Biophilia* is in them, in us, is who we are. Humanity *comes home* in *biophilia*. Yet we may forget who we are, and have lost our way – not in the forest but in discursive languages that take us away from our senses and presence. Ecology is an art of homecoming for the souls lost, not in wilderness, but in senseless discursivity of the mind fed on abstract and fragmented information that often passes as knowledge in schools. However, poetry-making and storytelling can return us to our bodies and senses, and to our indwelling presence. To us, *bibliophilia* in the form of poetry-making and storytelling is really the heart of environmental education. Hence poetry-making and storytelling are perhaps our best navigational devices that may lead us home – to *biophilia*. It is with this insight that we offer the following poem composed by Daniela Elza as the reader's homing device:

if bachelard were in verse II (Elza 2008)[1]

life begins well.
                  it begins   enclosed.
protected.   all warm in the bosom   (of the house.
it is body   and soul.
            it is the human being's
first world.
when   being is being-   well
in the well being   originally associated
                         with being.
in its countless alveoli   space
            contains compressed time.
            within the being
in the being of within
            an enveloping warmth welcomes
        (being
         reigns in a sort of earthly paradise
of matter.
         and the poet well knows that
the house holds childhood   motionless
in its arms.
         here space is   everything
for time ceases to quicken   memory.
           in this remote region
memory   and imagination remain   associated.
and even when we are   in a new house
the memories   of other places travel through

our bodies.   the house we are born in
is physically inscribed in us.   it is
         a group of organic habits.
the word   habit   too worn (a word)
to express
        this passionate liaison of the body
           which does not
forget.

         we are never   real historians
but always   near poets.

         and our emotion is   perhaps
nothing   but (an expression
of a poetry   that was lost.

Source: Reproduced by permission of *Educational Insights*. First published in 2008 in *Educational Insights* 12, no. 1.

Acknowledgements

We are grateful to our anonymous reviewers for their insightful criticisms. We appreciate the editors of this special issue for their support and patience. Also many thanks are due to Mina Elza for her wisdom and activism, and to Veronica Hotton for all manners of editorial support.

Note

1. Daniela Elza (2008), the poet, notes: 'As I read the French philosopher Gaston Bachelard, I was struck by how poetic his prose is at times. This is a poem where all the lines come from Bachelard (1964, 5–15). All I did was find them and arrange them and of course intervene stylistically'.

References

Abram, D. 1996. *The spell of the sensuous: Perception and language in a more-than-human world.* New York: Pantheon Books.

Bachelard, G. 1964. *The poetics of space.* New York: Orion Press.

Bai, H. 2001. Beyond educated mind: Towards a pedagogy of mindfulness. In *Unfolding bodymind: Exploring possibilities through education,* ed. B. Hockings, J. Haskell, and W. Linds, 86–99. Brandon, VT: The Foundation for Educational Renewal.

Bai, H., and G. Scutt. 2009. Touching the earth with the heart of enlightened mind: A Buddhist contribution to ecology as educational practice. *Canadian Journal of Environmental Education* 14: 92–106.

Bateman, R. 2000. *Thinking like a mountain.* Toronto: Penguin Books.

Benjamin, W., and M. Jennings. 1999. *Walter Benjamin: Selected writings, volume 2, 1927–1934.* Cambridge, MA: Harvard University Press.

Bettelheim, B. 1977. *The uses of enchantment: The meaning and importance of fairy tales.* New York: Alfred A. Knopf.

Bonnett, M. 1997. Environmental education and beyond. *The Journal of Philosophy of Education Society of Great Britain* 31, no. 2: 249–66.

Bowers, C.A. 1995. Towards an ecological perspective. In *Critical conversations in philosophy of education,* ed. W. Kohi, 310–23. London: Routledge.

Carter, R.E. 1995. *Becoming bamboo: Western and Eastern explorations of the meaning of life.* Montreal: McGill-Queen's University Press.

Dehò, V. 2007. *Children's corner: Artist books for children.* Mantova: PubliPaolini.

Denzin, N. 2003. *Performance ethnography: Critical pedagogy and the politics of culture.* Thousand Oaks, CA: Sage Publications.

Elza, D. 2008. If Bachelard were in verse II. *Educational Insights* 12, no. 1. http://www.ccfi.educ.ubc.ca/publication/insights/v12n01/poeticmoment/elza/index2.html.

Evernden, N. 1985. *The natural alien: Humankind and environment.* Toronto: University of Toronto Press.

Fromm, E. 1996. Having and being in daily experience. In *To have or to be,* 28–41. New York: Continuum.

Hanh, T. 1999. *Interbeing: Fourteen guidelines for engaged Buddhism.* Berkeley, CA: Parallax Press.

Hart, P. 2003. *Teachers' thinking in environmental education: Consciousness and responsibility.* New York: Peter Lang.

Leopold, A. 1949. *A Sand County almanac.* New York: Ballantine Books.

Littledyke, M. 2004. Primary children's views on science and environmental issues: examples of environmental cognitive and moral development. *Environmental Education Research* 10, no. 2: 217–35.

Martel, Y. 2001. *The life of Pi.* Vancouver: Seal Books.

Orr, D.W. 1994. *Earth in mind: On education, environment, and the human prospect.* Washington, DC: Island Press.

Panikkar, R. 1992. A nonary of priorities. In *Revisioning philosophy,* ed. J. Ogilvy, 235–46. Albany, NY: State University of New York Press.

Trousdale, A. 2008. An endangered relationship. *Journal of Children's Literature* 34, no. 1: 37–44.

Varela, F., E. Thompson, and E. Rosch. 1991. *The embodied mind: Cognitive science and human experience.* Cambridge, MA: MIT Press.

Vazquez, J. 2008. Growing up green. *BioScience* 58, no. 2: 884–6.

Zipes, J. 1987. *The complete fairy tales of the Brothers Grimm.* Trans. Jack Zipes. Toronto: Bantam Books.

Zwicky, J. 2008. Lyric Realism: Nature poetry, silence, and ontology. *The Malahat Review* 165: 85–91.

Remarkable-tracking, experiential education of the ecological imagination

Phillip G. Payne

Faculty of Education, Monash University, Victoria, Australia

Imagination might be understood as letting our senses, perceptions and sensibilities run free for no apparent reason. Here, for this special edition what might be 'remarkable' is the 'opening' of our imagination provided orally through storytelling. This opening involves the 'placing' of our own and our listeners' embodied selves in the spatio-temporal geographies of those stories and their more-than-human natures. The remarkable opening is an important experiential dimension of becoming aware of the ecological otherness of nature's places. Yet, opportunities for such embodied and storied encounters with nature's places, in the wildly imagined other, are less available to children in what, increasingly, is a fast, literate, urban, technologically saturated and consumptive postmodern world. Story, storytelling, art, illustration, song and poetry provide animated means that, pedagogically, might re-place children within an ecocentric sense of self. For over 30 years, the author has told gnome-tracking stories in mysterious places so as to invite young school children and pre-service teacher educators to sense, perceive and (re)imagine their (un)tamed ecological otherness and their intimate connections with more-than-human natures. This article briefly outlines the author's 'significant life experience' encounter with Robert Ingpen, illustrator and author of gnome stories. It highlights how the embodied dance of visual illustration and oral storytelling experienced in natural settings provides a playful means for listeners to explore, discover and relate to their inner, social and more-than-human natures and places. The article concludes with a series of cues about an 'ecopedagogy of imagination', whose end-in-view is to establish some grounds for artful pedagogues to nurture the still elusive reconciliation of human, social and more-than-human natures.

Storying gnomes

The 'first' playful hairy Pervuvian gnomes from the High Andes in South America arrived in the 'unchosen land' (now known as Australia) over 450 years ago after a remarkable voyage of exploration, adventure and discovery across the Pacific Ocean.

Only recently, the last survivor of the original eight, Teresa Verde (Green) told the untold story of that epic voyage from Callao, the Port of Lima in Peru, to Indented Head, near Melbourne, Australia (Ingpen 1980).

I don't dare define the terms 'remarkable' or 'imagination' in this account of the 'pedagogies of gnome tracking'; an ecopedagogy I have developed over the past 30

Figure 1.   The eight hairy Peruvian gnomes with baby Teresa (third from right).

years that seeks the (re)discovery of various signs of gnome inhabitation in a range of very special places. Below, I highlight the role and value in this ecopedagogy of the 'dance' of illustration – a form of visual representation, and storytelling – an oral art form. I describe how this dance with gnomes in their telling should also be embodied and 'lived' in real experiential encounters in those gnome's wild and untamed places. This ecology of the visual, oral and experiential 'placing' of storytelling and tracking combine as a form of embodied, sensory and intercorporeal perception and, hopefully, conception. Hence, a remarkable 'ecopedagogy of imagination'.

This autoethnographic account of gnome storytelling and tracking, as it might occur in a radically revised notion of 'ecoliteracy' in environmental, outdoor, place, art, musical, drama, literature and geography educations, is a sketch only, a thumbnail impression of what really and unreally cannot be said. Why gnome storytelling and tracking? Why the dance, or intersection, of oral, textual and visual representations, via storytelling and illustration that, when storied experientially in nature, act as remarkable literary catalyst of the 'environmental imagination' (Buell 1995) and, perhaps, ecocriticism (Dobrin and Kidd 2004; Garrard 2004) or the environmental criticism (Buell 2006) of the 'environmental turn' in the humanities, in particular its literary and cultural studies formations? Simply, promoting imagination about our edgy and othered relationships with various versions of natures – our own, others and the others 'out there' is, I argue, a pedagogical key to *becoming* something other beyond our rationally assumed and narrowed sense of self.

Ecoliteracy and ecocritically? Now I am in hot water! First, contemporary children's literature relies heavily on text, language and the alphabet. The visual dimension of literacy is less visible in the stories we tell while the sensory or experiential dimension is hard to find. David Abram (1996) has argued, often eloquently, how language, specifically the emergence of the phonetic alphabet in ancient Greek civilization, was a major factor in how the human species severed itself from animated nature and its special places. Abram argued that the new written literacies (and books) were a key development in replacing the previously sensuous and embodied experience of humans with objectified, static but easily transferrable representations of nature made mobile. That is, a very limited number of symbols replaced and, therefore, severed oral telling humans from their animated contexts and places in nature that, later, were substituted for paper, ink, letters and the page. For Abram, the phonetic alphabet (as well as numbers) is an abstraction, as has become its languages, technologies of writing, grammars and texts whose accelerating mobility and autonomy from nature is close to complete, barring some remnant indigenous cultures whose endangered oral traditions sustain some memory of an animated relationship with nature and place (Chatwin 1987). Two thousand years after the Greeks, with numerous other enculturating forces, most contemporary children's literature privileges the text, its pages and screens and, hence, the ongoing de-naturing of animated nature.

As will be explained shortly, telling stories *in, about, with* and *for* nature's places is part of my attempt to create a reanimated version of 'ecoliteracy', presuming the ongoing popularity of that term, which recommends oral story be told and experienced directly in nature. Reanimated, remarkably? So that the connections of story, nature and place are spontaneously and sensuously experienced. This ecopedagogy seeks in a small way only to introduce children to an imaginatively real encounter with nature. While restor(y)ing imagination in child and adulthood is not a panacea in its own right to that which ails our younger generation (Stanley, Richardson, and Prior 2005) or 'fixes up' the ecologically problematic human condition, we note here that only recently have environmental education scholars included children in their studies; their growing up, their experiences, their learning and voice (see Rickinson 2001; Chawla 2002; Payne 2006; Barratt Hacking and Hacking 2007).

The role of imagination in educational research has received little attention (for example, Fitzgerald and Nielsen 2008). The dance of story (making, telling, doing, living), visual illustration and imagination has only been indirectly addressed and, in environmental education, is non-existent, as far as I know. The notion developed here of an ecopedagogy of imagination of nature/place constitutes a major point of departure from those studies in children literature where pedagogies and literacy occur, typically, within the unimaginative and non-remarkable confines of the four walls of the classroom. This article seeks to overcome some of the (eco)pedagogical silences in both the research in children's literature and in environmental education.

My use over the years of Robert Ingpen's gnome illustrations and accompanying folktales is part of long effort to conceive and pedagogically enact a phenomenologically lived but symbolic and mythical experience for children of *being not* what is anticipated by the everyday society in which they live and, in schooling, are expected to be 'culturally literate' about. It is difficult in this everyday to see how children can imagine something other than the crisis and fear conditions of postmodernity. Climate change, war, economic collapse and disease are intensified and individualized in a constructed 'fast' childhood that, increasingly, is mirrored in the equally quick 'downloading' in education and pedagogy of techno–consumerist–entertainment imperatives (for example, Payne 2003/2006; Malone 2007). Remarkably, an ecopedagogy of imagination provides hope for children to slowly immerse in, experience and reclaim some of the their untamed and yet to be domesticated wild natures.

Bob Ingpen's works reflect an abiding commitment to the re-storying, and reimagining of the remarkable times, spaces, places of nature, conservation and the positive prospects for the human condition, especially children's. He works through the medium and form of illustration, tale and text. In my pedagogical work, I have helped children and pre-service teachers live, dance and embody Ingpen's visual and textual inspiration. Ingpen's story *becomes* my own that, in turn, might *become* that of others, hence the intergenerational hope of the passing down of oral storytelling and illustration in nature's places.

My gnome-tracking excursus into Ingpen's remarkable world started in 1978 when I was a young, recently graduated teacher of Year 3 primary school children. A serendipitous combination of events introduced me to Ingpen's gnome storying, telling and tracking. In my pre-service teacher education program at college, I recall that we weren't introduced to gnomes in the 'children's literature' class! But I have faint memories of reading the 'Beowulf' story, an oral tradition from about the eighth century AD that is linked by some to the genesis of the modern wilderness concept. Indeed, that might have been the sum total of my environmental education as a pre-service teacher!

Ingpen is a remarkable pedagogue that I sought to emulate after my second year of teaching. So, after this year-long encounter in 1978 with Ingpen, I resigned from teaching and undertook overseas postgraduate studies in outdoor/environmental education. I wanted to *become* an academic and influence the next generation of teachers to become more than ordinary. Thirty years and many gnome expeditions later, I still teach Year 3 students in a pre-service teacher education unit called 'Experiencing the Australian landscape' (Payne and Wattchow 2009). This time they are 21- to 22-year-old third year undergraduate students in outdoor, physical, environmental and health education. Like my pre-service training, they are far less imaginative, more sceptical (Payne 2006), and I think I know why!

The underlying notions of the remarkable, experiential and imagination that I focus on here are a strange mix of ecopedagogical concerns that reflect the chance encounter in 1978 with Robert, an illustrator/author and parent of one of the eight- to nine-year-olds in my Year 3 class at Drysdale Primary School. In Australia, 1978 provided an educational climate in primary schools where curricula were far freer and schooling was less prescribed than what currently exists, as were the more open children and their less-protective parents. The school was located in a partially developed town. The mix of the bush, the built and the bay fostered numerous opportunities for children to explore, play and discover who and what they were, and what nature can mean (Payne 1998). And this mix of geography, demography and opportunity encouraged those children into a timely sense of self in 'place' in the broader scheme of faster things and worldly affairs about which the children obviously knew very little. Or so it seemed! And as a recently minted graduate, I was professionally naive, or was it frustrated with the stultifying nature of teaching in the already sterile confines of the four walls of the classroom. These ingredients, and others, led me into the gnome tracking experiences I recount here as they exist as memories of the past that persist in the significant present (Tanner 1980).

Chancy encounters with Robert Ingpen

A sealed letter hand delivered to me in class by nine-year-old Tom asked if I was prepared to allow the letter writer to trial on the Grade 3 I was teaching a new book he was illustrating and authoring. All I knew of Robert Ingpen was that he was Tom's father. I agreed via a telephone call.

Apparently Tom was telling stories at home about some of the things we had been doing 'environmentally' in class. I was piloting an innovative curriculum model for a new environmental education subject devised by Faculty of Education academics at nearby Deakin University (Castro et al. 1981).

In practice, this Deakin pilot project had me leading 'expeditions' into the local community, with some mums, to investigate six everyday sites of interest to the children. The class had earlier 'voiced' and concluded there were three 'good' and three 'bad' changes to that local environment. These outside expeditions set the curricula for teaching inside the class – developing spelling lists of words newly used during the excursions; estimating distances and times walked; drawing maps; having guest-speakers from each site to tell us about the 'change' at each setting. The expeditions and spelling lists, and other things, were extended in class to reading and discussing storybooks (with environmental themes) like the *Wump world*, *Where the wild things are* and *Bunyip at Berkeley's Creek*. Finally, in accordance with John Dewey's notion of democracy in the classroom, the class voted about the personal importance of these six changes to their everyday, local environment. A drainpipe emptying into the bay was considered most worthy of further investigation and excursions with more mums and some dads.

Other wild things were happening in my class and, perhaps, being told at home by Tom (and others) to their parents: Mr Payne said it was OK to put on our raincoats and go outside to play even though (the Principal) had just announced over the school's speaker system that there would be no play time due to the 'bad' weather.

After agreeing to Ingpen's wish to trial a new book, the remarkable day came when Bob arrived with the draft text and illustrations for *The voyage of the poppykettle* (1980). Etched in my memory about the story and its reading and telling is the twinkle of his eye, the gaze, the timely display of each of the illustrations, the smooth voicing and gesturing of how over 450 years ago these eight hairy Peruvian gnomes, including baby Teresa (now elderly), descended from the high Andes to the coast and sailed in an earthenware poppykettle across the Pacific Ocean in a voyage of discovery to the 'unchosen land' (Ingpen 1981a) that by historically revisionist happenchance we now call Australia.

The class was spellbound! As was I. Ingpen, myself and another Year 3 teacher then organized (for some months later) a gnome festival for our combined 60 odd children, and their interested or curious parents, to Limeburner's Point, near Indented Head where the friendly dolphin had beached the storm-damaged poppykettle and spilled its brass key ballast into the dunes over 450 years ago. Those brass keys, stolen by the hairy Peruvian gnomes from the Spanish invaders of the Andean highlands, were found deep in a cliff at Limeburner's Point by lime diggers in 1847, exactly 263 years after the poppykettle crashed at Indented Head. Their discovery was documented by the then governor of the colony, Charles La Trobe, and is archived in what is now the State Museum. As an aside, Captain James Cook who is recognized as having 'discovered' Australia in 1770 never sailed into this part of the unchosen land. Others have hypothesized, possibly due to the brass keys, that Spanish or Portugese explorers might have first set foot on 'the great southern land'. But, we now know better!

Now, or then in 1978, our gnome tracking festival to Limeburner's Point had masses of children running, crawling, climbing, searching, high and low, here and there, for evidence of a gnome and, for enchanted and animated children who are not skeptics (unlike most mature and rational adults) the possibility of a sighting/siting. We had a gnome feast of sausages, mango chutney and poppyseed tea; the singing of the gnome national anthem; additional clues from Bob about how to track a gnome and, of course more and more searching and seeking of gnomes – maybe the garden gnome in the bush, the musical metrognome tuning an instrument high up in a tree or the vindictive marram grass gnomes who catapult sand into the faces of those people departing the beach but whom have been sighted, or sited, or cited,

Figure 2. Vindictive marram-grass gnomes riding the bulldog ant and catapulting a frond full of sand into the faces of pop-top littering people departing from a leisurely day-at-the-beach. Reproduced with permission from Robert Ingpen.

by those resident marram gnomes, for the crime of littering the sands and dunes during the day.

This chance encounter with Ingpen happened 30 years ago. Much could be said and written about the unfolding of an ecopedagogy of imagination but is summarized below in accounting for how I am now significantly positioned by these events. Ingpen and I struck up a (lifelong) friendship. I visited his home and we talked about gnomes, reality, imagination, stories, illustrations, teaching, knowing, children, learning, ticket sellers, side tracks and many other matters that mixed commentary, whimsy, wisdom, dreams, concerns, hopes and joys, worries and disappointments and many 'what next's?' His timbered voice, twinkling eyes and gaze were and remain both fixating and alluring. The real was not real and the not real was real; Ingpen's irreal was my introduction to metaphysics – the wild, untamed, edged and othered in us, nature and the world, lost somewhere from our memories of childhood that now gestures imaginatively and empathetically to the re-storying of nature, and critique of what now passes as education and pedagogy – thus ecocriticism.

Robert Ingpen

Bob Ingpen's career and contribution to pictures and stories is a remarkable one (Ingpen with Page 1980; Ingpen with Mayor-Cox 2004), as is the story of the poppykettle told to him by Teresa Green, the baby stowaway and, now, 450 years later, remaining survivor of that voyage to the unchosen land.

Figure 3.   Robert Ingpen and Teresa at Brickenden Barn, 'marking time' somewhere near Longford, Tasmania. Reproduced with permission from Robert Ingpen.

A distinguished and prolific illustrator and writer, Ingpen's contribution crosses more genres than just children's literature. Ingpen was awarded the internationally prestigious Hans Christian Andersen Award for Children's Literature in 1986. For the purposes here, Ingpen's publications for children and adults about cultural history and geography (for example, 1979a), indigenous and natural heritage (for example, 1981b), and conservation in general, are prescient in the way they foreshadow, both visually and textually, many of the motifs we now ascribe to the discourses of environmental ethics, social and/or deep ecology theory and place pedagogy. Ingpen has always enjoyed close links with various educational institutions, be it as a founding member of the Council of Deakin University in the late 1970s, a lifelong commitment to the Geelong College and, indeed, to the Year 3 class at Drysdale Primary School where I was a young teacher.

Numerous things can also be said about Bob the person, Angela – his lifelong partner – and family, his career and its moral–political message by stealth (a point that escapes many), but I won't. For Ingpen is a beguiling bit of an outsider and in-betweener whose 'play' on the 'difference' between possible facts and fiction, the explainable and unexplainable, the real and irreal, the visible and invisible, gives imaginative life to the otherwise empty academic calls for the jargonized 'other'. Ecopedagogical imagination gives presence to this other. Gnome storytelling and tracking is easy, simple and practical – a discourse event that spontaneously embraces the openness of childhood and denials of it in adulthood.

Design, it must be added, looms very large in Ingpen's background and horizons, and the ways in which he constructs his work. But, Sarah Mayor-Cox (Ingpen with Mayor-Cox 2004) observes that 'joining the dots' about Ingpen's 'work' demands that the reader/viewer be attentive to those dots Ingpen confesses to deliberately leaving out. Those dots, metaphorically speaking, are part of what makes the dance of illustration, tale and text imaginative, simple and, potentially, ecocentrically wild for newcomers like me – to play with the dots I think are missing when I retell gnome stories . The missing dots in Ingpen's design have shaped much of my own post-poppykettle aspirations and efforts in environmental education pedagogy, curriculum development and (critical/post-phenomenological) approaches to research design and methodological inquiry and critique. Ingpen is less concerned about 'artistry' and 'colouring in' the dots than what he is about intelligent conceptual creation and the will to imagine and de-sign more than what is available, or present.

The slow discovery of the remarkable

The design just outlined has lived on for me and now takes the form of a 'slow ecopedagogy' in which gnome storytelling and tracking are a key part of a three-day discovery 'experiential learning program' (*elp*) I facilitate with university students. This ecopedagogy is described elsewhere (Payne and Wattchow 2008), as is its phenomenological role in the deconstruction of texts, including those that deconstruct other texts (Payne and Wattchow 2009). As part of a semester-long study of 'Experiencing the Australian landscape' the three-day 'Discovery *elp*' is conducted at the aptly named Bear Gully, near Cape Liptrap, on the coastal edge of SE Australia in late summer. Another three-day 'Rediscovery *elp*' revisits the same location some six weeks later in early winter when the place and its nature has changed considerably. The second *elp* is a further opportunity to sense and conceptualize what a 'place experience' might be by immersing in and, potentially, attaching to Bear Gully's natural qualities and cultural characteristics. Six half-day academic learning program (*alp*) seminars held at university before, in-between and after the two *elps* are designed recylically to slowly embody the learning experiences. Following Dewey's (1938/ 1988) prescient call for an intelligent theory of experience in education, the slow pedagogical dancing conversation of *alps* and *elps* acts as a model for the still chronically undertheorized notion of 'experiential education' (Fox 2008).

Prior to the first Bear Gully 'Discovery *elp*', the third year students are informed that the three-day experience will be different. Gnoming is not mentioned. Indeed, the three days are de-signed and de-vised in a way that prepares 'students' to 'strip away' various personal assumptions, social baggage and cultural constructions often associated with outdoor/environmental education. For example, equipment 'needed' and distance 'to be travelled' are downplayed; boots, tents, jackets, maps, compasses and activity driven notions of walking 20 kilometres from a to b in so many hours are replaced by nine locally placed 'experiences' of a few hours each that enact 'different ways of doing, as meaning-making/knowing' (Payne 2005). Rockpooling, shoreline art, water floating, beach strolling, sleeping under tarps in groups of 10 and preparing 'slow food' group meals with locally grown ingredients sourced from within 100kilometres of campus are some of these experiences. Over the three days most students will have remained within a kilometre or so of the Discovery camp.

I retell and show the *The voyage of the poppykettle* (Ingpen 1980) in a secluded spot a few hundred metres from camp on an edge-place in-between the sand and rocks meeting the coastal scrub and dunes. Dressed in a Peruvian poncho given to me many years ago in the Altiplano of the High Andes, I tell the story from memory, add bits when I feel the time is right, show the illustrations, glance carefully at students to retain eye contact, especially for the abundant sceptics, and move creatively amongst the group seated-in-the-sand.

But preceding the telling, I wander along the sandy and rocky edge-place, seemingly aimlessly and distracted by the surrounds, stopping, listening, pausing, looking – all of which are bodily pedagogies, or nonverbal cues and clues, for what I know in advance is the way most students will make meaning of the story and then track for gnomes in the dunes and bush.

Before the poppykettle retelling, I provide a 'real' history of Australian settlement. I read (not tell) fragments from two of Ingpen's factual and illustrated accounts of (white) Anglo-Australian social and cultural history. I introduce poppykettle with the observation that those factual stories are one account only of the historical record and that others remain, often untold or not chosen and certainly not textualized. The 'other' historical story of the poppykettle's voyage to the 'unchosen land' (Ingpen 1981a) and the facts surrounding the finding of the keys and documentation by Governor La Trobe is retold, steadily, with eye contact sustained – but occasionally distracted by more environmental cues, like the calling of a crow, and clues about gnomes (some marram grass I pause at and 'handle' on the edge space but do not name) known only to the storyteller. The clues will be revealed in a conclusion to the

Figure 4. The author telling gnome stories at the discovery of Bear Gully. Photograph reproduced with permission of Brian Wattchow.

storying that leads into my invitation for student pairs to explore the immediate edge area for a possible sighting of a gnome or, at least, the finding of some evidence of possible gnome inhabitation. Eventually we regroup, discuss our 'findings' and, in some instances, record via sketch or/and words in an 'experiential log', some of the shared evidence.

As might be expected, there are a wide variety of responses and contributions. For the most part, the openness I encourage is taken up by students with many searching, discovering, or pretending to, and then verbally sharing the imaginative experience. At its 'end' I ask the group to not 'let on' to the other groups what has happened. Over the remaining times of the *elp*, where and when appropriate, I 'drop' more non-verbal and verbal cues to individuals or a group. For example, I might listen intently to sounds in the high up branches that might, indeed, be the sound of metrognomes tuning their instruments.

I have collected data from the trackers of gnomes over the years, invariably a number of weeks after the first *Discovery*. In response to the question, 'What is your overwhelming memory of the gnome storytelling and tracking?' a random sampling of responses include:

It felt like hearing about Santa Claus all over again. It encouraged me to believe again in the irrational. Kids have it – a beautiful imagination. We now have to force that back on ourselves. It was about making something out of nothing – a kid mentality that is lost. (Greenleaf, male, 29)

Knowing that I was going to be given the opportunity to do what I love most was my favorite memory. The anticipation and excitement of being able to tap into an alternative reality – and create and explore the possibilities of the gnome world. I loved the freedom of living in that world – and being with the experience of valuing all things – and everything worldly holds an infinite and connected story. (Fairy Sparkle, female, 24)

It was a bit silly but the more I tried to get into it, the more I was curious about what was going on. (Troll, female, 21)

It made me feel a bit naïve. In China, where I'm from, only small children are told by the teacher to do that. I haven't experienced it since kindergarten – the interaction of story and real nature. I've never seen a teacher take fun all so seriously. I liked it – very memorable. (Sun, male, 22)

Since the early 1980s, I occasionally bump into ex-students who, amongst other things, chat fondly about the gnome experience. Some contact me to describe how they have taken up 'gnoming', often with a class they are teaching, but also with their own children. One mother recently wrote to me:

Over twenty years ago you introduced me to Robert Ingpen. Since then I have had two children and they both know all about the gnome culture in Geelong. Many years ago, my son had a great time climbing over the Poppykettle in the park at Geelong. About three weeks ago, my daughter brought out 'The Poppykettle Papers' from the bookcase and has been getting me to read a chapter each night. She already has got 'Australian Gnomes' lined up as the next book to read. Thank you for sharing the special world with me so many years ago.

An annual 'Poppykettle festival' for children occurs in Geelong, near my first gnome tracking expedition to Limeburner's Point in 1978 with the Year 3 primary school children. It is regularly attended by Robert Ingpen. The event is a tangible expression of imagination by children in that it seeks to presence that remarkable possibility.

Remarkable pedagogies

Gnomes and their visualization played out through the sensuous dance of illustration, storytelling, pedagogical cueing and experiential tracking, in nature's classroom, is one example of a slow ecopedagogy of imagination. It aspires to be ecocentric and intercorporeal – that is, nature's places socially guide the embodied meaning-making and 'learning' of the participants. In schooling, the majority of literacies occur indoors, are primarily of the text and, therefore, mind and, mostly anthropocentric. Experiential and embodied 'openings' and the lure of the 'wild' of nature might not be accessible, or available, because texts and words reflect the tamed nature of the domesticated indoors.

Here, beyond the descriptions of gnome storying and tracking outlined above, is not the space to prescribe an ecopedagogy of imagination. That would be counterproductive! It would defeat for other creative teachers and researchers the possibility of other remarkable alternatives. But, in moving to the temporary end of this account, there are some broad dimensions of an ecopedagogy of imagination that the interested, possibly imaginative reader, might like to consider.

I concede the role of imagination is not a pedagogical aim for all teachers. Some might see it as a luxury. Undergraduates are often difficult to work with (in my experience) in that there exists a great deal of scepticism to that which is non-factual, or extraordinary, and speaks to the values of perception, imagination and exploration of the wild or the other. On the other hand, there are many who will welcome the possibility of a pedagogy of imagination, even an ecocentric and intercorporeal one. Children's story, telling, illustration and visual dimensions of literature can sustain childhood and nurture the wellbeing of their (and our) human condition. It can reinvigorate many of the assumptions we make about practices of education, including how meaning-making in experiences can contribute to the much-sought after engagement of learners. Viewed in this way, for the ecocentric purposes pursued here, children's literature can be a 'voice' *in*, *with*, *about* and *for* the environment and against the ecological problematic and what that entails for the next generations. They will inherit what we currently can't or don't want to see, or reimagine. Openings are needed.

Beyond the numerous cues, clues and exhortation described above, noting numerous dots are missing from that text, what non-prescribed dots about imagination do need to be joined, identified very generally and briefly coloured in as a textual account of an ecopedagogy of imagination?

It has been said many times that the human species is a storytelling one, ranging from grand narratives, scientific and moral truths to folklore, myth and superstition. We struggle to tell, or listen, to the right, true or correct story. Indeed, different stories, narratives and discourses are constantly told, rehearsed and lived. In education, we are too often confronted with the teaching and telling of a particular state-sanctioned curriculum story, or document. Children's literature, potentially, and the arts, potentially, retain the possibility of being different, other or wild. We need to grasp that possibility in education, including environmental education. That opportunity, potentially, is the source of a revitalized means of promoting the sensual, perceptual and conceptual dimensions of an aesthetic education, in this instance an ecoaesthetic opening in 'experiencing', 'living', *being* the story and *becoming* other than what we currently are. Their confluence might well be the remarkable.

An ecopedagogy of imagination invokes that which can't normally be accessed, or isn't anticipated, expected and accepted. If so, and beyond the above characterization of gnome tracking, there are some indicators of an ecopedagogy of imagination worth mentioning, in conclusion, so that we might begin to contest and reimagine dominant views of pedagogy in education and how they are reproduced in environmental education, sometimes according to the imperative of pedagogical content knowledge as it might now inform the emerging popularity of the notion of ecoliteracy.

First, to what extent are our current pedagogies aware of the shift entailed in moving towards the possibility of an ecocentric approach to education? To what extent do we encourage the body and its experiences of stories in making meaning of our connections and, therefore, intercorporeal relations with environments, places and natures? Children's literature, inclusive of story, illustration, telling and experiencing, can make a crucial contribution to an aesthetic education that is pleasing and meaningful to a range of ages. The main limit to a pedagogy of imagination is, ironically, our own imagination. There is, for example, an imaginative place in the slow ecopedagogy pedagogy referenced above for gnome storying but also silences and stillness that nature might tell not in words and not language, but in the strange, the wild, the moment, the now and nature's call on our individual and collective memory. We, as pedagogues, educators and researchers, might not feel the rushed need to 'fill' pedagogy (or published papers) with preconceived notions of accelerated learning (outcomes) and predetermined content and its assessment/evaluation.

What, therefore, is harder to imagine in the practices of an ecopedagogy of imagination? And how might children's literature contribute in ways that other curriculum areas associated with environmental education can consider? Here, I am in murkier waters! But my list includes the importance of fostering the suspension of belief that, unfortunately in the negative, recommends the need for us all to cast off, even momentarily, the existing assumptions and presumptions that we anthropocentrically bring to teaching and learning. But I think we can reasonably conclude that the perceptual–sensory nurturing of imagination and its pedagogical embodiment requires much more time than what we can ordinarily commit to, or our timetables dictate to us. Be it the very slow telling of a story in the classroom, allowing children much more time to 'look at' and interpret illustrations, or re-timetabling children's schedule to encourage 'reflection' on the story told and shown. Or, as I have described above, the dance of slow time 'opens up' when we recycle the telling and experiencing of the story on site in that place (as we do at Bear Gully) with other different spaces, such as the classroom, as modelled in the Deakin pilot project.

The experiential nature of on-site storying immediately invites into our formulation of an ecopedagogy of imagination the emphatic role and value of the sensing and perceiving body, its corporeality and intercorporeality with others, be they human or more-than-human. And here, in conceiving a notion of the dancing relationship between imagination and embodied experience of story, a degree of importance can be attached by storytellers, artful pedagogues and craft-ful researchers to, for example, the sensuous spatiality of the body and 'geographies of physical activity in time'. Here, I depart quite assertively from story read or told only within the confines of the indoor classroom, typically a disciplined space of, essentially, sedentary body engagement in learning that consistently targets cognitive growth only.

As an underlying dimension of human experience, but with a particular relevance to younger children, the spatialities and geographies of pedagogical experience are only ever implied in the discourses of environmental education and, to my limited knowledge, in children's literature and 'story' theory. While children might well anthropocentrically listen to the social nature of stories about their selves, or gender issues, and so on in the classroom, the embodied/experiential connection I am recommending with open spaces and more-than-human 'natures' places a heavy burden on environmental education pedagogues, storytellers and ecoliteracy/criticism researchers to go outside into those other, wilder, edgier places, spaces and versions of nature.

Notwithstanding these challenges, it seems to me that the storied suspension of belief and phenomenological/experienced suspension of time and the playful and sensuous connections of bodies and different versions of nature are some of the more vital ingredients of an ecopedagogy of imagination that might, indeed must, be developed in children's (eco)literature. And, potentially, adults! But, in reiterating the scepticism of the many about such gnome-like matters, I must also acknowledge there are other challenges. One of the Grade 3 children I taught in 1978 was not allowed to participate in the gnome festival or Deakin project due to religious reasons. Also, to not indicate that there is potentially a downside to imagination and the various forms in which it can be negatively promoted, or manifested, would be a serious oversight here given how certain images, constructions and expectations act across the broad spectrum of human endeavour and, potentially, anti-social and/or environmental behaviours. For example, some 'games' and their texts and narratives ask their owner to imagine themselves as a 'killer' and so on, all of which are contrary to the positive connotations of the remarkable pedagogies of imagination outlined here.

On this note of caution, clearly much of the work on the value of imagination, the role of story, the possibility of the remarkable, the wild and the open in children's (eco)literature is speculative and subjective. While the notion of imagination in education has attracted recent attention (for example, Egan 1997), Thomas Nielsen's (2004) book is one of the rare examples in education of an empirical study of imagination. His grounded theory study of Steiner classrooms helps elaborate some of the preceding ideas indicated above about a pedagogy of imagination. Nielsen felt that Rudolf Steiner's philosophical interest in imagination required empirical qualification and updating, particularly with how young postmodern children presented a different sort of pedagogical challenge to those children Steiner was writing about in the late nineteenth century/early twentieth century. Not surprisingly, Nielsen's longstanding motivation to study imagination drew autoethnographically on his 'childhood memories from school' where his 'unbearable anticipation' of the marking of his fourth grade 'imaginative story' was soured by a teacher who accused him of copying it from a book. Nielsen recalls how his now discredited 'gaze' returned to 'out the window' (3). Subsequently, Nielsen's ethnographic and phenomenological study of three Steiner classrooms identified three modes of pedagogy and seven methods of teaching. The methods included exploration activities, empathy, story, art, discussion, drama and routine or order while the overarching modes are described by Nielsen as 'leaving', where the teacher designs activities for pupils to imagine on their own; 'sharing', where imagery is negotiated between child and teacher; and 'immersing', where children are ensnared in a 'net' of imagery.

Ecopedagogies of imagination

Mindful of Nielsen's (2004) rare empirical study of the notion of imagination, and related speculative works (Fitzgerald and Nielsen 2008), and my autoethnographic restorying of 30 years of gnome storytelling and tracking experiences with various populations, I conclude with some observations.

There is a profound difference between 'story'-reading, telling and making or authoring and their 'doing' and how each might influence the experience of the senses, the growth of perception and imagination, and other learning outcomes. 'Story', to be sure, has different genres, such as the 'tale', 'tall', 'folk' or factual narrative, and so on. The physical or experiential setting of the story 'performance' will also be influential – in the classroom is, essentially, a vicarious experience that is easily and immediately accessed – but, at the end of the day, is abstract and primarily of the mind or intellect only. Story for more ecoliterate and broadly imaginative environmental criticism (Buell 2006) purposes can be performed orally (not textually) 'on-site' in nature's places or rehearsed outside, possibly in the real contexts, proximal spaces and geographies of the physical activity of that story and, if so, encourage a 'direct' embodying, sensing and perceiving of wilder, in-between possibilities of that 'place'.

The dance of story, illustration, performance, exploration and drama developed within the realm of sensory and ecological affordances of 'nature' will further open the imaginative into the realms of the remarkable. Eco, intercorporeal options enter freely into the magic of the pedagogical transaction as those stories are told, danced and 'lived' in an embodied manner on the 'real' stages of that which has been storied – the body(ies) ecopedagogically imagined story.

So, to the magical storyteller, read David Abram's (1996) *Spell of the sensuous*. It is a remarkable philosophical source for anyone contemplating an environmental education through story and literature. Telling imaginative stories imaginatively is disinterested in technique. Like Ingpen, know your story inside out and outside in. Understand its messages, overt and covert. Use the dynamics of your voice, mood, gesture, positioning, eye contact. Understand the importance of timing, tempo, rhythm, silences, pausing and stillness, even silliness in the telling. The teller holds and releases eye contact with the audience, sometimes intensely with a listener looking beyond the surface of his/her eye; other times roaming around and wiling/inviting the listener to share the uncertain moment. Gazes and pauses allow the place a voice in the telling. The teller can 'work' the spatiality of his/her movement, orchestrating a dynamic geography of activity in some of those more-than-human spaces important to the places inhabited by the children. What features of localized nature and places can be embedded in the oral telling (and mimicking) – for example, the morning warble of the lyrical magpie, a stand of old trees, the distant, recyclical roars of the crashing waves.

So, reflect upon some strategies for suspending and animating one self and the audience and letting nature speak through the story you select to tell. Know your environments – outdoors and indoors, school, playgrounds, gardens and parks and the bush, sea or coast – if outdoors nurture a 'drawing-in' of and for the environment, as that 'place' *becomes* co-storyteller and interpreter or embodied prompt for exploration and discovery. Understand the experience of the child and in the transactional nature of the ecopedagogy of imagination and its interactive positioning of teacher and active, participatory audience. Allow children to invent and tell their stories about the place the teacher has storied. In other words, a remarkable ecology of the (oral) story (telling) beckons pedagogues and researchers.

Acknowledgements

Robert Ingpen, Thomas Nielsen and Rosie Rosengren are thanked for their contributions to earlier drafts of this manuscript and for their longstanding friendship and support for the more-than-ordinary and untamed. Thanks to the Faculty of Education at Monash University for grant D01009 225 8520 that supported the color reproduction of plates for this publication.

References

Abram, D. 1996. *The spell of the sensuous.* New York: Vintage Books.
Barratt Hacking, E., and R. Barratt. 2007. Childhood and environment. *Environmental Education Research,* 13, no. 4: 419–23.
Buell, L. 1995. *The environmental imagination: Thoreau, nature writing, and the formation of American culture.* Cambridge: Harvard University Press.
Buell, L. 2006. *The future of environmental criticism: Environmental crisis and literary imagination.* Oxford: Blackwell.
Castro, A., J. Evans, L. Fitzclarence, J. Henry, I. Robottom, and M. Wright. 1981. *Environmental education.* Geelong: Deakin University Press.
Chatwin, B. 1987. *The songlines.* London: Picador.
Chawla, L. 2002. *Growing up in an urbanizing world.* Paris: UNESCO.
Dewey, J. 1938/1988. Experience and education. In *John Dewey, Volume 13: 1938–1939,* ed. J.A. Boydston, 3–62. Carbondale: Southern Illinois University Press.
Dobrin, S., and K. Kidd. 2004. *Wild things; children's culture and ecocriticism.* Detroit: Wayne State University Press.
Egan, K. 1997. *The educated mind: How cognitive tools shape our understanding.* Chicago: University of Chicago Press.
Fitzclarence, L., and P. Payne. 1981. The curriculum design model in practice: Drysdale case study. In *Environmental education,* ed. A. Castro, J. Evans, L. Fitzclarence, J. Henry, I. Robottom, and M. Wright. Geelong: Deakin University Press.
Fitzgerald, R. and T. Nielsen. 2008. Imaginative practice, imaginative inquiry. *Proceedings of the Sixth International Conference on Imagination and Education.* Canberra: University of Canberra.
Fox, K. 2008. Rethinking experience: What do we mean by this word 'experience'? *Journal of Experiential Education* 31, no. 1: 36–54.
Garrard, G. 2004. *Ecocriticism.* London: Routledge.
Holt, N. 2003. Representation, legitimation, and autoethnography: An autoethnographic writing story. *International Journal of Qualitative Methods* 2, no. 1: 1–22.
Ingpen, A., with M. Page 1980. *Robert Ingpen.* Melbourne: Macmillan.
Ingpen, R. 1979a. *Marking time: Australian's abandoned buildings.* Adelaide: Rigby.
Ingpen, R. 1979b. *Australian gnomes.* Adelaide: Rigby.
Ingpen, R. 1980. *The voyage of the poppykettle.* Adelaide: Rigby.
Ingpen, R. 1981a. *The unchosen land.* Adelaide: Rigby.
Ingpen, R. 1981b. *Australia's heritage watch: An overview of Australian conservation.* Adelaide: Rigby.
Ingpen, R., with S. Mayor-Cox 2004. *Pictures telling stories: The art of Robert Ingpen.* Melbourne: Lothian.
Leopold, A. 1966. *A sand county almanac.* New York: Ballantine.
Malone, K. 2007. The bubble-wrap generation: Children growing up in walled gardens. *Environmental Education Research* 13, no. 4: 513–28.
Murdoch, J. 2006. *Post-structuralist geography.* London: Sage.
Nielsen, T. 2004. *Rudolf Steiner's pedagogy of imagination. A case study of holistic education.* Bern: Peter Lang.
Payne, P. 1998. Children's conceptions of nature. *Australian Journal of Environmental Education* 14: 19–27.
Payne, P. 2003/2006. The technics of environmental education. *Environmental Education Research* 12, nos 3–4: 487–502.
Payne, P. 2005. 'Ways of doing' learning, teaching and researching. *Canadian Journal of Environmental Education* 10: 108–24.

Payne, P. 2006. Gnome tracking vs. the sceptics: Experiential education and the early childhood setting. *Every Child* 12, no. 2: 10–11.

Payne, P., and B. Wattchow. 2008. Slow pedagogy and placing education in post-traditional outdoor education. *Australian Journal of Outdoor Education* 12, no. 1: 25–38.

Payne, P., and B. Wattchow. 2009. Phenomenological deconstruction, slow pedagogy and the corporeal turn in wild environmental/outdoor education. *Canadian Journal of Environmental Education* 14: 15–32.

Rickinson, M. 2001. Learners and learning in environmental education: A critical review of the evidence. *Environmental Education Research* 7, no. 3: 207–320.

Stanley, F., S. Richardson, and M. Prior 2005. *Children of the lucky country? How Australian society has turned its back on children and why children matter.* Sydney: Pan Macmillan.

Tanner, T. 1980. Significant life experiences: A new research area in environmental education. *Journal of Environmental Education* 11: 20–4.

Children's literature as a springboard to place-based embodied learning

Linda Wason-Ellam

College of Education, University of Saskatchewan, Canada

Globalization makes living in the world more complex. Many children live as social cyborgs attached to the digital spaces of the virtual play worlds of television, video and computer games rather than connected to their own local places. The impact of this change may well be that children lack acquaintance with their local places and may never develop the ecological literacy or the positive attitudes toward place that is so crucial to its sustainability. This paper presents an autoethnographic study of a third grade class engaged in reading picture story books that featured place-based settings in partnership with embodied learning textually and visually through art, photography, poetry, story writing and environmental journals of class field experiences along their local river valley. Combining place-based education with social constructivist pedagogy fostered places for learning for children to create a knowing that they, too, can take action for places where they live throughout their lives.

Introduction

Globalization makes living complex (Bowers 2005; Reisberg 2008). As a cross-cultural researcher, I have observed many children who spend long hours living as social cyborgs[1] engaged within the digital spaces of virtual play worlds of television, video or computer games. With a click of a mouse, channel selector, joystick, keypad or other rapid-fire mechanical devices, these children electronically enter into screen worlds situated in cyberspace (Wason-Ellam 2005) which are digital places that estrange them from their own natural place (Louv 2005) by presenting abstract images simulating other place worlds. Payne (1997) reminds us that the postmodern world has become increasingly a '"technoscape" where individuals are constantly surrounded by, preoccupied with and engaged by an ever increasing range of technological artifacts, economic imperatives and necessities and other lifestyle complexities and demographic/geographic realities' (136). Globally, the norm for today's children is a daily routine of viewing animated images depicting dehumanized characters and constructed environments, which constantly distorts the reality of everyday life or as Bowers states 'deplaces' them (1997) for these built worlds are mass commodities rarely worlds of possibility. Children depend upon commodity consumption not just for survival but for participation and inclusion in social networks (Seiter 1993, 3;

Wason-Ellam and Li 1999) or affinity groups centred on being viewers of storied icons such as Disney characters and collectors of their mass-marketed commodities. The lack of sentiment for a local place, that is a belonging or attachment to their outdoor community, is often a by-product of the pervasive characteristics of living in the homogeneous screen-scape environments (Gradle 2007, 392) as children yearn to 'talk about' or 'be in' global places like Disney World so that the natural places of their own community become other and elsewhere. Because places are often bounded sites in which children build experiences and hold emotional attachments – such as 'the place where I found a robin's egg' or 'putting graffiti or breaking people's property is wasting their money 'cause they have to fix it up and use more wood and paint' – both the local and social aspects of place have become central concerns in the exploration of how a sense and responsibility of place may be encouraged in class-rooms. In explaining the importance of attachment to place, Kruger (2001) reminds us that 'we cherish places not just by what we can get from them but for the way we define ourselves in relation to them... [as] places with stories, memories, meanings, sentiments and personal significance' (178).

Central to this paper is the description of my work with a primary teacher in an urban school. Together we reimagined how classrooms could be centres of inquiry and critical thinking about place that expectantly could lead to a consciousness of and respect for environment. We grappled with the question of how critical place-based pedagogy (Gruenewald and Smith 2008; Gruenewald 2003) could be open to chil-dren's interest in things worth knowing and be responsive to building on their ideas and meanings through integrated art and literacy activities. Place is a setting but it is often linked to memory, imagination, or embodied experiences. As Graham (2007) points out, 'Place-based education aims to strengthen children's connection to others, to their region, to the land, and to overcome the alienation and isolation that is often associated with modern society' (378). Gruenewald (2003) reminds us that essentially, environmental issues are on the margins of education so what we wanted to establish was 'places for learning' (Ellsworth 2005) for young children so we could offer them multi-disciplinary and aesthetic possibilities for nurturing a sense of place within the local environment. At the same time, we were eschewing the traditional classroom script about reading and talking about environment and then testing the content (Bowers 2001) and setting benchmarks.

McKenzie (2008) suggests the need for more attention to the pedagogical 'balanc-ing' of critical and emotional/embodied engagements (Gruenewald 2003), but rather the possible productivity of looking more closely at how we might understand learn-ing as cognitive and embodied intersubjective experiences. With a background in art, children's literature and photography, I realized that there were many possible places of learning beyond the school walls. In the paper, I begin with a discussion about a growing trend relating to an abundance of high-quality Canadian children's picture storybooks featuring the natural environment as a purposeful setting and its potential as a springboard to exploring childhood identity and meanings about environment. I then discuss an autoethnographic study of a focal classroom where environmental experiences were 'learning in the making' (Ellsworth 2005) as children explored place-based experiences through children's literature in addition to field walks inte-grated with more embodied experiences such as art, photography, poetry, reflective writing, map-making and dialogue with peers. The theoretical basis for this experien-tial approach was grounded in the Deweyan notion that authentic learning necessitates having children engaged with real-world activities and real-world problem-solving

(1938). Most intriguing is his reference to the mind–body intersect (Dewey 1988, 191) or embodied knowledge which is more than an acknowledgement of the sensory input; rather, it is a recognition of the embeddedness of thought in experience as it emerges in our interactions. In the classroom, we used a social constructivist pedagogy, which implies that learning occurs in situated sociocultural contexts and that knowledge is apprehended and appropriated in and through social interaction, dialogue, negotiation, and contestation (Kukla 2000). Of particular importance to our work in urban neighborhoods is the consideration of the 'who' we are teaching, a point that we as educators need to keep in mind. Social constructivism is grounded in the viewpoint that learning is individualistic so it is important to take into account the background and culture of the child throughout the learning process, as background helps to shape the knowledge and truth that the learner creates, discovers and attains throughout the learning process (Wertz 1997). Social constructivism not only acknowledges the complexity and the uniqueness of the learner but also encourages and rewards it as an integral part of the learning process. Furthermore, feelings of attachment, respect and responsibility that children express toward a particular place become articulated in and through social interactions (Bakhtin 1981; Wells 2000) with peers, adults and the physical world. Therefore, this research is based on the notion that, the collaborative and social aspects of the learning process or social constructivism are also integral to knowledge production as children learn through situated learning (Lave and Wenger 1991) working alongside more knowledgeable peers. In conclusion, I will consider what characterizes this study as place-based learning, as well as socially constructed, embodied and experientially-based that emerges primarily out of more non-conventional pedagogies to education, including those integrated activities that occur outside the school boundaries.

Picture storybooks and new landscapes

Picture storybooks create multiple meanings with a blending of illustrations and text. As visual representations of the words, illustrations add to the information and help make the text more understandable (Huck et al. 1997) and personally meaningful to the reader. In viewing picture books, the illustrations engage the reader both cognitively and emotionally as the story progresses thus adding a multi-layered richness and depth to the author's words. Squire (1996) suggests that literature expressly written for children often serves as a medium of cultural communication as it is often integral to both individual and collective identity and the meanings in one's life. Largely, literary communication is facilitated by images of landscape.[2] Consequently, 'there is an intrinsic geography to many literary texts and, correspondingly, such geographic representations may both foster and help to make possible a range of culturally defined meanings, attitudes and values' (75). Literary theorist Perry Nodelman (1997) agrees when he writes that one of the characteristics of 'Canadian literature for children is its fascination with the land' (16). When reading full page illustrations and stories of children camping at the edge of the forest, canoeing on a lake, hiking in the mountains, watching birds on a flyway or searching for shells in the tide pools one immediately senses that these are not just stories of any *place*. These atlases of images are of the vast and varied Canadian terrain. Like other nations such as Australia, Canada is a land of dramatic physical contrasts (Bainbridge and Thistleton-Martin 2001). As a northern geography, it is shaped by glaciers whose moving ice has carved valleys, forged mountains and left behind crystal lakes and fine loam in the prairies.

Books brimming with these settings invite young readers to build on emerging layers of experiences with natural environments, which are in contrast to the manufactured environments as presented in video or computer playgrounds. As stories unfold in settings of pristine arboreal forests, high bluffs, marshy bottomlands, or in the prairie grasslands, the young reader/viewer connects both aesthetically and cognitively (aligning their ideas, attitudes, and experiences) to be socially aware, reflective, and transformational as this is a 'place to be'. The multi-layered visual settings run deep like a river as they honor traditional cultural knowledge interweaving the local knowledge, indigenous knowledge (Bowers 2001) or cultural knowledge of place (Gruenewald 2008). Descriptive texts layered with illustrations, narratives, poetry or photographs become the pedagogical pivot points as children visually and textually experience stories about outdoor activities that could possibly sensitize them to care for other places belonging to Mother Earth. When reading and discussing messages embedded in these imaginative pictorial atlases children begin to dialogue about developing an environmental ethic of caring (Noddings 1992) of the world in which we all dwell. Years of researching in the classroom has shown me that in quality children's literature, vistas widen when conversations address relationships in social ecology and how we relate to one another, or physical ecology and how we relate to the land and resources. When children read both illustrations and narratives on winter camping, fishing in trout streams or hiking on rocky cliffs, there are moments of still-ness, moments of intersection, moments of enlightenment, and moments of shared inquiry. Stories beget other stories. As children walk on their own ground, by foot or in their minds, they can relate memories of similar experiences that transport them back to craggy coastlines, majestic forests, or rolling prairies with expansive horizon lines. Story initiates query, roots them in place and keep their connections alive. Stories help them see where they are, how others live here, and how they themselves should live. Story then realizes several things that information does not for stories are analogies for living life. Meanings articulated in prose or poetry creates relationships, translates information into image and excites imagination or sense of wonder. Like-wise in other cultures such as in Australia, Jeannie Baker's wordless picture stories beckon children to comment about the environmental changes to place in *Window* 1991) and the reclamation of place in *Home* (2004). In Baker's work, story reaches inward to awaken the heart and mind, which is a way of understanding, experiencing, and gaining empathy for and imagining oneself in the natural world. Reading alone is not just sufficient. It is in classroom learning communities as children dialogue, inquire and respond to story with others that they develop cultural values, beliefs, and practices (Bakhtin 1981) that can contribute to sustainable relationships with the environment (Bowers 1997) and the community. Dewey (1938) would concur when he wrote that learners need educational experiences, which enable them to become valued, equal and responsible members of society.

An autoethnographic study

To illustrate, I use an autoethnographic perspective to document how children attending an urban prairie third grade participated in reading adventures where both setting and place positioned them in an experiential and participatory approach to environmental learning. With many walking trips to the nearby river, a taken-for-granted feature of the familiar landscape was re-negotiated as a social space, a place of play, learning and ecological significance that fostered environmental understanding as well as place appreciation and attachment (Gruenewald 2002). I used autoethnography[3] as it considers the study of one's own culture, which for me is being a privileged white woman working in the social geography for many years in the same neighborhood school (Wason-Ellam and Ward 2003; Wason-Ellam 2005). I position myself in Haig-Brown's (1990) category of border-work for as a professional educator I chose to remain and work in society's margins 'outside of my postcode' in a supportive and bridging role helping to problematize the inequalities in schools and its hegemonic practices while advocating for culturally responsive resolutions (Giroux 1992). For me, border is a meeting place where cultures sometime intersect or collide in complex ways or come to full resolution as we find ways to make learning respectful for all.

Specifically, autoethnography provides the opportunity for me to become reflective and introspective, for gaining a critical perspective on the everyday occurrences (Fiske 1990) of school life (Fiske 1990), and for resituating the self within a cultural context (Reed-Danahay 1997) as my work across borders. As a flexible mode of inquiry, it allows me to research and envision intentions of change that can take place in educational institutions and classroom practices. Throughout the writing of research, I intertwine field texts written over the span of one school year to explicate how children's picture storybooks became the catalyst for critical classroom dialogue about understanding the local place. Participant observation, dialogical inquiries, reflective writing, photovoice[4] and in-depth conversations were the primary data-gathering tools used to capture moments in time to understand how a diverse group of children came to learn about the social cultural meaning of place. When I suggest social cultural meaning in autoethnographic research, I deem that critical to being a researcher is an expanse of 'lived time' or historicity doing field work in urban neighbourhoods so that I am are able to thoughtfully interpret and respect the lives of children and families who live there. As a field researcher, I have been involved in both individual and collaborative projects that explored the social, cultural and economic worlds of family and community literacies in urban prairie neighborhoods.

In this study, I sketch how children engaged in a place-based pedagogy as they participated in creating their own photos, art, poetry and writing journals to document their enriched story meanings for illustrations/texts intersecting with reflections of class trips in their local river valley.[5] Stories such as *Morning on the lake* (Waboose 1997) or *The elders are watching* (Bouchard 1997) planted seeds of thought (Cajete 1994) and deep reflection of eco-justice issues (Bowers 2001) as the children responded about why we should respect the environment. Stories called to children as they encountered new ways of sense-making about the local environment for an appreciation for place precedes any commitments to stewardship, and ultimately the goals for sustainability (Stedman 2003). Learning from the local fostered opportunities for children to think about creating long-term caring and in knowing that they, too, can take action for places where they live throughout a lifetime.

Located in the inner core of the city, the elementary school was just footsteps away from adjacent strip malls, fast food outlets and bingo halls. The city centre straddles the banks of a wide river,[6] which meanders through the downtown core following the natural contours of the land making it a picturesque vista in startling contrast to the windswept prairies. The river with its ease of access and navigation was once the primary gateway to the rich fur-bearing regions nearby, but currently it is both a source of water and recreation. In close proximity to the school, there were access points to the riverbank imbued with wide-open spaces and walking trails. For the children, the neighboring river was 'always there' as an ever-present part of their daily lives. Yet, while the river was familiar to them, it represented a taken-for-granted aspect of their immediate surroundings. Over time, it became an ideal place to spend time observing the seasonal rhythms over the school year while at the same time fostering a sense of ecological place just beyond the classroom. Early in the study, the children found special 'places to be' on field walks along the river such as a large boulder that they named the 'sitting-rock'. 'My big brother took me to the river,' stated one child when he commented on the river viewing place as a personal sanctuary, 'I showed him our sitting-rock and we sat there so we could see the river for a long way. It made us feel better to know that we have a quiet place to go when things are bad.'

The neighborhood

Learners in the study were representative of the patchwork quilt of families residing in Canadian cities. The neighborhood was a mix of long time residents, newcomers from African, Asian, Middle Eastern and Eastern European countries. Alongside were urban Aboriginal[7] families. In the early days of this region, the colonial settlements had dispossessed these groups of the land of their ancestors; consequently some lived in cities while others lived farther a field or on northern reserve land. For many of the children in this school community, they live their lives in flux within the cycle of poverty and transience, thus putting down few roots or attachments to any place. Many live in unbalanced home environments tempered by temporary guardianship, single parent families, the cycle of addiction and the violence that often characterize inner-city neighbourhoods. For most of these families, literacy resources such as high quality books or computers were not affordable or accessible and it was in school time that this classroom teacher could provide an alternative world or in her words, 'to give all children an equal opportunity to live a good life'.

The classroom teacher used a social constructivist pedagogy (Vygotsky 1978) to eschew the stale teaching and irrelevant curricula that often subjects children of poverty to what Haberman (1991) has termed as a 'pedagogy of poverty' or a basic urban style based upon memorization, rote learning and 'one size fits all' commercial programs based on teaching skills, drilling and then testing those skills to obtain a decontextualized score. Curriculum is never neutral, especially ones that are selected by people remote from the circumstances of the learners nor does it always honor children's background and experiences. Building meaningful understandings is critical for young learners, especially for those who come to school with a culture different from the dominant society. Freire (1972) advocated for a dialogical teaching approach that allows learners to become teachers of their own experiences which in this study means that learning was enriching the ways of knowing of the children rather than just assimilating them into mainstream ways of knowing. Expanding Freire's idea, social constructivism assumes that all knowledge is social in nature and in this study converges with place-based pedagogies advocated by Bowers (2001) and Gruenewald (2008, 2003). Although tensions exist about the differences in executing place-based pedagogies, the rupture could be best served by expanding the places of learning that include integrated activities in embodied spaces that could address both sociological and ecological issues. Learning occurs in a context of social and dialogical interactions, bringing the community into the school and taking the students into the community and the natural environment (Gruenewald 2003; Reisberg 2008). Learners are active risk takers who accept challenges and understand how and why to learn.

They are given opportunities to restructure information in ways that make meaning personal (Wertz 1997). The teacher realized that schools are not able to replicate traditional values and a sense of spiritual connectedness to the land when the earth beneath the children's feet is only concrete pavement. However, in her professional practice the teacher was aware that there is a growing sensitivity to the communication styles and participation structures needed to be more culturally responsive to children's own lives, especially those in her multi-lingual classroom (Ladson-Billings 1994). As educators, Bateson (1994) argues that we often keep students in our 'peripheral vision'. We may be aware of their presence, but we need to be reminded that we seldom turn to really see them or really hear them.

Pedagogy of place

Initially, when I went to the classroom I listened to the Grade 3 chatter which was not about books read or the enjoyment of the river valley; instead the chatter was the ubiquitous focus on hunkering down in front of a wide screen television or a Playstation viewing the latest video or game. Contemporary culture is popular and pervasive so it is not easy to set aside. To interrupt the daily rehash of home–media routines, the classroom teacher read picture storybooks with a strong Canadian setting to help the children identify beyond the classroom to their local prairie experience. The intention was to develop both care of and a sense of place in synergy with the local region. Like other educators, the teacher felt it was critical that children have opportunities to have a 'third-space', an in-between dialogical space somewhere between formal schooling and home that negotiates broader, cross-cultural and creative interactions (Ikas and Wagner 2008). Theorists such as Ellsworth (2005) view that as a liminal space in which learners can engage in low-stakes exploration with emerging ideas. With an increased emphasis upon inclusion of immigrant and Aboriginal participation in the local schools, dialogue began with the knowledge that the identity is inextricably bound with a pride in one self. To facilitate a learning community, the teacher felt obliged to build on the cultural capital (Bourdieu 1986) that the children brought to school such as their sense of identity, resilience, and home reference points. Tapping children's own sense of place could be that starting point.

The teacher's goals echoed Sobel (1996) who contends, 'what's important is that children have an opportunity to bond with the natural world, to learn to love it, before being asked to heal its wounds' (10). At the onset of the study, the class began with sharing the catalyst story, *If you are not from the prairies* (Bouchard 1999), a poetic tribute that invites readers to view the extraordinary beauty of the prairie – a land of extremes. Each page begins with the phrase, 'If you're not from the prairie...' and follows with 'you don't know the sky', 'you don't know the wind', etc. In snatches of verse and illustrations, descriptions of the prairie emerge – the blazing light, the cutting wind, an endless sky and the piercing cold. The realistic, intensely colored paintings show settings in which children board a school bus, repair a bike, engage in a snowball fight, or play in a streambed. Many of these outdoor activities were located in the background and were not always central to the story line but the young readers made comments about how 'The kids were having fun outside' or 'It is nice to be in wide open field looking for grasshoppers'. In viewing the images, children discovered new meanings and what Maxine Greene (1978) calls 'unsuspected angles of vision' (16). Culturally, the children read the landscape, romancing their own place-based remembrances in the third spaces as they tried on their ideas. In connecting to the book, the rhythmic pattern of the story spawned many parallels to their own sense of place as reflected in some of the comments as children wrote in their journals and illustrated at the paint stand the following: 'If you are not from the prairie, you do not know playing tag with the wind' or 'If you are not from the North, you will never know the peacefulness of the trap line' and 'If you are not from here, you will never know what it is like to hide in the tall prairie grass'. In sharing stories, queries arose. The teacher initiated open-ended probes that gave all children dialogical space with an equal chance of responding in pairs or in small groups:

- Can you describe the setting and is it like any place you know?
- How would you feel about being here…? What might you do in this place?
- What have you experienced in your own life that is similar to this? Or different from this?

In addition to reading about place, she used an assemblage of meaningful engagements including photography and language experience stories[8] to be more responsive to the learners, their language and existing knowledge to keep them in view.

Lundin (2004) reminds us that literature is like an atlas, an imaginative map of the universe as well as a guidebook (114) leading children to both new and familiar horizons. When readers step out of an illustrated book and rethink what they know, they mentally cast themselves out of that text and reenter their own world-making. It is here that they can learn from the text and visuals as they make connections to the landscapes of the story and to places in their own lives. Initially, Bouchard's work (1999) opened the children's lens for dialogue about his words and the illustrations. They read the story as a panorama of local landscapes that are socially constructed, a concept predicated on the values and ideals of their own experience. Nonetheless, these were not just any landscapes; these were like theirs, a place just a few blocks away. Place, then, became the construction of stories that these learners told themselves that arose from frameworks of place-based identity, ideology, narrative tradition and imagination. Class time was for engaged reading and viewing as the visual messages embedded in the stories or in their watercolor paintings require response, interpretation and critical assessment. The children talked with one another about their meanings attributed to the place-based settings and the people who inhabited them. Questions such as what are the people doing in the outdoors led to pondering about the lives of others. The images became catalysts for discussion, as they ascribed many meanings to both illustrated place-based books and photos they had snapped on some of their class walks along the riverbank. Themes began to emerge from the data – a sense of identifying with the local places and self-discovery or gaining perspectives through awareness of environmental experiences. 'The river' became 'our river' as children felt new connections and lessened the estrangement many of the children had with the local environment. They used the watercolors to capture and preserve the sense of awe, mystery, beauty and tranquility that evoked their deeper connection to observations of the natural world. Although, the interaction between the viewer and images varied widely because of learners' prior knowledge and cultural perspectives, the artwork enabled the learners to identify peak or significant moments during or after the experiences. The placed-based environment provided occasions to look at life from new vantage points and vistas.

Other books led to more dialogue, art, poems and stories. Children's literature can be a mirror for shifting attitudes and values. Books such as *Prairie summer* (Hundal

1999), *A winter's tale* (Wallace 1997), *Prairie alphabet* (Bannatyne-Cugnet 1992), *How cold was it?* (Barclay 1999) or *Prairie year* (Bannatyne-Cugnet 1994) all have finely detailed paintings of children appreciating the windblown fields, scudding clouds and snowy landscapes of the prairie or the North. These were reminders of the joy of childhood and the thrill of discovery. In a time when children's entertainment has become increasingly formal and high-tech, these books illuminated to children the joy of unstructured play and the pleasures to be found in the explorations of and embodied knowledge of the natural world around them.

When children stand in this position to text or images, they reflect on the things they have done and places they have been. Something they have encountered in the place-based text – an event in the plot structure or an image plunges them back into their past to consider other possibilities. Meaning-making is multiple, dynamic and situated within personal experience. Not only can readers learn about other cultures, eras and even their own lives from the text, but also they can sometimes become cognizant of the information they are learning from it. Readers are not always provoked to rethink their lives as they read. However, when they do find points of congruence as in dialogue with others, they can use their own words to describe it. Place becomes personal for they turn to another and respond to the basic questions: who we are, where we came from, where we are going. When the young readers turn to others[9] to share or what Bakhtin (1981) calls addressivity, they are making and sharing connections as they connect their knowledge of the ecological world with their reading, images, or memories of experiences. Meier (2000) names this as 'I'll-put-in-and-then-you-add-on' strategy that encourages learners to 'self-scaffold… through the experiential knowledge of their own lives' (37).

Places are also cultural myths of sense making that exist at a deep, unconscious layer (Lundin 2004, 113). Over the course of the school year, the learners viewed the river valley in all the seasons. The children commented about fall with its autumnal tints in the bushes and trees: 'It looks like somebody has painted all the trees and bushes red, yellow, and orange'. They began to view the river as a new horizon, as Gruenewald (2008) nudges us: 'Exploring places can deepen empathetic connections and expand the possibilities for learning outward' (316):

> It is really peaceful here and you can listen to the songs of the trees when the wind blows briskly.

> The river is a fly way and you can hear all the cries of the birds as they fly overhead. Sometimes they fly in a V shape.

> But, it isn't really quiet along the river as we still can hear the r-r-r of cars along the roads. They are going so fast, they don't take time to look at the river.

> Long ago, my ancestors fished on this river and hunted nearby… Now, most of my family lives on the reserve.

Like other Aboriginal families, the children are distant from their life-ways and the physical bond to river valley no longer exists. *'I want to canoe on the river someday',* wistfully said another. In Freeze-up,[10] they observed the frost on the fields and kept track of the river as it began to ice-up. 'When the river ices up most of the geese and ducks fly south to get away from the cold'. In winter, with its naked trees that are entanglements of gnarled and twisting branches along the river pathways, one boy made an observation. 'I think the branches look cool in the winter 'cause you can see how the tree is actually made'. Break-up was a foreshadowing time for the prairie began to warm. 'The snow is turning to mud. The ducks and geese will be returning!' Viewing spring was a time for the children to see re-growth. 'The baby ducks and geese are here already swimming on the river', said one child who visited the river on the weekend. The arrival of the pelicans, who are special visitors, was a harbinger of summer, 'The pelicans are by the weir fishing... I've seen them. They have come all the way from Mexico!' It is these explorations of personal story that learners had with places of learning that lends to the ability for place identity (one's perception of the self in relation to the physical context in which lived experiences unfold). According to Gruenewald (2008), 'explorations amount to a guided, ecological approach to a Freirean reading of the world' (316).

Personal story is an imaginative rehearsal for living as it involves 'living through the experience'. It can be characterized as exploring a horizon of possibilities. The stories told explore emotions, relationships, motives and reactions, calling on all that the children knew about what it is to be living on Mother Earth. For children dwelling in the city core, I knew as a researcher that there exists a risk in asking them for stories about in-door home experiences and what those stories often reveal. In such circumstances, local places serve as ideal laboratories or places of embodied learning, and that presenting students with opportunities to touch, view, smell and listen outdoors in an interactive and social setting may acquaint them with their surroundings which can be the seeds to story writing, art, photovoice or poetry.

Ongoing conversations

There were other prairie stories introducing environmental issues in an approachable way that led to deeper levels of dialogue. The stories chosen were all well-crafted and enjoyable for themselves but could also provide an opening to critical thinking. The reading of *The dust bowl* (Booth 1997), a reminiscence of the hardscrabble times during the droughts of the 1930s, challenged children to think of the courage and resilience needed to live on a prairie farm in the face of the hardships caused by nature. In reflecting on the data, it seemed to me that the important learning for the children was it inculcated in the mind of the learners the nature of the situation and the causes and consequences of why things (drought) are the way they are. The children generated mindful questions to ask each other:

How would you feel about being here...?

What have you experienced in your own life that is similar to this?

Critical moments occur during some of the walking trips along the nearby river valley. On one occasion, the children were conducting an environmental scan to query how the local municipality was honoring its program intended to maintain the ecological integrity of the area. At the time, the city was restoring the damaged areas or preserving natural areas in the valley, and enhancing or creating wildlife habitat areas. As demonstrated in students' comments below, the frequent outings provided opportunities for extending students' existing perceptions of the local river to include in-depth observation understanding of its function and significance to our community.

Our river has no factories nearby to pollute the water and make it poison.

It looks nice along the river because there are lots of trash containers for people to get rid of their garbage. Most people do not litter there.

But there is a water treatment plant nearby. How do we know whether those people are being good protectors of the river from pollution?

Children in the classroom experimented with voice and identity as viewers, speakers and writers filling their discussions with thoughtful inquiry. The eco-justice discussions (Bowers 2001) were like magnets that pulled learners along, as they experienced new terrains of concepts and knowledge that will further promote their capacity to develop as caring for the river valley and the earth in general. They talked about litter, noxious fumes and air pollution. They worried that the speed boats on the river might erode the soil of the river banks or the shiny flip top lids from pop cans being tossed in the river would become lodged in the throats of the ducks. They wondered if speeding motorcycles on the roadway might frighten the pelicans away for good. As Smith (2002) points out, 'The primary value of place-base education lies in the way that it serves to strengthen children's [and adults'] connections to others and to the regions in which they live' (593–94). Moreover, Nieto (1999) advises educators pursuing transformative learning to keep in mind that "learning begins when students begin to see themselves as competent, capable and worthy of learning (123). 'Seeing children capable of contributing and worthy of learning' was what the classroom teacher felt was her most important task throughout the study.

Lessons learned

Bateson (1994) explains that when we as educators learn a 'deeper noticing of the world' (109) and use 'broader vision' (110) to illuminate what lies in our peripheral vision, we will see the worlds our students live in and learn about their diverse experiences. Autoethnography or the study of lived experiences (Ellis and Bochner 1996) can realize Bateson's goals. As a researcher in the classroom the happenings could not be fully understood while it is being experienced, but only retrospectively as I sifted through the mounds of field notes and texts, it was then I could widen my lens so that I could ask myself, 'in what ways were children learning?' Through the process of autoethnographic writing which is reflexive in nature, I became distanced from the moments and thus able to assume a more thoughtful, intuitive and critical viewpoint, allowing myself to recognize in hindsight the essence of the experience and the hidden significance of the study. So, when I tethered my thoughts, repeatedly I pondered what *is* important about this work. Such reflexivity does not arise merely in response to an academic query; rather it tends to absorb me, the researcher, who lives the question throughout the ongoing pursuit of meaning as I look forward and inward throughout the interpreting process always with the goal of thinking about how our schools offering children.

This study of one classroom and their atlas of place-based literature combined with their embodied open-ended experiences in the river valley are meant to be only an example of the way ecological concerns can be imagined. The narrative accounts sprinkled throughout the text are an attempt to de-homogenize the learners and recognize them as individuals while sketching the unexpected moments of their discovery about place. In doing so, I crossed the borders carrying back stories and artifacts to collect about our year and ourselves together as I sought to understand the dialectics of self and culture (Neumann 1996). The written text provides the reader with a means of vicariously observing and experiencing the cognitive and embodied moments during the study while at the same time giving me the opportunity to critically examine some underlying assumptions and viewpoints. In autoethnography, I became the primary participant/subject of the research in the process of writing personal reflections based upon the narratives of the children and accounting for the culture of the experiences. Narrative as a writing tool presses me to find a relationship between the theoretical and the practical detailed business of living in the multi-lingual classroom so that a closer look at one case study might encourage this kind of research in the future as children recurrently learn about natural ecological connections. Maxine Greene (1978) offered me inspiration as I journeyed along with her words that were forever lingering in my thoughts, 'The caring teacher tries to look through students' eyes, to struggle *with* them as subjects in search of their own projects, their own ways of making sense of the world' (120).

Wells's (1999) work is useful in explaining how dialogue between individuals is one of the central tools for knowledge building as each of the learners interprets, reflects upon (comparing new information to previous conceptions) and responds accordingly to solve problems and advance understanding. In practice, it is through exploratory and collaborative cognitive and embodied activities that dialogic opportunities leads to the co-construction of meaning and knowledge, which can be facilitated among children, peers, teachers and others jointly, involved together. This research explored a blending of textual, visual, aesthetic and place-based pedagogy that was a counter-narrative to the decontextualized program-based learning that permeates the school. To enhance the environmental learning of urban children, a high emphasis was continually and consistently placed on the relevance of the content and contexts of reading place-based literature, as well as the concreteness of learning experientially in the field. Environmentally illustrated stories read and the stories told were an open window into the world of human experiences and emotions, allowing the children to learn more about who we are in this world. A social constructivist view of knowledge and learning was useful as it implies that learning occurs in situated sociocultural contexts and that knowledge is apprehended and appropriated in and through social interaction, dialogue, negotiation, and contestation. In the blend of 'traditional' and 'newer' information environments, children had the options of drawing upon diverse sources of information and means of communication.

Throughout this paper, it has been critical to invite children's narratives because voice reveals the deeper meanings and perspectives of individuals and reflects learners' personal realities. It is the insights we as educators gain about them as individuals from listening to their stories that can lead us to develop more thoughtful and culturally responsive teaching practices (Ladson-Billings 1994) and to expand and enrich our sense of what it means to teach place-based pedagogies. When teachers learn new ways of crossing boundaries between the known experiences of learners' experiential backgrounds and the more unfamiliar worlds of placed-based environments then they are better equipped to work with children from many different backgrounds, with diverse beliefs and culturally-based expectations. The need to care for the environment is one of the most discussed topics in the global society. As educators, we need to teach future generations about the importance of caring for their world, but it is not always easy to convey such 'big picture' concepts as global footprints and greenhouse gas emissions to young minds. Nevertheless, this study identifies opportunities for ongoing learning textually and visually enhanced by place-based experiences that enable young learners begin the journey by finding a *place* in their communities.

Notes

1. Cyborg refers to a rejection of the rigid boundaries that divides 'human' from 'animal' and 'human' from 'machine'. Cyborg theory thus asserts that technology merely comprises material extensions of the human body as in the work of Donna Haraway.
2. In this paper, landscape is used for images and illustrations as interpreted through book illustrations or other visual representation. In contrast, place represents environment as a specific reality.
3. Autoethnography is a form of personal narrative that explores the researcher/writer's experience of life. The overarching goal of autoethnographic writing is to bring about an understanding of oneself and one's culture through the detour of other, as well as the inverse; understanding others through the increased awareness of self (Ellis and Bochner 1996).
4. Photovoice promotes critical dialogue about important issues through group discussion of photographs. This relates to Freire's principals of collective consciousness.
5. Once important as a fur-trading route, the river basin provides hydro-electric power and contains Canada's largest irrigation district.
6. The habitat variety includes riverbanks and channels, oxbow wetlands, boulder-strewn slopes, cliffs, slump blocs, fluvial terraces, permanent wetland basins and seeps, riparian forests and scrublands.
7. Aboriginal refers to the Indigenous peoples who were the original inhabitants of Canada.
8. Language experience stories are collaborative writings that are about children's own shared experiences. They become the reading stories for the class based upon the children's own language, thoughts and experiences.
9. Bakhtin (1986) calls these moments addressivity, which is the act of turning to someone to share ideas or perceptions.
10. Traditionally, in the local Cree culture there are six distinct seasons that being spring, summer, fall, freeze-up, winter and break-up.

References

Bainbridge, J., and J. Thistleton-Martin. 2001. Canadian literature: Vehicle for transmission of national culture and identity or the victim of mass-marketed globalization? Paper presented at the Annual Meeting of the Australian Meeting of Research in Education, June 6–11, in Freemantle, Australia.

Baker, J. 1991. *Window.* New York: Greenwillow.

Baker, J. 2004. *Home.* New York: Harper Collins.

Bakhtin, M. 1981. *The dialogical imagination.* Austin, TX: The University of Texas Press.

Bakhtin, M.M. 1986. *Speech genres and other late essays.* Ed. C. Emerson and M. Holquist. Trans. V.W. McGee. Austin: University of Texas Press.

Bannatyne-Cugnet, J. 1992. *A prairie alphabet.* Illustrated by Y. Moore. Montreal: Tundra Books.

Bannatyne-Cugnet, J. 1994. *The prairie year.* Illustrated by Y. Moore. Montreal: Tundra Books.

Barclay, J. 1999. *How cold was it?* Illustrated by J. Donato. Montreal: Lobster Press.

Bateson, M.C. 1994. *Peripheral visions: Learning along the way.* New York, NY: Harper Collins.

Booth, D. 1997. *The dust bowl.* Illustrated by K. Reczuch. Toronto: Kids Can Press.

Bouchard, D. 1997. *The elders are watching.* Illustrated by R. H. Vickers. Vancouver: Raincoast Books.

Bouchard, D. 1999. *If you are not from the prairie.* Illustrated by H. Ripplinger. Vancouver: Raincoast Books.

Bourdieu, P. 1986. The forms of capital. In *The handbook of theory and research for the sociology of education,* ed. J. Richardson, 241–8. Westport, CT: Greenwood Press.

Bowers, C.A. 1993. *Education, cultural myths, and the ecological crisis.* Albany, NY: State University of New York Press.

Bowers, C.A. 1995. *Educating for an ecologically sustainable culture: Rethinking moral education, creativity, intelligence and other modern orthodoxies.* New York: State University of New York Press.

Bowers, C.A. 1997. *The culture of denial: Why the environmental movement needs a strategy for reforming universities and public schools.* Albany: State University of New York Press.

Bowers, C.A. 2001. *Educating for eco-justice and community.* Athens: The University of Georgia Press.

Bowers, C.A. 2005. *Rethinking Freire: Globalization and the environmental crisis.* Mahwah, NJ: Lawrence Erlbaum Associates.

Cajete, G. 1994. *Look to the mountain: An ecology of indigenous education.* Durango, CO: Kivaki Press.

Dewey, J. 1938/1997. *Experience and education.* New York: Macmillan.

Dewey, J. 1988. Experience and education. In *John Dewey the later works 1925–1953,* ed. J.A. Boydston, 13: 1938–1939, 1–62. Carbondale, IL: Southern Illinois University Press.

Ellis, C., and A.P. Bochner. 1996. Autoethnography, personal narrative, reflexivity: Researcher as subject. In *Composing ethnography: Alternative forms of qualitative writing,* ed. C. Ellis and A.P. Bochner, 733–68. Walnut Creek, CA: AltaMira Press.

Ellsworth, E. 2005. *Places of learning.* New York: RoutledgeFalmer.

Fiske, J. 1990. Ethnosemiotics: Some personal and theoretical reflections. *Cultural Studies* 4: 85–99.

Freire, P. 1972. *Pedagogy of the oppressed.* Harmondsworth: Penguin.

Giroux, H.A. 1992. *Border crossings: Cultural workers and the politics of education.* New York: Taylor and Francis.

Gradle, S. 2007. Ecology of place: Art education in a relational world. *Studies in Art Education* 48, no. 4: 392–421.

Graham, M.A. 2007. Art, ecology and art education: Locating art education in a critical place-based pedagogy. *Studies in Art Education* 48, no. 4: 375–92.

Greene, M. 1978. *Landscapes of learning.* New York: Teachers College Press.

Gruenewald, D.A. 2002. Teaching and learning with Thoreau. Honoring critique, experimentations, wholeness, and the places we live. *Harvard Educational Review* 72, no. 4: 515–41.

Gruenewald, D.A. 2003. The best of both worlds: A critical pedagogy of place. *Educational Researcher* 32, no. 4: 3–12.

Gruenewald, D.A. 2008. Place-based education: Grounding culturally responsive teaching in geographical diversity: Local diversity. In *Place-based education in the global age,* ed. D.A. Gruenewald and G.A. Smith, 137–54. New York, NY: Lawrence Erlbaum.

Haberman, M. 1991. The pedagogy of poverty versus good teaching. *Phi Delta Kappa* 73, no. 4: 290–94.

Haig-Brown, C. 1990. Border work. In *Native writers and Canadian writing,* ed. W.H. New, 229–41. Vancouver: University of British Columbia Press.

Huck, C.S., S. Hepler, J. Hickman, and B.Z. Kiefer. 1997. *Children's literature in the elementary school.* Boston, MA: McGraw-Hill.

Hundal, N. 1999. *Prairie summer.* Illustrated by B. Deines. Toronto: Fitzhenry and Whiteside.

Ikas, K., and G. Wagner. 2008. *Communicating in the third space.* New York: Routledge.

Kukla, A. 2000. *Social constructivism and the philosophy of science.* New York: Routledge.

Kruger, L. 2001. What is essential is invisible to the eye: Understanding the role of place and social learning in achieving sustainable landscapes. In *Forests and landscapes: Linking ecology, sustainability and aesthetics,* ed. S.R.J. Sheppard and H.W. Harshaw, 173–87. Wallingford, Oxon: CABI Publishing.

Ladson-Billings, G. 1994. *The dream-keepers: Successful teachers of African-American children.* San Francisco: Jossey-Boss.

Lave, J., and E. Wenger. 1991. *Situated learning: Legitimate peripheral participation.* Cambridge: Cambridge University Press.

Louv, R. 2005. *Last child in the woods: Saving our children from nature-deficit disorder.* Chapel Hill, NC: Algonquin Books of Chapel Hill.

Lundin, A. 2004. *Constructing the canon of children's literature. Beyond walls and ivory towers.* New York: Routledge.

McKenzie, M. 2008. The places of pedagogy: Or what we can do with culture through inter-subjective experiences? *Environmental Education Research* 14, no. 3: 361–73.

Meir, D. 2000. *Scribble scrabble: Learning to read and write. Success with diverse teachers, children and families.* New York: Teachers College Press.

Neumann, M. 1996. Collecting ourselves at the end of the century. In *Composing ethnography: Alternative forms of qualitative writing,* ed. C. Ellis and A. Bochner, 172–98. Walnut Creek, CA: Alta MiraPress.

Nieto, S. 1999. *The light in their eyes: Creating multicultural learning communities.* New York: Teachers College Press.

Noddings, N. 1992. *The challenge to care in schools: An alternative approach to education.* New York: Teachers College Press.

Nodelman, P. 1997. What's Canadian about Canadian children's literature? A compendium of answers to the question. *Canadian Children's Literature* 23: 15–35.

Payne, P. 1997. Embodiment and environmental education. *Environmental Education Research* 3, no. 2: 133–56.

Reed-Danahay, D.E. 1997. *Auto/ethnography: Rewriting the self and the social.* New York: Berg.

Reisberg, M. 2008. Social/ecological caring with multicultural picture books: Placing pleasure in art education. *Studies in Art Education* 49, no. 3: 251–68.

Seiter, 1993. *Sold separately: Children and parents in the consumer culture.* New Brunswick, NJ: Rutgers University Press.

Smith, G. 2002. Place-based education: Learning to be where we are. *Phi Delta Kappan* 83, no. 8: 584–94.

Sobel, D. 1996. *Beyond ecophobia: Reclaiming the heart in nature education.* Great Barrington, MA: The Orion Society and The Myrin Institute.

Squire, S. 1996. Landscapes, places and geographic spaces: Texts of Beatrix Potter as cultural communication. *Geo Journal* 38: 75–86.

Stedman, R. 2002. Toward a social psychology of place: Predicting behavior from place-based cognitions, attitude, and identity. *Environment and Behavior* 34, no. 5: 561–81.

Stedman, R. 2003. Is it really just a social construction? The contribution of the physical environment to sense of place. *Society and Natural Resources* 16, no. 8: 671–85.

Vygotsky, L. 1978. *Mind in society: The development of higher psychological processes.* Cambridge, MA: Harvard University Press.

Waboose, Boudreau, J. 1997. *Morning on the lake.* Illustrated by K. Reczuch. Toronto: Kids Can Press.

Wallace, I. 1997. *A winter's tale.* Illustrated by I. Wallace. Toronto: Groundwood Douglas and McIntyre.

Wason-Ellam, L. 2001. Living against the wind: Pathways chosen by Chinese immigrants, *Canadian Ethnic Studies* 33, no. 1: 1–39.

Wason-Ellam, L. 2005. Unpackaging reading: What counts as engagement? *English Quarterly* 36: 32–40.

Wason-Ellam, L., and G. Li. 1999. Identity-weaving in the places and spaces of a cross-cultural classroom. *Canadian Children* 24, no. 2: 23–35.

Wason-Ellam, L., and A. Ward. 2003. Community literacy: Commodifying children's spaces. *Language and Literacy* 6, no. 1: 1–20.

Wells, G. 1999. *Dialogic inquiry: Towards a sociocultural practice and theory of education.* Cambridge: Cambridge University Press.

Wells, G. 2000. Dialogic inquiry in education. In *Vygotskian perspectives on literacy research: Constructing meaning through collaborative inquiry,* ed. C. Lee and P. Smagorinsky, 51–85. Cambridge: Cambridge University Press.

Wertz, J.V. 1997. *Vygotsky and the formation of the mind.* Cambridge, MA: Harvard University Press.

The stories are the people and the land: three educators respond to environmental teachings in Indigenous children's literature

Lisa Korteweg, Ismel Gonzalez and Jojo Guillet

Faculty of Education, Lakehead University, Thunder Bay, Ontario, Canada

This article explores how Indigenous Canadian children's literature might challenge adult and child readers to consider different meanings and worldviews of the environment as a land-based value system. As three teacher educators from elementary and university classrooms, we use reader-response theory to explore a collection of rich alternative narratives of Indigenous land-based knowledge systems available in the work of Indigenous authors and illustrators of children's literature. Our study considers how Indigenous picture books might serve to decolonize environmental consciousness through offering accessible and immersive Indigenous stories of the land. As we respond to and analyze these picture books, we work from a prior commitment to decolonization as a critical self-reflexive political process in which one's colonized beliefs are explicitly pinpointed, challenged and countered by Indigenous worldviews and perspectives.

Introduction

I want to suggest how dialogue with Aboriginal people might be framed in different terms, looking for language that expresses Aboriginal perspectives and also connects with the aspirations of a wide spectrum of Canadians. Creating and sustaining a national community is an ongoing act of imagination, fuelled by stories of who we are. (George Erasmus, Baldwin-Lafontaine lecture, 2002)

Following the editorial lead of this special issue, our study explores the compelling need to acknowledge the role and power of children's literature in environmental education in providing both formative engagements with the land but also deeply mediating those encounters and our constructions of the Indigenous peoples of those lands.

Children's literature in general can enhance students' and teachers' awareness and appreciation of diverse constructions and understandings of nature, environment and place, but it is picture books in particular that immerse children and adults in a visual portrayal of the environment, be that of their own environments or those of other places.

Aesthetic responses to and socio-cultural interpretations of picture books may also suggest a beauty to inhabiting and re-inhabiting the 'land' that photographs or purely textual depictions cannot express. In this regard, we note Hunter's (2005) assertion that picture books 'are a polyphonic form that embodies many codes, styles, textual devices and intertextual references and which frequently pushes at the boundaries of convention' (128). Indeed, Indigenous children's literature may offer not only polyphonic forms of narrative codes and visual devices, but also through their arts-based representations, push at educators' conventional understandings of the environment or land. Thus, picture books can afford openings for dialogue about teachers' and students' environmental formations – their ways of being and relating to the land and its people – in relation to Indigenous peoples, territory issues and living together on the land. While in the case of environmental or land-based stories written and illustrated by Indigenous authors to reclaim their stories, land and cultural ways of knowing, they may also be invaluable sources of worldview narratives that help counter the constant marinade of colonization that non-Indigenous environmental educators, and all mainstream teachers, are steeped in (Smith 1999; Battiste 2000; Strong-Wilson 2007).

Strong-Wilson (2007), a literacy education specialist, observes that fictional narratives, including children's picture book stories, offer immersive 'perceptual horizons' or worldviews that run deep as 'touchstones': that is, they provide foundational or pivotal stories that impact perceptions and influence how we relate to the land and, equally as important, to the peoples of that land.

We present our study as an exploratory example of how Indigenous picture books can help the receptive decolonizing non-Indigenous teacher imagine counter-point stories to their own environmental formation and begin to transform or 'shape-shift' this formation. 'Shape-shift' is a term associated with the coyote trickster in many Indigenous legends (see King 2003). Coyote shape-shifts and transforms its outward appearance to suit the quest, lesson or trick needed and to keep people thinking and reflecting. We use this term to refer to environmental educators shifting their understandings towards an Aboriginal epistemology. By learning to move towards shape-shifting, we develop flexible ways of knowing and doing that permit us to begin to reflect and honour specific places and nurture a different environmental consciousness.

Thus in the collective auto-ethnographic study we present here cued by our deeply felt concerns about the ongoing presence of colonial imperatives, we investigate our responses as teachers to Indigenous concepts, stories and language of the land and the importance of their contribution to the literatures used in and as environmental education, as well as to the ongoing project of decolonizing environmental education (Gruenewald 2008; Lowan 2008; Simpson 2002; Agyeman 2003). Our work began as a process to illuminate and extend current perspectives on environmental education that focus on place (Gruenewald and Smith 2008), decolonization (Gruenewald 2003, 2008), re-inhabitation (Gruenewald 2004, 2008) and cultural commons to sustainable traditions (Bowers 2001, 2004). We soon discovered, however, that before encountering the Indigenous epistemologies of the land through the picture books, we first needed to grapple via an autoethnographic approach with our own relations with the land, and with our own formative stories of colonization, inhabitation and cultural commons.

Our article starts with these formative stories and contexts, and then discusses our methodological frame and methods for our inquiry. The findings point to the increasingly significant contribution that Indigenous children's literature can make to environmental education in forming and shifting educators' understandings of *land* (metaphorically, a term that conveys stronger historical, cultural and social meanings than the term 'place'). Further, the study suggests how we can employ literary tools, both textual and visual, to decolonize environmental teacher education and enable educators to develop conceptual tools (Grossman et al. 2000; Smagorinsky et al. 2007), a capacity for deep reflection (Harste et al. 2004) and an enlarged imaginary of land-based experiences, to contrast with their own colonized worldviews. We demonstrate this method through our own self-study process of ongoing decolonization towards more culturally responsive environmental education approaches, a responsibility we take seriously as treaty partners (Bishop 1996) on the land and traditional territory of the Anishinaabek.

Auto-ethnographic positioning as environmental educators and teachers

Our collaborative partnership and process in this study incorporate critical self-reflexivity (Pillow 2003), auto-ethnographic journaling (Jones 2005) and dialogic analysis of each other's responses (Galda and Beach 2001; Landis 2003; Kaufman et al. 2001) to the picture books. We came together for such a project based on our teaching experiences, our many critical conversations on Indigenous and non-Indigenous relations in school and university classrooms, our commonalities as settlers and treaty partners on Indigenous traditional territory, and out of grave concern as parents for our children's environmental inheritance. While we are three teachers with different schooling contexts and distinctive personal histories of cultural legacies and citizenship, we had already forged bonds of collegiality and friendship through previous research projects in pre-service and in-service teacher education. Each of us had also begun experimenting with and researching the integration of picture books into our culturally responsive teacher education projects. We describe here, in our own words, our reasons for engaging in this decolonizing environmental education study and our individual cultural positions located within the 'we' or collective stance of this article.

Lisa (Author 1)

I am a first-generation Canadian, non-Indigenous, born to a sixth generation Empire Loyalist mother and a White European immigrant English language learner father. I have long been concerned with how colonized my own relations are and others can be with Indigenous peoples in Canada and globally. I am also acutely aware of the colonial tragedies all educators inherit within Canadian schools: the education system of residential schools was the tool of linguistic assimilation and cultural annihilation of the Indigenous peoples of Canada.

As a teacher (12 years in upper elementary classrooms), a teacher educator (pre-service programs in a faculty of education) and a teacher–researcher (in-service teacher education projects in environmental education), I have become convinced of my own colonized education and cultural ignorance of Indigenous history, land knowledge and traditional rights. As I have become more involved with environmental and social justice issues in education, I have come to realize just how colonized my perceptions and 'molded images' (Dion 2007) of First Nations peoples are – the keepers of the knowledge of the land across Canada and of where I make my home.

Ismel (Author 2)

I am a university instructor of modern languages and a doctoral student and researcher in a faculty of education. I am also a new Canadian (10 years). Prior to engaging in this study, my relationship with the land as a male Latino (Cuban-Canadian) had been heavily shaped by western views in which nature was to be tamed and used to satisfy my most immediate needs, as opposed to thinking of nature as the provider to whom I had to be thankful for all she had already shared with me. Furthermore, my 'touch-stones' have been dominated by Euro-western story patterns. There is typically a climax to these stories. And whenever nature is involved, the bravery of the main character (usually a male figure) can often be determined by how well the hero conquers and tames her during the climax. Engaging in this study, I began decoloniz-ing my own 'touchstones', opening myself up to a whole new way of looking at stories and their possible figurations, including ones which could immerse me and generously provide alternative ways of seeing as well as very valuable knowledge of Aboriginal cultures and their close relationship with the land.

Jojo (Author 3)

I am a product of everything I carry in my blood memory and all the benefits and chal-lenges presented in this world. I am an Aboriginal/Indigenous woman. The challenges I face are not necessarily those of the larger group of Indigenous women represented by Statistics Government Canada data: I am not poor, I own a lovely home; I am educated; I am not involved in a relationship of abuse or violence. Educationally I am a product of the provincial urban education system, not the federal reserves school system.

Each day, however, I struggle with my Indigenous cultural identity. I constantly grapple with the concept of decolonization as I am a product of the colonial education system; however, I am not colonized. I am not a gatekeeper in this study of what counts as Indigenous, nor am I an expert on being 'Indian'. I am not in the position to speak for all Indigenous peoples of Ontario or Canada. I am I, and can only tell you of my journey in a respectful way and in my own voice. I too am a settler to the land where I live and work. While I am not Indigenous to this land as Ojibwe, I have been welcomed and treated here as family. Conversely, I have been discriminated against, and made to feel shame for my worldview and Aboriginal belief systems by non-Indigenous people. Each day, I struggle to retain and regain what is respectfully mine as an Aboriginal person. I am surrounded and immersed in an education system that does not recognize or place much value on my history or political views. My struggle then is to walk tall, use my voice and my words to reinforce the beauty of my legacy and my ancestral beliefs. To tell the stories of my elders and make this world good for my children, so, when I pass to the spirit world, my children will have to fight a little less to understand the views of our ancestors. I function in this world of colonialism as a word warrior, while I do not seek to become colonized, I contest it mainly through words. I know the rules and can play the game of the colonized education system, but I do not seek to proclaim it to be just, fair or good.

Representing and misrepresenting Indigenous cultures in children's literature

For the most part, North American children's literature has excluded Indigenous authors, peoples and themes from its contents (Bradford 2007; Johnston and Mangot 2003; Manning 2003). It has also romanticized Indigenous peoples' ways of life and misappropriated Indigenous traditions and ceremonies of the land (Francis 1992; Alfred 1999; LaDuke 1999). In their description of the different themes that have characterized Canadian children's literature since the beginnings of the nineteenth century, Edwards and Saltman (2000) observe that some of the earliest attempts to depict Indigenous peoples were those of Toye and Cleaver's collaborations in the 1960s. Their children's books were derived from recordings of Indigenous myths and legends and consisted of romanticized Indigenous peoples as 'peoples [who] live in the distant past of folktales' (2). Bradford (2007) comments that (non-Indigenous) children's literature:

> … as colonial narratives of exploration, adventure, and settlement produced and reinforced the givens of Western cartography, [while] alternative modes of mapping the world – the spacio-temporal cartographies of Indigenous peoples – were rendered invisible… (Bradford 2007, 147)

Consequently, the history of Canadian children's literature can be understood to dwell at an intersection of Indigenous space (the people and land) subjugated to European values, maps and time, albeit an uneasy, even dangerous, juxtaposition between land/scape and Eurocentric literature, and a mismatch of Indigenous land and Eurocentric stories (Edwards and Saltman 2000).

This literature, argues Saul (2008), contributes to a cultural imagination that has not yet located or articulated its own mythos or philosophy 'to live by' and 'live well together' on the land. The consequences in Canada of an erased, ignored or avoided *'Metis'* history (our mixed or woven history of Indigenous, English and French peoples) along with an impoverished shared cultural language to express these merged foundational values, Saul adds, have contributed to the environmental destruction of the land. Bringhurst (2002) summarizes the damage of historic and ongoing colonization in Canada on both peoples and lands – its endangering of Indigenous peoples, languages and traditional knowledges in particular – as:

> When you wipe out a community, a culture, and leave five or ten or twenty speakers of the language, you can claim that the language survives, that it isn't extinct. But what happens is every bit as terrible as when you clear-cut a forest and leave a strip of trees along the edge, to hide the clear-cut from the highway. It's true in both cases that something will eventually grow back – but what was there before is gone forever. (Bringhurst 2002, 11)

In an era when the United Nations has passed the Declaration on the Rights of Indigenous Peoples (2007), describing it as setting 'an important standard for the treatment of Indigenous peoples that will undoubtedly be a significant tool towards eliminating human rights violations against the planet's 370 million Indigenous people and assisting them in combating discrimination and marginalization' (1), we view this study as not only an opportunity to engage or re-engage ourselves with Indigenous values rooted in Canadian land, but timely for other (environmental) educators, to examine their own relations with Indigenous peoples and colonization, no matter the place or location.

Our study focuses on a series of Indigenous picture books published since the 1990s in Canada. They contest simplistic and romantic representations of Indigenous peoples, their cultures and their relationships with the land, and carry teachings of an Indigenous epistemology of the land that transcends national borders and can inform environmental educators who teach, travel or live with the planet's 370 million Indigenous people. A focus on Indigenous picture books coupled to a decolonizing framework transforms the complexity of Indigenous and non-Indigenous relations into a cultural strength not weakness. It also helps us engage in ways that communicate a collective imaginary or mythos centred on 'all our relations' – an expression of relational value with each other, the land, the animals, our intertwined histories and seven generations to come. Our goal then in this paper is to consider how deep currents of thinking, imagination and representation in Indigenous children's picture books can help non-Indigenous (environmental) educators recognize, explore and *disrupt molded images* (Dion 2007, 2009): those entrenched cultural perceptions that may be limiting our possibilities for changing environmental conditions and values – learning to live well on the land – while simultaneously promoting more equitable societies – learning to live well with the (Indigenous) people of the land. We call this shifting of colonized, settler, Eurocentric frames of reference towards imaginative possibilities and new culturally/environmentally responsive articulations, the decolonization of non-Indigenous environmental education.

Indigenous children's literature and decolonizing environmental education

Non-Indigenous scholars are now beginning to question the meanings of concepts such as decolonization (Gruenewald 2003, 2008a), place (Gruenewald and Smith 2008), re-inhabitation (Gruenewald 2003, 2008a), cultural commons and sustainable traditions (Bowers 2001, 2008), and how these concepts or foundational values may become root metaphors (Bowers 1997) that influence how we act upon the land/ environment and enact environmental education. Long before this moment in environmental education and research, Indigenous peoples in Canada, like other Indigenous peoples around the world, have been involved in struggles for environmental reclamation and protection of land as part of their demand for cultural integrity and self-determination (see Marker 2006; LaDuke 1999). While many Indigenous scholars have called for a foregrounding of Indigenous ways of knowing that reintegrate concepts of *land* and *relationships to land* in environmental education (Marker 2006; Barnhardt and Kawagely 2005, 2008; Cajete 1999), we recognize that it has been risky research for non-Indigenous educators to find appropriate representations and stories to work towards imagining new enviro-cultural values, compounded by the difficulty of working in ways that tries to embody respectful research in decolonizing environmental education (Battiste 1998, 2005; Dion 2007, 2009; Smith 1999; Haig-Brown 2001).

As two non-Indigenous researchers (Author 1, Lisa, and Author 2, Ismel) and one Indigenous educator (Author 3, Jojo) in a Northern Canadian university, we were excited to read as many Indigenous picture books as we could locate and then enter into conversations about what images and stories of land were communicated, how the stories were told and made public for a Canadian readership, and who was determining and telling the stories. We understand that making Indigenous knowledge of the land, history and culture publicly available is a critically important act of self-determination, even though such knowledge is endangered by having been subjugated, subsumed and eroded by gross misrepresentations in media, textbooks, curricula and research. We also knew that Indigenous knowledge and culture is embedded and passed on to generations through stories and the oral telling of the stories (King 2003; Bringhurst 2002), and thus it is a new era in Canadian children's literature to be able to read and learn stories of land and cultural history via artifacts that are in the control of Indigenous peoples. Furthermore, we believe that deep stories, delivered imaginatively and creatively with compelling images, can play a key role in shaping and decolonizing non-Indigenous teachers' ways of learning how to live well on this land and with Indigenous peoples (Dion 2009; Alcoff 2006).

Yet we also knew that we should begin this study in the spirit of reconciliation (Castellano, Archibald, and DeGagne 2008), as another means of moving towards fulfilling our promises as fair and responsible treaty partners (Bishop 1996; Saul 2008), learning to live well together with Indigenous peoples on this land called Canada (though we note that in our historical/legal understanding, all Canadian land is the traditional territory of Indigenous peoples). Thus we acknowledge how a European dominated worldview is too limited to reflect the multidimensionality, the historical–cultural triangulation of Canadian society: British, French and Indigenous peoples living and learning to live together (Saul 2008).

As noted above, with ambitious politico-historical philosophies by non-Indigenous Canadian scholars such as John Ralston Saul (2008) and Indigenous philosophers such as Tainaike Alfred (1999), Canadian society can be recognized as evolving and our social values are becoming increasingly recognizable as *Métis*. Saul, for example, describes Canadian society as resting on a triangular historical foundation composed of British, French, and Aboriginal pillars. Of these three, the Aboriginal or Indigenous is the senior and most important pillar, consisting of a set of shared values that have shaped who we are today as Canadian citizens. These shared values of acceptance, complexity, negotiation, balance, cooperation, inclusiveness, diversity, collectivity and adoption/adaptation originated with the Indigenous peoples and through living in close association during the first 250 years of Euro-Canadian history. Our Indigenous roots are what have made Canadian culture more oral than written, more circular than linear, and more accepting of complexity (multicultural), and thus could provide us with sources for solutions to our current deep problems, mainly environmental or land-based. For example, the Indigenous (Mohawk) proverb of 'the single bowl and spoon' of the Earth displays our dependence on the land and our need to be united as a people, Indigenous and non-Indigenous.

Reader response as design

The inquiry took place on the traditional territory of the Fort William First Nation, in a Faculty of Education in northern-central Canada and was conducted as an interpretive dialogic, auto-ethnographic collaborative study into our own individual and group reader responses to a set of Indigenous children's literature. As both the participants in and authors of this research, we are three distinct Canadians: a first generation Euro-Canadian (Lisa, Author 1); a new Canadian from Cuba (Ismel, Author 2); and an American-Canadian-Choctaw (Jojo, Author 3), that together represent a typical slice and mix of Canadian society, or what Saul (2008) refers to as our *Métis* nation. We also have three distinct education voices, those of an: environmental educator (Lisa), a modern languages educator (Ismel) and an Indigenous educator (Jojo), which converge upon a set of Indigenous children's picture books to read into our own molded images (Dion 2007) of place, land and environment.

We adopted and adapted a reader response approach (Rosenblatt 1938, 1978) as a methodological strategy for decolonizing our perspectives of the land, environment and Indigenous peoples in reading and discussing the children's picture book stories, language and images. Reader response theory focuses attention on the reading process and on the relationships between reader, text and images. As a critical approach to reading children's literature, the reading act is viewed as a transaction between readers and texts, in which readers use their lived experiences or 'touchstones', convictions, personal opinions and assumptions, to interact with the ideas and images in the text and create personal meaning as a result of their transactions (Hunsberger and Labercane 2002; Rosenblatt 1938, 1978; Iser 1978). Reader response approaches foreground deep aesthetic relationships with a text as literature is regarded 'an experience rather than an object' and readers 'active participants rather than passive consumers' (Davis 1989, 421) . Our reader response process treated the picture book experiences as a combination of written text and visual images where the illustrations communicated more directly and evocatively than a 'words-only' narrative (Nodelman 2005). The illustrations show readers what the world and worldview implied by a cultural story might look like as a complex visualization, and can thus engage emotions and evoke pleasure in ways that a 'words-only' text cannot (Nodelman 2005).

Sumara (1995) employs reader response theory to develop 'reading as a focal practice', a process to encourage a deeper aesthetic relationship between readers and texts. Sumara's (1995) theorization of reading and the reader's comprehension builds on the assumption that:

> ... 'literariness' is not something which is contained in the text; rather, it is a quality which emerges from the unique relation that the reader has with a text which is culturally announced as literary and, most importantly, which leaves enough space or indeterminacy for the reader to participate in the shaping of meaning. It is the process of anticipating, reading, and interpreting the text that announces what I am calling 'commonplace location' – an opening which functions to help the reader to shift perspective and understand his or her life differently because of the relation established with the text. (Sumara 1995, 20)

Focal practice may involve writing in a journal or in the margins of the book and in reviewing these reflections, readers have the opportunity to develop a relationship with a book which, in turn, allows them to experience reading as a place where memories of lived experiences might be found (25–6). Thus reading can become a deeper, reflective experience as we allow our reading responses to become subject to interpretation and reinterpretation, prompted by our other experiences and intertextual readings and/or by participating in a community of readers of the text(s) (23).

Sumara (2002, xv) also argues that engagement with literary texts can result in 'associational complexities' or transformative multidimensional opportunities to re-create, re-imagine and reinterpret our frames of reference and molded images. Every reader and educator has developed touchstones that shape our perceptual horizons or 'standpoints', against which we implicitly compare other narratives (Wilson 2003). We wanted to read these picture books to experience different storied landscapes and to immerse ourselves in the cultural visualizations or image-based portrayals of land (Kiefer 1995). And equally as important, we wanted to accept our responsibilities as non-Indigenous treaty partners, to address our privileged cultural position and our collective responsibility to read Indigenous stories, immerse ourselves in them and learn from them of how to live well on the earth.

Methods of focal practices to reveal and decolonize

Our individual and collaborative focal practices consisted of two main phases. In the first we selected a bibliography of 20 Indigenous children's picture books that we read alone and privately on a weekly basis (see references marked*). We then met briefly as a group three times to exchange our sets of books so that once we proceeded to the second phase, we had each read all of the books.

We used the reader response approach as a focal practice to reveal and disrupt our molded or colonized images of the environment and the people. We began by engaging and reflecting in a journal on our initial responses to the narrative and illustrations in the picture books. In the second phase, we joined together to discuss and respond to each other's journal reflections and reflected on each other's interpretations and re-interpretations of the books. We recorded our conversations, and re-listened to these recordings to individually analyze and then discuss critical themes as a group. These meetings constituted five literature circles (Sumara 1995), through which we charted our own decolonizing journeys via collective dialogue and respectful re-interpretations. Each author transcribed one of the meeting transcripts and we then met to pool codes, impressions and analyses. We worked with poster sheets to locate common language, issues, shifts and convergences. We paid close attention to themes of pivotal moments of disruption or revelation, themes that could provide clues as to how non-Indigenous educators' viewpoints or 'perceptual horizons' of relations with the land and people can shift, change or move.

We understand these multiple stories, re-storied memories and circular conversations (Kaufman et al. 2001) as part of the decolonizing process for non-Indigenous educators. What we wondered was whether or not our immersion into these stories and reliving them in dialogue and mutual story-sharing would help the two non-Indigenous educators move towards new literary touchstones that would influence or shape-shift our cultural relations with the land and its Indigenous people. In highlighting and writing from our conversations, we wanted to maintain the circular narrative paths of our decolonizing interactions, creating new stories and shifting values that we can live and teach by, as we learn to live well as treaty partners on this land and with the Indigenous people of the land. Displaying the multiple voices and layers of our reader and story-making responses, we hope to draw non-Indigenous environmental educators into the picture books stories themselves, and to engage in their own touchstone shifting and shape-shifting processes as allies with the land and the Indigenous peoples of the land.

We used three criteria informed by our purposes to select the 20 picture books: (i) a self-identified Indigenous author or illustrator of the picture book to ensure an Indigenous story and worldview; (ii) a land base or territory that was geographically Canadian to underscore our treaty responsibilities and history of relations with the Indigenous peoples of this land; and, (iii) nature or the land as a central character in the story to ensure an immersion into land-based values and an examination of environmental content. In the 20 picture books, we located four approaches in Indigenous writing of children's books: (a) an approach that affirms the contemporary applicability of traditional teachings of the land to all people (see Waboose 1997, 1999, 2000); (b) a resistant voice that quietly rages against systemic racism and stereotyping through education (see Littlechild 1993; Van Camp and Littlechild 1997); (c) an ironic voice that reminds children and educators of the distances yet to be traveled in knowledge and relations (see King 1992); and finally (d) a bridging voice that encourages Canadian society, both Indigenous and non-Indigenous, to be taught by Indigenous experiences and values (see Highway 2001, 2002, 2003).

Data for the study included transcripts from our five recorded literature circle meetings, the three reader response journals (each consisting of multiple entries) and the collections of Indigenous literature by Canadian Indigenous writers and artists.

What began on the surface as a quiet literacy study soon became a whirlwind of animated discussions, teachings, and critical insights into our cultural standpoints and how we can learn to live well with 'all our relations' (human, non-human and more-than-human) on a northern boreal land.

Shifting environmental education understandings of the land through three themes

Three land-based values themes became prominent, repeatedly highlighted and noticeably shifted through the journaling stage as well as during the analysis of the five literature circle transcripts. They each concern an Indigenous worldview of land or environmental relations that influences our shape-shifting decolonization process. They were: (i) how we humans are creatures embedded in the land; (ii) the concept of all our relations or deep circular connections of self-community-land-Creator; and (iii) the foundational knowledge of Indigenous languages carrying the stories of the land and the land embedded in the language/knowledge of Indigenous people.

These three concepts or teachings from the children's stories became points of convergence for our discussions and our re-interpretations or focal practice work. We were surprised at the affirmative, wondrous, fascinating tone in our close readings and retellings of our touchstone stories triggered by and merging with the Indigenous picture books. The non-Indigenous educators expected more disruption, discomfort, disbelief and discord with both the children's literature and with our colleagues' responses; however, the opposite occurred. Clearly, we had had different environmental education experiences or formative touchstones in our youth but we had very similar insights and many moments of connection with these children's books. It was a surprising set of convergences between three educators – two non-Indigenous and one Indigenous – which Lisa distilled into the comment, 'It's as if we were all very thirsty for these stories and these teachings'.

We are creatures embedded in and of the land

In these picture books, people are as integral to the land as the animals and spirit world. Land is portrayed as teacher through its gifts, visions and dreams. Relationality is experienced directly with the land, there is no interference or mediation through western models of curriculum or teaching (see Cajete 1999; Simpson 2002).

Jojo (Author 3) and Lisa (Author 1) identified closely with Jan Bourdeau Waboose's *Morning on the lake* (1997). This is the story of an Ojibwe grandfather, *Mishomis*, and his young grandson, *Noshen*, who set out in a birch bark canoe one misty morning. Together they watch a pair of loons and are rewarded by seeing the male loon perform his territorial dance. In the second story, 'Noon', the boy and his grandfather climb a rocky high cliff and are visited by an eagle whose presence, *Mishomis* explains, 'is a sign of honour and wisdom. As the Great Eagle is a proud protector of our people, I am a proud *Mishomis* of my *Noshen*'. The final story, 'Night', takes place in the dark of the woods where the boy and grandfather walk so that *Noshen* may see the nocturnal animals. They encounter a pack of timber wolves and *Noshen* is very afraid. But with the example of his grandfather, his wisdom and courage, *Noshen* is able to overcome his fear, to shape-shift, and stand his ground with the yellow-eyed gazes of the pack.

This book reminded Jojo of the presence of the elders in our daily lives (those in the physical world as well as those who walk in the spiritual world) and how their teachings are embedded in nature, hence, present everywhere we go. To Jojo, this book:

> ... reminds us that we're not stewards of the earth or each other, we're creatures to the earth and to each other, which is quite a different view of how we take care of each other, and our responsibilities to each other and to the earth are outlined in this relationship of being creatures of each other. When we make choices we are not isolated for ourselves, we act like ripples. (Jojo)

Lisa's interpretation of the book was linked to memories of her childhood and the summers she spent at her family's cottage where she could go 'roaming or wandering freely in the bush'. Her memories, however, were also permeated with the constant voice or presence of her parents hovering over her, even if they were not beside her during those moments of solitude in the forest. She wrote that:

> Even when wandering for the day – climbing trees, exploring 'wild' areas, observing animals – I was always aware of or listening for my mother's voice calling my name. I was regularly anticipating her calling me back for meals or bedtime as that voice had been instilled in me. If I did not heed her call, her authority, my parents would be angry and disciplinary. They never inquired, at least not much, about where I had traveled, what little discoveries I had made, or insights acquired, they were just glad that I had amused myself on my own. (Lisa)

Lisa and Ismel had similar experiences when they read Tomson Highway's *Caribou song* (2001), one of a trilogy of picture books entitled *Songs of the north wind*. *Caribou song* is set in northern Manitoba and shares the story of the land, peoples and customs in both English and Cree. Through the long winter, two brothers, Joe and Cody, dance and play the *kitoochigan* (accordion) and, in the spring, become part of a family adventure following the *ateek* (caribou) with a sled pulled by huskies. Brian Deines, the illustrator, adds to the feelings of warmth and joy using soft sensuous colours and a dreamy pointille technique that captures the warmth of the family as well as the powerful vastness of the land. There are no clear or harsh lines in the illustrations or in the depiction of wilderness; instead, a safe warm feeling exudes from the drawings of moss-covered rocks and a streaming sea of caribou bodies.

Again, when reading this book and engaging with the images, Lisa found a great contrast between western and Indigenous perception of 'benign' wilderness as well as a connection to parenting styles. She noted that western parenting, as she experienced, is more strict or fear-based towards many things, including nature, whereas the portrayal of Indigenous parenting is wiser and more liberating.

> I find this trilogy of books such a contrast to those early experiences of mine. In Tomson's trilogy, the parents are almost absent and the brothers are listening to a different voice, not a human parental authority but some other voice or calling from the land. (Lisa)

Similarly, Ismel found a stark difference between the spiritual connections the boys share with the caribou in Highway's book (2001) as contrasted to conventional western stories that focus on the danger/safety factors for children when encountering nature or wild animals.

Tomson Highway chooses to focus on a magical moment of spiritual connection between children and the environment in which rather than being afraid, the brothers just open their arms to embrace as much as they can of the stampeding caribous' spirits. I think this book also shows how clean or pure our spirits are when we are children and how we are taught, through colonial children's literature, to let go of these clean spirits and become part of the world of our parents. (Ismel)

These examples of our responses to questions of how our own 'touchstone' environmental stories correspond or do not correspond with the Indigenous picture books point to the strong character of the land reflected in these Indigenous stories. Rather than a fear or cautionary tale of what nature might do to humans, there is an embracing respect of and joy in the gifts nature has to offer. The stories in both the *Caribou song* and *Morning on the lake*, reveal encounters with nature that hold the potential for harm and risk but the illustrations engrossed us and subsumed our fear or tensions with a warm beauty of colours and textures, and delightful depictions of nature as enticing playground.

'All our relations' epistemology or relationality of self–community–land–Creator

The expression, 'all our relations', refers to a deep relational ethics of care, an epistemology directed toward the land and all its creatures, including the people of the land (Bishop 1996, 2005, 2009; Wilson and Wilson 1998; LaDuke 1999; Cajete 1999). Jojo and Lisa discussed the value of the relationality teachings in the picture books, Waboose's *Sky sisters* (2000) and Highway's *Dragonfly kites* (2002). In *Sky sisters*, two young Anishinaabeg sisters, Nishiime and Nimise, set out across the winter north country to Coyote Hill, where the Sky Spirits dance. The story and illustrations honour the mystery in the sky that is the Aurora Borealis and tell of the relational bond between sisters, generations, humans and nature. The images depict small wondrous details of nature such as warm breath clouds, icicles on spruce boughs and the Sky Spirits – the Northern Lights – dancing and shimmering in the night sky. Together, the images and the text capture the chill of a northern land, the warmth of family and cultural traditions, and the radiance of a child's communion with nature.

In *Dragonfly kites*, Joe and Cody, the two young brothers first introduced in *Caribou song*, live in a tent near a different lake each summer in Manitoba's Far North. Summer means exploring the world and making friends with an array of creatures. They catch dragonflies in order to gently tie a length of thread around their middles before setting their dragonfly kites free and then chasing them through trees and meadows, down to the beach, before watching them disappear into a dreamy night sky.

These two books prompted Jojo and Lisa to reflect on how important it is to live in relational harmony with the environment and how this harmony includes and returns so much more than simply self-awareness. In Jojo's words:

The images here remind me that the good of the collective is most important. The collective here is the Earth Sky, with millions of glimmering diamonds dancing in the blue-black sky. Breath is exhaled from the children as they bridge the gap between the expansive sky and each other – sharing oxygen and nitrogen, exchanging with the surroundings, trading with the forest that needs their exchange of carbon, and in turn provides the chance for their next breath. In walking the hill in the dark of night to find the Aurora Borealis or sky sisters, the girls are building awareness of self, to connect to family, to community, to the land and Creator. (Jojo)

For Lisa, *Dragonfly kites* conveys a relationship with the land that she tasted but which also significantly differs from the majority of experiences in her childhood. The impressionist paintings evoke the slowed pace and dreamlike quality of Cree family life in a vast wilderness of northern Manitoba lakes and boreal. Highway celebrates the freedom of children in nature and the imagination that arises from children being left alone and to their own devices. Deines' illustrations in oil are simple and gentle, yet rich, and capture the sensitivity of the text. It is an understanding of nature that Lisa very much desires, yet did not experience directly as a child. As she recounted:

> From my Eurocentric standpoint, one common theme that really struck me right across the three Tomson Highway picture books is the notion of fearless communion or unin-hibited relational being with nature. All three books give the impression of deep joy and freedom in and with nature. (Lisa)

This reflection even led her to question the problematic use a Eurocentric word such as 'freedom' because this term may imply that the children in these books were captive at some point or knew of this western dualism, freedom and captivity:

> I think the use of the term 'freedom' is a Eurocentric construct since there may have been no captivity anywhere in these brothers' lives or experiences in Highway's books – there is no 'town' or school or even a house – so, I may be applying an inappropriate use or intrusive construct of freedom onto these brothers, onto this Cree family, living on the northern boreal. (Lisa)

To conclude this theme of relationality, Jojo offers a reflection on what the land means for her as an Indigenous person, and how this relationship positions her views on environmental education:

> Place and space cannot be defined without recognizing and incorporating the connec-tions to land and ecology as well as responsible relationships with our selves, with each other, and the Creator. The Creator is directly connected to the elements that surround us in Nature and our environment. Actually, the term 'environment' does not exist in my Aboriginal worldview as it is not a place, but rather a concept of being. There is no word for environment in Ojibwe [Anishinaabe]. Environment is everything, so attempting to define a place it exists in, is not possible. We are creatures of the space and land we occupy, not caretakers of it, removed from the land. The land owns us, we do not own the land. (Jojo)

The language of the land is the language and stories of the people

The third theme we located across the discussions and journals was the pivotal role of Indigenous language in the picture books. Even when used sparingly, it conveyed an intimate expression of and foundational relationship with the land. For example, the inclusion of words in Indigenous languages such as 'Mishomis' (grandmother in Ojibwe), the rhythm of the stories themselves, the descriptive passages of minute but special natural details such as animals' eyes and tree bough icicles, all provide an immersive language that is also the centre of the language of the people. For example, Ojibwe is the language of the Ojibwe or Annishinaabe people and the expression of the boreal forestland in northern Ontario. The Indigenous authors in our literature set, Waboose and Highway in particular, represent the Indigenous language in both actual words and resonating images of the boreal land connected to the words.

In Waboose's *Firedancers* (1999), an Indigenous child travels by boat to an island with her grandmother one autumn evening. As night sets in and the fire crackles, the young girl is amazed when her grandmother invokes the spirits of their ancestors. She learns the spiritual *firedance* and creates a bond with her ancestors, the land, and all these relations that will last a lifetime. To express this joy, Waboose reveals details and specific images through English words to describe the spiritual levels of the story. As Jojo re-describes it:

> Grandmother feels the spirit, she puts on her moccasins and begins to dance round the fire in praise to all creation and all relations. The accompanying child hears, feels, and smells the drum of the earth and the ancestors who journeyed before dancing along with them. This is a story that reminds us that none of us ever travel alone. Each choice we make is representing all of those who came before us and brought us to this very point in time and space. Choices made for our selves – are not isolated to the self. We are ripples in a large sea and the direction we take impacts the past, the present and the future. The past, because the pains and joys that come out of the journey have created our worldview. The present, because all of the Creator's energies since time beginning have been used to create each of us. That is quite a commitment to the future because the actions of today create the future and future generations. (Jojo)

Ismel also commented upon the use of language by Waboose (1999) in one of his journal entries:

> As I was reading I could feel the chill in the autumn air and could hear the crackling leaves as the 'fast one' and her 'Noko' were on their way to a spiritual journey to meet the ancestors or firedancers, something that the child or 'fast one' cannot even imagine would happen as they walk to the lake to travel to Smooth Rock Island. (Ismel)

While for Ismel the connection with the land in this particular book was represented by the detailed description of the sounds of nature, for Lisa it was reflected by the solemnity and sacredness of what occurred in the story and illustrations. The story resembled a mysterious invocation told from the mystified perspective of the girl; the illustrations dark full colour oil paintings, surrounded by black, that amplified a powerful solemnity of a ceremony in the middle of the night:

> This story reminds me how important intergenerational learning and experiences on the land are in Aboriginal culture and all its systems. While I have sensed metaphysical connectedness in swimming in a lake at midnight or the intense stillness in the middle of a wilderness trip, I haven't had anything remotely close to this spiritual ceremony of connectedness with ancestors through the example of a grandparent in a particular place. I can intuit it and feel the significance of this particular island, of this spiritual power of the fire in the middle of the wilderness night, but, I appreciate that in Anishinaabek culture, these connections are deeper or what Evelyn Steinhauer (2002) calls the 'blood cellular level' when this ancestral knowledge is invoked. I would also imagine that this ceremony is all in the language and that it is very indirect. Always very appreciative that the type of teaching that grandparents and elders do is non-directive. You experience it, you witness it, but they don't tell you are going to do this now, you are going to listen to what exactly what they want you to learn. (Lisa)

Decolonizing environmental education through children's picture books

By reading these picture books, immersing ourselves in both the lyrical stories and the evocative illustrations, and then engaging in reflections on how these stories counterpoise our own formative environmental stories from childhood, the two non-Indigenous authors in particular were challenged and enlightened by the Indigenous perspectives. The contrast of these stories to our environmental formations, highlighting different ways of being and relating to the land/people, made us appreciative of how much more we could be in relation to Indigenous people and their land as well as how much more we could teach our children to live well as treaty partners and co-inhabitants on the land. For Lisa (non-Indigenous, first generation Canadian), the need to wander freely but in mindful awareness, to listen or observe intensely the details and teachings of the land, was in significant contrast to the internalization of a parental authoritative voice that distracted her from being in relation to her surroundings, to hear the land give its teachings. The visual immersion in the Waboose and Highway picture book illustrations allowed her access to alternative conceptualizations of learning from the land, a land very familiar to her (the boreal forest of her own childhood) but on which these characters have significantly different relations. Watching dragonflies at the edge of the lake was a wonder in her own environmental formation, but it did not reach the imaginary heights or joyful communion of flying into a mystical dream realm in soft transcendent colours, as portrayed in the images by illustrator Brian Deines in Highway's book, *Dragonfly kites*.

For Ismel (non-Indigenous, new Canadian), giving himself and his own young daughter space and time to experience nature directly as a worthy education, without interfering or directly teaching her in the experience, was affirmed in these stories. Also, as a language specialist, Ismel was reminded of the centrality of language to any communication but, in this case, the critically important knowledge that Indigenous languages contain of the land. Battiste (2005) describes this role and power of Indigenous language with the land in the following manner:

> Knowledge of Indigenous peoples is embodied in dynamic languages that reflect the sounds of the specific ecosystems where they live and maintain continuous relationships... All Indigenous knowledge flows from the same source: the relationship of Indigenous peoples with the global flux, their kinship with other living creatures, the life energies as embodied in their environments, and their kinship with the spirit forces of the earth. (Battiste 2005, 128)

Anishinaabe (Ojibwe) is the language of the boreal land in which we live and has special knowledge to communicate the land's ethics, epistemology and pedagogy. Whenever we can, we try to learn the Anishinaabe words for landmarks, animals, spiritual spaces and natural elements as we learn to live more respectfully on this land. The centrality of language to learn the culture and the land was reinforced for Ismel and continues to drive his doctoral research agenda, which includes Indigenous language revitalization.

For Jojo (Indigenous), reading the set of Indigenous picture books and engaging in this study re-affirmed her right and commitment as an educator, Indigenous curriculum specialist and teacher educator inside a provincial (non-reserve) urban school board. Her cultural understandings of her educator role were re-inscribed by many of the themes in the Indigenous children's literature collection, in needs to:

(a) bring traditional teachings of the land into mainstream classrooms and non-Indigenous or culturally responsive teacher education (see Waboose 1997, 1999, 2000);

(b) sustain cultural resilience by maintaining a resistant voice against systemic racism and stereotyping through education (see Littlechild 1993; Van Camp and Littlechild 1997);

(c) remain ironic and humorous in order to not become defeated by the distances yet to be traveled in knowledge and relations (see King, 1992); and

(d) maintain her work as a bridging voice that encourages teachers and students, both Indigenous and non-Indigenous, to be taught by Indigenous experiences and values.

Conclusions

As demonstrated in the previous sections, the reader response approach to reading children's literature as focal practice and the imaginary expansions elicited by the evocative illustrations provided three adult educators with the opportunity to develop an intimate relationship with the books we read. As our interpretations came together in the literature circles, we found ourselves illuminated and informed by each other's 'touchstone' stories of colonizing and decolonizing, of being Indigenous and non-Indigenous, of being (re)connected through a commitment to the land and environment. We believe we have achieved what George Erasmus (2002) called for in our epigraph, by engaging in dialogue with Indigenous authors and stories that were framed in their languages, stories and imagery, where picture books have provided a multisensory immersive representation that expresses Indigenous perspectives more authentically and holistically, connecting with the aspirations of a wider readership, Indigenous and non-Indigenous, beyond Canadian borders through picture book conventions and a deep attention to the land.

Remembering and re-storying our environmental formations through this auto-ethnographic approach to reflexive inquiry and research brought each one of the authors back to the particularity of our own storied horizons, for the purposes of recognizing our cultural standpoints or colonial formations as well as shifting our horizons through decolonizing moments. Shape-shifting is an analogy of the experiences in reading these meditative, affirmative Indigenous accounts of the land. Our educator horizons, our worldviews and our perspectives are confronted by the books' imaginative worlds, centred on Indigenous epistemologies of the land, taught through a pedagogy of stories. These books give the non-Indigenous reader the Other's language of historical critique (Spivak 1988) – to realize both what has been lost or damaged by imperialism and colonialism as well as what we are fast losing as a collective cultural knowledge/heritage. The sheer act of reading the picture books and being receptive to the environmental stories of Indigenous land was an act of recognition of Indigenous self-determination, an act of respecting Indigenous traditional rights, and an act of avoiding the daily tide of unabated colonization. For the three authors, it is not just a small personal act of recognizing Indigenous rights but a bigger step towards strengthening our decolonization processes.

The findings of this type of exploratory study have, potentially, important implications for teaching and teacher education. Our students, children and adults, in schools and universities, in pre-service and in-service teacher education programs, deserve opportunities to engage these rich artistic and cultural experiences of the land, from an Indigenous perspective and time immemorial relationship with the environment. Our findings are not prescriptive; however, they do demonstrate the opportunities that can be gained from including Indigenous sources of knowledge and worldviews in environmental education curricula, classrooms and teacher education, to reconsider the environmental crisis and global warming destruction as intimately intertwined with the colonial damage to Indigenous people, their traditional rights and lands.

From the standpoint of decolonizing education taken in this paper, we want to stress that the situation of decolonizing environmental education cannot be fixed solely by improving environmental educators' access to Indigenous picture books or by a greater number of these books on library and store shelves. We also do not want to portray environmental education through Indigenous children's literature as just teaching in a culturally appropriate way; rather, we want to stress that placing the stories at the centre of the curriculum and consciously responding to them allowed us to educate ourselves in an inherently cultural way (Simpson 2002).

Teacher educators in general and environmental educators in particular need to engage with such stories in order to remember their own formative experiences and stories of nature and land, to re-experience these touchstones in telling them, and to seek out and experience Indigenous 'counter-stories' that challenge their environmental foundational touchstones inherently, incrementally and revealingly. For environmental educators to shape-shift their learning, they need to confront their own culturally storied environmental formation (see Fawcett 2002) and transform these stories into new knowledge processes. The Indigenous picture books as content, the environmental crisis as context, and the reader response approach and literacy practices as pedagogy, can together activate a shape-shifting or decolonizing process for non-Indigenous environmental educators.

Given the current global environmental crisis, the deeply damaging colonization that persists and languages, cultures and species all disappearing at alarming rates, environmental education needs Indigenous picture books more than ever to help educators (and children) shift their perceptual horizons and environmental perspectives, to consider the strength and contribution of Indigenous land-based knowledge. Indigenous children's literature in environmental education can help to reveal and illuminate an alternative land-based knowledge system, a relational integration, and a respectful ethics of land and people. The stories in these children's picture books are the stories of the land and the Indigenous peoples of the land. As Battiste (2000, xxix, emphasis added) argues:

> The real justification for including Aboriginal knowledge in the modern curriculum is not so that Aboriginal students can compete with non-Aboriginal students in an imagined world. It is, rather, that *immigrant [or settler] society is sorely in need of what Aboriginal knowledge has to offer*.

All educators and all children deserve environmentally-conscious or land-based stories in their formational educational lives, and all non-Indigenous people sorely need Indigenous ways of knowing the land in order to imagine, empower and enact other ways of being on the Earth, no matter their place on the planet.

References

Agyeman, J. 2003. 'Under-participation' and ethnocentrism in environmental education research: Developing 'culturally sensitive research approaches'. *Canadian Journal of Environmental Education* 8: 80–94.

Alcoff, L. 2006. *Visible identities: Race, gender, and the self.* Oxford: Oxford University Press.

Alfred, T. 1999. *Peace, power, righteousness: An Indigenous manifesto.* Toronto, ON: Oxford University Press.

Barnhardt, R. 2008. Creating a place for Indigenous knowledge in education: The Alaska Native Knowledge Network. In *Place-based education in the global age: Local diversity,* ed. D. Gruenewald and G. Smith, 49–64. New York: Taylor and Francis.

Barnhardt, R., and A. Kawagley. 2005. Indigenous knowledge systems and Alaska Native ways of knowing. *Anthropology and Education Quarterly* 36, no.1: 8–23.

Battiste, M. 1998. Enabling the autumn seed: Toward a decolonized approach to Aboriginal knowledge, language, and education. *Canadian Journal of Native Education* 22, no. 1: 16–27.

Battiste, M. 2000. Unfolding the lessons of colonization. In *Reclaiming Indigenous voices and vision,* ed. M. Battiste, xvi–xxx, Vancouver: University of British Colombia Press.

Battiste, M. 2005. You can't be the global doctor if you're the colonial disease. In *Teaching as activism,* eds. P. Tripp and L. Muzzin, 121–33, Montreal: McGill Queen's University Press.

Bishop, R. 1996. *Collaborative research stories: Whakawhanaugatanga.* Palmerston North: Dunmore Press.

Bishop, R. 2005. Freeing ourselves from neocolonial domination in research: A Kaupapa Māori approach to creating knowledge. In *The Sage handbook of qualitative research,* ed. N. Denzin and Y. Lincoln, 109–38. Thousand Oaks, CA: Sage.

Bishop, R., M. Berryman, T. Cavanagh, and L. Teddy. 2009. Te Kotahitanga: Addressing educational disparities facing Māori students in New Zealand. *Teaching and Teacher Education* 25, no. 5: 734–42.

Bouchard, D. 2003. *The Elders are watching.* Illustrated by R. Vickers. Vancouver, BC: Raincoast Books.*

Bouchard, D. 2007. *I am raven.* Illustrated by Andy Everson. Vancouver, BC: MTW Publishers.*

Bowers, C.A. 1997. *The culture of denial: Why the environmental movement needs a strategy for reforming universities and public schools.* Albany: State University of New York Press.

Bowers, C.A. 2004. Revitalizing the commons or an individualized approach to planetary citizenship: The choice is before us. *Educational Studies* 36, no. 1: 45–58.

Bowers, C.A., V. Newman, P. Brawdy, and R. Egan. 2001. Toward an eco-justice pedagogy. *Educational Studies* 32, no. 4: 401–52.

Bradford, C. 2007. *Unsettling narratives: Postcolonial readings of children's literature.* Waterloo, ON: Wilfrid Laurier University Press.

Bringhurst, R. 2002. The tree of meaning and the work of ecological linguistics. *Canadian Journal of Environmental Education* 7, no. 2: 9–22.

Cajete, G. 1999. *A people's ecology.* New Mexico: Clear Light.

Campbell, N.I. 2005. *Shi-shi-etko.* Illustrated by K. La Fave. Toronto, ON: Groundwood Books.*

Campbell, N.I. 2008. *Shin-chi's canoe.* Illustrated by K. LaFave. Toronto, ON: Groundwood Books.*

Castellano, M., L. Archibald, and M. DeGagne. 2008. Introduction: Aboriginal truths in the narrative of Canada. In *From truth to reconciliation,* ed. G. Erasmus, 1–8. Ottawa: Aboriginal Healing Foundation. http://www.ahf.ca/.

Davis, J.N. 1989. The act of reading in the foreign language: Pedagogical implications of Iser's reader-response theory. *The Modern Language Journal* 73, no. 4: 420–8.

Dion, S. 2007. Disrupting molded images: Identities, responsibilities and relationships – teachers and Indigenous subject material. *Teacher Education* 18, no. 4: 329–42.

Dion, S. 2009. *Braiding histories: Learning from aboriginal peoples' experiences and perspectives.* Vancouver: University of British Columbia Press.

Edwards, G., and J. Saltman. 2000. Looking at ourselves, looking at others: Multiculturalism in Canadian children's picture books in English. Paper presented at the History of the Book in Canada's Open Conference for Volume III (1918–2000). http://www.hbin.library. utoronto.ca/vol3edwardssaltman_en.htm.

Erasmus, G. 2002. The Lafontaine-Baldwin lecture 2002. In *The Lafontaine Baldwin lectures, Volume 1: A dialogue on democracy in Canada,* ed. R. Griffiths. Toronto: Penguin Canada.

Fawcett, L. 2002. Children's wild animal stories: Questioning inter-species bonds. *Canadian Journal of Environmental Education* 7, no. 2: 125–39.

Francis, D. 1992. *The imaginary indian.* Vancouver: Arsenal Press.

Galda, L., and R. Beach. 2001. Response to literature as a cultural activity. *Reading Research Quarterly* 36, no. 1: 64–73.

Gruenewald, D.A. 2003. The best of both worlds: A critical pedagogy of place. *Educational Researcher* 32, no. 4: 3–12.

Gruenewald, D.A. 2008. Place-based education: Grounding culturally responsive teaching in geographical diversity: Local diversity. In *Place-based education in the global age,* ed. D. Gruenewald and G. Smith, 137–54. New York: Taylor and Francis.

Gruenewald, D.A., and G. Smith. 2008. Introduction. In *Place-based education in the global age,* ed. D. Gruenewald and G. Smith, xiii–xxiii. New York: Taylor and Francis.

Haig-Brown, C. 2001. Continuing collaborative knowledge production: Knowing when, where, how and why. *Journal of Intercultural Studies* 22, no. 1: 19–32.

Harste, J., C. Leland, K. Schmidt, V. Vasquez, and A. Ociepka. 2004. Practice makes perfect or does it? The relationship between theory and practice in teacher education. *Reading Online* 7, no. 4. http://www.readingonline.org/art_index.asp?HREF=harste/index.html.

Highway, T. 2001. *Caribou song.* Illustrated by B. Deines. Toronto: HarperCollins Publishers.*

Highway, T. 2002. *Dragonfly kites.* Illustrated by B. Deines. Toronto: HarperCollins Publishers.*

Highway, T. 2003. *Fox on the ice.* Illustrated by B. Deines. Toronto: HarperCollins Publishers.*

Hunsberger, M., and G. Labercane, eds. 2002. *Making meaning in the response-based classroom.* Boston, MA: Allyn & Bacon.

Hunter, P. 2005. *Understanding children's literature.* Florence, KY: Routledge.

Iser, W. 1978. *The act of reading: A theory of aesthetic response.* Baltimore: Johns Hopkins University Press.

Johnston, I., and J. Mangat. 2003. Cultural encounters in the luminal spaces of Canadian picture books. *Changing English* 10, no. 2: 199–204.

Jones, S.H. 2005. Autoethnography: Making the personal political. In *Sage handbook of qualitative research,* ed. N.K. Denzin and Y.S. Lincoln, 763–91. Thousand Oaks, CA: Sage.

Kaufman, J.S., M.S. Ewing, A.E. Hyle, D. Montgomery, and P.A. Self. 2001. Women and nature: Using memory-work to rethink our relationship to the natural world. *Environmental Education Research* 7, no. 4: 359–77.

Kiefer, B.Z. 1995. *The potential of picture books: From visual literacy to aesthetic understanding.* Englewood Cliffs, NJ: Prentice Hall.

King, T. 1992. *A Coyote Columbus story.* Toronto: Douglas & McIntyre.*

King, T. 2003. *The truth about stories: A native narrative.* Toronto: House of Anansi.

LaDuke, W. 1999. *All our relations: Native struggles for land and life.* Cambridge: South End Press.

Landis, D. 2003. Reading and writing as social, cultural practices: Implications for literacy education. *Reading and Writing Quarterly* 19, no. 3: 281–307.

Littlechild, G. 1993. *This land is my land.* Illustrated by G. Littlechild. San Francisco: Children's Book Press.*

Lowan, G.E. 2008. Outward bound Giwaykiwin: Wilderness-based Indigenous education. Masters' diss., Lakehead University.

Loyie, L. 2005. *As Long as the river flows.* Toronto, Ontario: Groundwood.*

Manning, E. 2003. *Ephemeral territories: Representing nation, home, and identity in Canada.* Minneapolis, MN: University of Minnesota Press.

Marker, M. 2006. After the Makah whale hunt: Indigenous knowledge and limits to multicultural discourse. *Urban Education* 41, no. 5: 482–505.

Nodelman, P. 2005. Decoding the images: How picture books work. In *Understanding children's literature,* ed. P. Hunter, 128–39. Florence, KY: Routledge.

Pillow, W.S. 2003. Confession, catharsis, or cure? Rethinking the uses of reflexivity as methodological power in qualitative research. *Qualitative Studies in Education* 16, no. 2: 175–96.

Rosenblatt, L.M. 1938. *Literature as exploration.* New York: Modern Language Association.

Rosenblatt, L.M. 1978. *The reader, the text and the poem: The transactional theory of the literary work.* Carbondale, IL: Southern Illinois University Press.

Saul, J.R. 2008. *A fair country: Telling truths about Canada.* Toronto: Viking Canada.

Simpson, L. 2002. Indigenous environmental education for survival. *Canadian Journal of Environmental Education* 7, no. 1: 13–24.

Smagorinsky, P., L. Wright, S.M. Augustine, C. O'Donnell-Allen, and B. Konopak. 2007. Student engagement in the teaching and learning of grammar: A case study of an early career secondary English teacher. *Journal of Teacher Education* 59, no.1: 76–90.

Smith, C.L. 2000. *Jingle dancer.* Illustrated by C. Wright. New York: Morrow Junior Books.*

Smith, L.T. 1999. *Decolonizing methodologies: Research and Indigenous peoples.* New York: Zed Books.

Spivak, G.C. 1988. Can the subaltern speak? In *Marxism and the interpretation of culture,* ed. C. Nelson and L. Grossberg, 271–313. Urbana: University of Illinois Press.

Steinhauer, E. 2002. Thoughts on an Indigenous research methodology. *Canadian Journal of Native Education* 26, no. 2: 69–81.

Strong-Wilson, T. 2006. Re-visioning one's narratives: Exploring the relationship between researcher self-study and teacher research. *Studying Teacher Education* 2, no. 1: 59–76.

Strong-Wilson, T. 2007. Moving horizons: Exploring the role of stories in decolonizing the literacy education of white teachers. *International Education* 37, no. 1: 114–31.

Sumara, D. 1995. Understanding reading as a focal practice. *English Quarterly* 28, no. 1: 18–26.

Sumara, D. 2002. *Why reading literature in school still matters: Imagination, interpretation, insight.* Mahwah, NJ: Lawrence Erlbaum Associates.

United Nations. 2007. *Declaration on the Rights of Indigenous Peoples.* http://www.un.org/ esa/socdev/unpfii/en/declaration.html.

Van Camp, R. 1998. *What's the most beautiful thing you know about horses?* Illustrated by G. Littlechild. San Francisco: Children's Book Press.*

Van Camp, R., and G. Littlechild. 1997. *A man called Raven.* Illustrated by G. Littlechild. San Francisco: Children's Book Press.*

Waboose, J.B. 1993. *Where only the elders go: Moon lake, loon lake.* Illustrated by H. Below. Manotick, Ontario: Penumbra Press.*

Waboose, J.B. 1997. *Morning on the lake.* Illustrated by K. Reczuch. Toronto, Ontario: Kids Can Press.*

Waboose, J.B. 1999. *Firedancers.* Illustrated by C.J. Taylor. Toronto, Ontario: Kids Can Press.*

Waboose, J.B. 2000. *Sky sisters.* Illustrated by B. Deines. Toronto, Ontario: Kids Can Press.*

Whetung, J. 1996. *The vision seeker.* Illustrated by P. Morin. Markham, Ontario: Fitzhenry and Whiteside.*

Wiebe, R. 2006. *Hidden buffalo.* Illustrated by M. Lonechild. Edmonton, Alberta: Red Deer Press.*

Wilson, S., and P. Wilson. 1998. Relational accountability to all our relations. *Canadian Journal of Native Education* 22, no. 2: 155–8.

Wilson, T. 2003. Bringing memory forward: Teacher engagement with constructions of 'difference' in teacher literature circles. PhD diss., University of Victoria.

What's there, what if, what then, and what can we do? An immersive and embodied experience of environment and place through children's literature

Geraldine Burke and Amy Cutter-Mackenzie

Faculty of Education, Monash University, Victoria, Australia

We describe an immersive investigation of children's contemporary picture books, which examines concepts of environment and place. The authors' experience occurred through and alongside a community of learners, of preservice teachers and young children, in an urban coastal community, as part of an undergraduate, pre-service teacher education unit. Participants were led through the experience utilizing techniques informed by immersive art pedagogy, to foreground the in-between dispositions of their roles as artists, researchers, and teachers (A/r/tography), and their emerging roles as environmentalists (A/r/t-*e*-ography). Our investigation of the relationship between picture books and inquiry into their embodied experiences with the books awakened an awareness of environment and place, taking us from *what's there?* to *what if?* to *what then?* to *what can we do?* This reflexive process provides an entry point into the second part of the article, a focused autoethnographic account of how environment and place might be treated pedagogically using Jeannie Baker's 1991 book, *Window*.

Contextualizing our experience, our place

> To learn about a tree go to a tree. (Matsuo Basho, cited in Kriesberg 1999, 79)

This article is grounded in a discussion of our experiences as teacher educators in an urban coastal university campus located approximately one hour from Melbourne.[1] Specifically, it presents an account of our experiences in an undergraduate teacher education unit entitled, Experiential Environmental Education. Students undertake this semester-long unit in the first year of their degree program. The unit is experientially driven and has replaced an environmental science unit devoted to an introduction to Australian ecology. The rationale for moving away from a traditional environmental science focus was to resituate the students' learning in a social–ecological framework pedagogically informed by experiential education principles. Thus, the reconceptualized unit starts from the view that personal positioning and the experience of the subject matter under study are crucial for learning to occur and accrue. When students can engage more meaningfully in 'authentic' experiences, including the opportunity for eco-biographies to be conceptualized experientially and textually constructed, they can more meaningfully elicit their felt interests and (embodied) memories of prior experiences in nature and through environmental education. The unit's sequencing moves from a deeply personal focus to a broader social and ecological focus, promoting interpretation of the phenomena experienced and, potentially, critiquing previously assumed, or given, understandings of environment and place.

Our intention as teacher educators is to encourage and facilitate these shifts throughout the unit. In the first instance, this is through an immersive investigation of children's picture books, whereby the students and their lecturers collaboratively and critically examine the pedagogical content and value basis of environmental and place-based picture books. As an immersive process, we deliberately focus on the attributes of visual qualities in picture books through encouraging sensory, experiential, perceptual, relational, cultural, and socially critical investigations of the environments and places featured in the books. Throughout this process, the characteristics and qualities of eco-literacy, an undertheorized concept within educational practice, are opened up for lively interrogation, discussion, and action (see, for example, Cutter-Mackenzie and Smith 2003). In this way, the picture book task is positioned as a medium through which students can look anew at their own embodied, memoried and storied connections to environment and place, as well as those of others. Our rationale for this approach is similar to that of Kriesberg's:

> Picture books are like bringing a storyteller to the class to act as a guide for the experience ... For thousands of years, the knowledge of place was continued orally, through stories. The best teachers are the best storytellers. There are stories that have the power to teach and to connect children [*and teachers*] to their place. (1999, xxi; emphasis added)

In this article, we focus on our experiences and those of the community of learners associated with the unit in 2008. We met, as authors, as teacher educators, with teacher education students, and with school children, to examine changing experiences and understandings of the notion of place over the course of several consecutive school-based learning experiences during a semester. This particular 'community of learners' consisted of 30 teacher education students enrolled in the Experiential Environmental Education unit, 15 school children from the Frankston community where the university campus is located, and two teacher educators (the authors). The two lecturers, now co-authors, led the teacher education students initially through an immersive investigation of picture books. Their collective investigations drew on multiple theoretical lenses, including immersion, embodiment, a/r/tography, and our reconceptualized extension of this notion into a/r/t-*e*-ography, eco-literacy, and visual literacy (Phase 1). As teacher educators, our eco-pedagogical process sought to develop a deeper and intimate relationship with the selected picture books for the unit. We foregrounded sensory, cognitive, and emotional ways of knowing such that the teacher education students could relate their own embodied responses of the books to those of their immediately proximal and temporally situated life world. Following this initial process of focused inquiry, together with our university students, we then worked with 15 children in a primary and middle school-based investigation of environment and place using Jeannie Baker's 1991 book, *Window* (Phase 2).[2] *Window* has no written text, instead revealing a series of images (through the same window) of a changing Australian landscape and community. It portrays a once natural and rural community that is transformed into a semi-urban community (through residential estates, infrastructure, and commercial outlets) over a 24-year time period. Indeed, the development of the community in Baker's picture book is akin to that of the Frankston community and its expansion.

Before presenting a vignette of our work with the children (an autoethnography of our experience – Phase 2), we set out our understandings of the notions of immersion and embodiment, followed by an autoethnographic[3] description of our approach to using a/r/t-*e*-ography and visual/eco-literacy attributes, as applied by the authors as teacher educators with our preservice teacher education students (Phase 1).

Phase 1

Immersion and embodiment

Our approach to an immersive pedagogical experience (Burke 2010) privileges the bodily engagement of the learner in the content or subject matter of an otherwise academically driven undergraduate unit. We hope that students are drawn, through deep interest and curiosity, into an embodied connection to the inquiry at hand. Immersive approaches encourage learners to identify and embrace a range of dispositions (such as those of environmental ideologies) through which they can (re)look, (re)think, (re)imagine, and (re)create meanings. By fusing together these diverse experiences, as teacher educators, we attempt to connect the learner with the subject matter through the added insights that might be afforded through these processes. Our approach was influenced by Burbules (2004) who suggests four features when considering the various qualities of experiences, namely, those of interest, involvement, imagination, and interaction. Burbules states:

> An experience is interesting to us when it is complex enough to allow us to pick out new elements, even with repeated encounters. ... An experience is involving to us when we have a reason to care about what we are experiencing: we pay attention to it because it concerns us in some way ... An experience engages our imagination when we can interpolate or extrapolate new details and add to the experience through our own contributions ... An experience is interactive when it provides us with opportunities to participate in it, not only perceptually or intellectually but also through embodied action and responses. (2004, 166–7)

Our approach to immersive learning was further informed by the a/r/tographic position on embodiment, which presupposes that sensory and perceptual experiences are valid means of knowing (Irwin and Springgay 2008). In addition, it was our intention that adopting an a/r/tographic disposition would lead participants to understanding relationships between embodiment and an ethics of being through giving explicit attention to 'understanding the relations between identities rather than in terms of describing identities, intentions, or acts of individuals or groups' (Springgay et al. 2008, 160). According to Spinggay et al., it is this a/r/tographic disposition to 'being-with and the in-between ... that enables the possibilities of an ethics of embodiment' (2008, 154). This was important to our approach as it allowed us to become consciously aware of our own perspectives across the roles we inhabit as teacher educators, authors, and researchers, as well as those of our students and the children we worked with. We also reflected on the multiple and interwoven roles of artist, researcher, and teacher as understood through a/r/tography (Irwin and de Cosson 2004; Irwin and Spinggay 2008). Thus, during the immersive process, we considered poetic and imaginative connections to place, through picture books, artwork, and narrative, which prepared the ground for further work exploring future environmental action/experience. For instance, in adopting our roles as *artists*, we created our own eco-windows and recorded our own narratives. This lived experience helped us develop meaningful questions and techniques to use in our teaching and research. Likewise, in our roles as *teachers*, we ensured that the process was overtly informed by research into eco and visual literacy. While as *researchers,* we theorized with and through our practice so as to learn from our emerging visual literacy skills, our art-making, and our experience of the teaching process.

Recognizing these multiple perspectives enabled us to create a working model, which in turn utilized visual and eco-literacy skills as a starting point for environmental education. Our intention is that future refinement and extension of our working model will further continue the cycle of art-making, researching, and teaching (as informed by a/r/tography), with the added goal of developing our approaches to environmental education as a consequence of our shared experiences and processes (which we here conceptualize in relation to a/r/t-*e*-ography).

Finally, we note that immersive art pedagogy informed our approach by connecting every day concepts (such as place) to the essential characteristics of art and environmental education (through picture books). It is our intention that immersive art pedagogy links creativity, art pedagogy, discipline, and local knowledge to sociocultural, socioecological, and critical ways of knowing. This in(-)formative approach was applied to how we addressed skill development, personally meaningful contexts, and aesthetics on the unit, so as to awaken the experiences to hand to imaginative and relational possibilities. That said, an immersive art pedagogy positions the notion of creativity as a central concern within the learning experience and highlights the idea that we need to build a self-conscious awareness of our personal creativity. In doing so, immersive art pedagogy contextualizes the participants (be they teachers/students/researchers/environmentalists) as dynamic investigators who actively reflect upon lived practice (Burke 2006).

Toward an a/r/t-e-ographic approach

Alongside our teacher education students, we undertook our own immersive investigations of 100 contemporary picture books, all of which broadly explored concepts of environment and place.[4] Utilizing techniques informed by immersive art pedagogy (Burke 2006), we undertook a tactile and complex cross-referencing of these books. By applying aesthetic, functional, and socially critical approaches to inquiry (Anstey and Bull 2000), we developed four key themes to the outcomes of this process (see Figure 1). These themes were further interrogated through the in-between (Grosz 2001) dispositions of artist/researcher/teacher (Grosz 2001; Irwin and de Cosson 2004) as well as those of the environmentalist.

The emerging themes provided an entry point for our teacher education students[5] who then employed visual and eco-literacy strategies (as discussed next) to further their immersive investigation of the very same picture books. So as to foster dialogic appreciation of each group's chosen books, we posed a series of provocations (see Table 1) to prompt a greater awareness of the visual strategies employed by authors and publishers and to foreground a more nuanced sense of environment and place (Jeffers 2003). During this stage of the process, we gained an awareness of how the inter-textual nature of picture books could help us explore relational (Bourriaud 2002;

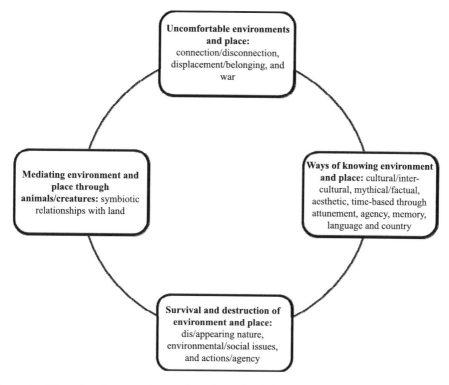

Figure 1.   Emerging themes – immersive picture book investigation.

Carter 2004), socially critical (Anstey and Bull 2000), and a/r/tographic (Irwin and de Cosson 2004) interpretations and expressions of the environment (Lippard 1997). This aspect of the work also allowed a platform from which to then consider the interrelated concepts of space and place as understood through experience (Tuan 1977). As Tuan (1977, 6) suggests, 'what begins with as undifferentiated space becomes place as we get to know it better and endow it with value'.

Adapting Bourriaud's (2002, 109) *Co-existence criterion*, as teacher educators, we pondered our relational connection to environment and place by asking ourselves: Whether the picture book, as an aesthetic production, could 'permit (us) to enter into a dialogue? Could (we) exist, and how, in the space it defines?' And further, as researchers and authors, we discussed whether the encounter between our own experiences of environment/place and that of the picture/text could enact a 'collective elaboration of meaning' (Bourriaud 2002, 15). Thus, we asked ourselves:

> What do these picture books *do* to environment/place and how are we, as beholders of their story, encouraged to connect? Are we called to be: activist, mentor, un/interested bystander, culturally informed person, environmentalist, inter/culturally aware, dis/empowered person/group, sustainable, imaginative, embodied, listener/communicator, aesthetically aware, maker?

Adapting Irwin and de Cosson's (2004) six a/r/tographic renderings as following (now rephrased as a/r/t-*e*-ographic for the purpose of this article[6]), we further troubled the interconnected notions of *environment and place*, thus opening up questions of local/global, place/space, and cultural/intercultural notions through our picture

Table 1.   A/r/t-*e*-ographic renderings.

Openings	How are notions of *environment and place* opened up through selected picture books; what co-construction of meaning develops as a consequence of our encounter?
Metaphor and metonym	What ideas and relationships about *environment and place* are made accessible through our senses as a result of engaging with these picture books?
Reverberations	How can other people's/your own artwork/research/teaching reverberate with these picture books to reveal and contextualize notions of *environment and place*?
Excess	Is there excess knowledge provoked by these picture books that offer complex ways through which to understand *environment and place*?
Living inquiry	How can we integrate the author/illustrator's and our own lived experience of *environment and place* through writing/dialogic appreciation and art-making?
Contiguity	How can the in-between/crossovers of our roles as students/artists/ researchers/teachers open new understandings of *environment and place* through picture books?

Source: Adapted from Irwin and de Cosson (2004).

book investigations. We also posed these as a series of questions to the students (see Table 1).

Our intention then was that an immersive investigation of picture books would enable us and the students to utilize visual literacy attributes, which in turn would open up a greater awareness of eco-literacy, and vice versa. By utilizing visual literacy perspectives as a means to explore notions of environment and place within children's picture books, we became conscious of the larger provocations posed by eco-literacy (Clacherty 1993; Cutter-Mackenzie 2009; Cutter-Mackenzie and Smith 2003; Orr 1992, 1994; Roth 1992; Stables and Bishop 2001; Sturdavant 1993; Weston 1996). But before discussing the immersive investigation process with the community of learners in detail, we briefly discuss each main concept.

Visual–eco-literacies

The term 'visual literacy,' despite popular uptake, is multifariously defined across disciplines, provoking debate concerning structural dichotomies between text-based and visual literacy (Langer 1942) and claimed competencies vs. limitations (Messari 1994). Kress and van Leeuwen (1996) argue for the new thinking as regards the interconnection of image, text, screen, and new media so as to enable greater meaning through multi-modalities. In 1969, Debes (1969) defined visual literacy as:

> a group of vision-competencies a human being can develop by seeing and at the same time having and integrating other sensory experiences. The development of these competencies is fundamental to normal human learning. When developed, they enable a visually literate person to discriminate and interpret the visible actions, objects, symbols, natural or man-made, that he encounters in his environment. (27)

More recently, Bamford (2003, 1) suggests that visual literacy involves interpreting, examining, and discussing an image's content, social implications, and 'purpose, audience and ownership'. She includes the perspectives of reader/viewer/maker by suggesting that a visually literate person should be able to 'successfully decode and interpret visual messages and compose visual communications'. On the other hand, Clacherty argues that an eco-literate person should possess:

> not merely an ability to 'read the environment,' but ... an ability to perceive, understand and work towards things which are not yet with us, towards a vision grounded in a fully conscious ... grasp of what is and what could be. (1993, 117)

The environmentalist and educator David Orr (1990, 1992, 1994) challenges that no student should graduate from any educational facility without knowing 17 key subject areas. Orr (1992) refers to this complex knowledge base as a syllabus for ecological literacy. He nominates over 100 articles and books as essential readings for all students and teachers. Orr (1992) draws works from distinguished philosophers, scientists, and commentators such as Ehrlich, Bacon, Kahn, Berry, Merchant, Emerson, Lovelock, Eiseley, Leopold, and Thoreau. Table 2 illustrates these subject areas.

Orr (1992) claims that it is this knowledge that enables educators, teachers, and citizens to ask, *what then*, while Sturdavant postulates that asking this question requires:

> Interrogating the interconnected layers of practices, trends, and assumptions upon which we construct our present life style will render those interconnections and their ramifications more explicit, thereby making their sustainability available to assessment. (1993, 209)

Table 2.   A syllabus for eco-literacy.

Syllabus no.	Subject areas
1.	How does the world work?
2.	Trends, forecasts, probabilities, possibilities, uncertainties
3.	The dynamics of the modern world: the project of modernization
4.	Some critics of the modern world
5.	Source of environmental problems
6.	The question of scientific knowledge
7.	The problem of technology
8.	Ideas of nature
9.	Ideas of human nature
10.	What is natural and what is it to us?
11.	The evolution of ecological consciousness: science
12.	Ecological consciousness II: religion and ethics
13.	The concept of sustainability
14.	Tools of analysis
15.	Tools for reinhabitation
16.	Models of sustainability
17.	Social change

Source: Adapted from Orr (1992, 109–24).

Through the teaching-focused research approach described above, we devised a working model for developing visual and eco-literacies through immersive picture book investigations. Our *in-progress* model (see Figure 2) attempts to highlight the ways in which we can *open up* visual and eco-literacies to immersive and experiential education as well as immersive art pedagogy as a pathway through which to encourage active participation within environmental contexts.

Foregrounding visual literacy strategies takes us from a descriptive awareness of given picture books to engaging imaginative and interpretive perspectives. This shift in perspective prompts us to value the 'as if' perspectives afforded by imaginative interpretation, allowing us to 'disclose possibilities – personal, social as well as aesthetic' (Greene 2001, 65). In our case, we include possibilities informed by environmental perspectives. In turn, the provocations and socially critical themes that arose from our 'as if' perspectives can provide a link into the 'what then' eco-literacy tenets suggested by Orr (1992). Together, visual literacy and eco-literacy strategies within an immersive context can afford a platform from which we can actively participate in our teacher education and community context.

Both our model and pedagogical process begin by recognizing that picture books are an artifact made possible by the visual (multi) literacy/ies of the illustrator/author, whereby the interplay of image and text opens up inter-textual possibilities that often allow for imaginative interpretations. We understand the notion of creativity as a centrally informing concept to this approach, in that it highlights the links between cultural/community and individual contexts across the domain, the field, and the individual. What follows is a description of our immersive starting point, here presented as an autoethnographic investigation of the processes involved.

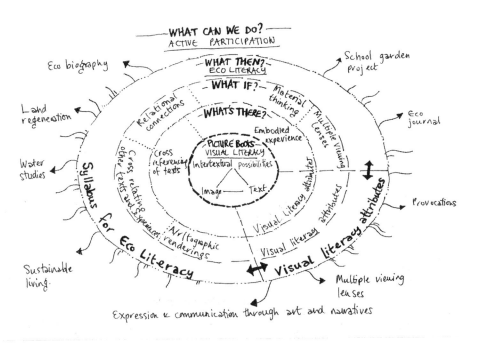

Figure 2.   Working model: 'Developing visual and eco literacies through immersive picture book investigations'.

What's there? Detective work

Our own developing visual literacy skills were fine-tuned as we immersed ourselves in a range of picture books that explored environment and place. We then physically interacted with these books by calling on our sense of touch, smell, and deep looking. We explored format, shape, layout, balance, focal points, rhythm, sequences, elements, and media. Through manual investigation, we turned pages, grouped, classified, and cross-referenced various pictures/texts/concepts as a means to question, discuss, and share diverse findings as they were revealed to us through dynamic investigation. All the while we consciously used our hands and eyes as physical tools through which we asked 'What's there? ... What do *I* see?'

What if? Imaginative and relational interpretations

Once we ascertained *what's there*, we then took on a more overtly imaginative disposition by pitting our developing inventory against the 'what if' of imagined scenarios. We explored relational connections made imaginable through the picture book genre. We pondered ... *How might we live in the space of these books/this environment/this place?* We adopted different viewing lenses by asking ... *how do our identities as artist, teacher, researcher and environmentalist affect our interpretation/s* We employed and adapted Irwin and De Cosson's (2004) a/r/tographic renderings so as to explore *metaphoric and metonymic* interpretations, the *excess* involved in our awakening sensibilities, and the *openings* that active inquiry enables, as related to the concepts that were brought forth by the picture books. Again we considered how the illustrator/author conveyed intended, unintended, and implicit ideas to us and how the attributes of visual literacy could be further understood through the aesthetic, functional, and socially critical trajectory, as identified by Anstey and Bull (2000).

All the while, we interrogated, postulated, and recreated notions of place and the environment inspired by these picture book contexts. In the process, we allowed ourselves to understand our findings in relation to personal experiences of environment and place, as well as other texts. We also expressed our findings through material expressions of thinking, be it through a painting, a photograph, or an installation; in doing so, we also developed our awareness of arts-based possibilities for research. At this point, we had become immersed in the picture book experience, and diverse investigations generated *what if* scenarios, as afforded by an imaginative and relational interpretation of the picture books.

What then? Visual and eco-literacy

A range of important questions opened up to us at this point as a result of our picture book journey through environments and places. Our evolving visual literacy skills were allowing us to explore bigger issues by moving between embodied, descriptive, imaginative, and relational interpretations. We began to think about sustainability, power play, action, and inaction. In essence, we were opening up to the *what then?* dispositions that Orr (1992) highlights through his 17 eco-literacy attributes. We found ourselves ready to explore major concepts within eco-literacy.

What can we do? Active participation

Orr's (1992) eco-literacy attributes provide a link from picture book immersion to active participation. Our immersive investigation of picture books awakened our awareness of environment and place, which we now primarily understood on an ecological level. From *What's there?* to *What if?* to *What then?*, we then came to ask, *What can we do? How can we become agents for change?* From this vantage point, we saw a segue to school garden projects, eco-journals, expression and communication of environment and place through art and narratives, land regeneration, water studies, and the uptake of various viewing lenses, so that we were better aware, informed, imaginative, relational, and active in respect to environment and place.

In sum, taken together, the visual and eco-literacy strategies that we employed within an immersive context created a platform from which we could better actively participate in community and urban places. To further contextualize and illuminate this immersive process, we now present a vignette that we developed to gauge the applicability of our immersive approach to children's visual and eco-investigations of a given picture book. In this vignette, we explore how children have applied the immersive framework and theoretical lenses presented previously to a focused investigation of environment and place, using Jeannie Baker's 1991 book *Window*.

Phase 2

Vignette: opening our minds to change

After our own immersive picture book experience and those with our teacher education students, we explored together our working model for developing visual and eco-literacies through immersive picture books investigations with a group of 15 children, aged 8–13 years. These children volunteered to be part of this experience via local primary and secondary school networks. What follows is a vignette (an autoethnographic account of our experience – Phase 2), which uses aspects of our model as a means through which to investigate Jeannie Baker's book *Window* as an attempt to make connections to our community (the places we live).

In this final section of the article, we introduce the book *Window*, followed by the immersive investigation with examples from the children's work.

About Window

As illustrated in Figure 3, *Window* has no written text. It allows one to cross language, age, and cultural boundaries in communicating messages of environment and place. Visual literacy skills are also honed as the viewer is led from page to page across a changing landscape.

Using our model's core provocations, we sought to highlight with the teacher education students and the school children that Baker's picture book allows for many interpretations regarding changing environments and places. The children undertook deep looking through detective-like investigations (*What's there?*), utilizing their visual literacy skills to enable a greater awareness of the ecological themes within the book. They then progressed to imaginative and relational interpretations by discussing *What if?* scenarios such as: *What if we could have a say about urban development? What if we could protect green areas in our neighbourhood?* From this starting point, children then made their own *window* that sought to depict an environmental issue that

Figure 3. *Window*.
Source: Reproduced by permission of Walker Books Ltd, London, SE11 5HJ and Jeannie Baker, copyright © 1991, 2002 Jeannie Baker (from *Window* by Jeannie Baker).

could potentially affect their community. In this way, children enacted changes to their chosen images through artful re-visitations across a range of layered sheets and recreated a given site with ecological issues in mind.

What's there? Responding to Window

We used Big Book versions of *Window* so as to truly immerse the children in the detail and textures of Baker's vision. We asked, *What is happening here? How do you relate to this place? How is the landscape changing?* Together, we spent time looking, pondering, and discussing the changing landscape that evolves throughout the book. In what follows, we present a selection of the children's comments as they describe the various views through the window, which change with every turn of the page:

> It's a backyard full of life ... I see a cat, butterflies, a kangaroo, eight birds, a duck ... and a Mum and a child ... and a drop toilet. (One child says our view at home is the next door neighbor's wall).

> He's two now ... the trees have gone, cleared; they've got a fence ... It's established, it's more of a home ... more of a backyard ... there are galahs instead of cockatoos. There's no more kangaroos, there's no more life ... (it's) more civilized.

> The kid is four now, his name is Sam ... there are pigeons now because the land is more cleared ... they've removed lots of gum trees, they've mowed the grass ... the pond has gone ... I wouldn't swim in it anymore, it's got pale ... there's horses and cars ... Look, he likes Richmond (football club) ... the teddy bear has a jumper and maybe it's knitted by the new neighbors ... it's turning into a town ... friendly neighbors.

> He's six ... there is serious development now because of the tractor ... there's no tyre in the tree ... now he has a (bought) swing ... and more neighbors ... the swamps gone ... there's high development ... he's starting to have pets ... like rabbits.

> I think he's ten now ... there's loads more houses and a shed ... the fence is better ... or worse.

It's a rural town now … He's a pigeon killer! … He's got a frog in a jar that he's about to kill! … the kid seems kind of mean now … he's captured a frog and kept it in a jar … it symbolizes that we are being mean to the environment.

They broke a window … the tree house has gone, all the mountains are cleared … they are cutting down the forest … there won't be oxygen for them to breathe … more people want to move to this nice place but they are destroying it.

The night view shows there are so many more neighbors now.

Oh look there's a mad cat lady … and the boy is making his own motorbike.

The next door neighbor has 12 … no 16 cats!! … ugh … and there is a painted background (of a landscape) to disguise the background (of houses).

There's graffiti … advertising … oh, no she has 24 cats!

Look, he's moved … he has a child … and there are house blocks for sale … the lizards are back and the birds are back … it's the same type of bird as on the front page … It should stay like this … we can leave the bush as it is and the other half O.K … at the same time it's kinda hypocritical because he's moved away from the built up area … I'd still make houses because I'd make money for it … but … small houses and parks, well spaced but keep it how it is (in this new place that he has moved to) … yeah, I'd probably put in a few more houses … but more mixed … like a bit of country and city … you want company but some peace as well.

What if scenarios: creating Windows *onto ecological change*

As they discussed their findings, the children's relational attitudes to the views became evident. Having seen *Window's* landscape change so drastically over time, we then asked them to respond to a local community site that they would like to change through human intervention. In line with the role of an a/r/t-*e*-ographic researcher, as teacher educators with our preservice teachers, we first undertook this exercise so that the educational experience would be informed by our own materialized expressions of thinking. Figure 4 represents one such response to this exercise, showing Burke's window depicting a smoggy, overcrowded space (Layer 1), which, through collage and drawing (Layer 2), is recreated into an environmentally pleasing, vibrant site (Layer 3). Alongside the developing images are Burke's spontaneous, in process, comments that articulate a sense of the changing layers and processes needed to travel from one layering to another.

The exercise also provided us with insight into the window-making process. In particular, as teacher educators and teacher education students, we realized that in order to understand how children can develop a sense of active participation through this exercise, we needed to ask them: *Why is our window vision important? How can we make this window happen? What do we need to do? How can we effect change (through what process)? Who do we need to speak to?*

In sessions we facilitated (and assisted by the pre-service teachers), the children were shown the images and narratives in Figure 4 and asked the above questions to facilitate their active involvement. The children then created their own windows, starting with a place they depicted as environmentally damaged and transforming it. Figures 5–7 provide three different examples of the children's work.

Layer 1

Smog and overcrowding, no green space.

Layer 2

We need to lower the buildings to see the view ... plant trees for cleaner air and to create a home for animals.

Layer 3

Encourage animals to come back, capture water and live in closer connection with the land ... allow beauty to be a consideration in town planning.

Figure 4.   Creating ecological change from an adult's perspective.

As with the adult example in Figure 4, the children provided narrative to accompany each layer of their window. Their images and narratives were then explored in interviews with us, so that the children could recount the thinking behind their window. Excerpts from these interviews are also included in each of the figures.

C (child): 13 years (male)

R (researcher)

Layer 1

This place is all disgusting. It is like a big junk yard and in the water there are pipes dripping tar and nasty stuff. There is a symbol of an angry God chucking up!

Layer 2

It's the same photo but I've just added a better bit of it … It blocks out the smog towers and the smoke … there are now waves and fish.

Layer 3

There is more green on the trees … It just grew.

Layer 4

My site has become a nice river … There is a sigh of relief … a big sigh of relief … The umbrella is there because it is all nice now. It's a place people like to visit!

R: What can we do to effect this change?
C: We need lots of people with a caring mind need to help. They will see the damage, assess it and then change it. They will have invented a better way than factories spewing out smoke.
R: Why are the changes in your window important?
C: because they save the world by moving the junk, and destroying the factories and planting new trees.
R: What jobs are needed to effect these changes?
C: Someone to make eco friendly factories … maybe that would be a scientist?

Figure 5.   Ecological change from a child's perspective (1).

C: 12 years (female)

Layer 1

There is a road and on both sides it is filled with cars. There are two exit lanes. There is a plane, a UFO and black smog ... lots of things in the air. It is very busy ... I'm going to make it have less lanes and only 2 or 5 cars ... there will be houses and bicycles ... there will be houses not apartments ... and solar panels and it will all be greener.

Layer 2

Grass takes over the car ... a few of the black clouds turn white ... all of the dead trees go green. A little creek appears. The plane turns into a bird. There is no more smoke coming out of the tower ... two car lanes are turned into bicycle, horse and walking lanes. There is only one driving lane.

Layer 3

All the black clouds turn white. The tower turns into a tree. Half of the city goes and turns into grass and random stuff ... and three houses are built on the grass area. The creek turns into a river.

R: How can we make your window happen?
H: We would need to contact the City council ... and lobby to get a bike path.
We would have to get groups involved ... plenty of the community ... And you could build a climbing ladder to climb up trees to see the pollution and for having fun. You could plant trees and make the sky cleaner. You could move all the cars.

Figure 6.   Ecological change from a child's perspective (2).

C: Eight years (male)

Layer 1

My picture is of rubbish city. They crush the green leaves to make the smoke. The smoke is bad for the animals. There is black smoke made from the trees. They are doing that because they are not aware of the nature.

Layer 2

The green shape says 'green.' The white is better than black and green smoke. The blue is sea ... It got cleaner and more animals come to a cleaner river.

Layer 3

There's a crab and a turtle because it's a better environment. They are happy living there because it's clean and fresh and they can play there.

R: What can we do to make these changes happen?
C: You can put barbed wire around the site, you know ... signs, you need people's support ... you need advertisements to show them what it used to be like ... and there is no people allowed on the marina until it is happy and better.

Figure 7.   Ecological change from a child's perspective (3).

What then? What can we do? Opening a window and developing notions of agency

As the children's own 'window' images evolved from an undesirable site to a preferred imagined place, we asked the children how they could enact such change. As beholders and creators of their site, we encouraged them to connect and create change in that environment. These changes signaled the need for participation as activists (cleaning up the land, lobbying the council), environmentalists (who suggest and enact greener cleaner places), aesthetically aware residents (who want a more beautiful place to be in), inventors (who recreate eco-friendly factories), mentors, and communicators (who make signs and posters to educate others).

Where to from here? Provocations and gaps

As the children thought through the active participation needed to affect changes in their sites, various provocations arose that suggest further possible inroads for eco-literacy development (e.g., *Is it the role of scientists to design eco friendly factories? Could we not move all the cars? No people are allowed in the environment until it is happy and better*). If taken up by teachers and students, such provocations could make for rich learning within an eco-literacy syllabus.

Missing from the children's insights was a clear view of the jobs and power paths through which their environmental changes could occur, as Hart (2003) has previously signaled. Greater participation in community action projects, so as to model the roles, systems, and career paths, needed to enact change in a given place could help address this gap. This, however, will form a focus in the next offering of this experience on the unit (during 2010).

Concluding thoughts

> Most significantly, I think we too often forget that the primary purpose of education is to free persons to make sense of their actual lived situations – not only cognitively but also perceptually, imaginatively, affectively – to attend mindfully to their own lives, to take their own initiatives in interpreting them and finding out where the deficiencies are and trying to transform them. And discovering somehow that there is no end to it, that there is always more to see, to learn, to feel. (Greene 2001, 206)

Visual literacy and ecoliteracy, as reconceived through an immersive investigation of children's picture books, can be used as a pathway to active community participation. A journey from '*what is here*' (the beholder of picture books) to '*what if*' (imaginative possibility) to '*what then*' (the ecologically literate) to '*what can we do?*' (active participation and sustainable action) can enable students and teachers to enact living inquiry at the heart of their educational experience. This process activated the four attributes of immersion as described by Burbules (2004), namely; *interest, involvement, imagination* and *interaction* and enabled students to explore immersive art pedagogy as a pathway through which to examine environment and place. In the process the personal insights, provocations and possibilities that students and teachers found within given content was privileged so as to encourage a belief in one's personal volition. This was an attempt to empower participants to *analyze, create, act* and *participate* for meaning making and sustainability, knowing that there are always more possibilities and provocations to explore. As such, the process also served to further advance the conceptualisation of ecoliteracy and experiential learning which is particularly timely given that these concepts are increasingly being deployed in environmental education research and practice but rarely elaborated upon.

Our vignette, phase 2 of the teaching/research process, also shows us that the children involved were able to identify and analyze the changing Australian landscape that indeed affects them but are overall less sure about their role (and adult roles) in effecting desired and actual change. However, this ecopedagogical process developed a deep and intimate relationship where the students (both our pre-service teachers and the children we worked with) could relate their own embodied responses of children's picture books to that of their immediately proximal and temporally situated life worlds through the creation of their own eco-windows. Arriving at this awakened position requires what Baker calls the reader to do in *Window* (1991, in the author's endnotes): 'by opening a window in our minds, by understanding how change takes place and by changing the way we personally affect the environment, we can make a difference'. This is a heartening thought.

Acknowledgments

We would like to sincerely thank and acknowledge Mira Reisberg for her helpful feedback in the initial conceptualization of this paper. We would also like to thank Jeannie Baker and Walker Books for granting permission to utilize the images from *Window*.

Notes

1. The location of the Peninsula Campus is Frankston. Frankston is located on the fringes of the greater Melbourne metropolitan. It is situated on the eastern shores of Port Phillip Bay and is considered one of the Melbourne's more sustainable suburbs. See http://www.frankston.vic.gov.au/index.aspx.
2. For the purpose of this article, we will refer to the initial stage as Phase 1, which only involved the teacher educators and pre-service teachers. The phase involving the children will be referred to as Phase 2. We initially discuss the Phase 1 process. In Phase 2, though, we primarily focus on the children's experiences and responses. We do not focus on the pre-service teachers' responses.
3. Autoethnography has many interpretations. We see the methodology as primarily interrogating our highly subjective, personal, and reflective experience. We are both the researchers and participants.
4. Selected books were sourced from Monash University's Picture Book Collection; a Victorian State Primary School library; the authors' personal collections (compiled as a consequence of their roles as primary school teachers, teacher educators, and parents). The selection of books reflects those that are generally accessible within Australian primary school contexts. A more comprehensive study from other locations is welcomed, so as to extend our understanding of environment and place as gleaned through picture books availability in other locations.
5. The authors facilitated a series of experiences centered on children's literature and environment/place.
6. Although environmental education was at the core of our approach, we were significantly inspired by a/r/tography. In this instance, our reasoning for the inclusion of the -e- in a/r/tography was an attempt to contextualize and connect these two dynamic research fields. We acknowledge our playfulness and reimagining in how a/r/tography can enrich or embody environmental education. We equally acknowledge that much more work is needed with respect to theorizing a/r/t-e-ography.

References

Anstey, M., and G. Bull. 2000. *Reading the visual: Written and illustrated children's literature.* Sydney: Harcourt.

Baker, J. 1991. *Window.* London: Walker Books.

Bamford, A. 2003. *The visual literacy white paper.* Sydney: The University of Sydney.

Bourriaud, N. 2002. *Relational aesthetics.* Paris: Presses du réel.

Burbules, N.C. 2004. Rethinking the virtual. *Computing in Education: Theory & Practice* 7, no. 1: 89–107.

Burke, G. 2006. Towards an immersive art pedagogy: Connecting creativity and practice. *Australian Art Education* 29: 20–38.

Burke, G. 2010. Immersive art pedagogy: (Re) connecting artist, researcher and teacher. PhD diss., RMIT University.

Carter, P. 2004. *Material thinking.* Melbourne: Melbourne University Press.

Clacherty, A. 1993. Environmental literacy and the technicist worldview: Towards a new conceptualisation. *International Journal of Environmental Education and Information* 12, no. 2: 107–20.

Cutter-Mackenzie, A. 2009. *Eco-literacy: The 'Missing Paradigm' in environmental education.* Saarbrücken, Germany: Lambert Academic Publishing.

Cutter-Mackenzie, A., and R. Smith. 2003. Ecological literacy: The 'Missing Paradigm' in environmental education (Part I). *Environmental Education Research* 9, no. 4: 497–524.

Debes, J. 1968. Some foundations of visual literacy. *Audio Visual Instruction* 13: 961–964.

Greene, M. 2001. The creative spirit: Keys, doors and possibilities (Address to the New York State Board of Regents, 1984). In *Variations on a blue guitar: The Lincoln Centre Institute lectures on aesthetic education,* 201–208. New York: Teachers College Press.

Grosz, E. 2001. *Architecture from the outside: Essays on virtual and real space.* Georgia, MA: Massachusetts Institute of Technology.

Hart, P. 2003. *Teachers' thinking in environmental education: Consciousness and responsibility.* New York: Peter Lang.

Irwin, R.L, and A. de Cosson. 2004. *A/r/tography: Rendering self through arts-based living inquiry.* Vancouver: Pacific Educational Press.

Irwin, R.L, and S. Springgay. 2008. A/r/tography as practice based research. In *Being with A/r/tography,* ed. S. Springgay, R.L. Irwin., C. Leggo, and P. Gouzouasis, xix–xxxiii. Rotterdam: Sense Publishers.

Jeffers, S. 2003. Gallery as nexus in art education. *Journal of the National Art Education Association* 56, no. 1: 19–23.

Kress, G., and T. van Leeuwen. 1996. *Reading images.* Melbourne: Deakin University.

Kriesberg, D. 1999. *A sense of place: Teaching children about the environment with picture books.* Englewood, CO: Teacher Ideas Press.

Langer, S. 1942. *Philosophy in a new key: A study in the symbolism of reason, rite, and art.* 3rd ed. Cambridge: Harvard University Press.

Lippard, L. 1997. *The lure of the local: Senses of place in a multicentered society.* New York: New Press.

Messari, P. 1994. *Visual literacy: Image, mind and reality.* Boulder, CO: Westview Press.

Orr, D.W. 1990. Environmental education and ecological literacy. *Education Digest* May: 49–53.

Orr, D.W. 1992. *Ecological literacy: Education and the transition to a postmodern world.* Albany, NY: State University of New York.

Orr, D.W. 1994. *Earth in mind: On education, environment, and the human prospect.* Washington, DC: Island Press.

Roth, C.E. 1992. *Environmental literacy: It roots, evolution and direction in the 1990s.* Columbus, OH: ERIC Clearinghouse for Science Mathematics and Environmental Education.

Springgay, S. 2008. An ethics of embodiment. In *Being with A/r/tography,* ed. S. Springgay, R.L. Irwin, C. Leggo, and P. Gouzouasis, 153–165. Rotterdam: Sense Publishers.

Stables, A., and K. Bishop. 2001. Weak and strong conceptions of environmental literacy: Implications for environmental education. *Environmental Education Research* 7, no. 1: 89–97.

Sturdavant, D.W. 1993. From thinking like a machine to thinking like a mountain: Educational Restructuring or ecological literacy. PhD diss., University of Oregon.

Tuan, Y. 1977. *Space and place: The perspectives of experience.* Minneapolis, MN: University of Minnesota Press.

Weston, A. 1996. Deschooling environmental education. *Canadian Journal of Environmental Education* 1: 35–46.

Exploring instructional strategies to develop prospective elementary teachers' children's literature book evaluation skills for science, ecology and environmental education

J. William Hug

Elementary/Early Childhood Education Department, California University of Pennsylvania, California, PA, USA

This article is an auto-ethnographic account of the development of a children's literature book critique assignment by a science teacher educator sharing instructional dilemmas and pedagogical responses. Prospective elementary teachers enrolled in an elementary school science teaching methods course in the US selected and evaluated children's literature books with science, environment and nature content. The book critique assignment sought to enhance prospective elementary teachers' ability to evaluate the quality of children's environmental literature books for use in elementary school classrooms. Prospective elementary teacher responses for two characteristics, scientific accuracy and anthropomorphism, are presented demonstrating a range of sophistication in their understanding of these concepts. The discussion explores insights into prospective elementary teachers' thinking with implications for science, ecology, natural history and environmental education.

Prologue: a pedagogical puzzle

After the elementary school science teaching methods class one of my prospective elementary teachers, 'Christy', lingered and tentatively asked the question on her mind, 'Is this children's literature book OK to use for my critique assignment?'

Other students had asked me the same question in other semesters so it did not take long to form the pedagogical response, 'So, can you explain some more about why you selected this children's literature book?'

Christy did not realize that I phrased this question in answer to her question with pedagogical purpose. In my view Christy anticipated the simple answer, 'Yes, this is a good book to use for your assignment'. In this context it appeared that she wanted confirmation that her book choice was 'right'. Yet as I thought about her question, Christy appeared to shift pedagogical decision-making from herself to me and in a sense asked the tacit question, 'You decide. If I select this book will I achieve a high grade on my assignment?' But I wanted Christy to decide – to practice deciding. I would not be present in the future to help her decide which books to use in her elementary classroom. As her instructor I believed that my duty in this context was to create opportunities for her to practice skills in the selection and evaluation of children's literature that help students learn about their environment. I wanted to listen to and assess those skills in order to offer targeted guidance. I had to get Christy past the simple yes or no answer. We had to get to why.

I waited patiently for Christy to take the risk to share her thinking with me, expressing non-verbal encouragement. Slowly she turned the children's picture book toward me and opened it to the first few pages. Tentatively she ventured, 'I really like the pictures. These animals are cute!'

This opening vignette is a composite of countless similar interactions I have experienced over the years as a teacher educator. It captures some of the challenges I have faced with prospective teachers in helping them select and evaluate high quality children's literature. Christy is a fictionalized archetype – but she would not be the first prospective or practicing teacher to use cute illustrations as the primary criteria for selecting children's books. Finding myself in such situations I have felt a variety of emotions: disappointment at what I considered low level book selection criteria; anger at an educational system that conditions students to respond passively with surface level critiques; and occasionally an overwhelmed sense at the immensity of the task of helping future teachers to become environmental educators in their classrooms. After many years of using a children's literature book critique assignment with prospective teachers, I now mostly feel empathy, demonstrate patience and remain hopeful. As my understanding of prospective teachers, teacher education and environmental education has grown, so too has my ability to visualize the influences of larger social and cultural systems at work in my student's questions and responses. I metaphorically imagine prospective teachers' responses as not really their responses alone but as a composite layering of cultural and previous school influences deposited over time in a kind of educational archeological site. I imagine myself, a teacher educator, as the educational archeologist systematically sifting through layers of dialogue to piece together from incomplete clues an understanding of the larger social–cultural influences that shaped their answer. When prospective teachers use what I consider surface level criteria such as cute pictures to select their children's literature books, I wonder why and explore what social–cultural influences informed their choice. Similar to this approach, Hart (2003) has advocated for explorations into teacher thinking in environmental education and described the efficacy of these methods.

I have to ask myself, how can I help prospective teachers such as 'Christy' develop more sophisticated ways of selecting and evaluating children's literature? In addition, how does my use of children's environmental literature in my science teaching methods course help future elementary school teachers learn about environment, ecology, and natural history? How can I treat the innocent individual prospective teacher with respect, kindness and encouragement while engaging in an assertive critical pedagogy (Bowers 1993; Gruenewald and Smith 2008) against salient cultural forces that enable the destruction of nature and my students' higher order thinking skills?

This article explores my own pedagogical choices to address these questions employing an auto-ethnographic approach (Ellis 1997). In what follows, I engage a range of personal pedagogical experiences, prospective teacher assignment data and literature. I also employ shifts in tense and style to signal different aspects of my presence in this auto-ethnography. I start with personal reflections on pedagogical dilemmas before moving on to discuss prospective teacher thinking on scientific accuracy and anthropomorphism represented in children's literature. The article concludes with reflections on my instructional approaches, development as a teacher educator and calls for further auto-ethnography research in environmental education.

Pedagogical issues: opening reflections

How do I understand prospective teachers' thinking and decision-making about the representation of environment, ecology and natural places in children's literature? My pedagogical problem-solving journey began with trying to address two dilemmas. The first dilemma concerned the realization that in their approximately 15 years of previous schooling, many of these prospective teachers had not acquired even the basic ecological and environmental content knowledge that should be expected of citizens, much less beginning teachers (McKeown-Ice 2000; National Research Council 2007). I was concerned that if prospective teachers think of themselves as deficient in content knowledge, they might avoid teaching environmental education in their future careers to circumvent their perceived fear of being asked a question to which they do not know the answer. In an effort to help them break through this thinking I wanted to find a motivating hook that these prospective teachers would find non-threatening as a way to begin to address their content knowledge deficiencies.

Second, my observations in elementary school classrooms lead me to believe that many practicing teachers do not teach science or environmental education in their classrooms. The challenging environment for environmental education, teachers explained, stemmed from 'adding one more thing' to a crowded curriculum, feelings of inadequacy in content knowledge, not having enough time for training or activity preparation, and school policies that prevented them from taking their classes outside. The situation, teachers told me, worsened after the passage in the US of the 'No Child Left Behind' Act. This reduced the already low number of weekly minutes devoted to science instruction in elementary schools by 33% (CEP 2008) as well as made it difficult for teachers to use a wide variety of children's literature in their reading programs (Williams and Bauer 2006). I needed to find a way in my elementary science teaching methods course to concretely demonstrate to prospective teachers that they are not confronted with an 'either environmental education or achieve proficiency on the achievement test' choice. They could do both simultaneously. One solution to these twin dilemmas consisted of using children's literature books as an entry motivator for deepening science, environment and ecology content in a non-threatening way.

This proposed solution presented a challenge: how do I help prospective teachers select high quality children's literature for use in their instruction (Christenson 2005)? Harvey and Goudvis (2007) estimate that approximately 5500 children's literature books are published in the US each year. Based on the science and environment related books I commonly see for sale in bookstores, it appears that manuscript publication decisions are primarily based on judgments about what will sell to the general public. This may or may not correspond with whether the books are factually accurate or portray appropriate environmental relationships for classroom use. Further, common literary techniques such as anthropomorphizing animals and creating character conflict have the potential to convey misconceptions about human/environment relationships. It seemed clear to me that prospective teachers need to become aware of these issues and use more sophisticated criteria to evaluate children's literature books for use in their future classrooms.

Another issue that eludes prospective teachers, in my experience, concerned the developmental appropriateness of children's environmental literature (Sobel 1999).

While it is fairly common for teachers to consider a book's reading level and match it to the reading ability of the student, my observation has been that many teachers do not consider a book's environmental content and match it to the developmental level of their children. For instance, I have observed teachers living far from the Tropics introduce young children to books about the destruction of tropical rainforests and the death of charismatic tropical animals. Young children often do not yet adequately understand their own ecosystem, much less a distant one they are unlikely to experience directly. In addition, early childhood learners may not have developed the ability to put into perspective complex human and environment relationships (e.g., cutting trees for forest products versus forest preservation) or the relative risks to ecosystems, plants, animals, people and self (e.g., 'Will rain forest fire burn me too?'"). This is not to suggest that teachers should ignore distant ecosystems and eliminate uncomfortable subjects, however it is important for teachers to consider when it is developmentally appropriate to introduce these topics to children. David Sobel (1999) proposed this strategy and suggested that parents, teachers and caregivers consider the environmental developmental appropriateness of materials for use with children.

Research methods and the 'auto' dilemma

It is clear to me that the prospective teachers I work with needed further practice in selecting, evaluating and using children's environmental literature books. The previous section illustrates some of the grounds for my instructional approaches to some of these issues. It also illustrates how one can utilize personal voice to focus on a practical pedagogical issue to provide a narrative that constructs one version of my lived experience as a science teacher educator.

In the educational research literature, qualitative methods generally and auto-ethnography specifically, describe a diversity of methods for such inquiries. Denzin's and Lincoln's work over many years (Denzin 1999; Denzin and Lincoln 1994, 2005; Lincoln 1990, 1995; Lincoln and Guba 1985), for example, provides the foundation for the general qualitative research aspects that inform this work. Their explorations of diverse research methods and various ways to represent the results of qualitative research powerfully inform the selection of auto-ethnography for this work. Ellis (1997) describes 'evocative ethnography' as the autobiographical impulse blended with the auto-ethnographic impulse. She describes a kind of looking outward at culture as well as inward to the self to produce descriptive stories of lived experience. Her auto-ethnographic examples include first person autobiographical text that purposefully disrupts the traditional academic voice of distance and citation. Hughes (2008) suggests that narratives should, 'embrace the conflict of writing against oneself as he or she finds himself or herself entrenched in the complications of their pedagogical positions' (128). His notion of 'good enough methods' reveals how even thorough, meticulous research can result in errors, uncertainties and blind spots. Thus he advocates the use of the personal, the value-laden and the critical in order to produce narratives that illuminate the inner and outer lived world of the teacher–researcher. And even while such strategies reveal auto-ethnography as subject to limitations – as one potential story out of many possible stories, for example – this situation can be recast as a strength: where description leads the reader to an increased understanding, empathy or resonance with the lived experience described.

Recent literature reviews, however, would suggest auto-ethnography has not been commonly employed in environmental education research (Reid and Scott 2008). So, how should one go about producing and evaluating quality auto-ethnographic research? Hart (2002) synthesizes the question of emerging research methods quality criteria and suggests:

> We should not be surprised at the impossibility of a single standard set of criteria. It is more productive to approach quality issues in research, from the perspective that a multiplicity of goals imply multiple ways of assessing quality. There is no one right way to do research. There is no one right way to assess it. (Hart 2002, 154)

There are many stories. There are many standards. Therein lies the 'auto' dilemma in writing for publication. Can an aspect of my lived experience actually be conveyed through academic text? What relevance does one story among many have for a scholarly journal?

I am reminded of Elie Wiesel's (1977) concept that the experience of the holocaust cannot be known by non-survivors, that survivors speak in code. He wrote that holocaust narratives must use words against words in an attempt to describe the undescribable. Wiesel notes that writing about the holocaust experience so that non-survivors will understand it, is ultimately a futile task. Yet, the holocaust survivor writer feels compelled to try because of the holocaust's significance.

In some meager fashion, my experience as an environmental educator and teacher educator parallels this idea. My sense of beauty, connectedness, respect and reverence for nature enhanced through thousands of outdoor experiences over many years seems like a code that few people share in the same way. Is it possible to describe my affinity for nature in text or through classes I teach to people who do not have a deeply felt and practiced environmental perspective? Is affinity for nature a code that cannot be known by those who have not yet experienced it? My attempt as a teacher educator to share this sense of nature with prospective teachers and through them their students is fraught with the possibility of futility. Can talking about the quality characteristics of children's environmental literature books really help prospective teachers become future environmental educators in their classrooms? In only a modest way then, can this auto-ethnography seek to account for one aspect of my practical pedagogical journey to help prospective teachers think about their relationship with nature and the ways culture represents nature through text, language and experience. The significance of the human–environment relationship and the imperative for people to understand it more completely compels me to engage in this work.

Strategies for using environmental children's literature with prospective teachers

One of the main expectations for teachers is that they know the content they teach (National Research Council 2007). Many of the prospective teachers in my classes know very little environmental content and appear reluctant to admit that this is the case because it conflicts with their conception of teacher as 'knower of the answers'. This presents barriers to their learning. In order to reduce the threshold for these prospective teachers to actively engage in developing their environmental content knowledge and children's literature evaluation skills, I have employed two main learning experiences. First, I model read-aloud strategies using environmental children's literature. Second, I require the students to select a children's literature book and critique it according to a set of criteria that focuses on the quality characteristics of children's environmental literature books.

I introduce children's literature books early in the elementary science teaching methods course, usually on the first day of class. I want to establish the classroom climate as supportive, help them redefine their understanding of the nature of science, and begin the process of revising their conceptions of teacher and teaching. One of the first books I share with them is *Molly goes hiking* (Radlauer 1987). This picture book shows Molly, a girl of about seven-years-old, packing a backpack, taking a solo hike, eating a lunch on top of a mountain, picking up her trash and going home. Recognizing that my physical attributes convey the white, male, middle class, university professor with eyeglasses that corresponds to popular media-fueled images of professors and scientists, I conscientiously select books that showcase alternatives to this image. Within the first minutes of class, I strive to set a tone that provides entry into a semester-long dialogue with my students about environmental content, literature, behavior and culture.

Another book I introduce early in the course to emphasize science process skills (Monhardt and Monhardt 2006) rather than science fact memorization is *Everyone needs a rock* (Baylor 1974). This book's narrator describes 10 flexible 'rules' for selecting a rock to keep as a friend and then encourages the reader to find his or her own rock. The rules are written in a way to encourage observation of rocks rather than the naming the rock type. Size, shape and color are mentioned as well as characteristics such as, 'feel jumpy in your pocket' and 'always sniff a rock'. In my experience, prospective teachers engage in learning about rocks more quickly through this children's literature experience than if I had passed out rocks and identified them as, 'gneiss, pottsville sandstone and quartz monzonite'.

To focus my student's attention on content, I read children's literature books such as *Owl moon* (Yolen 1987), the story of girl and her father who take a hike through snowy woods under a full moon in search of great horned owls. After the father's calls attract an owl to a nearby tree branch, father and daughter experience looking closely at an owl looking back at them. This children's literature book leads easily into hands-on classroom activities such as dissecting owl pellets and reassembling rodent skeletons. *Owl moon* provides an excellent entry into learning about food chains, animal adaptations, ecosystems and intergenerational informal environmental learning opportunities.

I find that the book *Pumpkin circle* (Levenson 1999) helps focus attention on plant life cycles. Many children's environmental literature books omit key concepts such as decomposition producing an incomplete view of natural cycles. The outstanding photographs in *Pumpkin circle* show sprouting, growing and flowering as well as time-lapse photos of a pumpkin decomposing over time with the explanation, 'back to earth you go'. The visual representation of the recognizable pumpkin turning into a pile of soil provides a powerful message for the reader. Books such as *Pumpkin circle* do not omit key aspects of natural processes and enable prospective teachers to engage with content in a non-threatening way.

Children's literature can play an important role in initiating conversations about animals, environment and people. *Salamander room* (Mazer 1991) provides an excellent entry into a discussion of what to do when a student catches an animal and asks to take it home or bring it into the classroom. The book begins when a young boy, Brian, catches a salamander and asks his mother to keep it in his bedroom. Through a series of questions, the mother asks about animal needs such as water, food and shelter. Brian explains with ever more fantastic inventions how he will provide for the salamander's needs. By the end of the story, as bedroom modifications are made,

Brian is sleeping outside in the salamander's home rather than sleeping in his own room. Discussions with prospective teachers after this story elicit rich stories about their own experiences with animals and the ethics of keeping classroom pets. Following these conversations, books such as *Salamander rain: A lake and pond journal* (Pratt-Serafini 2000), *Near one cattail* (Fredericks 2005) and *Song of the waterboatman* (Sidman 2005) offer excellent opportunities for deepening prospective teachers content knowledge when paired with hands-on instructional activities such as nature journaling (Leslie and Roth 2003), map-making (Sobel 1998), water quality monitoring (Mitchell, Stapp and Bixby 2000) and species identification (Watts 1998).

A final example of a book I use in my science teaching methods course is *Secret place* (Bunting 1996). It describes an urban environment where the children discover animals and plants living tucked away in the corners of a city. I use this book to initiate a discussion of environmental education activities and issues in urban settings and to demonstrate the need to select a variety of children's literature that connects with the diverse student contexts present in an elementary classroom.

Evaluating environmental children's literature

One challenge with using children's literature to engage prospective teachers in learning environmental content rests in evaluating scientific accuracy. Several authors have demonstrated that children's literature can convey misinformation and serve to reinforce science misconceptions on important science topics (Ford 2006; Trundle and Troland 2005). Like any instructional strategy, there are positive and negative benefits to using a particular children's literature book in the classroom. A key question is: How do teachers select, evaluate and use the books meant to instruct children in environmental content?

In order to provide prospective teachers practice in selecting, evaluating and using high quality children's literature I designed a children's literature book critique assignment based on an earlier assignment (Campbell 1992). The assignment required prospective teachers to select a book that they could use to teach a specific science or environment and ecology academic standard, and critique the book according to a list of quality considerations.

The children's literature quality considerations are an essential aspect of the assignment. Based on my lengthy experiences of using the books described above, I revised Campbell's (1992) quality criteria for use with prospective teachers in my classes in order to help them look beyond surface criteria such as 'cute pictures' in their selection of children's literature books. The current quality considerations (see the appendix) are based on a synthesis of a variety of sources such as: the National [United States] Science Teachers Association (2003); the American Library Association (2009); Donovan and Smolkin (2002); Eggerton (1996); Martin (2003); and Rice (2002). In preparing this article I became aware of the work of Atkinson, Matusevich and Huber (2009). Their work confirms in many ways that similar quality criteria are being used by many organizations and individuals. It seems clear that healthy classroom dialogue should include discussions about the multiplicity of children's literature quality criteria as well as questions about who determines children's literature quality criteria and for what purpose.

I use several strategies in the classroom to prepare students for their assignment, including supporting them through modeling, guided practice and independent practice. First, I model reading quality children's literature aloud with instructional pauses to demonstrate my 'teacher thinking' about the positive and negative quality characteristics of the book. Next, in small groups students read and practice evaluating books using the quality criteria. Individual conversations occur as students ask questions and I interact with the working groups to focus their attention on understanding the latent aspects of the quality criteria. Students are then shown on-line searchable databases of children's literature books and the locations of award winning book lists. The prospective teachers then independently select a book, use the quality criteria to review their book, and write a book review using direct quotes and examples from their book. The aim of this critique assignment is to deepen their understanding of children's literature quality characteristics beyond that exemplified by Christy's response in this article's prologue.

Common student responses

While prospective teachers do exhibit a variety of responses they tend to ask similar questions while completing their children's literature book critique assignments. One common response is, 'I can't find *any* children's literature books for my academic standard'. In some cases this is the result of laziness or inability to search children's literature databases properly. In other cases, they select non-fiction 'fact' books because these books are conceptualized as 'science' books while children's literature 'storybooks' remain outside their definitional boundary of a book that could be used to teach science, environment and ecology. I believe this is evidence of the larger cultural influences on their thinking about the environment. Based on my conversations with these prospective teachers over the years, I believe their difficulty in finding a children's literature book is mainly a symptom of their initial constricted selection strategy. I find that many prospective teachers, schooled in classroom cultures that reward vocabulary memorization, tend to search for the vocabulary words to get their 'correct answer'. For instance, if the assigned academic standard involves animal adaptations, the students typically search children's literature books for the word 'adaptations' in the book title or in the text. A Caldicott Award-winning book such as *Owl moon* (Yolen 1987) does not explicitly mention adaptations in the title or text, but provides extraordinary opportunities to examine the physical features that enable the owl survive in its environment. My inference is that prospective teachers use this initial selection strategy of looking for exact text matches due to their low levels of content knowledge, their prior schooling experiences emphasizing vocabulary memorization and naïve view of the nature of science as 'facts'. This realization inspired my decision to read children's literature books aloud in class and explicitly state examples of connections to academic standards. For additional support, I added a small group task where prospective teachers read a book and together brainstormed a list of academic standards connected to the book. This strategy helps many prospective teachers become more familiar with academic standards, the connections to children's literature books, and works toward broadening their conceptions of science.

Another common issue involves evaluating the accuracy of the book's content. Initially, some prospective teachers will evaluate the accuracy of a children's literature book's content by the copyright date, reasoning that a recent book is more accurate. Based on many conversations with students over the years, the use of the publication date as the indicator of content accuracy has tended to reflect low level of content knowledge on the part of the prospective teacher. In response, my instructional strategy has shifted to involve deepening their content understanding through associated hands-on activities and helping them to verify environmental content accuracy from reliable sources.

In the following section, I use selected prospective teacher work samples to illustrate aspects of their scientific accuracy understanding as demonstrated in their children's literature book critique assignments. The examples were selected to show the range of responses I received from many students over multiple courses.

The typical response at one end of the range provides little information about the student's evaluation strategies: 'The content in this book is up to date and clear'. It indicates a judgment without helpful information about how the evaluation was made. It essentially restates the quality criteria and is perceived as a safe generic response.

The next example, frequently found in the prospective teacher responses, demonstrates the close connection the prospective teacher makes between the publication date and information accuracy. The instructional goal of fostering outside research to confirm the environmental content was not met by this student's response:

> This book tells a story while still informing readers of accurate facts about octopuses. It enlightens readers about the life of an octopus. It covers the fact that they need sea water to survive, that they change colors to match their surroundings, that they grow weak when they lay eggs, and that they die shortly laying those eggs. At the end of the book, the author includes a page with additional information about octopuses. This book was written in 2003; therefore, the information within the text is fairly recent.

It circumvents making a determination by focusing on description and use of the copyright date to support the judgment that the content in the book is scientifically accurate.

The following example is typical of those prospective teachers who use information within the text to evaluate the book. It appears that 'science facts' resonate with the prospective teacher's conception of scientific accuracy. In effect, the prospective teacher states, 'there are science facts in the book' rather than 'the science information presented is accurate'. Again, there is no outside confirmation of the content based on independent research outside of the existing book text or existing knowledge base of the prospective teacher:

> The content information about wolves and their existence in Yellowstone National Park is very thorough in this story. The author is able to depict the necessary activities the wolves need to survive in an up-to-date manner. The author also goes into detail of how their existence in Yellowstone has leapt from a thriving member of the ecosystem, to non-existent, to once again an important species. As shown in the following text, the author is factual even by date of disappearance and the return of the wolves.

The final example represents the other end of the range of responses. It describes moving outside the student's own existing content knowledge base and beyond the information in the children's literature book to engage in outside research verification of the content in the book:

> Surprisingly enough, the book is quite accurate (according to the web). I checked online to make sure that each occurrence had indeed happened, and each one was there for me to view. One instance however was false; the book states that a tornado had plucked the feathers right off of a chicken. This seems to have been a fabricated story, and there was no evidence that this could or did happen.

This passage shows how the prospective teacher indicated an outside source to verify the content accuracy in the children's literature text. Although there is mention of outside research (the web), I wonder how honest the prospective teacher was in representing the depth of the outside research as well as the accuracy of the websites used to confirm the children's literature book content. The instructional goal of the critique assignment is to illuminate the characteristics of high quality children's literature books, but it is also to provide practice in the broader professional expectation, of continually verifying and developing content knowledge over a teaching career.

Children's literature books and anthropomorphism

Anthropomorphism is a common literary device used by authors of children's books yet Anderson and Henderson (2005) argue that anthropomorphism has the potential to shape the human/environment relationship in negative ways. For the purposes of this article, anthropomorphism refers to the practice of imbuing animals or objects with human characteristics, behaviors or values. Examples of anthropomorphism in environmental children's literature could include animals wearing human clothes, talking to each other or interacting as human families. Anderson and Henderson also point out that anthropomorphic portrayals of animals invites stereotypes such as turtles are slow, rabbits are fast, owls are wise and snakes are evil.

The following scenario exemplifies the case for the negative impact of extensive cultural anthropomorphism exposure. Imagine a person encountering a baby bird hopping on the ground and chirping loudly. They conclude that the bird has fallen out of its nest, misses its mother and is hungry. Not seeing the mother around, they further assume that the mother has abandoned the baby bird, which results in their decision to pick up the baby bird, take it inside the house and call the local nature center or zoo or wildlife officer to inquire about how to feed an abandoned baby bird. In reality, the baby bird was probably learning to fly and was being fed on the ground by adult birds that flew away upon the approach of the human. In this example, the action of 'rescuing' the baby bird is based on inaccurate projection of human characteristics and behaviors onto the bird. Human babies cannot survive without adults and human mothers do not normally 'abandon' their children, therefore we must 'save' the baby bird. Nature centers and wildlife organizations in the US commonly handle these kinds of requests for assistance every spring.

Can reading children's literature with anthropomorphic characters shape children's conception of the human–environment relationship? It is reasonable to suggest that in some instances reading anthropomorphic children's literature books could contribute to detrimental environmental behaviors as described in the scenario above. However, anthropomorphic devices in children's literature might also produce positive benefits. It seems possible that the anthropomorphic aspects of books can allow children to first develop empathy for animals and a sense of wanting to protect them before learning the complexities of biology, ecology and environmental science. I argue that prospective teachers should understand anthropomorphism when they select children's literature books and be able to develop classroom activities appropriate for their students that call attention to environment/human relationships, critically examine them and provide a range of action choices. Ideally, teachers should help children critically examine the received cultural fabric rather than to act unconsciously within it. Calling attention to anthropomorphism in children's literature is but one small example of the more general endeavor to help citizens understand the natural world, their relationship within it and how human actions contribute to the natural community's health or ill health.

When I asked prospective teachers to critique the use of anthropomorphism in children's literature books, I received a variety of responses. The quote below represents a typical response that indicates a lack of understanding of the term:

The only anthropomorphic statement that would be misleading to students is that there are nine planets in the solar system when really there is only eight. All other aspects of this book did a great job of explaining the factual information about the solar system.

In the next example, the prospective teacher's response indicates that she has begun to grasp anthropomorphism but does not yet have an in-depth understanding:

The descriptions written of the various animals in this book incorporate some human characteristics, but in such a subtle manner that it could be debated as to whether or not they constitute as being anthropomorphic. Some examples include: '(one salmon) leaps with a splash, fish-dancing', 'he (the moose) twitches one ear and I creep close to see if we'll be friends' and 'her (the eagle) wings whistle a song'. These examples show friendly, descriptive features about the creatures and not humanistic traits that would give children the wrong idea about the animal.

The next examples demonstrate that the prospective teachers have begun to grasp anthropomorphism and describe its use in the children's literature book they selected:

Yes, in this story there are a few examples of imposing human values on wildlife. One example of that is, 'Friendly daddy longlegs that never bite'. This statement says that daddy longlegs are 'friendly' which is giving a spider a human quality. Also, another part of the book suggests that caterpillars have 'tiny feet' again this is giving caterpillars human qualities.

The frogs appear to have smirks on their faces (not all). Other than that the animals are just animals. None of them speak, dance or wear human clothing.

There is a lizard in the story that does seem to have human emotions placed on it. One illustration of the lizard in a 'scary' part of the story looked scared or unsure and hiding under the covers of a bed. In another picture it looks curious, and in another the students placed a pair of the 'magic glasses' on it. The story does not give voice to the lizard only visual emotions.

In my experience, prospective teachers exhibit a range of comprehension of anthropomorphism in children's literature. They often are not familiar with the concept and rarely demonstrate awareness of its potential impact on children's conceptualizations of nature or how to address the issue instructionally in their classrooms. In many of the books these prospective teachers select for their assignment, anthropomorphism is prevalent. In the worst cases it is often accompanied by gross environmental, ecological and biological misinformation. The instructional goal is to engage the prospective elementary teachers in a critical conversation about the human–environment relationship through identifying and examining anthropomorphism in children's literature books. Through classroom discussions and the book critique assignment the ideal circumstance is to cause the prospective teacher to move from an unconscious, unaware, taken-for-granted stance toward anthropomorphism into the first steps toward questioning how culture, in this case children's literature, shapes the human–environment relationship. As an early semester experience, this opens the possibility for further explorations of how we live within received cultural frameworks and the role of the teacher in helping students learn academic content as well as critically examine the framework within which it rests.

Conclusion

The choice to use children's literature in my science teaching methods course, like any instructional strategy, has advantages and disadvantages. On the one hand, I am convinced that including children's literature provides an opportunity for prospective teachers to begin to think of themselves as teachers of science and environmental content. It allows them to start the process of envisioning themselves as successful environmental educators. These prospective teachers are also exposed to the characteristics of high quality children's literature for use in environmental education. They learn how book characteristics such as anthropomorphism and scientific accuracy can contribute positively or negatively to the human–environment relationship. On the other hand, by advocating the use of children's literature in elementary school classrooms to teach science and environment content I run the risk that prospective teachers will select children's literature that perpetuate naïve or damaging conceptions toward the environment in their learners. I wonder how many of these prospective teachers will use their experiences in the science methods class to select high quality children's literature and develop critical pedagogy activities to examine the cultural influences of the human–environment relationship. These and other questions will guide future research.

I think about my development as a teacher educator through this process. Based on these experiences, it seems clear that there is much the science educator can do to help develop prospective teacher's understanding of the environment. Although this children's literature book critique assignment is conceptualized as early semester awareness activity, the next progression of the assignment should include more explicit emphasis on environmental content knowledge research skills. I should also employ more explicit strategies later in the semester to critically examine the received cultural frameworks. It would be beneficial to study individual cases of prospective teacher thinking as it develops through the children's literature assignment.

Upon reflection, I remember my own environmental children's literature experiences, which included a wide variety of children's literature books, some of which I would evaluate today as poor and others excellent. I remind myself that children's literature is only one small instructional event that contributes to a person's environmental understanding and perspectives. In my experience, children's literature provides a motivating, easy access, low fear, early semester entry point into discussions about the nature of science, the idea of evaluating children's literature for use in classrooms, developing environmental content knowledge through additional research throughout a teaching career, examining the human–environment relationship and using developmentally appropriate environmental children's literature books. This auto-ethnographic narrative provides one teacher educator's constructed narrative about practical pedagogical dilemmas and instructional strategies to develop prospective teachers' ability to select and use high quality children's literature books for environmental education. In my view, the environmental education research literature would clearly benefit from other auto-ethnographic narratives from a variety of people, places, cultures and contexts.

Epilogue: pieces to a pedagogical puzzle

I looked carefully at the illustrations in the children's literature book Christy held up for me to see. She was right. The animals were really cute. My eyes moved from the page and held her uncertain glance for just a moment before I said, 'You're right. These animals are really cute. What else do you like about this book that makes it especially good for teaching about the environment?' I noticed her shoulders relax slightly and knew we could continue talking about the characteristics of high quality children's literature books for environmental education.

Acknowledgements

I would like to thank the anonymous reviewers and guest editors of *Environmental Education Research* for their invaluable comments on earlier drafts of this manuscript.

References

American Library Association. 2009. *Caldecott award terms and criteria.* www.ala.org/ala/mgrps/divs/alsc/awardsgrants/bookmedia/caldecottmedal/caldecottterms/caldecottterms.cfm.

Anderson, M.V., and A.J.Z. Henderson. 2005. Pernicious portrayals: The impact of children's attachment to animals of fiction on animals of fact. *Society and Animals* 13, no. 4: 297–314.

Atkinson, T.S., M.N. Matusevich, and L. Huber. 2009. Making science trade book choices for elementary classrooms. *The Reading Teacher* 62, no. 6: 484–97.

Baylor, B. 1974. *Everybody needs a rock.* Illustrated by P. Parnall. New York: Macmillian Publishing Company.

Bowers, C.A. 1993. *Education, cultural myths, and the ecological crisis: Toward deep changes.* Albany: State University of New York Press.

Bunting, E. 1996. *Secret place.* New York: Clarion Books.

Campbell, L.M. 1992. *SCIED 458 syllabus/course packet.* State College, PA: The Pennsylvania State University.

Center on Education Policy. 2008. Instructional time in elementary schools: A closer look at changes for specific subjects. A report in the series *From the capital to the classroom: Year 5 of the No Child Left Behind Act.* Washington, DC: Center on Educational Policy.

Christenson, M.A. 2005. Teaching multiple perspectives on environmental issues in elementary classrooms: A story of teacher inquiry. *Journal of Environmental Education* 35, no. 4: 3–16.

Denzin, N.K. 1999. Interpretive ethnography for the next century. *Journal of Contemporary Ethnography* 28, no. 5: 510–19.

Denzin, N.K., and Y.S. Lincoln. 1994. *Handbook of qualitative research.* Thousand Oaks, CA: Sage Publications.

Denzin, N.K., and Y.S. Lincoln. 2005. *The Sage handbook of qualitative research.* Thousand Oaks, CA: Sage Publications.

Donovan, C.A., and L.B. Smolkin. 2002. Considering genre, content, and visual features in the selection of trade books for science instruction. *The Reading Teacher* 55, no. 6: 502–20.

Eggerton, S. 1996. Balancing science and sentiment: The portrayal of nature and the environment in children's literature. *Science and Children* 33, no. 6: 20–3.

Ellis, C. 1997. Evocative autoethnography: Writing emotionally about our lives. In *Representation and the text: Re-framing the narrative voice,* ed. W.G. Tierney, and Y.S. Lincoln. Albany, NY: State University of New York Press.

Ford, D.J. 2006. Representations of science within children's trade books. *Journal of Research in Science Teaching* 43, no. 2: 214–35.

Fredericks, A.D. 2005. *Near one cattail.* Illustrated by J. DiRubbio. Nevada City, CA: Dawn Publications.

Gruenewald, D.A., and G.A. Smith. 2008. *Place-based education in the global age: Local diversity.* New York: Taylor and Francis.

Hart, P. 2002. Narrative, knowing, and emerging methodologies in environmental education research: Issues of quality. *Canadian Journal of Environmental Education* 7, no. 2: 140–65.

Hart, P. 2003. *Teachers' thinking in environmental education: Consciousness and responsibility.* New York, NY: Peter Lang.

Harvey, S., and A. Goudvis. 2007. *Strategies that work: Teaching comprehension for understanding and engagement.* Portland, ME: Stenhouse Publishers

Hughes, S.A. 2008. Toward 'Good Enough Methods' for autoethnography in a graduate education course: Trying to resist the matrix with another promising red pill. *Educational Studies* 43, no. 2: 125–43.

Leslie, C.W., and C.E. Roth. 2003. *Keeping a nature journal: Discover a whole new way of seeing the world around you.* North Adams, MA: Storey Publishing.

Levenson, G. 1999. *Pumpkin circle: The story of a garden.* Berkeley, CA: Tricycle Press.

Lincoln, Y.S. 1990. Toward a categorical imperative for qualitative research. In *Qualitative inquiry in education,* ed. E.S. Eisner and A. Peshkin, 277–95. New York: Teachers College Press.

Lincoln, Y.S. 1995. Emerging criteria for quality in interpretive inquiry. Paper presented at the annual meeting of the American Educational Research Association, in San Francisco, CA.

Lincoln, Y.S., and E.G. Guba. 1985. *Naturalistic inquiry.* Newbury Park, CA: Sage Publications.

Martin, D.J. 2003. *Elementary science methods: A constructivist approach.* Belmont, CA: Wadsworth Publishing.

Mazer, A. 1991. *The salamander room.* Illustrated by S. Johnson, and L. Francher. New York, NY: Alfred A. Knopf.

McKeown-Ice, R. 2000. Environmental education in the United States: A survey of preservice teacher education programs. *Journal of Environmental Education* 32, no. 1: 4–11.

Mitchell, M.K., W.B. Stapp, and K. Bixby. 2000. *Field manual for water quality monitoring: An environmental education program for schools.* Dubuque, IA: Kendall/Hunt Publishing.

Monhardt, L., and R. Monhardt. 2006. Creating a context for the learning of science process skills through picture books. *Early Childhood Education Journal* 34, no. 1: 67–71.

National Research Council. 2007. *Taking science to school: Learning and teaching science in grades K-8.* Washington, DC: National Academy Press.

National Science Teachers Association (NSTA). 2003. Outstanding science trade books for students K-12. *Science and Children* 40, no. 6: 33–8.

Pratt-Serafini, K.J. 2000. *Salamander rain: A lake and pond journal.* Illustrated by K.J. Pratt-Serafini. Nevada City, CA: Dawn Publications.

Radlauer, R.S. 1987. *Molly goes hiking.* New York: Simon and Schuster.

Reid, A., and W. Scott. 2008. *Researching education and the environment: Retrospect and prospect.* London: Taylor and Francis.

Rice, D.C. 2002. Using trade books in teaching elementary science: Facts and fallacies. *The Reading Teacher* 55, no. 6: 552–65.

Sidman, J. 2005. *Song of the water boatman and other pond poems.* Illustrated by B. Prange. New York: Houghton Mifflin Company.

Sobel, D. 1998. *Mapmaking with children: Sense of place education for the elementary years.* Portsmouth, NH: Heinemann.

Sobel, D. 1999. *Beyond ecophobia: Reclaiming the heart in nature education.* Great Barrington, MA: Orion Society.

Trundle, K.C, and T.H. Troland. 2005. The moon in children's literature: How to avoid the pitfalls of introducing misconceptions when reading about the moon. *Science and Children* 42, no. 2: 40–2.

Watts, M.T. 1998. *Tree finder: A manual for the identification of trees by their leaves.* Rochester, NY: Nature Study Guild.

Wiesel, E. 1977. The holocaust as literary inspiration. In *Dimensions of the holocaust,* 4–19. Evanston, IL: Northwestern University Press.

Williams, N.L., and P.T. Bauer. 2006. Pathways to affective accountability: Selecting, locating and using children's books in elementary school classrooms. *Reading Teacher* 60, no. 1: 14–22.

Yolen, J. 1987. *Owl moon.* Illustrated by J. Schoenherr. New York, NY: Philomel Books.

Appendix.   Children's literature book quality considerations

Accurate content. The book's science/environmental content is scientifically accurate and consistent with the latest up-to-date information

Observation and factual information is clearly distinguished from opinions, judgments and inferences

Reality is clearly distinguished from fantasy. Sections of the book that are fiction or fantasy are clearly identified in the text and separated from sections that describe real observations or factual information

Generalizations are supported by evidence. The book provides clear accurate empirical evidence that clearly supports the generalizations that are advanced

Avoids over-simplification. The complexities of science concepts are presented in a developmentally appropriate way but are not over-simplified or 'dumbed down' to the point where the information becomes misleading

Includes relevant information. All information related to the scientific or ecological concepts are included rather than omitted

Realistic passage of time. The passage of time is portrayed in a realistic way in presenting the science concept or clearly distinguished from unrealistic circumstances

Avoids stereotypes and is free of gender, ethnic and socioeconomic bias. Provides a variety of positive role models for children to emulate

Avoids anthropomorphic statements through the imposition of human characteristics, behaviors or values on wildlife or natural objects

Emphasizes science process skills. Emphasizes people (especially children) involved in the process of science inquiry or actively participating in environmental action projects

Encourages student decision-making. The book portrays students conducting inquiry projects based on their own interests, developing their own procedures and self-monitoring their progress

General literature quality:
Logical and clear presentation of material
Appropriate content level for intended audience
Compatible text and illustrations
Illustrations that are accurate representations in size, color and scale
Appropriate size and format for intended age group
Well-organized layout that advances the text
Quality of binding, paper, reproduction and appropriate of typeface

Developing environmental agency and engagement through young people's fiction

Stephen Bigger[a] and Jean Webb[b]

[a]Department of Education, University of Worcester, Worcester, UK; [b]Department of Arts and Humanities, University of Worcester, Worcester, UK

This article explores the extent to which stories for young people encourage environmental engagement and a sense of agency. Our discussion is informed by the work of Paul Ricoeur (on hermeneutics and narrative), John Dewey (on primacy of experience) and John Macmurray (on personal agency in society). We understand fiction reading about place as hermeneutical, that is, interpreting understanding by combining what is read with what is experienced. We investigate this view through examples of four children's writers: Ernest Thompson Seton, Kenneth Grahame, Michelle Paver and Philip Pullman. We draw attention to notions of critical dialogue and active democratic citizenship. With a focus on the educational potential of this material for environmental discussions that lead to deeper understandings of place and environment, we examine whether the examples consistently encourage the belief that young people can become agents for change. We also consider whether the concept of *heroic resister* might encourage young people to overcome peer pressure and peer cultures that marginalize environmental activism. We conclude by recommending the focused discussion of fiction to promote environmental learning; and for writers to engage more with themes of environmental responsibility and agency.

Introduction

> There seems to be no reason to do a book unless there is a point to it, particularly reflecting what is happening in the world … I am not doing books for children. I am doing books for the next generation of adults. (Michael Foreman, author and illustrator)[1]

Our opening quotation exemplifies the view that some fiction writers deliberately seek to fuse entertainment with instruction in their works for young people. Peter Hunt's (1994, 3) introduction to children's literature equally claims that:

> It is arguably impossible for a children's book (especially one being read by a child) not to be educational or influential in some way; it cannot help but reflect an ideology and, by extension, didacticism. All books must teach something, and because the checks and balances available to the mature reader are missing in the child reader, the children's writer often feels obliged to supply them … Children's writers are, therefore, in a position of singular responsibility in transmitting cultural values, rather than simply 'telling a story'.

In this article, we focus on four writers for young people, two from the early twentieth century and two from the early twenty-first, whose works differently illustrate matters of personal agency and the potential of children's literature to foster environmental learning. The writers are: Ernest Thompson Seton (1860–1946), author of Canadian stories about wildlife and outdoor adventure; Kenneth Grahame (1859–1932), whose *The wind in the willows* depicts a romanticized English countryside; Michelle Paver (born 1960), whose stories engage the pre-scientific beliefs of Stone Age ancestors; and Philip Pullman (born 1946), whose trilogy *His dark materials* promotes a humanistic mission to improve our world. The first two were influential in different ways to earlier generations of children despite their opposite ideas about place; the contemporary writers each express distinct approaches to human responsibility for the physical and social world. Because we view stories as potentially empowering for young people, we also consider the extent to which the reading of stories stimulates attitude formation, behaviour change and personal agency in young readers with regard to social and environmental responsibility.

Fiction, education and experience of place

Bernard Crick, reporting on education for citizenship in England, articulates a widely held concern that the majority of its young people are not actively involved in community and democracy (Crick 2004; Qualifications and Curriculum Authority 1998). However, reducing serious issues of citizenship and democracy to textbooks and worksheets does not change mindsets. As Illich (1971) and Weston (1996) have argued, education is better viewed as a willed community activity rather than an enforced and disempowering government hegemony. Undeniably, most fiction is read by children outside of school, with teachers having a responsibility to encourage it. Recent environmental education research and scholarship suggest that broader underpinnings and dimensions are needed for our discussion. For example, regarding curriculum integration through place-based learning, McKenzie (2008) argues for the importance of intersubjectivity, and sees a role for literature to stimulate this; while Sharpe and Breunig (2009) advocate fostering 'pedagogical kinships', linking diverse areas of study – for example, the sciences and arts. The importance of youth agency to early adolescence (being able to 'take a stance') has been examined by Blanchet-Cohen (2009), while Davis (2009) reports agency for the environment as widely neglected in literature-based approaches to early childhood environmental education. Moreover, given that young people learn through experience, Barratt Hacking, Barratt, and Scott (2007) recommend engaging young people through participating in local environmental research and its representation in relevant forms, while Schusler et al. (2009) emphasize the importance of youth environmental action to engendering active forms of citizenship both immediately and in young people's future lives.

We link this integration of effort with the reading of fiction to encourage young people to see themselves as agents for change. This journal has already problematized the notion of 'critical pedagogy of place' (see Gruenewald 2008); readers trained to be critical link their encounter with the characters, plots, relationships, dilemmas and places presented and can thereby interrogate their stance on the environment. Fiction juxtaposes different opinions, requiring the reader to deliberate and decide, to take a stance – differently expressed, it is polyvocal and polyphonic, enabling dialogue and dialectic. Drawing on Ricoeur's philosophy, which maintains that one's understanding of the world is generated through dialogue, we note his comment that storytelling in:

the post-Enlightenment age has displayed ominous symptoms that point towards a collapse of the very capacity to tell stories and to listen to stories. The destruction of any genuine sense of tradition and authority in conjunction with the abusive prevalence of the will to dominate, exploit and manipulate the natural environment of humankind – and consequently human beings themselves – amounts to an *increase of forgetfulness*, especially that of the past sufferings of humankind, which is the ultimate cause of the impinging death of the capacity for storytelling. (Ricoeur 1995, 238, emphasis in original)

Pre-scientific societies used stories politically to understand their world and communicate values (Bigger 2009b); today, reading stories is largely recreational but also can establish an inner dialogue between reader and text about 'worlds' and values. Dialogue, as a confrontation with the 'other', introduces different perspectives and requires readers to reconsider attitudes and concepts enriched by new perspectives. Engagement with story can stimulate inner dialogue between reader and text; a discussion of the story with others offers broader perspectives, interpretations and applications. Räthzel and Uzzell's (2009) self-reflexive transformative work in environmental education fits well with this agenda.

Methodology: our approach to the texts

This is a part autoethnography, part conceptual inquiry. Autoethnography is the study by observation and discussion of a field of which the writer/researcher has intimate knowledge, normally as an insider. Hayano (1979/2001, 82) emphasizes that autoethnography involves 'ethnographic reflexivity', should include insiders, 'voices from within', and should benefit others. Commonly used currently for reflexivity on one's own arena of work, it has been called 'writing emotionally about our lives' and 'evocative autoethnography' (Ellis 1997, 116–39).

An autoethnographic dimension underpins the conceptual aspects of our inquiry in three ways. First, both authors are teachers and educators who use stories with young people. Webb studies children's literature as an academic subject; Bigger's interests are in values, ethics and empowerment. Bigger (2008) has used oral stories with troubled young people close to expulsion from school: the young listeners enter the narrative as themselves, interact with characters of their own creation, and construct a 'wise character' as an inner discussion partner. Second, our views and arguments are underpinned by our reading histories. Bigger had rural formative experiences, and research expertise in children's literature between 1930 and 1960, especially that written during 1939–1945. Webb had an urban childhood in the post-war slums of London's East End, and has a research interest in Victorian and Edwardian literature. For both, reading vibrant, sensitive stories brought other landscapes and other worlds into being beyond their localities. It has supported our belief in the importance of literature to opening up new worlds for young people, and to contributing to the development of their personal values and enthusiasms. We also study the childhood reading passions of adults, including teachers and parents; and we believe that young readers are developing similar understanding to influence their own world in these and other ways in the future. Third, we are each concerned with story writing: Webb through working with authors, Bigger as a writer of children's stories for school use. How story might be developed to meet twenty-first century challenges is therefore of academic and practical interest to us.

Drawing on the strategy of *deep reading* within the literary critical tradition, in this article we interrogate passages in stories that illustrate the issues under discussion. Reading a text demands *exegesis*, searching for *original* meaning and significance; and *hermeneutics*, that is, interpreting texts to comment on contemporary issues (Ricoeur 1974, 3). Actually there is an interplay, a continuum. Reader's minds are clouded with interpretation(s). So, although people approach texts exegetically, the ideas engage them as readers and are filtered through their understanding. Ricoeur (1990, 2004) explores how texts speak to contemporary circumstances and to people's lives and memories, partly rooting his work in Husserl's phenomenology (Husserl 1989; Kockelmans 1994), that is, as the study of how we experience everyday life. How people *experience* place is a phenomenological question (Payne 2003); how this experience is put into words, understood and explained is hermeneutical. Husserl's ontology sought to determine what might be considered 'real' about experiences, that is, the ability to see things *as they are* rather than *as we conceptualize them through words*. According to Ricoeur (1995, 3), all descriptions of phenomena draw on conceptual frameworks, so that Husserl's search for pure experiences *not mediated by dialogue* is idealistic. In effect, we slot experiences into broader understandings. Phenomenological 'reduction' (termed *bracketing out*) attempts to separate the 'real' from the 'constructed'. Payne (2003) regards problematization as helpful 'subversion' in environmental education, transforming the bracketing process into what he terms the 'post-phenomenological' in that ambiguities enrich understanding. He seeks a *philosophy of experience* in and through environmental education (Payne and Wattchow 2009). Reading about something is not experience of it: a *phenomenology of reading* is still to be written.

Followers of John Dewey link learning with experience and democracy, and emphasize experience as a learning mechanism (Dewey 1938/1963; McDermott 1981). For Dewey, philosophy must be true to experience, and tested by experience, so he resisted non-experiential theorizing (*Experience and nature*, in McDermott 1981, Part IV). Experience of *reading about the world* and experience *of the world* are separate but can interact in both directions. Keith and Pile (1993), writing on postmodern geography, make a similar point: there is an inner dialogue between the two. Reading fiction can be an interpretative tool to assess past experience, and to structure new experiences. This is the essence of hermeneutics.

We argue, following Ricoeur (1990), that human experience is *storied*. Whatever we experience slots into our life story and our community story, past (retrospective) and future (prospective), and is informed by stories that we have found meaningful. Understanding this web of interpretation (viz. hermeneutics) precedes phenomenological reduction: it analyses what has been bracketed out. Conversely, and proactively, fiction might equally 'story' experience. Brett's notion (2008, 150) of 'storied space' in postcolonial contexts (his example is of the land claims of indigenous nations in Australia and America) shows how myth and folk history structure place awareness, emphasizing that storying places might be done historically, culturally, spiritually, ethnographically and/or personally.

Early twentieth century writers: Seton and Grahame

We now present a focused exegesis of two writers from a century ago. Popular and influential in their day, they held diametrically opposed views about place and environment.

Ernest Thompson Seton

Seton was founder of the American scouts and mentor to Baden-Powell in Britain after writing a series of wilderness stories for boys first published in the *Ladies Home Journal* (Anderson 1986; Smith 2002; Seton-Barber, online). Seton's work encouraged boys into 'woodcraft' and championed the First Nations; he also encouraged similar guidance for girls (Beard and Beard 1915). His tales show respect for hunted animals through stories of their courage and bravery, contrasting this with the greed of the hunters. *Wild animals I have known* (1898), *Lives of the hunted* (1901) and *Animal heroes* (1905) present stories of particular animals in realistic contexts with love, danger and death represented. Detailed observations of animals are enhanced by his line drawings on most pages. *Animal heroes* is dedicated 'To the Preservation of Our Wild Creatures' and emphasizes 'our kinship with the animals by showing that in them we can find the virtues most admired in Man [*sic*]' (9) – that is, dignity, love-constancy, sagacity, obedience, fidelity, mother-love, physical force and love of liberty. He concluded:

> My chief motive, my most earnest underlying wish, has been to stop the extermination of harmless wild animals; not for their sakes, but for ours, firmly believing that each of our native wild creatures is in itself a precious heritage that we have no right to destroy or put beyond the reach of our children. (12)

Monarch, Seton's (1904) story which explores human cruelty to a grizzly cub, unfolds with a lifetime of the eponymous bear being hunted for no purpose, and finally ending his days angrily, imprisoned in a zoo. A different kind of story, *Two little savages* (Seton 1903) depicts two young white American boys experiencing the wilderness, learning woodcraft and pretending to be native American Indians. His explicit purpose is to show that outdoor adventure develops *character*. The outdoors is depicted as an adventure playground: hunting, tracking, wigwams, campfires and fighting are all a game, but with serious intention. Young people are encouraged to be enterprising and self-supporting with a strong sense of personal agency.

Kenneth Grahame

In contrast to Seton, *The wind in the willows* (1908/1983) celebrates the security and peace of an idealized English rural landscape and way of life symbolized by the riverbank. It also demonstrates a critical awareness of the threat of urbanization and underlying unrest in Edwardian England. Grahame depicts an idyllic riverbank world: orderly, controlled, satisfactorily divided into social classes from the rabbits up to aristocratic, unruly and uncontrolled Toad. Mole, the worker emerging from his 'dark' and 'lowly little house' which he has been industriously cleaning and decorating, luxuriates in his new found sense of freedom:

> It all seemed too good to be true. Hither and thither through the meadows he rambled busily, along the hedgerows. Across the copses, finding everywhere bird building, flowers budding, leaves thrusting – everything happy and progressive and occupied. (2)

Industry is related to the bountiful state of nature in springtime. Grahame creates a safe world for Mole as he explores and discovers the river:

> Never in his life had he seen a river before … The mole was bewitched, entranced, fascinated. By the side of the river he trotted as one trots, when very small, by the side of a man who holds one spellbound by exciting stories. (2)

This is a wholly new experience of life above ground for Mole, and the river itself becomes a quasi-narrator. Grahame combines the notions of the natural environment as enabling safe exploration, joy and emotional upliftment with story and narrative as means of experience, expression and education. For Mole, this discovery of life as bounteous nature is combined with emergence from a singular mode of being, for here in the riverbank he meets with the Water Rat. Ratty takes Mole into his care, educates him into the ways of river life, such as travelling by rowing boat, and welcomes him into the community of the riverbank. This is a complete pastoral idyll where environment, landscape and society are in harmony.

However, it is not without threat, as Ratty explains to Mole. Socially each group understands their position and the stratified set of relationships which enable life to continue harmoniously whilst each keeps to a sense of position and place. The riverbank is bounded by The Wild Wood, where weasels, foxes and rabbits live. Ratty admits that 'they are alright in a way' (6) and that he is friends with them and passes the time of day when they meet, but they are prone to 'break out'. There are subtle references here to the sense of unrest in the late nineteenth and early twentieth centuries. Peter Green (in Grahame 1983/1908, ix) writes of Grahame as a:

> traditionalist living in an era of increasingly rapid social change, when age-old customs – and worse, a largely stable class pyramid – were in imminent peril from the aftermath of the Industrial Revolution. Political violence was in the air.

Representative of a stable yeomanry, Badger is the symbol of safety, conservative wisdom and the values of Englishness. When lost in The Wild Wood, Mole finds sanctuary at Badger's door. Life can be ordered and controlled within the remit of nature but beyond is the industrial Wide World, typified by smoking chimney stacks. This is the ultimate threat to the ideal community as envisioned by Grahame and beyond the imagination or desire of Ratty and his friends:

> 'And beyond the Wild Wood again?' he [Mole] asked. 'Where it's all blue and dim, and one sees what may be hills or perhaps they mayn't, and something like the smoke of towns, or is it only cloud drift?'

> 'Beyond the Wild Wood comes the Wide World,' said the Rat. 'And that's something that doesn't matter, either to you or me. I've never been there, and I'm never going, nor you either, if you've got any sense at all. Don't ever refer to it again, please. Now then! Here's our backwater at last, where we are going to lunch.'

> Leaving the main stream, they now passed into what seemed at first like a landlocked lake. (Grahame 1908/1983, 6)

The riverbank community are happy to live their lives actually and metaphorically out of the mainstream and in a landlocked safe paradise. There is always a place of natural harbour and safety there.

In addition to the poetically veiled industrialization, the gentle life by the river is invaded by Toad and his uncontrolled passion for the motorcar. Toad states that the car 'is the future', perhaps belying Grahame's awareness of Futurism and the cult of the machine and speed which arose in Italy in the early twentieth century. Grahame was an eminent banker and widely travelled (Prince 1996, 313). Toad the aristocrat is easily tempted by 'adventure'. His irresponsibility almost threatens the downfall of his stately home, Toad Hall, but Badger (the yeomanry) and friends (the workers), stand united in the face of threat to the social order. Grahame's story promotes protection-ism for a pastoral idyll, and at its centre is the depiction of landscape. A decade later the social structure was severely disrupted by World War One and that pastoral idyll would never return. Furthermore, urbanization and the disappearance of the English rural landscape continued to the extent that in 1947 the Government instituted Green Belt legislation to protect the countryside.

The wind in the willows was a bestseller throughout much of the early and mid twentieth century. For young people reading it today, the class distinctions of rich – professional – ordinary citizen still work to some extent, although routes to richness are more varied. Being becalmed in a safe spot is more psychological than locational; the wide world now is less of a fear than a lure. Young readers might find sanctuary in the story; but intelligent discussion of its implications could engage deeper meanings and messages. It is the ordinary citizens who sort out problems; and it is compulsive rich toad who causes them. There are people like badger who take community responsibility; but it takes cooperation to enable all to work together effectively.

Contemporary fiction for young people: Paver and Pullman

In the two contemporary storywriters considered, the places they depict are not 'our world': readers enter imaginatively into fantasy worlds and are explicitly invited to reflect upon social, political and environmental values.

Michelle Paver

Paver's contemporary series *Chronicles of ancient darkness*, starting with *Wolf brother* (2004) features two courageous young people in the Stone Age. Paver explains, positively assessing Stone Age people, 'They were superb survivors. They knew all about the animals, trees, plants and rocks of the Forest. When they wanted something, they knew where to find it, or how to make it' (author's note, 243–4). Drawing on archaeology, she depicts life in the forest and carefully constructs a pre-scientific mythic mindset based on her familiarity with anthropology. The characters believe animals to have souls and that misdirected souls, whether human, animal or elemental, can become death-demanding demons. The young protagonist Torak, a magic-imbued redeemer, is charged with resetting the balance of humankind with nature which had been jeopardized to the point of destruction by human mania for power. Torak learns to understand and respect the natural environment, and those clans which live in harmony with nature. He has a close companion, a wolf and later a girl, Renn. These three are independent yet interdependent. Power is shared, and each shares an emotional bond with the other. The world of Torak is one where humankind, animals and the environment are locked into holistic cooperation for survival and fruition. Everything the Stone Age people have is made from the natural world around them. They must depend on their understanding of the characteristics of the natural materials from the forest, the rivers, plants, sea and animals in order to create what they need to survive. Nothing can be wasted, nor can they take from this world without giving thanks and acknowledging the spirit world for the gifts of food and tools which they will take and make from nature. A very necessary meal is shared with the spirits and with Wolf; the bones make tools. Humans and animals are locked into the need for cooperation. They each depend upon their environment which is variously threatened by fire, flood and sickness.

Disasters and pestilences emanate, we gradually learn, from human desire for power. In this Stone Age world, natural disasters threaten because there are characters who upset the spiritual balance by seeking the powers which lie in the moral darkness of the spiritual underworld. In contemporary society, we might view our world as environmentally out of balance because of desires for wealth, power and oil where no account is taken of the irrevocable damage which is being done. The story reveals that choices are as complex as human nature itself:

> It wasn't only the evil of the Soul-Eaters which Fin-Kedinn feared. It was that within Torak himself... 'Evil exists in us all, Torak' [he said], 'Some fight it. Some feed it. That's how its always been'. (Paver 2006, 135).

Paver's universe does not easily translate to our modern scientific world where magic and supernatural power are not taken literally. Yet, although individuals no longer 'save' the world, except in fiction, young people can discuss how, in small ways, they can overturn evil and work towards a better world.

Philip Pullman

The fantasy trilogy, *His dark materials* (1997–2000) rejects religious authoritarianism and, through the courage, determination and example of two young people, Lyra and Will, promotes demythologized rational responsibility. Central to this is the notion that one's mission to improve the world is a lifelong process involving hard work and study, finding and learning to rely upon one's authentic self, represented as an animal-shaped 'daemon'. In one of Pullman's worlds (Pullman 2000), live the Mulefa, strangely constructed intelligent creatures with trunks, no hands and four legs on a triangular skeleton. Their way of life is ecologically friendly, harmonious and cooperative. The health of their world depends on their protection and use of particular seedpods; oil derived from these gives them knowledge, and their use of the seeds as wheels helps the seeds to germinate:

> as more seed pods fell, they showed their children how to use them. And when the children were old enough they began to generate the *sraf* [viz. *conscious knowledge*] as well, and as they were big enough to ride on the wheels, the *sraf* came back with the oil and stayed with them. So they saw that they had to plant more seed-pod trees, for the sake of the oil, but the pods were so hard that they seldom germinated. And the first mulefa saw what they had to do to help the trees, which was to ride on the wheels and break them, so mulefa and seed-pods trees have always lived together. (2000, 237)

The ungainly mulefa ride upon the wheels which prepares the pods for germination, maintains the trees and receive understanding through the oil. The mulefa represent cooperation with others and synergy with their environment (or '*biophilia*', using Erich Fromm's – 1965 – terminology for a passion for life). They are set in contrast to the beautiful but destructive tulapi water birds, which destroy the pods and the homes of the mulefa (representing Fromm's *necrophilia*, a passion for death and destruction). The trilogy shows these two opposing motivations at war with each other. Pullman enables his characters to find answers, to find peace and to make decisions as to where their future lies; here also Lyra and Will discover their adult love, which will sustain them in their differing 'biophilic' futures. This is the world of *knowledge* of good and evil, a re-mythologizing of the biblical Garden of Eden myth in a positive direction, with a focus on *including* rather than *excluding*. Embedded in this creation of the imagination, this new public story to replace the old myth, are humanistic moral and ethical values which are directly pertinent to inclusive citizenship and environmental responsibility.

Agency and engagement: towards a hermeneutic of place

The four writers present different models of relationship of the young person with their surroundings – Seton shows the environment as an adventurous place; Grahame as a haven or hell; Paver as a vulnerable place and Pullman as a place requiring long-term cooperative custodianship. These are each part of the complexity of place, and experience of place, which young people encounter in coming to terms with the significance of place *for them*. Personal experience of places that readers bring to the act of reading are broad, having both individual and relational dimensions and associations, for example, affective responses coming from memories of friendships and pleasant activities. Reading about places offers vicarious experiences and invites readers to reflect and share. Reflection on experiences of different places with others stimulates awareness of other perspectives. An implied dialogue takes place between the writer and the reader, between the reader and the characters, and another between readers discussing the book. Discussion of broader issues can then develop.

Environmental responsibility is encouraged when young people are brought face-to-face with dilemmas and contested values, and encouraged to make up their own minds. Engaging with fiction is a mechanism for this and can offer young people different perspectives and role models to consider. Bakhtin frames this in terms of dialogicality, polyvocality and heteroglossa: the engagement with other generates meaning (Bakhtin 1979/2000; Gardiner 2002). A story may stimulate inner debate, which others can enrich. In considering what kinds of people the characters are and how appropriately they behave, readers can reconsider their own lives and the lives of others.

When writers communicate significant issues, their work has a moral purpose. By championing good over evil in stories, authors intend readers to identify with the good, encouraging them to become engaged resisters and activists. Understanding the range of characters in stories may help readers better to understand themselves, others and human nature in general. In the real world, people tend not to be heroes. Yet Zimbardo (2007, 444f; and see Bigger 2009a) praises 'heroic resisters' in an analysis of Milgram's 1971 Stanford Prison Experiment and more recently the Abu Ghraib and Guantanamo prisons. Only one of the experimental subjects resisted expectations of intimidation of prisoners. Nazi atrocities were made possible by lack of robust resistance by the whole population, so that heroic resistance by a minority could easily be crushed. Holocaust survivor Milgram tested just how far people would go under orders from 'authority' (Blass 2004), concluding that around three quarters of participants (within the covert simulation) were prepared to kill if ordered to do so, and felt absolved from responsibility when doing so. The exceptions, a minority, were the *resisters*. The implications of this for responsible action are profound.

Arendt coined the phrase 'banality of evil' to highlight when evil is *just a job* (Arendt 1994). Discussion of good and evil, using fiction as a stimulus and in this particular context, focusing on questions of environmental quality, is one way of preparing young people to become champions for good, generating the 'banality of heroism' (Zimbardo 2007, 483–7) – affirming that it is normal to stand up for good.

Heroes stand up firmly against social pressures, facing personal risk for reasons of principle. Young people's fiction is full of heroic resisters as role models for readers. There are also anti-heroes, from whom different lessons can come about selfishness, greed and power.

'Critical readers' interrogate texts they encounter within a meaningful personal philosophy. This includes ethical and moral reasoning, emotional understanding and a willingness to interact positively with 'the other' as part of their developing concept of self. *Critical studies* have the specialized meaning of working towards justice and human emancipation (see Horkheimer 1993). Macmurray (1957a, 1957b; Conford 1996) argued that people are defined by actions (the self as agent) and relationships (self in relation), that individual lives are intertwined with others. Stories illustrate 'self in relation' emphasizing that success is a group achievement, that people need to work together to solve problems. These paired concepts of *agent* and *in relation* encourages critical discussion about how to become active participants in the locality and community.

Unlike in fiction, the story of one's life is not fixed. Young people can *restory* their past and their potential futures through the understandings generated by reading. The notion of lives as stories or scripts has been used therapeutically in Transactional Analysis (Steiner 1990) and Narrative Therapy (White and Epston 1990). One's life story (the interpretation of the past and projection of possible futures) can be revised, so negative expectations can be restoried into positive aspirations. Critical engagements with stories can examine community, environment and place and thus enable young people to identify and readjust their own attitudes and behaviours. Fiction can speak hermeneutically to contemporary circumstances and change lives if insights are internalized. People experience place phenomenologically by being there, alongside others, and their insights from literature can help to make sense of their experiences. Dialogue and discussion interiorizes diverse points of view and challenges latent prejudices.

Reflections

Fiction for young people can provide one mechanism to encourage thought and understanding about the environment, especially when open dialogue and debate are encouraged. However, it is not a strategy without problems. We have selected four writers with interesting and different things to say about taking a positive stance about environmental involvement, but apart from farming and nature books for young children, environmental themes do not dominate the market. Readers will not automatically become environmentally educated by the fiction available, which has a mix of motives and messages. Fantasy is popular, but is detached from the real world. If readers are helped to *critique* whatever they read, or view on film or television, they can learn to approach literature in personal, social and ethical ways.

Storywriters start with the plot and characters, but issues are secondary. Nevertheless, the writer's values (positive and negative) are implied behind the story and are perhaps more powerful for not being explicit. The woodcraft values of Seton are explicit, and so in a more sophisticated way are Paver's and Pullman's redeemer agendas. The readers are assumed to be siding with the heroine/hero and not with the enemy, although a degree of ambiguity increases tension. Not all who seem friendly are so. Grahame's values within *The wind in the willows* are implicit, so the reader encounters them unexamined, on trust. The big wide world is threatening, progress is to be feared, the hero conserves the rural idyll. For young readers to develop criticality, a young reader may need some help to disagree with a story's omniscient and persuasive narrational voice.

Places gain significance through valued stories. That this significance can follow young people through to adulthood is evidenced by the popularity of societies devoted to the work of children's authors and visits to places associated with these stories and their writers: The E.T. Seton Institute and the Kenneth Grahame Society are examples, and there are many others, reflecting adults treasuring fiction they once read. This nostalgic comradeship of fellow readers focuses on storied places, environments made familiar through childhood reading.

Current and future writers of fiction for young people could address more explicitly the environmental issues challenging the twenty-first century, in ways which could similarly stay with young readers into adulthood and promote attitudinal and behaviour change. It is not the only way to affect attitudes, but story can be remembered when instruction is forgotten. Robert Owen, the idealist industrialist, for example, is well remembered in Britain and the US: New Lanark (Scotland) and New Harmony (Indiana) have become 'storied places' attracting visitors, in Scotland in association with the Scottish Wildlife Trust. One dramatized story associated with these places is of a future girl, Harmony, from the year 2200, explaining what environmental action had been necessary in the two centuries between us and her.[3]

For a fiction writer, creating believable characters is like adopting a family who live in the head. Each character has independence and is not a wooden puppet of the writer's ideas. What they do or say can be a blend of what real children have said and done but, coming up from the creative imagination, the results can be unexpected even to the writer. Bigger has written pedagogically for 8- to 12-year-olds in local schools stories about children in their own locality.[4] A dialogue-rich text can encourage the dialogic process we have discussed above, presenting various points of view. When they become adults, the young readers of today will have the very serious job of running their world and making responsible decisions. Their willingness and ability to be critical and dialogue with others are features of active citizenship, helping them to be strong-minded heroes who are forces for good.

Conclusions

We have argued that stories for young people can be part of the educative process of encouraging environmental engagement and a sense of agency. From Ricoeur we stress the process of applying texts to real concerns; from Dewey we emphasize how experience underpins understanding, and how experienced is 'storied'; from Macmurray we link personal agency to social responsibility; from Zimbardo we expand the notion of 'heroic resister'. We have argued that fiction texts require hermeneutic application, readers (with teacher support) using fiction texts to reflect upon their lives. Our four examples use story to discuss the environment, bringing out ideas of active involvement in woodcraft (Seton), conservation and heritage (Grahame), respect for life (Pavel), and cooperation within a non-authoritarian commonwealth (Pullman). We argue that fiction's concern for heroic action and the victory of good over evil supports the development of 'heroic resisters' who will fight actively against peer pressure, injustice, irresponsibility and unethical behaviour, and who can become agents for change. This is unlikely to happen without a process of discussion (hermeneutics) with peers and adults, which parents and teachers can provide. We note that fiction texts explicitly about the environment are rare, and hope for writers to engage with themes of environmental responsibility and agency. Our next task is to write and use such stories with children and study the outcomes.

Notes

1. From his notebook, displayed in the Truro Museum, 2007.
2. The outdoor theme has been developed in stories by others. Grey Owl (1935, 1937), a hunter-trapper environmentalist in Canada, featured wilderness and its animals. The scouting movement and the philosophically more cooperative Woodcraft Folk (Paul 1951) linked story to practice. Other writers have used Seton's technique of animal biography to good effect: Church (1941) with squirrels, Adams (1972) with rabbits and Horwood (1980) with moles.
3. http://www.newlanark.org/download/upload.46.rtf.
4. Some of these stories can be found at http://fiction4children.blogspot.com/2009/08/jake.html.

References

Adams, R. 1972. *Watership Down.* London: Rex Collings.
Anderson, H. 1986. *The chief: Ernest Thompson Seton and the changing west.* Allen: Texas A&M University Press.
Arendt, H. 1994. *Eichmann in Jerusalem: A report on the banality of evil.* New York: Penguin.
Bakhtin, M.M. 1979/2000. *The dialogic imagination. Four essays by M.M. Bakhtin.* Austin: University of Texas Press.
Barratt Hacking, E., R. Barratt, and W. Scott. 2007. Engaging children: Research issues around participation and environmental learning. *Environmental Education Research* 13, no. 4: 529–44.
Beard, L., and A.B. Beard. 1915. *An outdoor book for girls.* New York: Scribner.
Bigger, S. 2008. *Executive summary and evaluation report on the Swindon Youth Empowerment Programme.* http://eprints.worc.ac.uk/380.
Bigger, S. 2009a. Review of *The Lucifer effect: How good people turn evil*, by Philip Zimbardo, Rider/Ebury Press, 2007. *Journal of Beliefs and Values* 30, no. 1: 88–91.
Bigger, S. 2009b. Ethno-spirituality: A postcolonial problematic? *Alternation: Interdisciplinary Journal for the Study of the Arts and Humanities in Southern Africa*, Special Issue 3, 'Religion and diversity': 218–36.
Blanchet-Cohen, N. 2009. Taking a stance: Child agency across the dimensions of early adolescents' environmental involvement. *Environmental Education Research* 14, no. 3: 257–72.
Blass, T. 2004. *The man who shocked the world: The life and legacy of Stanley Milgram.* New York: Basic Books.
Brett, M.G. 2008. *Decolonizing God. The Bible in the Tides of Empire.* Sheffield: Phoenix Press.
Church, R. 1941. *A squirrel called Rufus.* London: Dent.
Conford, P. 1996. *The personal world: John Macmurray on self and society.* Edinburgh: Floris Books.
Crick, B. 2004. *Essays on citizenship.* London: Continuum.
Davis, J. 2009. Revealing the research 'hole' of early childhood education for sustainability: A preliminary survey of the literature. *Environmental Education Research* 15, no. 2: 227–41.
Dewey, J. 1938/1963. *Experience and education.* New York: Collier Books.
Ellis, C. 1997. Evocative autoethnography: Writing emotionally about our lives. In *Representation and the text: Re-framing the narrative voice*, ed. W. Tierney, and Y. Lincoln, 115–40. New York: SUNY Press.
Fromm, E. 1965. *The heart of man: Its genius for good and evil.* London: Routledge.

Gardiner, M. 2002. *Mikhail Bakhtin* (4 volume set). London: Sage.

Grahame, K. 1983/1908. *The wind in the willows.* Oxford: Oxford World Classics.

Grey Owl. 1935. *The adventures of Sajo and her beaver people.* London: Peter Davies.

Grey Owl. 1937. *The tree.* London: Peter Davies.

Gruenewald, D.A. 2008. The best of both worlds: A critical pedagogy of place. *Environmental Education Research* 14, no. 3: 308–24.

Hayano, D.M. 2001. Auto-ethnography: Paradigms, problems and prospects. In *Ethnography: Analysis and writing in ethnography*, ed. A. Bryman, vol. IV, 75–85. London: Sage.

Horkheimer, M. 1993. *Between philosophy and social science.* Cambridge, MA: MIT Press.

Horwood, W. 1980. *Duncton Wood.* London: Hamlyn.

Hunt, P. 1994. *An introduction to children's literature.* Oxford: Oxford University Press.

Husserl, E. 1989. *Ideas pertaining to a pure phenomenology and to a phenomenological philosophy.* Dordrecht: Kluwer.

Illich, I. 1971. *Deschooling society.* Harmondsworth: Penguin.

Keith, M., and S. Pile. 1993. *Place and the politics of identity.* New York: Routledge.

Kockelmans, J.J. 1994. *Edmund Husserl's phenomenology.* West Lafayette, IN: Purdue University Press.

McDermott, J.J. 1981. *The philosophy of John Dewey.* Chicago, IL: University of Chicago Press.

McKenzie M. 2008. The places of pedagogy: Or, what we can do with culture through intersubjective experiences. *Environmental Education Research* 14, no. 3: 361–73.

Macmurray, J. 1957a. *Persons in relation.* London: Faber.

Macmurray, J. 1957b. *Self as agent.* London: Faber.

Paul, L. 1951. *Angry young man.* London: Faber and Faber.

Paver, M. 2004. *Wolf brother.* London: Orion Children's Books.

Paver, M. 2006. *Soul eater.* London: Orion Children's Books.

Payne, P.G. 2003. Postphenomenological enquiry and living the environmental condition. *Canadian Journal of Environmental Education* 8: 169–91.

Payne, P.G., and B. Wattchow. 2009. Phenomenological deconstruction, slow pedagogy and the corporeal turn in wild environmental/outdoor education. *Canadian Journal of Environmental Education* 14: 15–32.

Prince, A. 1996. *Kenneth Grahame: An innocent in the wild wood.* London: Allison and Busby.

Pullman, P. 2000. *The amber spyglass.* London: David Fickling Books/ Scholastic.

Qualifications and Curriculum Authority. 1998. *Education for citizenship and the teaching of democracy in schools.* London: Qualifications and Curriculum Authority.

Räthzel, N., and D. Uzzell. 2009. Transformative environmental education: A collective rehearsal for reality *Environmental Education Research* 15, no. 3: 263–77.

Ricoeur, P. 1974. *The conflict of interpretations.* Evanston, IL: Northwestern University Press.

Ricoeur, P. 1990. *Time and narrative.* Vol. 2. Chicago, IL: University of Chicago Press.

Ricoeur, P. 1995. *Figuring the sacred: Religion, narrative and imagination.* Minneapolis, MN: Fortress Press.

Ricoeur, P. 2004. *Memory, history and forgetfulness.* Chicago, IL: University of Chicago Press.

Schusler, T.M., M.E. Krasny, S.J. Peters, and D.J. Decker. 2009. Developing citizens and communities through youth environmental action. *Environmental Education Research* 15, no. 1: 111–27.

Seton, E.T. 1898. *Wild animals I have known.* New York: Scribners.

Seton, E.T. 1901. *Lives of the hunted.* New York: Scribners.

Seton, E.T. 1903. *Two little savages: A book of American woodcraft for boys.* New York: Doubleday.

Seton, E.T. 1904. *Monarch: The big bear of Tallac.* London: Constable.

Seton, E.T. 1905. *Animal heroes.* New York: Scribners.

Seton-Barber, D. A short biography of Ernest Thompson Seton. *The Ernest Thompson Seton Institute.* http://www.etsetoninstitute.org/biobydee.htm.

Sharpe, E., and M. Breunig. 2009. Sustaining environmental pedagogy in times of educational conservatism: A case study of integrated curriculum programs. *Environmental Education Research* 15, no. 3: 299–313.

Smith, M.K. 2002. Ernest Thompson Seton and woodcraft. *Encyclopedia of Informal Education.* http://www.infed.org/thinkers/seton.htm.

Steiner, C.M. 1990. *Scripts people live: Transactional analysis of life scripts.* New York: Grove Press.

Weston, A. 1996. De-schooling environmental education. *Canadian Journal of Environmental Education* 1: 35–46.

White, M., and D. Epston. 1990. *Narrative means to therapeutic ends.* New York: W.W. Norton.

Zimbardo, P. 2007. *The Lucifer effect: How good people turn evil.* London: Rider.

The Lord of the Rings – a *mythos* applicable in unsustainable times?

Alun Morgan

Graduate School of Education, University of Exeter, Exeter, UK

This article explores the relevance of J.R.R. Tolkien's *The Lord of the Rings* to environmental education and contemporary concerns about social and environmental injustices. It presents an account of the relationship between Tolkien's environmental biography and those aspects of the story that highlight the connection between his personal experiential *informal* environmental education learning journey in the real world and his imaginative 'sub-creation'. *The Lord of the Rings* is also considered a work of 'fantasy' or 'speculative fiction' that holds the potential to re-enchant the world by engaging the *mythopoetic* imagination, through a focus on its treatment of place, character and environmental ethics. In particular, it is argued that the story implicitly promotes, and is grounded in, a 'Creation-centred' ethic of stewardship. The article concludes with a discussion of pedagogical considerations on the continuing importance of the story as an inspirational work of literature, and its potential and limits as a source of inspiration for those engaged in challenging social and environmental injustices.

Introduction

J.R.R. Tolkien's *The Lord of the Rings* (*LOTR*) is an epic tale set in the mythological realm of Middle-earth. Unfolding across a vast canvas of environmental and societal degradations and injustices wrought by the industrial–militaristic complex of the Dark Lord Sauron and his servants, the story traces the ultimately successful resistance offered by the seemingly inconsequential Hobbits and their allies. Whilst a self-contained work of fiction set within a fabulous realm and age, the 'Battle for Middle-earth' provides a host of themes relevant – or as Tolkien would have had it, 'applicable' – to the contemporary world, and would therefore seem a fruitful topic for exploration in terms of environmental education.

The story has represented a cultural phenomenon for nearly 50 years and has had a global impact, particularly in recent years with the highly acclaimed and popular adaptation for the screen by Peter Jackson (2001, 2002, 2003). But the films cannot be the only explanation – the books had already been translated into over 30 languages decades before the films were released. There is something, or rather, many things, about *LOTR* and the whole Middle-earth *Legendarium* which speak to people, young and old, from a wide variety of cultural backgrounds. In particular, this paper argues that the story has had, and crucially continues to have, a significant impact upon the environmental and moral imaginaries of many of its readers. Whilst coined in the popular technical sense some decades after publication, it would seem appropriate to use the term 'sustainability' in describing some key themes (social, economic and environmental) which emerge in *LOTR*. Furthermore, the story, it will be argued, possesses significant pedagogical potential, albeit implicit in nature, and more likely to be efficacious through processes associated with 'self-education', autodidacticism or 'free choice' learning than with formal educational approaches.

Tolkien was at pains to deny both the allegorical and topical nature of his imagined world. Yet he acknowledged the potential 'applicability' of the story in the minds, and to the lived experience, of readers (Tolkien 2007, xxvi). In environmental education terms, applicability can be discerned both in terms of its powerful evocation of environments and places; and more normatively in the implicit environmental and social justice messages contained within the narrative. One can, for example, discern messages concerning 'right'/'just' or 'wrong'/'unjust' ways to behave in relation to the environment and other 'people' (be they human or otherwise). The first flush of real popularity only occurred when the story was adopted by the counter-cultural movement in the 1960s, to whom it spoke directly in an era of Vietnam, Civil Rights and a proto-environmental movement. The story was similarly adopted by protestors within the Soviet Bloc in the 1980s (Curry 1998). Whilst the films in part account for the current renewed popularity, on a deeper level it may also speak of a renewed applicability expected of *LOTR* to the globalized and unsustainable world of today.

An ecocritical approach informed by environmental education research

The analysis offered here follows that of ecocriticism since it is concerned with exploring *LOTR* in terms of 'issues of environmental imagining and representation… place as a fundamental dimension of both art and lived experience… and strong ethical and/or political commitment' (Buell 2005, viii–ix). Ecocriticism has emerged from, and is still broadly allied to, literary criticism. It is particularly concerned with the relationship between literature and the environment although the focus of the field has broadened recently to consider other cultural artefacts such as film and media. What makes ecocriticism an innovative and important analytical field is its attempt 'to evaluate texts and ideas in terms of their coherence and usefulness as responses to environmental crisis' (Kerridge 1998, 5). As might be expected given the inherent complexity of both the environmental movement and the field of literary criticism from which it has emerged, ecocriticism offers more of a broad research orientation than a prescriptive methodology. Consequently, the field is characterized by many alternative and sometimes antagonistic approaches and 'readings'.

LOTR is a large work and offers a range of options for ecocriticism. For example, one might simply wish to critically evaluate the 'science' implicit in a narrative – for example, was *LOTR* based on now outdated understandings of succession and 'steady state' ecosystems? Alternatively, one might choose to focus on the rhetorical strategies and 'environmental tropes' such as 'pollution', 'wilderness', 'pastoral' or 'apocalypse' employed by the author; and to what effect, whether intentional or otherwise (Garrard 2004). From a more overtly ecofeminist reading, one might critically evaluate the text in terms of its gendered treatment of character and environment and the relationship between them. Thus for some ecofeminists, *LOTR* represents a problematic work given the relative absence of female characters and the emphasis on 'masculine' settings such as 'wilderness' (as a 'macho' context for challenge and adventure) and 'the battlefield' although certain male characters (such as the Elves and Ents) and settings (such as Rivendell and Lothlórien) do exhibit decidedly feminine traits (for a further exploration of this theme, see Rawls 1984).

Whilst acknowledging the value of pursuing such ecocritical trajectories, this article adopts a more focused and positive approach to its analysis. I seek to evaluate the narrative in terms of its relevance to contemporary environmental debates as a moralistic tale that Dickerson and Evans (2006, xvi) have argued 'provides a deep and complex ecological vision incorporating many elements and spanning a broad spectrum of approaches, including positions compatible with both conservation and preservation in modern environmentalism'. As such the paper follows the admirable ecocritical analyses undertaken by Curry (1998) and Dickerson and Evans (2006) and my indebtedness to these works must be acknowledged. However, the paper extends the observations of these and other authors by drawing on concepts and lenses from environmental education research (such as on place attachment, significant life experiences, ecobiography and ecospirituality) to shed further light on how the book came to be written in terms of the significance of Tolkien's own personal *informal* environmental education journey; and why the story still has such a powerful reaction in readers including, but not exclusively, children. As such it represents a case study of sorts that attempts to integrate several significant themes in environmental education using an ecocritical engagement with *LOTR* as its focus.

It is appropriate at this point to acknowledge myself as one such reader who has had a powerful yet intermittent engagement with the work both in adolescence and, in preparation of this piece, adulthood – a period spanning two decades. This engagement presents several issues that must be acknowledged and addressed from the outset. First, an ecocritical approach necessarily involves the reflexive *subjective* engagement of *an* ecocritic (myself in this instance) with a literary text and other related materials. The relationship between reader and text can hardly be otherwise and, consequently, a claim to objectivity is never possible in such an analysis. Actually, as noted by Myhill (2007), to engage subjectively in reading a text or story is to:

> participate in creative transformations of words to ideas, understanding and imaginative engagement. It is a constructive endeavour of making personal meaning from text, not one of passively absorbing a message coded by the author of the text. Moreover, reading makes use of our social, moral and cultural understanding. (53)

Second, what follows in the analysis isn't based on primary research (other, that is, than an important personal engagement with the work and other sources, as considered in the next section). No attempt has been made to obtain say, through questionnaire, interview, reflective journal or other empirical methods, firsthand reports from current or recent readers of *LOTR* since these are not requirements for undertaking ecocriticism, as understood or practised here. Furthermore, such an approach would be too time-constrained to allow respondents to report reflexively on the impact *LOTR* has had on them over an extended period of their lifetime – 20 years in the case of the present author – which represents an important theme of this article. Occasionally though first person voices are presented from secondary sources precisely because they demonstrate such a more reflexive and lifelong engagement with the story.

Third, the purpose of this inquiry has not been to provide any detailed pedagogical recommendations. This is not to suggest that more concrete educational planning isn't possible or desirable, merely that it is beyond the scope of the article. This reticence

is for two reasons. Firstly, as an educator with a background in geographical education, environmental education and education for sustainable development, I do not
have the requisite experience to do this work justice unlike colleagues with expertise
in the teaching of literature. Secondly, there is a complex relationship between the
educative/didactic vis-à-vis entertainment purposes and processes of storytelling.
Sometimes this can be synergistic, a principle exploited in 'edutainment'; sometimes
it can prove antagonistic leading to disengagement and resistance on the part of learners. Added to this is the simple fact that it would be extremely challenging to handle
a work of such length within the confines of the formal curriculum or typical informal
educational programmes. Furthermore, external motivators and frameworks can prove
inimical to the processes through which stories operate best autodidactically through
'free choice' or 'self-learning'. You cannot, neither should not, *make* people read
LOTR, dictate their engagement with it, nor expect them to be edified by it.

This reader and writer

Given the preceding discussion concerning the importance of personal engagement to
ecocritical methods, it is important to outline some relevant personal background. My
first encounter with the book was somewhat accidental or serendipitous. Nearly 25
years ago I was mesmerized by the innovative although flawed Bakshi (1978)
animated adaptation which inspired me to go to the original source. I must admit that
as an undergraduate merely seeking distraction I found the written text hard going on
occasion and very nearly gave up. Similarly, my personal re-engagement with *LOTR*
was first and foremost precipitated by Jackson's films. The not inconsiderable effort
needed to re-read the book was partly sustained by the desire to respond to the call for
papers which gave rise to this special issue of *Environmental Education Research*
(i.e., to write this article). However, as I found the efforts personally worthwhile I can
also now attest to the potential for profound and unexpected personal learning to arise
from such seemingly superficial extrinsic motivations.

I note too that the informal learning I experienced through reading *LOTR* as a
callow youth was qualitatively inferior to the more recent given the intervening
quarter-century of lived experience and maturing of my mythopoetic imagination (see
below). The reflexively ecocritical engagement required in order to write this article
was also significant for making this second encounter a more meaningful learning
experience. For example, apart from the benefits of engaging in reflexive intellectual
work, my own enjoyment of *LOTR* has also been greatly enhanced by significant spells
in the outdoors in the kinds of places (moorland, woodland, mountain, marsh) that
Tolkien describes so well. I have 'felt' transported to Middle-earth because the various
environments (but thankfully not all) felt familiar. Indeed, my second encounter
proved much richer than the first partly because I also now have a wealth of specifically *environmental* experiences upon which to draw after nearly 20 years as a
geographical and environmental educator.

In addition to such generic environmental experiences, I have developed a deeply
personal and meaningful connection to the story as a consequence of discovering
some significant coincidences between Tolkien's and my own 'environmental biography' in the course of researching this article. Significant coincidences include
Cannock Chase and Great Bridgeford, Birmingham and Moseley, the Worcestershire
Landscape and the Alps. The significance of these particular places for Tolkien is
detailed below but it suffices to say that these are all places that I too have significant

lived experience of and very close attachment to. It was also personally gratifying to learn that Tolkien chose Welsh as the basis of one of his Elvish languages thanks to its beauty since this is my heritage (although I am currently a non-Welsh speaker). Finally, it is important to recognize a particular affinity I have come to feel for the story which is informed by an understanding of Tolkien's Creation-centred spirituality and focus upon mythology and mythopoetics which represent key themes I explored in my doctoral thesis (Morgan 2007).

A fairy story for children or an adult *mythos*? The lifelong educational potential of *The Lord of the Rings*

LOTR is undoubtedly popular with children and young adults including readers as young as 10, and it is often to be found in school libraries (including Primary) and in the 'children' and 'adolescent' sections of bookshops. In this respect, *LOTR* may be legitimately treated as 'children's literature' since children read it. However, whilst originally conceived as a sequel to *The Hobbit* (undisputedly a children's story), *LOTR* quickly took on a darker and more adult tone (Tolkien, Letter 34, cited in Carpenter 2006, 41) and Tolkien actually thought it 'quite unfit for children' (Tolkien, Letter 124, cited in Carpenter 2006, 136). Although he was pleased to hear that children enjoyed aspects of the story, it concerned him that they would encounter the work 'too early' when 'they must fail to understand most of it' (Tolkien, Letter 234, cited in Carpenter 2006, 310) and then wouldn't bother to read it again when they *were* 'ready'. He needn't have worried since many who encountered the book at a young age have sustained a lifelong engagement with it, often rereading it repeatedly throughout their youth and into adulthood; or coming to it again with the film versions, or when, as a parent, they choose to share it with *their* children. This desire to revisit Middle-earth could be seen as mere nostalgia and a desire to recapture lost youth. Yet, an alternative explanation can be proffered – people find that they 'grow' with the story as they mature to the extent that the 'child' vis-à-vis 'adult' readings, whilst equally legitimate, may be very different. Consider this father's reflections on re-reading the *LOTR* to his nine-year old son:

> For a long and magical run of nights, I journeyed together with my son through the great three-volumed world of Middle-earth … But Sean did not hear the same book as the one I read to him.

> What he discovered was the same book I had discovered that sleepless night in the land of Long Ago and Far Away – the single best adventure story ever written. As an adult, however, I found that during my long absence it had transformed into something else entirely. It was now the saddest book in the world … This is a book sad with wisdom. It moved me in ways my son could not feel. (Swanwick 2003, 35–7)

Thus *LOTR* represents a work which arguably straddles 'children's', 'adolescent'/ 'young-adult' or 'adult' literature. Consequently, this article wishes to extend the horizons within which *LOTR* may be considered appropriate as a potential vehicle for environmental education from childhood to 'lifelong learning', and to direct consideration to its varying significance at different phases of the lifespan.

The fact remains, however, that many consider *LOTR* as juvenile (see Moorcock 2004). Why is this? And how can it be refuted? In answer to the first question, the most likely explanation is that, as a work of 'fantasy', it is considered obviously '*for* children'. Tolkien happily acknowledged the former contention whilst vehemently denying the latter. He wanted to rehabilitate the fairytale and 'myth' as an adult genre (Tolkien, Letters 159 and 181, cited in Carpenter 2006, 209, 232–3). Of course Tolkien's concern was not with childish 'fairies' in the Victorian nursery sense but with adventures and explorations into the 'Perilous Realm of *Faërie*' and its 'shadowy marches' (Tolkien 2001). *LOTR* should properly be considered a work of 'speculative fiction' which imaginatively explores a fantastical alternative 'world'. Such works, both in their production and consumption, exercise what has been referred to as the mythopoetic imagination because they involve 'a different approach to reality, an alternative technique for apprehending and coping with existence. It is not anti-rational but para-rational; not realistic, but surrealistic, superrealistic; a heightening of reality' (Le Guinn, cited in Hunt 2003, 10). Rather than using our default workaday cognitive capacities, such literature stretches us intellectually, stimulates the imagination, and engages our creativity. From such a perspective the:

> interface between children's literature and adult fantasy is a fruitful continuum that has led many younger readers into adult fantasy and that has helped preserve childhood's pure delight in imagination well into adulthood for many readers and writers of fantasy. (Mathews 2002, 17–18)

For this reason the comic fantasy *Discworld* series author, Terry Pratchett, speaking in defence of Tolkien specifically and fantasy generally, says:

> that fantasy is one of the best things a growing mind can read because it's kind of like an exercise bike for the brain. It doesn't actually take you anywhere but it really tones up the muscles that will. (Pratchett in the documentary *Ringers* [Cardova 2005])

A recognition of the educational value, as opposed to error, of engaging the mythopoetic imagination through fantasy may be extended to a consideration of the personal and cultural importance of 'myths'. According to Armstrong (2001), humanity has evolved two modes of thinking, *logos* and *mythos*: the former is concerned with application of rationality to solve practical problems and gain knowledge about the phenomenal world; the latter, conversely, is concerned with the search for meaning in the face of the existential, psychological and metaphysical dimensions of life. Both modes are considered important and complementary. However, with the advent of Enlightenment and Modernity, the championing of *logos*-centric rationalities has been at the expense of the devaluation of *mythos*-centric possibilities. The world has consequently become disenchanted.

Turning the popular understanding of 'myth' as untruth on its head, 'other world' genres and 'mythic' narratives are concerned with deep 'truths' about our existential 'being-in-this-world' which a prosaic instrumental rationality obscures: 'It was in fairy-stories that I first divined the potency of the words, and the wonder of things, such as stone, and wood, and iron; and tree, and grass; house and fire; bread and wine' (Tolkien 2001, 60). This provides a very strong case for using fantasy literature of 'other worlds' with young people (Hunt and Lenz 2003) and to look for opportunities to exercise the mythopoetic imagination across and beyond the curriculum by both learners and teachers (Leonard and Willis 2008). This can also be seen as crucial concern of certain discourses within environmental education and education for sustainable development which see such mythic re-enchantment of the world as the precursor to developing a deep affection for, and ethic of care and reverence towards, the environment (see Abrams 1997; Dyer and Hodgson 2003). In support of this perspective, Armstrong (2005, 143) argues that the 'mythic' dimension of human experience is needed:

> to see beyond our immediate requirements, and enable us to experience a transcendent value that challenges our solipsistic selfishness. We need myths that help us to venerate the earth as sacred once again, instead of merely using it as a resource.

She further argues that contemporary western society can re-engage with this mythic dimension through art, music and literature in addition to religious or spiritual practice.

Tolkien clearly shared this view. He agreed with the assertion that fantasy literature is 'escapist' but argued that it assists the 'good escape of the prisoner' *into* reality, rather than the 'flight of the deserter' from it (Tolkien 2001). Such is an escape from familiarity borne of possessiveness and appropriation (Tolkien 2001) into 'wonder' which works by leading us out of 'the drab blur of triteness or familiarity... [to the freedom to see] things as we are (or were) mean to see them – as things apart from ourselves' (58). Thinking specifically in environmental education terms, *LOTR*:

> serves to reintroduce us to the wonders and beauties of the natural world around us, which we tend to accept rather than to wonder at as legitimate Things of Marvel. He [Tolkien] also turns to the materials from which fantasy is made – materials which lie all around us – showing how fantasy enlarges and underscores our appreciation of the real world, the Primary World. (Carter 2003, 75)

For Tolkien fantasy, myth and the fairy tale allow the satisfaction of 'primordial human desires': 'One of these desires is to survey the depths of space and time. Another is ... to hold communion with other living things' (Tolkien 2001, 13). These require the exercise of childlike (as opposed to childish) qualities on the part of both creator and receiver such as 'the joy of invention and discovery, the wonder at variety and ingenuity – the fresh view of the different, the other' (Hunt 2003, 4). However, the aim is clearly not to arrest the 'learner' in infantilism; nor is it restricted to the earliest phases of lifelong learning. According to Dickerson and Evans (2006), 'Tolkien suggests that the shaping of the imagination paradoxically involves both the development of maturity and the recapture of a childlike understanding of the world' (256). In Tolkien's own words:

> Children are meant to grow up, and not to become Peter Pan's. Not to lose innocence and wonder; but to proceed on the appointed journey: upon which it is certainly not better to travel hopefully than to arrive. But it is one of the lessons of fairy (if we can speak of the lessons of things that do not lecture) that on callow, lumpish, and selfish youth peril, sorrow, and the shadow of death can bestow dignity, and even sometimes wisdom. (Tolkien 2001, 45)

Thus, Tolkien thought in terms of a lifelong journey of personal (moral and spiritual) growth towards wisdom which he hoped to facilitate through his works of fiction. Indeed, part of *LOTR's* 'enduring appeal [is] because nearly every member of the Company undergoes immense moral and spiritual growth' (Wood 2003, 84) with which readers can identify. In this sense, *LOTR* could be seen as a *Bildungsroman*, a story detailing the journey to maturation of its chief protagonists. But as has already been noted it might not be the same story at all life-phases. For its part, *LOTR* explores such existential themes as mortality, loss, sacrifice and proper conduct in the face of despair. These are the 'sad' dimensions that the maturing mind is more likely to fore-ground in the story, and from which wisdom ensues; and which Tolkien feared would be lost on 'immature' or inexperienced minds. Consequently, *LOTR is* as much an adult as a children's story and it is the contention of this paper that it holds great poten-tial in terms of environmental education for *both* young *and* older readers, a point attested to by the legion of Tolkien fans of all ages who acknowledge the work as having transformed them deeply and for the better (the *Ringers* documentary contains numerous such *vox pop* admissions). The efficacy of the tale in this respect is signifi-cantly a consequence of the particular (environmental) biography of the author, to which we now turn.

Midland-Earth and beyond: Tolkien's formative years

> If you really want to know what Middle-earth is based on, it's my wonder and delight in the earth as it is, particularly the natural earth. (Tolkien cited in Carter 2003, 2)

One crucial dimension or task of literary criticism is 'to question who wrote the book, why they wrote it, and what values and opinions are embedded in the book' (Myhill 2007, 54). In order to understand how the imaginative world of Middle-earth was created, it is helpful to consider the 'leaf mould' of memories (Tolkien, Letter 324, cited in Carpenter 2006, 409) from which Tolkien drew inspiration, his own 'environ-mental education' and ecobiography (Doerr 2004). Tolkien exhibited a very strong 'Place Attachment' (Altman and Low 1992) to, and 'Place Identity' (Proshansky, Fabian, and Kaminoff 1995) with, the 'English Midlands'. This strong sense, or need, for rootedness through both familial and geographical ties was a consequence of tumultuous events in his early life which largely account for the story's emphasis on loss and recovery (Mathews 2002). He lost both parents at an early age and was never settled for long. Yet, Tolkien's strong regional identity wasn't merely a self-conscious and romantic identification with a nebulous and socially constructed 'Imagined Community' (Anderson 1991). His formative years were largely spent in Birmingham and the surrounding countryside where he developed a strong experien-tially based connection to the landscapes, ecology and people. He had, in environ-mental education research terms, 'significant life experiences' (Chawla 1992, 1999, 2002), both positive and negative, which greatly informed the world of Middle-earth he created.

Invariably his times in the countryside were idyllic and contrasted strongly with his enforced periods in the rapidly industrializing and urbanizing city. From 1896 to 1900, the Tolkiens' famously moved to the hamlet of Sarehole in the Cole Valley just outside the city, which instilled a deep and abiding love of the countryside and nature, and trees in particular. He reflected on these four years as being 'the longest seeming and most formative part of my life' (cited in Carpenter 2002, 42). Some notable features and events associated with this period provided the inspiration for 'the Shire', the idyllic if somewhat parochial home of the Hobbits. Thus Sarehole Mill, the local fords and the 'wonderful dell with flowers' (Tolkien cited in Ezard 1991) reappear as Sandyman's Mill, the Ford of Bruinen, and a host of places such as the Old Forest, Fangorn Forest and the Midgewater Marshes (Blackham 2006). The garden party to celebrate Queen Victoria's jubilee in 1897 provided the likely inspiration for 'the Long-expected Party' (Tolkien 2007, 35–40). Similarly, Tolkien's memory of being chased by a farmer for picking mushrooms is projected onto Frodo (Tolkien 2007, 122). The doors of local forges were horseshoe-shaped which might have provided the inspiration for the round hobbit doors (Blackham 2006); and he adopted the local term for cotton wool – 'gamgee' – as Samwise's surname. Through this early biography, Tolkien was able create an imaginary place – the Shire – which has had such enduring appeal as 'homely' because he was effectively writing about the places he himself called home and cared deeply about. Mathews has characterized *LOTR* as a work concerned with the 'struggle to survive and recover from loss… of geographical, social, political, and moral systems' (Mathews 2002, 61). All are relevant in terms of the current discussion of the relevance of *LOTR* to sustainability although perhaps the first – geographical – is particularly pertinent. One might say that on one level *LOTR* mythically recounts the struggle for physical *and* psychological survival and recovery of 'place' or vibrant, locally distinctive and convivial places in the face of modern processes advancing both diminished generic 'non-places' (Augé 1995) and geo-social anomie or 'placelessness' (Relph 1974).

While the 'significant life experience' literature is usually focused on positive experiences, it should also be noted that significance can accrue from negative experiences of place. Middle-earth is also replete with awesome, fearful and/or degraded landscapes which can also be accounted for in terms of Tolkien's environmental biography. *The scouring of the Shire* (Tolkien 2007, 1306–35) tells of its degradation which paralleled that observed by Tolkien as the metropolis inexorably encroached upon Sarehole: 'The country in which I lived in childhood was being shabbily destroyed before I was ten, in the days when motor-cars were rare objects (I had never seen one) and men were still building the suburban railways' (xxvi–xxvii). The young Tolkien once observed that a favourite willow had been cut down in a seemingly wanton act: 'They didn't do anything with it: the log just lay there. I never forgot that' (cited in Carpenter 2002, 39). Indeed he didn't and the episode is likely to have been the inspiration for both Treebeard's description of the behaviour of the Isengarders: 'Some of the trees they just cut down and leave to rot – orc mischief that' (Tolkien 2007, 617); and the destruction of the party tree:

> 'They've cut it down!' cried Sam. 'They've cut down the Party Tree!' He pointed to where the tree had stood under which Bilbo had made his Farewell Speech. It was lying lopped and dead in the field. As if this was the last straw Sam burst into tears. (Tolkien 2007, 1330)

Sarehole Mill presented the young Tolkien with a vision of large-scale mechanization which he took to be out of place in the landscape. It reappears as a polluting presence as part of Sharkey's (aka Saruman) 'redeveloped' and exploited Shire. Tolkien's less than welcome spells in Birmingham presented him with ample inspiration for scenes of hubris and mal-development associated with the emerging machine age. He encountered large, ornate towering buildings which no doubt provided inspiration for the many towers which populate Middle-earth. Tolkien would also have drawn on his experiences of the metallurgical and extractive industries at various places within the city and surrounding Black Country for the industrialization of Isengard:

> Once it had been green and filled with avenues, and groves of fruitful trees, watered by streams that flowed from the mountains to a lake. But no green things grew there in the latter days of Saruman. The roads were all paved with stone-flags, dark and hard; and

beside their border instead of trees there marched long lines of pillars, some of marble, some of copper and of iron, joined by heavy chains.

Many houses there were … so that all the open circle was overlooked by countless windows and dark doors. Thousands could dwell there, workers, servants, slaves, and warriors … The plain, too, was bored and delved. Shafts were driven deep into the ground … Iron wheels revolved there endlessly, and hammers thudded. At night plumes of vapour steamed from the vents, lit from beneath with red light, or blue, or venomous green. (Tolkien 2007, 723–4)

Or compare the following fictional but realistic description of the Black Country in Francis Brett Young's *Far forest* –

a sunless, treeless waste, within a crescent of mournful hills from whose summits a canopy of eternal smoke was suspended above a slagged desert, its dead surface only variegated by… mounds on which the mineral and metallic waste of these [industrial activities] had been tipped, as on gigantic middens; by drowned clay-pits and sullen canals whose surface appropriately reflected an apocalyptic sky. (Cited in Hooke 2006, 229)

– with:

here neither spring nor summer would ever come again. Here nothing lived, not even the leprous growths that feed on rottenness. The gasping pools were choked with ash and crawling muds, sickly white and grey, as if the mountains had vomited the filth of their entrails upon the lands about. High mounds of crushed and powdered rock, great cones of earth fire-blasted and poison-stained, stood like an obscene graveyard in endless rows, slowly revealed in the reluctant light. They had come to the desolation that lay before Mordor: the lasting monument to the dark labour of its slaves that should endure when all their purposes were made void; a land defiled, diseased beyond all healing – unless the Great Sea should enter in and wash it with oblivion. 'I feel sick,' said Sam. Frodo did not speak. (Tolkien 2007, 825)

But for biographical inspirations for the more awesome and horrific events and landscapes one must also look to Tolkien's 'significant life experiences' beyond the Midlands and Britain. Before he left South Africa (where he was born), he was bitten by a tarantula, an experience which possibly provides the origins of Shelob, one of his most fearsome creatures. In 1911, at the age of 17, Tolkien joined family friends on a trip to the Swiss Alps which enabled him to write evocatively about the Fellowship's abortive attempt to cross over Caradhras. Surely the grimmest part of Tolkien's younger life was spent in the trenches of the Somme. Here, as Tolkien himself admitted (Letter 226, cited in Carpenter 2006, 303), are the origins of the horrors of the Dead Marshes. He was spared the fate of so many of his friends through contracting 'trench fever' which was a debilitating and recurring disease, an experience which allowed him to write with some authority on the progressive physical, emotional and even spiritual debilitations endured by Frodo as Ring Bearer.

By 1917, when Tolkien began writing the tales that would evolve into his whole *Legendarium* whilst convalescing in Great Haywood in Staffordshire (close to where he had undergone his basic training in Cannock Chase), he had had the key experiences which would provide the 'leaf mould' for his imaginative creation. From this point on, Tolkien drew on these experiences as well as his intimate knowledge of Anglo-Saxon, Norse and Celtic myths to develop, through the exercise of his mythopoetic imagination, his own personal mythos. This he undertook over the remainder of his life purely for his own enjoyment (Tolkien, Letters 163 and 328, cited in Carpenter 2006, 211, 412) or, more probably, because he was driven to do so as an act of 'sub-creation' (Tolkien 2001). This use of personal narratives and personal mythologizing giving rise to an imaginal world has been identified as a powerful approach to personal growth in humanistic and transpersonal psychology (Rowan 1993, 2001). However, Tolkien was also motivated to 'create a myth for England' (Letter 131, cited in Carpenter 2006, 144–5), a mythological geography which could be gifted for the edification of his compatriots.

Inspiring places, people and environmental ethic

> Tolkien gave us wonderful characters, evocative prose, some stirring adventures and exciting battles … but it is the place that we remember most of all. (Martin 2003, 3)

Hunt (2003) distinguishes between literary 'otherworlds' that are 'mappable' and therefore convincing as a 'place' or 'realm' as opposed to those that exhibit a 'nebulous geography' in which things just happen. Middle-earth is most certainly of the former type and is generally recognized as a particularly veridical one. This ability to evoke places, landscapes and a coherent geography is one of the greatest strengths of Tolkien's writing, and part of the joy of reading *LOTR* is to be transported by the narrative into the places themselves, places which stay in the memory:

> I can still remember the luminous green of the beechwoods, the freezing air of the mountains, the terrifying darkness of the dwarf mines, the greenery on the slopes of Ithilien, west of Mordor, still holding out against the encroaching shadow … I remember it at least as clearly as – no, come to think of it, *more* clearly than – I do many of the places I've visited in what we like to call the 'real' world … Middle-earth is a place I went to. (Pratchett 2003, 81–2)

Tolkien's powers of description are legendary although readers are better able to appreciate these imaginary places if they have an experiential frame of reference as a guide as noted earlier in terms of my auto-ethnographic engagements. Equally, one may take Tolkien's imaginary places 'back' into the real world in a deeply experiential manner. Thus Duane, describing a visit to the Alps, was shocked to find that:

> I looked across the great blue gulf of air and saw them there, as perhaps he did …: Celebdil, Fanuidhol, and Caradhras the Cruel; Silvertine, Cloudyhead, and the terrible Redhorn. For just a flicker of time, genuinely, physically, I was in Middle-earth. (Duane 2003, 127)

Turning from the landscape, *LOTR* is populated by a range of traditional and invented fantasy creatures and 'peoples' or races. The chief protagonists are, of course, the Hobbits, often referred to as Halflings due to their diminutive stature. Hobbits are portrayed as a people close to nature, who love growing things and who value craftsmanship. Orcs, in contrast, value clever, labour saving devices or those of 'mass destruction' and enjoy destroying things. Hobbits manage their affairs communally with very little hierarchical leadership and exhibit a simple 'joie de vivre' based on friendship, singing, dancing and feasting. Parties are occasions for distributing material wealth much like the traditional *potlatch* of the Pacific North West (Dwarves and Dragons, in contrast, are hoarders). This simple, non-accumulative yet hardworking lifestyle enable them more than any other people to withstand the influence of the Ring of Power, although they are not completely immune.

Clearly, Tolkien was not drawing inspiration from contemporary environmental utopian thinking but it is interesting to note the resemblances of the Shire to the societal ideals advocated by the bioregional movement (Carr 2004; McGinnis 1999) and the 'municipal communalism' envisioned by social ecologists (Clark 1990). Tolkien however provides a much needed caution against overly fetishizing the 'local' which is sometimes a characteristic of environmental utopian thinking. The parochialism of the Shire makes the Hobbits easy prey to Saruman/Sharkey and it is only through the intervention and leadership of the now worldly wise Hobbits of the Fellowship that the 'Scouring of the Shire' may take place. Tolkien also makes other implicit recommendations for 'right social relations'. He advances a preference for 'unity-in-diversity' (a motif in accord with Tolkien's Christian Trinitarianism): the heterogeneous alliance of autonomous individuals or peoples working collaboratively and selflessly towards a common goal for the Greater Good. This is exemplified by the Nine Walkers of the Fellowship specifically and the Free People of Middle-earth generally, once they have overcome their internecine squabbles, that is. These are set in opposition to the Nine Riders (the ghostly Ring Wraiths who have become de-individualized and homogenous drones of Sauron) and the dark forces of both Sauron and Saruman (who are motivated by fear and greed and are constantly quarrelling amongst themselves).

Turning more specifically to environmental ethics, Saruman quite literally exhibits a technical–scientific instrumentalist rationality: 'He has a mind of metal and wheels; and he does not care for growing things, except insofar as they serve him for the moment' (Tolkien 2007, 616). His goal is 'Knowledge, Rule, Order' (338) and the desire to become a 'Power' (161) which he pursues at the expense of both landscape (Isengard and the Shire) and vulnerable people (e.g., Hobbits) which are considered expendable. This is an unsustainable ethic that gives rise to both social and environmental injustice which have echoes in the 'many of the destructive outcomes of political and commercial globalization today' (Elder 2006, xi). Saruman can be contrasted with Tom Bombadil – an enigmatic character who does not appear in the films. Tolkien described him as 'the spirit of the (vanishing) Oxfordshire and Berkshire countryside' (Tolkien, Letter 19, cited in Carpenter 2006, 26) and as a non-instrumentalist:

> exemplar, a particular embodying of pure (real) natural science: the spirit that desires knowledge of other things, their history and nature, *because they are 'other'* and wholly independent of the enquiring mind, a spirit coeval with the rational mind, and entirely unconcerned with 'doing' anything with the knowledge. (Tolkien, Letter 153, cited in Carpenter 2006, 192)

Bombadil neither seeks, nor is beholden to, any Power, but is in tune with, and supremely of, the Created world, perhaps making him something akin to a Daoist master – 'He is his own Master' (Tolkien 2007, 346).

The actions of Sauron and Saruman and their acolytes are clearly unsustainable. Fortunately, the story also presents alternative visions for engaging with and caring for the environment. Dickerson and Evans (2006) identify three: *agriculture* practiced by the Hobbits in the Shire; *horticulture* associated with the Elves and Entwives; and *feraculture* – the care of 'wilderness' exemplified by the Ents. The first two management regimes admit a greater degree of manipulation of nature whereas the third is more in keeping with a 'deep ecology' ethic (Devall and Sessions 1985; Naess 1989) and it is perhaps unsurprising that the Ents are particularly popular with 'Deep Greens':

We saw the Ents as characters who represented defenders of the environment. And in that we really saw some solidarity between what they were after – defending the forest – and what we're after as Green Party members which is also defending the forest. So we've used them as sort of a mascot for today. (Derek Iversen in *Ringers*)

The general principle which connects 'right' management of the biophysical *and* social realms throughout *LOTR* is Good Stewardship, 'the benevolent, selfless custodial care' (Dickerson and Evans 2006, xx) of that which we do not own but has been entrusted to our care, be it the environment or community. Denethor, who occupies the position of 'Steward of Gondor' is actually a Bad Steward for whom 'stewardship is all about rule and authority' (38). He refuses to relinquish his illegitimate power with the *Return of the King*; and when his personal future looks bleak, he simply falls into a paralysing and ultimately suicidal despair. Gandalf, in contrast, is a paragon of the Good Steward who says:

> the rule of no realm is mine … But all worthy things that are in peril as the world now stands, those are my care. And for my part, I shall not wholly fail of my task, though Gondor should perish, if anything passes through this night that can still grow fair or bear fruit and flower again in days to come. For I am also a steward. (Tolkien 2007, 992)

This ethic of Stewardship was based upon Tolkien's own Creation-centred Catholic faith: right action concerns the celebration, preservation and restoration of Creation. Those responsible for marring it or who try to manipulate it for self-glorification are guilty of sin and need to be opposed. But such opposition should not itself be used as a vehicle for self-aggrandizement (a further sin of which Boromir and Denethor are both guilty) but rather based on thoroughly Christian virtues of love, humility, pity, compassion and service to others – virtues exhibited by Gandalf, Frodo, Sam, Aragorn and Faramir amongst others. Yet, responsibility for the defence and rehabilitation of Creation may not be at first recognized; nor might the correct course of action be immediately apparent. Like the Ents, and the Shire Hobbits at the end of the story, people may need to be both roused to action and empowered or *conscientized* (Freire 1970) to become a 'change agents' capable of, on the one hand, resisting the seduction of power (which all too often leads to sin in the senses noted above), and, on the other, taking affirmative action to overcome injustice (Freire 1970). These are themes and processes of particular significance to transformative and socially critical interpretations of environmental education, including matters touched on in a recent article in this journal by Hitzhusen (2007) and also has particular relevance to some more 'critical' readings of pedagogies of place (see Gruenewald 2003a, 2003b, and below).

Sam, perhaps the 'chief hero' of the story (Tolkien, Letter 131, cited in Carpenter 2006, 161), is the character who matures most to become the Good Steward of the Shire. When he briefly becomes a Ring Bearer due to Frodo's incapacitation by Shelob's sting, he successfully chooses to resist its alluring powers because he recognizes that his needs are simple and his station in life humble:

> he knew in the core of his heart that he was not large enough to bear such a burden … The one small garden of a free gardener was all his need and due, not a garden swollen to a realm; his own hands to use, not the hands of others to command. (Tolkien 2007, 1178)

Indeed, Sam is a gardener *par excellence* and he is the chief restorer of the newly Scoured Shire, selflessly using Galadrial's gift of bountiful dust and the Mallorn seed for the benefit of everyone (Tolkien 2007, 1338–9). The Appendices reveal that Sam also becomes steward of the community as seven-times elected Mayor (Tolkien 2007, 1441–2).

In many ways then, Sam is the exemplary embodiment of the virtues of Stewardship noted by Dickerson and Evans above. Cooper's (2006) meditations on the primary object of such stewardship return us to the question of our relation to the land. For Cooper, the 'meaning' of gardens and gardening is one that can afford 'epiphanies'. Cooper first advances a 'modest' proposal: that gardening can awaken an appreciation of the 'unity between human beings and the natural world, an intimate co-dependence' (136). He then goes on to advance a 'further' proposal of a more mysterious 'epiphany' possible, that of the 'co-dependence of human existence and the "deep ground" of the world and ourselves' (145). Thus, the garden may yield intimations of transcendence; and the practice of gardening, conducted with the right 'enlightened sensibility' 'to the world as a gift that "needs" us, its creative recipients' (150) is conducive to the realization of such transcendence. Sam as 'gardener', and in the final scene, cultivating his cottage garden, provides a literary vehicle that exemplifies both senses of 'epiphany' and, as such, ably illustrates the ethical and metaphysical core of *LOTR*. It is no less than appropriate that the story ends with Sam's homecoming (Tolkien 2007, 1349).

Conclusion

> We're in solidarity with the People of Middle Earth. In support of the environment and social justice. (Derek Iversen in *Ringers*)

In the words of Gandalf, 'he that breaks a thing to find out what it is has left the path of wisdom' (Tolkien 2007, 337). Tolkien's implicit disapproval of such an analysis also suggests an important caution for educators keen to formulate a prescriptive environmental education programme or scheme of work based on *LOTR* which might unintentionally destroy the 'magic' or efficacy of the story through the exercise of an instrumentalist rationality.

As this article has hopefully demonstrated:

> a literary study that articulates Tolkien's emphasis on restraining our individual appetites, defending beloved landscapes against the ethical and technological challenges symbolized by Mordor, and fostering sustainability in our communities can amplify the author's potential for exercising an impact on present-day values and practices. (Elder 2006, x)

It points to the desirability of promoting ecocritical, reflexive engagements with *LOTR* for environmental education, providing these are sensitively handled. Certainly, this kind of inquiry has proved personally fruitful. The hope is that it will prove so also for the wider environmental education community and provide a stimulus for further environmental education informed ecocriticism to be undertaken as an end in itself into *LOTR* in its various other incarnations; or, indeed, into other works of 'speculative fiction'. It remains to be seen how such studies could then be utilized in the design of environmental education interventions catering for wider constituencies.

It might also be hoped that the renewed popularity of *LOTR* provides a reason for young people to actually get back into the landscape and the emerging 'place based education' (PBE) movement (Gruenewald and Smith 2008) has much to commend it in this respect. However, PBE is itself a contentious issue within environmental education scholarship as demonstrated by the lively exchanges in a recent issue – Volume 14, Number 3 – of this very journal (e.g., Bowers 2008; Greenwood 2008; Smith 2008; Stevenson 2008). Indeed efforts are being made, sometimes dubiously, to connect Middle-earth *with* real world places such as the New Zealand tourist industry, the Sierra Norte de Madrid region of Spain or the countless attempts by fanatical fans at recreating Middle-earth in 'live action role-playing' (LARP) games. An additional pedagogical recommendation might simply be to encourage firsthand environmental experience in the types of places encountered in the narrative. More specifically, this could represent a call to experiential environmental education and/or adventurous outdoor programmes designers to consider using *LOTR* as an inspiration for getting learners out into the landscape. Indeed, such programmes might, if carefully crafted, go further by deliberately seeking to stimulate the mythopoetic imagination in outdoor settings in the manner advocated by Dyer and Hodgson (2003), perhaps using LARPs as a template. Of course, such efforts would need to be handled exceedingly sensitively to avoid having the opposite effect of actively 'turning learners off' from authentic encounters with both the environment and their mythopoetic imagination.

LOTR is, in the first and last analysis, not an educational or environmental education tool but a 'ripping yarn'. It can, and indeed has proved to be edifying and morally (even spiritually) transformative for very many, although obviously not for all readers. Yet, this has invariably occurred independently of deliberate external interventions. Consequently, encouraging others to engage experientially with the story (in the dual sense of a deep personal engagement with the narrative *and* in the kinds of places encountered therein) when it seems right for them might be the simplest, safest and ultimately most powerful educational recommendation to make. *LOTR* is a complex and carefully crafted narrative that transports the reader along with the protagonists on a personal journey of maturation in a world which is at one and the same time fantastical and familiar. Tolkien was driven to write a personal mythology that might also form a myth for the English people. However:

> the fact that the books have been translated into languages all over the world, the fact that the films are playing to audiences all over the world suggests that what [Tolkien] actually did was to create, or perhaps re-create, a mythology for the world, a mythology for mankind, humankind. (Sibley in *Ringers*)

Similarly, 'in the context of global modernization and the resistance to it, his stories have become an animating and inspiring new myth' (Curry 1998, 25). If he has achieved these things, it is because he applied 'the best magic – the ability to make reality itself more real' (Duane 2003, 128) and his work 'aspires to the elvish art of enchantment' (Carter 2003, 75). Such enchantment works best unmediated on those young and old prepared to let it – my younger and older selves included. Long may it!

References

Abrams, D. 1997. *The spell of the sensuous: Perception and language in a more-than-human world.* New York: Vintage.

Altman, I., and S.M. Low. 1992. *Place attachment: Human behavior and environment.* New York: Plenum Press.

Anderson, B. 1991. *Imagined communities: Reflections on the origin and spread of nationalism.* London: Verso.

Armstrong, K. 2001. *The battle for God.* Edinburgh: Canongate Books.

Armstrong, K. 2005. *A short history of myth.* Edinburgh: Canongate Books.

Augé, M. 1995. *Non-places: Introduction to an anthropology of supermodernity.* London: Verso.

Bakshi, R. 1978. *Lord of the Rings.* United Artists.

Blackham, R.S. 2006. *The roots of Tolkien's Middle Earth.* Stroud: Tempus.

Bowers, C.A. 2008. Why a critical pedagogy of place is an oxymoron. *Environmental Education Research* 14, no. 3: 325–35.

Buell, L. 2005. *The future of environmental criticism: Environmental criticism and literary imagination.* Oxford: Blackwell.

Carpenter, H. 2002. *J.R.R. Tolkien: A biography.* London: HarperCollins.

Carpenter, H. 2006. *The letters of J.R.R. Tolkien.* London: HarperCollins.

Carr, M. 2004. *Bioregionalism and civil society: Democratic challenges to corporate capitalism.* Vancouver: UBC Press.

Carter, L. 2003. *Tolkien: A look behind Lord of the Rings.* London: Gollancz.

Chawla, L. 1992. Childhood place attachments. In *Place attachment: Human behavior and environment*, ed. I. Altman and S.M. Low, 63–86. London: Plenum Press.

Chawla, L. 1999. Life paths into effective environmental action. *Journal of Environmental Education* 31, no. 1: 15–26.

Chawla, L. 2002. Spots of time: Manifold ways of being in nature in childhood. In *Children and nature: Psychological, sociocultural and evolutionary investigations*, ed. P.H. Kahn, Jr. and S.R. Kellert, 199–225. Cambridge, MA: MIT Press.

Clark, J. 1990. *Renewing the Earth: The promise of social ecology – A celebration of the work of Murray Bookchin.* London: Green Print.

Cooper, D.E. 2006. *A philosophy of gardens.* Oxford: Oxford University Press.

Cordova, C. 2005. *Ringers: Lord of the fans.* DVD Planet BB Entertainment.

Curry, P. 1998. *Defending Middle-earth: Tolkien, myth and modernity.* London: HarperCollins.

Devall, B., and G. Sessions. 1985. *Deep ecology.* Salt Lake City, UT: Peregrine Smith Books.

Dickerson, M., and J. Evans. 2006. *Ents, Elves and Eriador: The environmental vision of J.R.R. Tolkien.* Lexington: The University Press of Kentucky.

Doerr, M.N. 2004. *Currere and the environmental autobiography: A phenomenological approach to the teaching of ecology.* New York: Peter Lang.

Duane, D. 2003. The longest Sunday. In *Meditations on Middle Earth: New writings on the worlds of J.R.R. Tolkien*, ed. K. Haber, 117–28. London: Earthlight.

Dyer, A., and J. Hodgson. 2003. *Let your children go back to nature.* Milverton: Capall Bann Publishing.

Elder, J. 2006. Foreword. In *Ents, Elves and Eriador: The environmental vision of J.R.R. Tolkien*, ed. M. Dickerson, and J. Evans, ix–xii. Lexington: The University Press of Kentucky.

Ezard, J. 1991. Tolkien's Shire. *Weekend Guardian* 28 December: 4–6.

Freire, P. 1970. *Pedagogy of the oppressed.* Harmondsworth: Penguin.

Garrard, G. 2004. *Ecocriticism.* London: Routledge.

Greenwood, D.A. 2008. A critical pedagogy of place: From gridlock to parallax. *Environmental Education Research* 14, no. 3: 336–48.

Gruenewald, D.A. 2003a. The best of both worlds: A critical pedagogy of place. *Educational Researcher* 32, no. 4: 3–12.

Gruenewald, D.A. 2003b. Foundations of place: A multidisciplinary framework for place-conscious education. *American Educational Research Journal* 40, no. 3: 619–54.

Gruenewald, D.A., and G.A. Smith. 2008. *Place-based education in the global age: Local diversity.* Abingdon: Lawrence Erlbaum.

Hitzhusen, G.E. 2007. Judeo-Christian theology and the environment: Moving beyond scepticism to new sources for environmental education in the United States. *Environmental Education Research* 13, no. 1: 55–74.

Hooke, D. 2006. *The west midlands.* London: Collins.

Hunt, P. 2003. Introduction: Fantasy and alternative worlds. In *Alternative worlds in fantasy fiction*, ed. P. Hunt, and M. Lenz, 1–41. London: Continuum.

Hunt, P., and M. Lenz. 2003. *Alternative worlds in fantasy fiction.* London: Continuum.

Jackson, P. 2001. *The Lord of the Rings: The Fellowship of the Ring.* New Line Cinema.

Jackson, P. 2002. *The Lord of the Rings: The Two Towers.* New Line Cinema.

Jackson, P. 2003. *The Lord of the Rings: Return of the King.* New Line Cinema.

Kerridge, R. 1998. Introduction. In *Writing the environment: Ecocriticism and literature*, ed. R. Kerridge and N. Sammells, 1–9. London: Zed Books.

Leonard, T., and P. Willis. 2008. *Pedagogies of the imagination: Mythopoetic curriculum in educational practice.* Dortrecht: Springer.

Martin, G.R.R. 2003. Introduction. In *Meditations on Middle Earth: New writings on the worlds of J.R.R. Tolkien*, ed. K. Haber, 1–5. London: Earthlight.

Mathews, R. 2002. *Fantasy: Liberation of the imagination.* London: Routledge.

McGinnis, M.V. 1999. *Bioregionalism.* London: Routledge.

Moorcock, M. 2004. *Wizadry and wild romance.* Austin, TX: MonkeyBrain.

Morgan, A. 2007. Minding the world: Integral transformative learning for geographical and environmental wisdom. PhD diss., Institute of Education, University of London.

Myhill, D. 2007. Reading the world: Using children's literature to explore controversial issues. In *The challenge of teaching controversial issues*, ed. H. Claire and C. Holden, 51–65. Stoke-on-Trent: Trentham Books.

Naess, A. 1989. *Ecology, community and lifestyle.* Cambridge: Cambridge University Press.

Pratchett, T. 2003. Cult classic. In *Meditations on Middle Earth: New writings on the worlds of J.R.R. Tolkien*, ed. K. Haber, 75–83. London: Earthlight.

Proshansky, H.M., A.K. Fabian, and R. Kaminoff. 1995. Place-identity: Physical world socialization of the self. In *Giving places meaning*, ed. L. Groat, 87–114. San Diego, CA: Academic Press.

Rawls, M. 1984. The feminine principle in Tolkien. *Mythlore* 10, no. 4: 5–13.

Relph, E. 1974. *Place and placelessness.* London: Pion.

Rowan, J. 1993. *The transpersonal: Psychotherapy and counseling.* London: Routledge.

Rowan, J. 2001. *Ordinary ecstasy: The dialectics of humanistic psychology.* Hove: Routledge.

Smith, G. 2008. Oxymoron or misplaced rectification. *Environmental Education Research* 14, no. 3: 349–52.

Stevenson, R.B. 2008. A critical pedagogy of place and the critical place(s) of pedagogy. *Environmental Education Research* 14, no. 3: 353–60.

Swanwick, M. 2003. A changeling returns. In *Meditations on Middle Earth: New writings on the worlds of J.R.R. Tolkien*, ed. K. Haber, 33–46. London: Earthlight.

Tolkien, J.R.R. 2001. On fairy-stories. In *Tree and leaf*, ed. J.R.R. Tolkien, 1–81. London: HarperCollins.

Tolkien, J.R.R. 2007. *The Lord of the Rings.* London: HarperCollins.

Wood, R.C. 2003. *The gospel according to Tolkien: Visions of the kingdom in Middle-earth.* Louisville, KY: Westminster John Knox Press.

Reading *The Lorax*, orienting in potentiality

Amy Sloane

Departments of Curriculum and Instruction, and Forest and Wildlife Ecology, University of Wisconsin-Madison, USA

The Lorax by Theodor Seuss Geisel (1971) is a popular children's book with a strong environmental message. Previous scholarship on *The Lorax* has focused on questions about the message and the process of its transmission from the Once-ler to the child. In contrast, in this study I inquire into the activity of transmission itself. Guided by the work of Agamben and Foucault, I analyze *The Lorax* and the activity of transmission as matters of human potentiality. I first present an analysis of the logic and function of potentiality itself. Then, with *The Lorax* as an example, I expose and critique the activity of transmission as one orientation in potentiality. I also indicate ways in which environmental education theory and practice maintains itself in this orientation. Beyond this, I show how *The Lorax* indirectly presents another orientation which offers a different way of conceiving the child, reading and critique.

Introduction

One of the most well-known children's books on the environment in the Anglo-American world is *The Lorax* by Theodor Seuss Geisel (1971), more popularly known as Dr Seuss. It depicts human and natural communities in crisis. On the 'Street of the Lifted Lorax', humans and nature merely survive. The Once-ler is abandoned to himself in his tower and nature is utterly exhausted. The book's popular American contemporaries echo the crisis, from Kelly's (1972) *Pogo*: 'We have met the enemy and he is us'; to Rachel Carson's (1962, 3): 'the people had done it themselves'.

Geisel's books are well known for teaching reading–readiness (see Fensch 2005). But *The Lorax* is also a message book, and one of the angriest books he wrote. Showing this crisis scenario Geisel expressed frustration with what he saw as the problem of human violence to natural life. He also noted how this problem was the book's message, and an objective of environmental education:

> Every once in a while I get mad. *The Lorax* came out of my being angry. The ecology books I'd read were dull… In *The Lorax* I was out to attack what I think are evil things and let the chips fall where they might; and the book's been used by ministers as the basis of sermons, as well as conservation groups. (Geisel cited in Cott 2005, 118)

In environmental education the object of most scholarship that considers *The Lorax* is this message (see Henderson, Kennedy, and Chamberlin 2004; Gough 1999). Studies either presume the message to be true and correct, question and disagree with it, or rework it. The important point is that the message is treated as the key object of study and however interpreted it is transmitted from the enlightened Once-ler to the child. For the Once-ler, the child is the dream of a way out. The child receives the message passed to him and there is hope. With this message, transmitter and receiver, researchers may question anything about them alone or in combination: for example, how to transmit, who receivers are and should be and how we are to conceptualize them, in what situations and places, and what warrants transmission.

This inquiry does not attempt to take a position on any of these possible questions. I do not ignore them, but I do not directly address or confront them either. This is because the object of my inquiry is not *about* the message, nor its transmitter or receiver. The object is the activity of transmission itself. This is a crucial distinction. In existing studies the questioning occurs *about* the message and presupposes trans-mission. That is, *transmitting and receiving beings exist and a message is passed from one to the other* (Agamben 1999). In contrast, the object of this inquiry is this activity of presupposing transmission.

Further, the conception of transmission I present is different from the common notion of an enlightened expert passing content (in this case a message or objective) to a novice, just as at the end of *The Lorax* the seed is passed from the Once-ler to the child. Years of research about environmental education gives evidence that this notion of transmission – tantamount to '*telling* someone to behave in a certain way and providing sound reasoning to support that command equals *teaching behaviour*' – continues to operate as a premise of the field (Heimlich and Ardoin 2008, 231; italics in original). In a crucial if unstated sense, Heimlich and Ardoin's review of behaviour–change research exemplifies the proliferation over several decades of pars-ing and linking concepts and categories to establish causal theoretical models of environmentally sound behaviours yet without actually producing consistent lasting desired behaviours. At the same time, while research challenging these models has called attention to even more ways that transmission fails in conceiving and achieving its objectives – for example, through arguments of environmental ethics, identity constructedness, problematic metanarratives or metaphors and other discursive elements of representation – this research has yet to resolve the very failures of trans-mission it makes visible (see McKenzie 2005; Hart 2007).

Presupposing transmission continues to be a foundational activity of environmental education scholarship and practice in at least two ways. First, presupposing transmission or the existence of transmitters, receivers and a message, is a necessary condition of articulating theories, policies, sets of best practices, curricula, and so on. In addition to its function as a condition for articulating theory and practice it has an ordering function. To presuppose transmission is to order a transmitter and receiver in a relation. The transmitter and receiver may be a teacher and learner, older and younger generations, government and citizens, or nature and human. But in each case they are separate and in a relation of transmitting and receiving. Hart (2005) notes how the existence of this relation remains unproblematized in mainstream environmental education research (including much of the behaviour–change research discussed above); and though it is problematized in 'post'-research that operates in tension, straining against the very legitimation and representation of this relation it deploys, apprehension remains about the ambiguous inconsistent ground from which to critique.

Guided by the work of Agamben and Foucault, I consider *The Lorax* and problems of transmission as matters of human potentiality. A potential is generally conceived not as an act but a quality *about* a human being that exists yet is immaterial (Agamben 1999). It also has an ontological status, meaning the quality is an essential *thing* possessed, being able to be or do this or that, which one decides to actualize or not. In this inquiry, instead of presupposing the potential to transmit as a quality and taking its existence as a premise, my goal is to analyze *how this potential comes about and in what way it exists.* It is to raise a philosophical question that neither accepts the potential to transmit as a premise, nor accepts that all potential is presupposed leaving it at that (Agamben 1999). The question requires an analysis that holds in focus and describes the logic and functions of potentiality itself, which I present next.

Method

The guiding question of this inquiry is: What is the task of the child in environmental education? The purpose is to expose the activity of transmission and open a way of reading *The Lorax* without transmission. This way of reading does not directly answer the guiding question. Rather, it is an experience of potentiality without presupposition which orients the task of the child and of environmental education in a different way. Further, it makes orienting itself the key matter of environmental education.

To describe the methodological approach I turn to Agamben and Foucault. It begins with a challenge: the method must avoid the very presuppositional activity of transmission I am trying to expose, yet still be able to expose it. This means, first, that I cannot presuppose the work of Foucault and Agamben, treating it as true principles and simply apply their conclusions to *The Lorax* and environmental education. Second, the method must not be an interpretive lens, a theory, or framework since these notions function to say, 'here is what I presuppose'. Agamben's work guides this inquiry in that he experiments with conceiving an ontology of potentiality irreducible to its presupposed transcendent existence (see Casarino 2002). But I do not deploy his conceptions as a theory or teaching. Rather, I realize my method as the movement of thought this experiment enacts, a movement that both exposes presuppositional activity and, at its limit, illuminates and realizes a different experience of potentiality. This experiment is not Agamben's. It belongs to a philosophical project whose recent history is expressed in the thought of contemporaries including Foucault, Derrida, Nancy and Deleuze and predecessors including Benjamin, Kafka and Spinoza. Hence, third, to conceive the method as either a subjective experience possessed or a universally valid real position would remain in the meshes of presupposition.

With these precautions in mind, I now present the method (or movement) of exposure, opening and experience and clarify the position from which it happens. I present the method formally by describing Agamben's account of how Plato and Aristotle each conceived human potentiality. This is a generic account; through it I describe the potential to transmit, the case in question. After this formal presentation I discuss *The Lorax* as an example.

In Agamben's reading, according to Aristotle and Plato, every potential is double, 'all potential to be or to do something is always also potential not to be or not to do' (Agamben 1999, 245). Thus transmissibility is the potential to transmit and at the same time the potential not to transmit. This double existence is not a trivial distinction from how potential is commonly presupposed. It allows one to expose the activity of transmission, and illuminates the opening to an experience of potential that is not presupposed. For this reason it is crucial to detail the way this double potential functions.

For both Aristotle and Plato, a human potential such as transmissibility comes about by suspending its double potential, dividing and removing the potential not to transmit from the potential to transmit. Double potential is decomposed 'into a being *about which one speaks* and… a quality and a determination *that one says of it*' (Agamben 1999, 33; italics in original). Thus transmission exists in the form of a human being who possesses the quality of being able to transmit. The key point is that the activity of presupposing gives the human positive existence as having the potential to transmit, while the potential not to transmit is removed from positive existence. Both Aristotle and Plato realized the activity of presupposing is groundless in that it exists without substantive content (Agamben 1999).

At this point Agamben reads a distinction between Aristotle and Plato. While Aristotle and Plato conceived this activity of potentiality in the same way, they oriented and positioned themselves differently within it. This distinction of orientation and position is crucial for the present inquiry. According to Agamben (1999), Aristotle's orientation is to give primacy to the activity of presupposing. In this orientation, the suspension and division of the double transmissibility, and removal of the potential not to, are given the status of an *absolute presupposition*. This means the potential not to transmit is permanently removed or abandoned, outside and inaccessible to any human potential. In Aristotle's orientation, humans have the potential to transmit but at the cost of abandoning the potential not to transmit and existing groundlessly with no content to actualize.

How, then, does a potential without content actualize? Agamben (1999) suggests Aristotle's solution as follows. The activity of presupposing must suspend itself, and the potential to transmit must seize a referent through which it can actualize. The referent seized is the potential not to transmit. In other words, what was established as absolutely external and inaccessible is now seized. This amounts to a second abandonment of the potential not to transmit. Actualizing human potential is a paradox since it is seizing what was already abandoned to the outside. Aristotle treated this paradox as a fact of existence. This is a second act of presupposing in which the potential not to transmit exists as an 'other' always available to human potential, and the human activity suspending, dividing and abandoning exists as a fact of human existence.

To summarize Agamben's analysis, Aristotle's orientation entails what I will call two 'orders' of functioning. The first order is the presupposing activity of suspension, division and abandonment of the potential not to transmit that brings into existence a human possessing the potential to transmit. The second order is the activity of suspension and seizing the potential not to transmit again in abandonment, as the referent through which the potential to transmit can actualize. As such, his position is the presupposing activity that is the potential to transmit.

In contrast Plato's orientation was to remember that this presupposing activity bears a weakness it cannot overcome (Agamben 1999). Since it divides from and abandons the potential not to transmit in order to come into existence and actualize, it can never express transmissibility's being double or restore being double. Only if the potential not to speak exists irreducible to the potential to transmit *and* is given primacy, can a restoration of double transmissibility happen. Hence for Plato, the potential not to transmit does not mean withdrawing or deciding not to actualize, for these are negative forms of the potential to transmit. It is not an act at all in the sense of doing, causing, praxis, and it can never be possessed. *It is that which allows human potential to exist and actualize by submitting to its own abandonment.* Plato's position then focuses on the potential not to transmit, which can be experienced at the moment when the potential to transmit has no more referents to seize and there is only being abandoned itself. It is an opening to restore double transmissibility in the primacy of the potential not to transmit.

Foucault's histories of the present, perhaps more than any other work in the twentieth century, show the primacy today of this presupposing activity of potentiality, or what Agamben has shown as Aristotle's orientation (see for example Foucault 1977, particularly the essay *Theatrum Philosophicum*). Naming this activity an exercise of biopower, Foucault's work highlights the bringing of humans into existence who have the potential to violate life. This is the potential that made Geisel so angry and that constitutes *The Lorax*'s message. Foucault analyzed biopower precisely as a presuppositional activity:

> … what I would like to show is… how a particular regime of truth… makes something [biopolitics] that does not exist able to become something. It is not an illusion since it is precisely a set of practices… which established it and thus imperiously marks it out in reality. (Foucault 2008, 19)

His method, a history of the present, was to expose this activity in its history, emphasizing how it constitutes humans and nature in their existence in a relation of violence, and establishes biological life and death as the stake (1966/1973, 2003, 2007, 2008).

With this formal discussion of potentiality I now fully describe my inquiry's method. The problem of transmission I raise in respect to *The Lorax* and the field of environmental education is not *about* the message, nor does it presuppose transmission. *The problem is to exhibit the activity of presupposing the potential to transmit and the potential to violate natural life, as what it is to read the book and to reason in the field of environmental education.* My inquiry is positioned with the potential not to transmit, the Truffula trees abandoned twice in *The Lorax*, in order to expose this activity. Later on in the article, I will show the orientation of the common reading of *The Lorax*, and I identify correspondences to much environmental education suggesting it is the same orientation, in the form of provisional theses.

This method reaches a matter of environmental education different from any issue or question *about* transmission or the message, which concerns the task of the child. It is the matter of orienting in transmissibility. At issue in orienting is what it is to critique, since one's orienting will determine the problem, object and position of critique. *The Lorax* is an example of the matter of orienting. As an example: 'the text is no more and no less than its way… it takes place nowhere else other than in its modality of being' or orientation (Casarino 2002, 89). The text Dr Seuss narrates is the Aristotelian orientation. But *The Lorax* is as irreducible to this text as Geisel was to Dr Seuss. *The Lorax* also allows a reading in the Platonic orientation, which is not narrated and not presupposed and in which reading is an experience of the potential not to transmit. In this reading there is an opening to the matter of orienting. Orienting is a decision on how the child is conceived in his task. Without favoring one orientation to the exclusion of the other, *The Lorax* indirectly presents a way of conceiving critique that occurs in the potential not to transmit. This is its offering to environmental education.

Reading *The Lorax* with the potential not to transmit

I have formally presented how the logical activity of potentiality *is* the practical form of transmission. In this section I read *The Lorax* with the potential not to transmit. Because this way of reading is unfamiliar and also considers the illustrations, it may be worthwhile to consult a copy of the text.

This section follows the text but reads with the potential not to transmit, making visible the book's presentation of potentiality. It begins in the crisis of the potential to transmit in the Aristotelian orientation. Then the reader is taken back in the Once-ler's past to a mythical beginning, his once. The Once-ler's story narrates the first, then second order activity of division and abandonment. Each of these moments – crisis, mythical beginning, first and second order – is exposed as a way presupposition happens, as reading *The Lorax* and doing environmental education. I state provisional theses on how an Aristotelian orientation occurs in environmental education. I am aware the field is not monolithic, yet my theses suggest different theoretical and methodological approaches to environmental education may share the same presuppositional activity of transmission. I do not attempt to defend the theses here. They are to invite the reader to take a look empirically at how those concepts and relations in environmental education presupposed as real, exist. They are not end points but conditions of opening to the matter of orienting.

'The Street of the Lifted Lorax'

The first pages of *The Lorax* depict the Once-ler and nature in loss and brokenness. At this 'far end of town', nature has become entire loss of life, and human existence entire lack of community. But neither is dead. Here in the second order there is no more nature available for the Once-ler to seize as a referent, yet something remains of each.

The remnant of human existence is the Once-ler's way of life, 'lurking' silent in the shell of his factory, unable to actualize his potential to transmit. He is biologically alive, but absent anything that would make him recognizable as part of the human community. The remnant of nature is being abandoned by humans. It is actual loss of life without death. The bird struggling to fly; Grickle-grass; scraggly plants difficult to distinguish as dead or alive – all expose this relation. One hesitates calling any of these natural. Having abandoned nature, the Once-ler seeks nothing in it. Entirely spent by humanity, nature offers nothing.

Witnessing these remnants shows survival is a common existence in division and abandonment for both humans and nature, a community of lack and loss irreducible to notions of biological life and death. Yet this community is the external reference environmental education seizes in order to articulate pedagogies of living. My first provisional thesis is that humans violating life is not environmental education's problem but the condition it needs to exist. For instance, the learner must never live as a greedy Once-ler, instead he/she must discipline him/herself in environmental pedagogies as she participates in community. And this street is the unnatural place the learner must never live since no referents are present to ground a human community.

As long as it refuses to acknowledge its activity presupposing this potential environmental education cannot resolve the problem of human violence. Nor can it recognize that transmission ends in meaningless survival, a real non-existence that is also not biological death. How is environmental education to think through this problem and orient? Seuss introduces the Once-ler's story.

'Now I'll tell you... how the Lorax got lifted and taken away'

To transmit his story the Once-ler must speak but he lives on a street in which he no longer transmits. It is Seuss the non-existent narrator who narrates three questions as the sphere of the story. 'What *was* the Lorax?/And why was it there?/And why was it lifted and taken somewhere...' (italics in original) presuppose that there is transmission. This guarantees the message as a quality *about* the potential to transmit. Further, it guarantees the Once-ler transmits and the child receives the message.

Seuss' presupposition of transmission makes it possible for the Once-ler to speak. Yet his story is already destined to be a re-iteration of the potential to transmit. His narrative cannot move beyond this orientation, nor can any critique within this narrative for that matter. To actualize his potential the Once-ler needs a referent, the child, whose valueless offering starts the Once-ler's story.

First order dividing and abandoning

The Once-ler wanders in darkness and non-belonging, his covered wagon traversing unknown wilderness. Only his arms and hands are visible. Suddenly he comes upon a 'glorious place' and beholds its harmonious Truffula trees, Swomee-Swans, Bar-ba-loots, Humming-Fish. The Once-ler's story begins here, the first order where transmission is already an absolute presupposition. External glorious nature is not an actual original historical past during which the Once-ler had a better or more harmonious relation to nature. It is the potential not to transmit brought into existence in the form of a past divided and abandoned by the wandering Once-ler. In this orientation the Once-ler has never belonged and can never belong in nature.

The second thesis is that environmental education critiques involving a historical relation between humans and nature take form first of all as absolute presupposition in which human and nature are divided (otherwise there can be no relation). The problem of separation as one of presupposing transmission generally goes unrecognized. This leads to thinking the problem can be overcome by relating, and without questioning where the presupposition itself comes from. Hence the activity of this presupposition gains the status of reality, and environmental education critiques become caught in a never-ending need to try to overcome the separation while unable from the outset to succeed.

For instance, critics of narrative such as Bergthaller (2006) acknowledge this limit of the Once-ler's narrative but continue to insist that all solutions are bound by the position of the Once-ler. This is a reification of the separation between the Once-ler and 'pure nature' commonly called anthropocentrism. In other scholarship, goals such as restoring harmony with nature, getting back to the land, or living according to knowledge of nature, may be noble and even temporarily succeed but fail to expose the division that perpetuates the need for these goals. Furthermore, to achieve them either the human community must withdraw entirely from nature or live totally in accord with nature. Both are impossible to achieve. More importantly to try to achieve them is actually to try to fulfill the division, not overcome the need for one.

Withdrawal is absolute division from nature, and living according to nature is living without anything that would distinguish one as human.

Even 'post'-scholarship that interrogates epistemological–ontological foundations may repeat this division, by both presupposing it as the problem and reifying it as the answer. On one hand there is effort to destabilize representations and positions of legitimacy, in some cases to the point of showing the groundlessness of all claims to transcendence. But this is precisely in order to make new representations and legitimations, in the name of multiplicity and change. What in the literature is variously called messiness, layering, complexity, ambiguity, continual reframing are ways of grasping human groundless division as a real value. This does not solve the problem of transcendence but reifies a position of abandoning ontology (Casarino 2002). In this position any presupposition may be legitimately questioned and its groundlessness revealed. But it remains unacceptable to allow this being groundless to be, without transmission. Instead, groundless existence is itself seized as a referent of incessantly critiquing and re-making human relations to nature. 'Engaged', 'committed', 'collaborative', 'constructed', 'mutually constituted' communities that emerge through absolute presupposition can only ever share the absolute value of searching for and seizing places in abandonment, endlessly re-making placeless existence.

Second order dividing and abandoning

Continuing to read with the potential to transmit, after the Once-ler touches the tree there is a suspension in which 'this glorious place' full of colour becomes a white blank. Through it the Once-ler recognizes his potential to transmit, 'a great leaping of joy in my heart./I knew just what I'd do!' He stops his wagon. The glorious Truffula tree of the first order is now a natural resource available to him, the referent of his incipient community.

This activity constitutes second order. The Once-ler actualizes his potential, unloading his axe and building a shop. Then wielding the axe he literally divides the Truffula Tree, seizing the tuft and abandoning the remnant stump. 'I am doing no harm./I'm being quite useful'. The community that forms from the Once-ler's call acts in expanding cycles of dividing and abandoning, or 'biggering' and 'getting rich'. This is not merely an unhealthy community as if it had the choice to act healthy. This community cannot do otherwise since its existence depends on actualizing by abandoning trees. Numerous illustrations depict seizing nature and bringing inside the factory the resource that was once the external glorious place. There is also an exemplary illustration of knitting the tuft of the felled Truffula tree propped on the Once-ler's window ledge.

Each time the community seizes a tree it leaves new groundless existence and a remnant stump and thus a new referent tree, or a hundred, must be seized. This activity compels itself along, as the words 'biggering' and 'growing' indicate. 'And, in no time at all,/in the factory I built,/the whole Once-ler Family/was working full tilt'. The factory and its technologies proliferate with the stumpage as well as 'smogulous smoke', 'Gluppity-Glupp and Schloppity-Schlopp', while an increasing diversity of creatures is abandoned homeless and must seek refuge elsewhere. This activity of seizing nature in abandonment actualizes human and nature to the point of reciprocal crisis.

A third thesis is that in environmental education the establishment of pedagogies is a realm of actualizing second order potential to transmit. The process is as follows.

A given pedagogy is called into question by a critique of its premises. For instance, scholarship has been critiqued for its post-positivist premises, for rhetorical–linguistic premises including narrative configurations and metaphor, for historical–political premises including social injustices, capitalism, anthropocentrism and ecological illiteracy, and for ethical premises including Christianity and capitalist values such as competition.

Yet what ultimately legitimates critiques of all premises is that the insufficiency of any pedagogy can be shown since pedagogy is a groundless presupposition. When the problem of orienting is not realized, a different premise simply creates the need to find and seize another referent ground through which to actualize pedagogy. To actualize pedagogy is to re-actualize the second order, abandoning the newly recognized referent learner or child. If it is not the child's behaviour that is recognized then it is his values, attitudes, critical thinking skills, responsibility, reflexivity, ethics, parents, peers or social structures that influence him (see Rickinson 2001).

While this process of actualizing new pedagogies may appear to move toward a concept of improvement from the status quo it only expands environmental education's referents or who needs to participate in environmental education, and techniques of actualization. For instance, over the course of the last four decades, national and international policies on environmental education, and meetings such as those at Tbilisi, Thessaloniki and Durban, have variously extended the scope of who is identified as in need of environmental education, the ramifications of human potentials deemed problematic, and multiplied the techniques to normalize these potentials. Several articles in the April 2009 volume of *Environmental Education Research* (15, 2) note this expansion in differing ways. Yet the essential element taught or transmitted in all these is that there is transmission and how to actualize it. What remains is to offer a mode of teaching without transmitting.

Existence in the second order

Having thrown his goods out of his wagon, established a shop and cut down a Truffula Tree, the Once-ler knits a Thneed. 'This thing is a Thneed./A Thneed's a Fine-Something-That-All-People-Need!' The Thneed is not merely a thing but the object existence of human and natural communities in second order presupposing.

Thneed, or thing-need, neatly displays the paradox of the second order. On the one hand to buy a Thneed is to quite literally become some*thing*. The first Thneed covers the face of the man who buys it, exhibiting human facelessness and the need to seize a referent to become some*thing*. On the other, human facelessness and the need to seize a referent cannot be fulfilled by a Thneed. Just the opposite, in covering the man's face it exposes his face as groundless taking possession of some*thing*.

Environmental education points to a crisis of human and natural communities by pointing to remnants such as those depicted in *The Lorax*: diversity loss, contamination, exhaustion of resources and fragmentation of systems to the point of collapse. It voices a demand to live a different way. Yet if it understands these crises as at bottom a factual need of biological existence with biological consequences at stake, then its voice transmits this orientation as the common face that unites all humans and nature in abandonment. The fourth thesis is that the concept of community in environmental education is a Thneed, and what unites a community is experience in a common orientation. Any position that registers the need for community is already divided in the potential to transmit, and ends up reproducing the fragmentary existence in abandonment humans share. Teaching ways of negotiating meaning, creating open-ness for challenge and debate, or constructing shared understandings is teaching that we must endlessly seek knowledge or make meaning without being able to be fulfilled. To settle for this paradox is not enough. But to think it through may require relinquishing this object existence as an ultimate goal, and accept and attest to human being groundless without being empty, nothing.

In the remnant stump the Lorax appears.

Responsibility

The mysterious Lorax appears warning and accusing the Once-ler. The Lorax is commonly read as the protagonist of the book, upholding the true, right approach to the matter and attempting to confront the Once-ler's despoiling greed. But this is a misreading.

The Lorax asserts, 'I speak for the trees, for the trees have no tongues', and demands, 'What's that THING you've made out of my Truffula tuft?' In this inter-rogation the Lorax has already presupposed nature as his. The misreading is in not recognizing he is no different than the Once-ler. In acting responsibly, 'speaking for' and being 'in charge of' nature, the Lorax exposes the impossibility of being respon-sible. The Lorax exclaims, 'Sir! You are crazy with greed'. He repeatedly takes the Once-ler by the hand and shows the damage he causes and the refugees he produces, Bar-ba-loots, Swomee-Swans, Humming-Fish. Yet every attempt to transmit this irresponsibility fails to enlighten the Once-ler. The Once-ler dismisses him as a 'poor stupid guy' and excuses himself stating remorse and ethical intent: 'I… felt sad', 'I meant no harm'. At wits end the Lorax leads each mobile natural existence away without knowing where it will go, preserving them in an indefinite wandering existence.

This taking-leave repeats until the Once-ler's final rebuke, 'I have my rights, sir, and I'm telling you/I intend to go on doing just what I do!' Entirely severing from and abandoning the Lorax, the Once-ler abandons himself to himself. Then, the human community experiences the 'sickening smack' of 'The very last Truffula Tree of them all'. This precipitates the community's abandonment of the Once-ler where nothing is left but 'my big empty factory…/the Lorax…/and I'. At the other end, 'The Lorax said nothing. Just gave me a glance/Just gave me a very sad, sad backward glance…/as he lifted himself…' It is a scene of reciprocal crisis in which the Once-ler has abandoned the natural community entirely, and the Lorax responds by withdrawing nature from the human community.

To read with the Lorax is merely to trade one's conception of external nature (produced through the first order of transmission) from an original 'glorious place' to an original ineffable mysterious accuser. This accuser does not overcome the realm of guilt in which the Once-ler stands, since the Lorax forecloses a solution to the refugee status he is complicit in establishing. Squarely in this realm the Lorax is 'the cipher of a guilty humanity that denounces its own guilt to the point of accusing the very legal order to which it belongs' (Agamben 1999, 150). He is ethical in the same way as the Once-ler. To side with him is not adequate to the task of overcoming human violence to natural life.

In environmental education to admit this is to admit the insufficiency of conceiv-ing the problem–solution as a matter of responsibility for some*thing*. Insufficient since teaching responsibility for the environment is firstly transmitting damage to learners, presupposing them as bearers of guilt and obligation, without this activity being registered as such. Presupposing may take the form of a juridical content of codes and/or rights; an ideological content; or as relational 'process' like critical thinking, or contested stories and meanings 'that constitute our social reality' (Jickling 2005, 21). In the last example, 'process' concepts function to transmit damage as the registering of relations of abandonment in the stories told. One learns ways humans abandon others and reflects on one's complicity in that relation. Either the relation is presupposed as a universal quality of human existence. Or a respect of differences (respecting reciprocal abandonment) is presupposed as a universal ethic. In both cases ethics is returned to responsibility, in which despite enlightenment about differences it is impossible to overcome them since the relation of abandonment remains their ground. Further, responsibility is insufficient since such imputations lead to accepting guilt and making changes only when learners are willing.

The fifth thesis is that humans are ultimately as incapable of assuming responsibly for planetary life as of spanning the gap between teacher and learner; adult and child; human and nature; one's ethics and one's practice of life. This incapability or impotential is not due to a human lack. It is a consequence of the fact that transmission cannot fill the gap, repair or overcome the divisions and differences it establishes because it enacts them in order to function.

Grasping how presupposing transmission takes form – as reciprocal crisis, mythical beginning or origin, and first and second order transmission – allows environmental educators to leave Seuss's question of how the Lorax disappeared and can return, whilst also putting to rest environmental education's theoretical tensions and contorted messiness, and stop presupposing the gap (which is its groundlessness) with its paradoxes as the common existence by which novel pedagogies must be transmitted.

With this grasp of the activity of transmission, an opening can occur to another mode of impotential. This other mode is not with the Lorax but the Truffula tree, my analytical bearing from the start. What remains in reciprocal crisis is the Truffula stumps abandoned from the beginning. They cannot withdraw with the Lorax since they are immobile. They transmit nothing since they *are* without language. They are not mysterious but simply there, actual loss of life without death. Without them the Once-ler suffers an anxious, meaningless existence on the 'Street of the Lifted Lorax'. At this moment their being abandoned opens him to an impotential that can end transmission, and to orienting.

Child and reader

The analysis and book are now at an opening where it is possible for the reader to experience the potential not to transmit. In the book the child arrives on the rocks left by the Lorax. Throughout the book he is mute since he must receive the message for transmission to succeed.

In the common reading the reader presupposes the child has listened and accepted the Once-ler's story as a message of responsibility. The Once-ler sees the child as the 'Unless' or future hope of human and natural communities. In this way he opens toward the child. But this opening to a possible future is foreclosed as the Once-ler throws the child the seed, seizing him in abandonment. The seed embodies responsibility in the same orientation as the Once-ler. Catching it, the child is simultaneously thrown into a community of irresponsible people, and divided and abandoned outside it. Only the child's arms and hands are depicted, just as with the Once-ler in the covered wagon. And his task is to restore the Truffula trees that 'everyone needs', which makes the trees a Thneed. This is an opening to a life of incessant responsibility to grow and protect that the child can never fulfill. Contrary to the common reading this is not a hopeful act. He comes into the human community a Lorax. His goal is survival.

But this foreclosure is not necessary and inevitable. With the child one may experience a different kind of opening than that which the Once-ler establishes. Another look at the last page shows the presence of a different orientation. With the child, the reader can accept that the child has not caught the seed and that *transmission itself remains suspended in the air*. In this suspension the reader may suffer the simple, difficult actuality that transmitting the Once-ler's message she withdraws from the child, consigning him to non-belonging in human and natural community. She may suffer herself in her own transmitting. Now, turning toward him without abandoning him she can experience what she never was, her potential not to transmit. Without reading, she can realize the seed as transmissibility itself and the white plume as the groundless opening of an orienting decision. Now readable is not only Seuss' narrative but readability itself or the white space, what Geisel never wrote or coloured in *The Lorax*. From the first letter of the book the reader has actualized her potential to read. But with the child she can interrupt her reading and orient in a different way.

White space

The white space is the key to reading *The Lorax* as an experience of the potential to transmit and at the same time not to transmit. The white is the medium that is, without text or colour, *which allows transmission to exist by submitting to its own abandonment.*

If the reader reads *The Lorax* again, contemplating transmission in this white medium, what is realized is that all the white in the book can be read in both orientations. One is the reading already exposed, wherein transmission is presupposed and actualized as narrative and colour. In this orientation white is a *thing* on which the story is transmitted. It is the suspension of the Once-ler's groundlessness as he touches the Truffula Tree; the suspension from which he stops and builds his shop; the path on which the Thneed-faced human travels; the end of the human community that extends with every axe-chop; the gesture of the Bar-ba-loots' becoming refugees; and more.

The white can also be read in itself, irreducible to the narrative and colour, the medium in which double potential can divide itself and let itself take place as transmission. In this orientation, without reading the reader reads the first gesture of the book, the 'A' not written on the first page. This is the critical moment in which medium exhibits itself in its primacy. Reading *The Lorax* in this medium, it does not teach a pedagogy of the Lorax or even of a post-Lorax. It says nothing. It is not a source of knowledge about the child, human community or nature. It has no depth of meaning. Language and color merely cover it (Nancy 1993/1997). It is unpresupposed, dwelling in language and color, giving forth itself, the white opening by which humans and nature exist in transmission.

The thing, the white, is the potential not to transmit. When primary, it is not a form of negativity; it affirms human potentiality without abandoning and being abandoned.

It is two drips of water passing from the pipe outside the Once-ler's dwelling affirm the presence of potentiality itself. The eyes of every Bar-ba-loot in 'this glorious place' indirectly indicate an experience of the potential not to exist in non-belonging and darkness. 'This glorious place' full of color, now gone white allowing transmission to take place. The white in which the Lorax withdraws 'through a hole in the smog', an idea of human potential not to exist through a relation to nature. And the plume on the last page indirectly affirming the experience of restoring transmissibility, double potentiality.

A matter of critique

The approach of this inquiry has been to think through how the activity of presupposing the potential to transmit and the potential to violate natural life may be a problem in reading *The Lorax* and doing environmental education. It reaches what is perhaps an unforeseen outcome, that *The Lorax* presents both modes of transmissibility's existence and expresses their distinction, indicating the matter of orienting. In so doing it attests to the potential not to transmit that can remain unrecognized in environmental education's messages and criticisms. On the 'Street of the Lifted Lorax' in a crisis of human–nature relations, there is a starting point for environmental education, with the potential not to transmit, in which the matter of critique is orienting.

The work of exposing the potential to transmit permits theses suggesting forms the Aristotelian orientation takes in environmental education teaching. These theses are not intended as declarations, but openings for reading in the potential not to transmit. They indicate a number of ways environmental education preserves the primacy of transmission over the potential not to transmit, and thus reflects on its problems and pedagogies in the same orientation that produces them:

> Benjamin... wrote that the past must be saved not so much from oblivion or scorn as from 'a determinate mode of its transmission', and that 'the way in which it is valued as 'heritage' is more insidious than its disappearance could ever be. (Agamben 1999, 60)

Perhaps environmental education can save the past by realizing that the child's task, if it can be called one, is not to receive a message but to play without it. Playing, he [sic] is the community's ever-present experiment in the potential not to transmit. What comes into play with the child is the experience and decision of orienting, and an experiment in unteachability or primacy of the potential not to, that *is*, without pedagogy. *The Lorax* invites us to consider what we are, without narrative and color and without violence to natural life. While it cannot teach this experience, it need not retreat from the 'fire' through which relations are constituted between learners, and between humans and nature (Hart 2007). This fire can offer itself the 'leaping spark' that kindles in the human an experience in potential not to (Plato 341c in Agamben 1999, 29).

Acknowledgements

The author wishes to thank Tom Popkewitz, Laura Hewitt, Svetlana Karpe, Bob Ray and the reviewers for their feedback and suggestions.

References

Agamben, G. 1999. *Potentialities: Collected essays in philosophy.* Stanford, CA: Stanford University Press.

Bergthaller, H. 2006. 'Trees are what everyone needs': *The Lorax,* anthropocentrism, and the problem of mimesis. In *Nature in literary and cultural studies,* ed. C. Gersdorf and S. Mayer, 155–76. New York: Rodopi.

Carson, R. 1962. *Silent spring.* New York: Houghton Mifflin.

Casarino, C. 2002. Philopoeisis: A theoretico-methodological manifesto. *Boundary 2, 29,* no. 1: 65–96.

Cott, J. 2005. The good Dr Seuss. In *Of sneetches and whos and the good Dr Seuss: essays on the writings and life of Theodore Geisel,* ed. T. Fensch, Jefferson, 99–123. NC: McFarland.

Fensch, T. 2005. *Of sneetches and whos and the good Dr Seuss: Essays on the writings and life of Theodore Geisel.* Jefferson, NC: McFarland.

Foucault, M. 1966/1973. *The order of things.* New York: Vintage.

Foucault, M. 1977. *Language, counter-memory, practice.* Ithaca, NY: Cornell University Press.

Foucault, M. 2003. *Society must be defended: Lectures at the College de France, 1975–76.* New York: Picador.

Foucault, M. 2007. *Security, territory, population: Lectures at the College de France, 1977–78.* New York: Palgrave.

Foucault, M. 2008. *The birth of biopolitics: Lectures at the College de France, 1978–79.* New York: Palgrave.

Geisel, T.S. 1971. *The Lorax, by Dr Seuss.* New York: Random House.

Gough, N. 1999. Rethinking the subject: (De)constructing human agency in environmental education research. *Environmental Education Research* 5, no. 1: 35–48.

Hart, P. 2005. Transitions in thought and practice: Links, divergences and contradictions in post-critical inquiry. *Environmental Education Research* 11, no. 4: 391–400.

Hart, P. 2007. Exploring relational politics in social learning: Dilemmas of standing too close to the fire. *Southern African Journal of Environmental Education* 24: 46–62.

Henderson, B., M. Kennedy, and C. Chamberlin. 2004. Playing seriously with Dr Seuss: A pedagogical response to *The Lorax.* In *Wild things: Children's culture and ecocriticism,* ed. S.I. Dobrin and K.B. Kidd, 118–48. Detroit: Wayne State University Press.

Heimlich, J., and N. Ardoin. 2008. Understanding behavior to understand behavior change: A literature review. *Environmental Education Research* 14, no. 3: 215–37.

Jickling, B. 2005. Ethics research in environmental education. *Southern African Journal of Environmental Education* 22: 20–34.

Kelly, W. 1972. *Pogo: We have met the enemy and he is us.* New York: Simon and Schuster.

McKenzie, M. 2005. The 'post-post period' and environmental education research. *Environmental Education Research* 11, no. 4: 401–12.

Nancy, J.-L.. 1993/1997. *The gravity of thought.* Atlantic Highlands, NJ: Humanities Press.

Rickinson, M. 2001. Learners and learning in environmental education: A critical review of the evidence. *Environmental Education Research* 7, no. 3: 207–320.

AFTERWORD

Openings for researching environment and place in children's literature: ecologies, potentials, realities and challenges

Alan Reid[a], Phillip G. Payne[b] and Amy Cutter-Mackenzie[b]

[a]Department of Education, University of Bath, Bath, UK; [b]Faculty of Education, Monash University, Victoria, Australia

This not quite 'final' ending of this special issue of *Environmental Education Research* traces a series of hopeful, if somewhat difficult and at times challenging, openings for researching experiences of environment and place through children's literature. In the first instance, we draw inspiration from the contributors who have authored, often autoethnographically, some of the art and craft of their respective ecopedagogies and research efforts. We then proceed with a reminder of the lurking presence of fear found in some of the articles published here and elsewhere, opening up the fear factor at large in broader everyday, social, political and global discourses to further scrutiny and a more optimistic quest when engaging children's literature, its risks and its hopes. Our aim here, as noted in the Editorial, is to develop the discourse and practice of environmental education research in this area. Thus, we also explore how children's literature has a pedagogical place in the positive social construction of intergenerational ethics focusing on how and what, and in what ways, textual and visual messages can be passed on to that next generation, and how and what they might take up creatively and imaginatively, in practice and conceptually. To do this, we offer thoughts on how children's literature might draw selectively from broader aspects of the eco-literature and humanities, and finally, on the basis of this collection, present a series of possible research issues and further deliberations to broadly nurture the development of research in this area.

Not quite once upon a time

I have argued that it is through narrative that we create and re-create selfhood, that self is a product of our telling and not some essence to be delved for in the recesses of subjectivity. There is now evidence that if we lacked the capacity to make stories about ourselves, there would be no such thing as selfhood.

Dysnarrativa, a severe [neurological] impairment in the ability to tell or understand stories … is deadly for selfhood … The construction of selfhood, it seems, cannot proceed without a capacity to narrate.

Once we are equipped with that capacity, we can produce a selfhood that joins with others, that permits us to hark back selectively to our past while shaping ourselves for the possibilities of an imagined future. We gain the self-told narratives that make and remake our selves from the culture in which we live. However much we may rely on a functioning brain to achieve our selfhood, we are virtually from the start expressions of the culture that nurtures us. And culture itself is a dialectic, replete with alternative narratives about what self is or might be. The stories we tell to create ourselves reflect that dialectic. (Jerome Bruner 2002, 85–7)

In this final article we revisit the themes of our Editorial and relocate the thrust of the special issue into a broader ecoculturally informed sweep about children, their experiences and literature, to open up questions about how we understand and research what (in)forms and shapes these aspects to their lives and education. In the first instance, we note that the collection raises a series of questions about our critical awareness of where stories for environmental education come from and how these stories are created, drawn on and contested, in or as an environmental education through work with children's literature. Thus, after Bruner, researchers, teachers and activists in this field might inquire as to how narratives, stories, ecologies and culture serve to enframe the discourses of environment, place and nature in educational settings, and how each are inflected therein: that is, how they provide both the *context* and *text* for a socio-ecologically grained selfhood engaged through and by the possibilities of environmental education.

Earlier work, as typified by Paul Hart (2002, 143) in relation to the narratives and lives of environmental educators, has argued that:

> According to Bruner (1990) narrative sensibility involves knowing and recognizing our own stories within the myths, folklore, and histories of our culture. As frames for our identity, narrative inquiry entails finding a place within one's culture. The challenge is one of becoming conscious and critically reflective (about, for example, how environmental education fits or differs from other curriculum goals and purposes). The challenge is to recognize the beguiling nature of narrative inquiry as a window into consciousness because it may merely be a mirror to our own. Narrative is as much a way of knowing ourselves as a way of organizing and communicating the experience of others. In our environmental education inquiries we came to see value in some form of intersubjective debate as essential to communication of other people's narratives about who we are, what we believe and why we follow one course of inquiry rather than another.

Yet for Hart as for us, whilst important, auto-ethnographic and narrative inquiries remain but one option and priority, and limited at that if we do not attend more deeply to probing what constitutes an 'eco' dimension to stories and selfhood and its claims on our literatures and lives. Indeed, given the context of a special issue, existing scholarly work as represented in two earlier special issues of this journal by Barratt Hacking and Barratt (2007)[1] and Rickinson (2001) might also inform such deliberations. In this case, both special issues raise important challenges about engaging children's lives and research issues around their voice, participation and environmental learning. However, we note that neither directly considers the role of narrative, story or literature to their review of research: the 'neuro-' and 'eco-logical' and hence arguably somaesthetic importance of which is signalled by Bruner above and by Young and Saver (2001, 72) as follows:

> Narrative is the inescapable frame of human experience. While we can be trained to think in geometrical shapes, patterns of sounds, poetry, movement, syllogisms, what predominates or fundamentally constitutes our consciousness is the understanding of

self and world in story. Not only our texts, but also our lives, gain meaning only through narrative-motivated words, words that acts as a story with a coherent sense of wholeness bound to a beginning, middle and end, as a series of events situated diachronically and with referential specificity, wrapped together by a governing sense of consequence or logic, enacted by agents, and structured by a discourse that defines a point of view.

Hart's work is known in this field for its exploration and examination of the import of such understandings to the field's research and practice, and particularly to epistemologies, methodologies and ontologies (e.g., Hart 2008). He notes the importance of an active, empowering and reflexive engagement with the demands of story-telling, story-making and story-reworking, alongside their dialectics and challenges in terms of experiential bases, writing (Hart 2002, 147):

> To act is to theorize, says Pagano (1991). I cannot describe my day or a moment in my classroom without recourse to intentions or assumptions. We act in ways that reflect our beliefs about the way the world works. Teachers' theories are stories about the kind of world we want to live in and about what we need to do (with children) to make that world … My stories reveal my values and attitudes, my sense of my cares and responsibilities, whether as teacher or as researcher. To know ourselves then becomes a teacher's or a researcher's primary obligation. Education is meant to change people, as is research; not through colonizing their consciousness but by bringing them to a place where they can go on to make up their own stories (Pagano 1991).

Thus, if we are to build upon notions of 'teachers as researchers' and 'children as researchers' or involving children and adults collaboratively in research (Barratt Hacking, Cutter-Mackenzie, and Barratt, forthcoming; Fielding 2004; Kellett 2005), we will need to consider not just recent stories and storyings, but theories and theorizings of environmental learning (e.g., Dillon 2003; Rickinson, Lundholm, and Hopwood 2010). These include engaging how they relate to the significance of certain childhood experiences, framings and voices in growing up and as possible pathways to environmental action (e.g., Chawla 2002), to issues of intergenerational learning (e.g., Ballantyne, Fien, and Packer 2001) and their eco-ethico-political qualities, to the recent neglect of family dynamics in understanding the possibilities and outcomes of ecopedagogies, including via children's literature and lifeworlds (e.g., Payne 2010a). Thus, while a number of contributions to this collection link the telling of and engaging with children's literature with experiencing place, we echo Barratt Hacking and Barratt's (2007) plea for a critical examination of childhood experiences of the environment and nature, and their links to significant life experiences, as well as to claims of positive learning and associated health and well-being benefits.

With such cautions in mind then, in this Endpiece we use a three-layered format to encourage the continuing of such 'conversations', where the very juxtaposition of the layers may lead to some novel, unexpected and non-linear unfoldings of this vitally important dimension of environmental education experience and its research. We also encourage wider discussion so that debate can be re-engaged (Robottom and Hart 1993) about an emerging 'body of knowledge' in environmental education research crucial to the inspirations, aspirations and fostering of an intergenerational ethic: children, meaning-making and the means and ends of that (e.g., literature), ecological types of experience and environmental learning (or eco'literacy'), and what shapes that end-in-view of a more positive sense of ecological being and becoming. As will become obvious in the remainder of this article, this special issue somewhat distinctively incorporates an (eco)aesthetics into the various theorizations of environmental education as a curriculum and pedagogical practice, but it also deliberates on a range of ways that researchers might frame their inquiries, as eloquently and sometimes poetically envisioned and environed by many of our contributing author/researchers.

Finally, we understand environmental education and its research as having a reflexive warrant, to examine its own assumptions and progress, or lack thereof (Reid and Scott 2006). We remain intrigued by the open question of the value(s) and useful-ness of research (Hart 2003), and in our drawing on Hart (2002), we note he has argued that in this context, we must learn (143):

> to recognize stories for what they are – versions of reality that resonate with the commu-nity (or do not). In seeking to uncover and surface unconscious, incomplete, partially coherent, or implicit thoughts as narratives, we also learn how to help teachers do that for themselves, to accept critical appraisal, to rely on intersubjective and negotiated understandings that help us adhere to reasonable levels of trustworthiness.

Thus, while considerable attention in environmental education and its research is devoted to learning and teaching, to pedagogies and ecopedagogies, including the place of children's literature as demonstrated in this special issue, we feel it is appro-priate but overdue that this warrant extends to relocating such developments towards a broader framing and thus the debating of scholarly inquiry that can offer a more comprehensive engagement of the field with new imaginaries (see, for example, McKenzie et al. 2009). In this regard, it interests us that Rishma Dunlop, who contrib-utes a Primer entitled 'Alphabet for the New Republic' to the *Fields of green* (2009) collection, previously observed (Dunlop 2002, 33) at a conference on 'Telling Our Stories' in environmental education that:

> Stories are theories, I tell my students, they are theories, opening up the scars of history, geography. Stories map us. Every work of research is in some sense a narrative, a fiction. Tell me your story and I will tell my own in new ways. I read you, reread you, see myself anew, retell our stories intertwined, tangled and the hallways of our ivory towers will breathe and pulse with the beating of hearts and wings and blood and aper-tures of hope.

A gap, or invisible, or missing in much previous work, as made clear in the focus of this special issue, is an 'aesthetics' that might sit as an equal partner with an ethics and politics of environmental education and its research, be that comfortably or uncom-fortably. Thus, while we note that the 'larger' or 'harder' ethico-political dimension appears to have waxed and waned in some quarters of the discourse of environmental education research over the past two decades, inquiries as to the place of children's literature, conceived broadly, can make a valuable and useful contribution to making visible some aspects of such an elusive aesthetics and, as we see in a number of the contributions, gestures to an ethics or/and politics. Yet, we must still ask, has such work grappled with their interconnections, contradictions and possibilities, noting Jim Cheney's (2002, 89–90) observations at the Stories conference noted above, that:

> A culture is best understood as a people enacting a story relating humans, nature and the sacred … the basic contrast [is] between stories rooted in fear and stories rooted in trust … I ask my students to try on the these stories by Leopold et al., to wear them for a while, see how they fit, see what differences they make to their perception and sense of being-in-the-world.

They are simply asked to live with the 'world' of the story, to live on its terms. This exercise makes it possible for students to read Leopold, Snyder, Berry and House as stories as lives lived – lives lived within larger lives, stories within larger stories – rather than as arguments in competition with one another.

But some stories are destructive, not conducive to ecosystemic health. The story that Western Culture whispers in our ears … is that the world was made for man and man was destined to conquer and rule – a tragic scenario that excludes other stories and reduces a rich and varied ecosystem in the direction of monoculture. How do we evaluate stories? How do we tell good stories with (and about) our lives? How do we learn to tell comedic stories … of the Earth and its human and other-than-human citizens?

How should we understand stories? They seem, many of them, to be at once descriptive and evaluative. They orient us, it seems, by telling us what our world is like and how we might be good citizens within it. They may seem to point to moral norms suggested by (or derivable from) presumably true (though storied) accounts of the world. Other stories … seem to be merely prescriptive: they are simply storied forms of telling us what we ought to do.

In the three layers of interpretation and commentary about the contributions to this special issue that follow: first, we broadly consider how the discourse of fear perpetuated by a variety of media in the lives of the younger generation often overwhelms the positive nexus of risk and hope we think has an 'ir/real place' in children's environmental and place literatures, as found in the contributions to this collection. Then we consider how children's literature, as an emerging research question for environmental education, can partially be relocated, re'placed' and re-imagined in the broader development of the 'eco' in the humanities, literature and cultural studies, for example, in ecocomposition, ecopoetics, ecoart and environmental criticism. And third, we derive from the contributions to this collection a range of hopefully compelling questions, illustrations and deliberations that might further engage the development of environmental education inquiries in these and associated areas.

The ecology of fear

The transition from a mechanistic to an organismic image of the earth and the accompanying shift in attention from the geosphere to the biosphere fundamentally alters the human perception of time upon which all definitions of human security are based. The linear time frame of geospheric politics will have to be bent into the cyclical loop of the biospheric processes. The notion of an ever-accelerating rate of production and consumption rushing into an open-ended cornucopic future has led us to the present environmental and economic crisis. In the name of progress, we have mortgaged our planet's future and made our children's world far less secure. Reorienting the time frame of human culture to make it compatible with the circadian, lunar, and circannual cycles of the biosphere will mean rethinking the most essential features of our temporal values. (Jeremy Rifkin 1991, 264–5)

It's all a question of story. We are in trouble just now because we do not have a good story. We are in between stories. The old story, the account of how the world came to be and how we fit into it, is no longer effective. Yet we have not learned the new story. Thomas Berry (1990; cited in David Hicks 1998, 165)

New stories

It is far riskier to reposition children's literature, broadly defined as we have encouraged in this special issue, beyond *matters of ecoliteracy and into, for example, an aesthetics whose momentum in the humanities, arts and cultural studies is being taken up in the burgeoning fields of environmental rhetoric, ecocomposition (e.g., Killingsworth 2005), ecopoetics (e.g., Bate 2000; Brady 2003; Peters and Irwin 2002), ecocriticism (e.g., Garrard 2004; Glotfelty and Fromm 1996) and environmental criticism (e.g., Buell 1995, 2001, 2005). A spectrum of hope, fear and criticism can be found in these theoretical and/or conceptual vantage points from which the 'work' of environmental education research in relation to 'story' and 'image' in children's literature (and indeed others) can be found and deliberated about. In listing these newer scholarly vantage points that might be 'valuable' and 'useful' in emerging genres of inquiry (Hart 2003), we note here the legacy of the genre of nature writing that has made such an important intergenerational contribution to the notion of environmentalism and literature (see, for example, the Cheney*

Children's literature and the realities of environmental education

We are living at the end of a story. That is to say the end of a period of history that had great attractions to it, although it also had an underside that we are only beginning to feel. But it's the end of the industrial story. That was our own invention as humans, and it is only one way that we have been in the world. We have to remind ourselves that we have only been in that period called modern-industrialism a short time. But in that short period of time, we have had a devastating impact in terms of how we have invented ourselves.

This technozoic story that we're living in is a terminal story, although it is glossed, in terms of advertising, as the direction we have to go. What is needed in that sense is a deep discernment, to be able to actually look through, and see through, that type of story. That is not a life-giving story and it is not an inspiring story … I think that sense of a journey is important in terms of our stories, as part of a story about the journey of our lives. And so, in that way, I appreciate the stories that are actually fighting for the sense of the differentiation of the creativity of the universe in which we live in, the ones that express the deep sense of subjectivity. That is to say, the different types of interiority, and also the expanse of stories of communion – differentiated communion is so important – to have that kind of discernment, to move away from the things that do not do that,

Twenty years ago, in the *Wall Street Journal*, Stephen Hicks (1991) claimed that 'global problems are too big for little kids' (A20). While environmental education research and policy rhetoric sometimes position children as catalysts for change (Ballantyne, Connell, and Fien 1998), they often negate that this so-called empowerment is overwhelmingly fed by fear (adult fear). Children and young people appear to feel either disempowered and therefore disenfranchised, all the while being summoned or constructed by particular interests as 'planet savers' and 'earth warriors'. What are they being asked to do? Hicks (1991, A20) alleged:

> **If we want our six and seven year olds to be ready to deal with acid rain when their time comes, teach them now how to care for a 30-gallon aquarium ... If we want them to be in a position to handle the Saddam Hussein's of the world ... Do not ask them now what they would do if terrorists exploded chemicals weapons above their town or what we do if the food chain irreparably were damaged by pollution ... Frightened or apathetic children are not going to grow into the adults who will be able to solve the world's problems.**

quotation in layer 1, cf. note 2). But while we suggest these newer 'eco' fields of theory about literature, narrative and image are, indeed, a renewed effort to legitimize the relationship between literary studies, environmental concerns and cultural production, most recent legitimizing efforts are truly adult concerns, as any cursory glance of the contents of the 'new' journals of ecopoetics and ecocriticism will reveal. Children, their cultures and their literatures (including Dobrin's reference in this issue to Ulmer's notion of networked 'elactracy') are absent from consideration. So too, is how story, telling and sensory/perceptual immersion can occur experientially in embodied ways in nature's places, as a number of contributors to this collection have described, explained or recommended.

Yet linking children's literature to deeper understandings of, for example, ecocomposition, ecodrama, ecopoetics, ecoart or environmental criticism is a risk-taking venture we feel is worth recommending for two basic and interrelated reasons. First, environmental education research must face the challenge of developing a credible literature base and, perhaps more discerningly, establishing bodies

> and move toward those things that make life joyful and beautiful. (Ed O'Sullivan in Bob Jickling et al. 2002, 286–7)

> Our society has become a recited society, in three senses; it is defined by *stories* (*recits*, the fables constituted by our advertising and informational media), by *citations* of stories, and by the interminable *recitation* of stories. (Michel de Certeau 1984, 186)

A key point of departure in our Editorial was to illustrate some of the everyday and possible experiences and realities of children's literature. Throughout this collection, and the different layers of this Endpiece, we have continued that work. Yet while other contributions to this special issue have hinted at it (Bigger and Webb, Burke and Cutter-Mackenzie, Dobrin, Morgan, Sloane), it is Payne who most directly highlights how the 'irreal's' entanglements with 'reality' might have significant value to our ongoing deliberations about environmental education practice, theory and research. Irreality is a notion that alerts us to the not quite reality of what we take to be real and the reality of that we take to be non- or unreal.[3] It affords a reopening to questions of the (pre?)supposed realism, and hence stability and multiplicity, of environmental

How much has changed since the 1990s? We can fairly confidently state that today's children have many hopes, fears, uncertainties and, often, boundless optimism worth preserving despite the cultures and discourses of fear that dominate in the everyday. Children's environmental fears are all too often characterized by popular media as soaring with an environmental apocalypse (Garrard 2004) described elsewhere as the 'new bogeyman' [sic] of the twenty-first century (Chua 2009). Research about children's fears is inconclusive but death, illness, spiders, snakes and being invaded/bombed are included in many children's lists of most common fears (Muris et al. 1997; Ollendick and Yang 1996; Salcuni et al.

of knowledge that foster a greater degree of 'insightfulness' on a range of thematic or applied fronts (Gray-MacDonald and Selby 2008; Reid 2009). Near and dear to many of us, pedagogy – better still, ecopedagogy, for want of shifting to a more discerningly ecocentric disposition informing the learning transaction between adult teacher and child learner (and their environments and places) – is one such thematic orientation, noting the Greek term paidagogeo *emphasized the art and craft of teaching, or leading of young children (boys only, sic). We might ask what is the artfulness of the craft of pedagogy? An aesthetic is, at least, implied but now perhaps forgotten as pedagogy becomes more of a technical enterprise driven by outcomes and measurable standards of rationality, literacy and numeracy, increasingly driven and mediated by the technologies of globalization and abstraction. A challenge we see coming out of the above, and the new theoretical vantage points listed earlier, is the invitation to revisit,*

education and its imaginaries more broadly, and not just as confined to the special place of children's literature. In this regard, modernity with its various commitments and admonishments has been seen as a kind of victory for realism – and more often than not for naive rather than critical forms in environmental education (e.g. Hart 2005; McKenzie 2005). Put sharply, when operating in a realist genre only, educators risk proceeding with an unwitting collapsing of the senses and the sense that might be made in and through this particular version of environmental education (Reid 2003).

Put otherwise, our point about the elision of the ir/real is that literature and its musterings highlight how a reader can be amenable to a beyond oneself experience including to other-than-human nature. As a (public) text, children's literature might thus be understood as a fictive vehicle for communicating as well as contesting a 'true(r?) reality' beyond its material manifestations and representational capacities. This irreality necessarily invites further considerations of mediations (e.g., processes and practices of visualizing, cajoling, revealing and informing) as well as the specific attitude and status of a suspension of disbelief that is commonly supposed in our encounters with literature. In short, a mediation shouldn't go unnoticed, nor is the suspension automatic. Equally, neither should be regarded simplistically, particularly given the profound nature and enchanting possibilities that may be afforded by our experiences of reading and writing.

Furthermore, rather than perhaps assume in this field that education is a relatively transparent representation or mirror of reality itself through its various curriculum selections and the experiences and capabilities environmental education fosters (see Hardy 2006), if we acknowledge that education works as a medium too we might then ask, what of its particular role as an 'illusion of reality' in its various and specific

2009). Yet, a looming environmental crisis is not widely, let alone universally, identified. It appears that two different stories are being told. The first positions the child in an ecology (or imaginary) of fear. The second is more focused on the internal workings of the child and a fear of their ecology (biophobia). In any case, real or imagined, fear appears omnipresent in the minds of the young.

According to Greg Garrard (2004), there are clear challenges and risks of advocating some ecocritical approaches to literature in lieu of others, particularly when we trace their logics. For instance, he suggests (2004, 71–2):

carefully consider and reimagine the pedagogical (and research) art and craft of the stories we 'tell' to the next generation and each other.

Second, there exists the closely related challenge for environmental educators and researchers that by drawing from the outside *in on stories about and notions of ecocomposition, ecocriticism and ecopoetics that those, potentially, 'harder-to-reach' varieties of theory, research and discourse might enrich, enliven and extend current framings of and research about ecoliteracy and its formation as an interdisciplinary 'end-in-view' focus of ecopedagogical development and scholarly inquiry. Conversely, as indicated, research already undertaken on the* inside *of environmental education about children's environmental voice, learning, experience and budding ecoliteracies should reciprocally inform emerging notions of ecocomposition, ecopoetics and ecocriticism so as to intervene early, qualify, resist or avoid the downloading*

affordances and potentialities (Sloane 2010)? Arguably no matter what the public and private 'aspirations', 'ceremonies' and 'rituals' of authoring and reading children's ecoliterature are as 'an education', in light of this special issue they along with the texts themselves no longer need to be the primary objects or ends of inquiry. Rather we might do better to embrace questions as to how an experience of literature serves to reconfigure or even transform the wider social–ecological–cultural relations with which embodied selves do, can or might engage. Thus, not only are researches of the eco-experiences of children's literature a matter of investigating the possibilities for new knowledge and accommodation of that knowledge, but as an embodied, immersive, playful and engaged relation, opportunities to broach questions as to whether they are also about engendering new entities: reconfiguring social–ecological ontologies, transformed by and transforming the everyday (sometimes opaque) practices of both reading and producing children's books, stories and illustrations in this and related fields of practice and inquiry (Dobrin 2010).

To be clear, children's literature often supported by visual representations variously implies a *narrator and artist* (perhaps sometimes inarticulate or even painfully expressive?), *narrative and form* (perhaps compelling, novel, hackneyed ...?) as well as a *recipient* of the *narration and imagery* (perhaps amenable or obdurate, be they the child or adult co-reader?). Through its diegesis and mimesis, literature in general offers intrigues, descriptions, drama, discourse, ideologies, a refraction of the writer's or illustrator's lived experience, etc. But our point about the irreal is not to precipitate a rush to interpret particular children's literature in these terms alone, but to grapple further with the notion's 'eco-nomy' of mediated intimacies and presences, and of their effects. Thus, it may be to reposition the 'remarkability' of the imagination as

Deep ecology … has conspired with some American ecocriticism to promote a poetics of authenticity for which wilderness is the touchstone. To critique this is not to argue for the abandonment of wilderness to the tender mercies of ranchers and developers, but to promote instead the poetics of responsibility that takes ecological science rather than pantheism as its guide. The choice between monolithic, ecocidal Modernism and reverential awe is a false dichotomy that ecocriticism can circumvent with a pragmatic and political orientation. The fundamental problem of responsibility is not what we humans are, nor how we can be better, more natural, primal or authentic, but what we do. Ecocriticism would not then be seeking a more truthful or enlightening discourse of nature, but a more effective rhetoric of transformation and assuagement.

of adult versions of 'environmentalism' that undoubtedly are part of the problem, as Hicks identified earlier in the Wall Street Journal.

With these hopes and risks in mind, we reiterate the call for papers for this special issue. It noted that while children's literature may afford some children their first significant contact with nature and animals, albeit vicariously and abstracted, it is still a formative influence. Thus, with a stake in enhancing the notion of ecopedagogy and ecoliteracy and their respectively undertheorized relation with (children's) literature, image and different types of networked and/or experientially embodied 'tellings' in places, some of the major ideas from these outside in *vantage points merit engaging in ways that seek to advance that literature and environmental education research about and for it. There is not the space here to differentiate sharply between nature writing, environmental rhetoric, ecocomposition, ecopoetics and ecocriticism,*

that of a structure that allows significations to take place (e.g., Payne and Wattchow 2009). And, when experiencing children's literature, to invite consideration as to what that might then imply about the lifeworlds of author and recipient of the text, ecocentrically viewed and otherwise: the immediate mileux of 'actors' and characters socio-ecologically, the affordances and limitations of the world of consciousness of N, as well as that of the constitution of communicative action, be that on the page, in the classroom or out in the field (see, for example, Sloane 2010).

Regarding education as an institution and setting for releasing the imagination, as Maxine Greene (2000) has observed, is but one well-known way of engaging these matters further. Another is to consider how an environmental education through the experiencing of children's literature serves to connote and express in a range of ways and evocations, through their images *and* words, because each can be 'gateways' to the imagination given their very power to (re)present. Thus, in our inquiries another potential point of departure may be to give attention to matters of the role of the unconscious and the symptomatic in constituting the lifeworld – not just our dispositions or learned habits of reading. Moreover, as Dobrin (2010) argues, an analytical hiatus to be avoided is disassociating word from image and image from word, e.g. in 'discourse analysis', particularly given the shifts in the 'technics' available to our 'green eyes'; put otherwise, the challenge is to reconcile rather than divorce an analysis of the complex jouissance of reading 'with' the (ir)real from that of the means of production of an ecoliteracy of reality, narrowly to broadly conceived.

Yet by a similar token, the irreal of environmental education might also be engaged via another route: that is, through recourse to a reckoning of our notions of the sublime. Doing so could invite consideration of whether this notion directly or

Notwithstanding the risks associated with conventional pedagogical approaches, is there then a more hopeful and imaginative prospect that education can contribute to rather than lapse into? According to David Sobel (1996), as with Hicks, much environmental education is developmentally inappropriate particularly with respect to young children. Where classrooms in a globalizing condition of education all too often focus on exotic and distant ecological environments (and their crisis-like threats) in unknown or nameless places/spaces, children become disassociated as a consequence of those environments and their ecologies' premature abstraction (Sobel 2008; cf. Payne 2010a). Like many others,

let alone how they might be reconfigured in children's cultures and environmental literatures (Dobson and Kidd 2004). Elements and characteristics of each and all can be found in the contributions to this collection but, overall, there still appears to be a lack of thematic coherence or sustained convergence on, potentially, the harder-to-reach varieties of theory such as that which can be found in, for example, the eclectic understandings of environmental criticism and environmental education that seems to stretch across the different vantage points mentioned above (see Buell 2005; Garrard 2010). Moreover, re-examining the links between children's story, literature, art, the discourses of environmental criticism and, for example, schooling, preservice teacher education, parenting or curriculum theory might add further credibility and, hence, legitimacy to different cues that can already be found in environmental education research; consequently, this commentary seeks to push some of the needed structures

should inform some of the concepts and experiences sought via the language, media and instantiations of environmental education. This is because it readily speaks to something of the realm of surprise, fascination, awe and astonishment that experiences of and 'epiphanies' via nature and its representations might, or are claimed, to afford. Thus, while an essential aspect of language theory is examining the conditions for its possibility to be intelligible and translatable, in *The critique of judgement*, Kant (1790/ 1987) argues against the common sense presumption that a sublime feeling comes from 'out there', as if the object (e.g., nature encountered) were prehensible without relation. Rather it is taken to suggest an index of a unique state of mind that recognizes its present incapacity to find expression adequate to the sublime feeling.

In that Payne's contribution argues for greater attention to how educators and learners engender an embodied and 'ecocentric sense of self' when faced with the irreal, including the role that pedagogical devices, structures, technologies and peda-gogues play in this, similar interpretations and implications can be drawn from Dobrin's and Sloane's contributions (among others less directly). Revisiting this in relation to a Kantian interpretation of the sublime, such a feeling borne of a somaes-thetic environmental education activity – such as journeying through and with Ingpen's (or Tolkien's) imaginative universe, as an extended case in this collection – may well serve to challenges one's existing understandings, language and competence in the need to make way for such imaginaries, since, as Payne notes, some do or may find them fundamentally unpresentable or incomprehensible in their current terms.

How then might such a person – learner, reader, embodied self – proceed in this situation? Try, perhaps 'like a child', to find a way of making 'it' imitate what it refers to – e.g., via an onomatopoeia? Or should they, perhaps 'like an adult', try to

including Barratt Hacking and Barratt (2007), Sobel (1996, 10) argues that environmental education must allow children to 'have an opportunity to bond with the natural world, to learn to love it and feel comfortable in it, before being asked to heal its wounds'.

Although generally lacking in this collection, among those contributions where children's voices are featured (Burke and Cutter-Mackenzie, Payne, Wason-Ellam), children tend not to be positioned as catalysts, warriors, saviours or even as 'empowered'. Rather, they are positioned in individualized local contexts, engaging with and caring for their local places in imaginative,

identified by Lawrence Buell and by Dobrin (2010) and these are further elaborated below.

A snapshot of hope and risk! Ecocomposition might pithily be described as an evolving refinement within the field of environmental rhetoric in that it shifts our attention and interest to the act *of writing (or other modes, genres and styles of representation) which, in their own right, is an ecopedagogy (Bai et al. 2010) and, for example, can occur immersively in the places of its production (Burke and Cutter-Mackenzie 2010). We witnessed this in the 'older' genre of nature writing. Ecopoetics, too, is probably more phenomenological in nature in that it draws much of its inspiration from the (romantic) 'lived' experience of (sublime) nature but in doing so may also (less naively) signal critical and political concerns (for example, Bowerbank 1999), as ecocriticism more overtly tends to do (see Merchant 1995). Ecopoetics, it*

domesticate 'it', grafting it onto another meaning, and in effect, create a hypertext? Or seek to engage 'it' or represent 'it' through arts-based or non-linguistic practices? Or, might this example actually offer another opening on to the ir/real of/in environmental education, and thus we might (once) again temporarily 'suspend disbelief' and see where that leads more widely (without shedding our longstanding critical and reflexive dispositions, of course). In effect, the latter option is to recognize once more that while we may not always be able to account for phenomena in and of themselves, we may still need to re-evaluate the principles and explanations that they have some bearing upon, particularly in adjudicating claims made that such and such an 'eco-experience' (via children's literature) is singular or stand alone, unique or irrevocably valuable as a contribution to an environmental education worthy of the name.

Equally, we should note that positing an irreal as necessary to ways of remaining curious about the status of realism and rationality in environmental education and its research is always already but one approach to engaging the structures and mean(ing)s of the real in this area. Increasingly, wider scholarship has gone elsewhere, or further, tying these inquiries to notions of the imaginary and symbolic too. The 'trialectic' of real, imaginary and symbolic is quite familiar in structuralist and poststructuralist circles in their concerns with the connexions between writing, subjectivity and culture, as in the latter's radical questioning of otherness and the subject–object relation (as befits a modernist epistemology), but also in how these are taken up and consolidated in pedagogies, such as in terms of the dispositions they seem to articulate or foreclose when engaging the 'imaginations' at work and play in a pedagogic field such as environmental education (e.g., Barrett 2008). And yet all this remains relatively unexplored in the Anglophone discourse of environmental education research (cf. the awakened, critical, creative, embodied, playful and reflexive ways facilitated through children's literature. Children's literature provides an entry point, opening or address for environmental education where locally based stories and their visual and embodied accompaniments drive curriculum and pedagogy. This paints quite a different picture to that of Maslin's, as cited in Sobel (1996, 2):

> The familiar old tales of ducks and bunnies may not have conveyed as many facts, but they were filled with whimsical possibilities that have no place in today's didactic children's literature. Bedtime stories of the past served the magical purpose of

must be pointed out, is not restricted to nature poetry or environmental poems. The Greek term poiesis *connotes the artistic and poetic aim, as a process of 'making', and a form of 'bringing forth', 'cultivation and flowering' or 'blossoming' of the blossom. In education discourse, particularly the almost forgotten role of curriculum theory, there are distinct similarities with the notion of* currere *(Huebner 1999).*

Within the contemporary mood of paidagogeo *and* currere, *we are promoting ecopedagogically their aestheticized mirrors as derived from the contributions to this special issue. There are numerous mediums of the modern 'utopian' and/or postmodern 'imaginary' through which ecopoetics might bring forth a worldview different or other to those that dominate (Bai et al. 2010; Payne 2010b), noting Dobrin's (2010) double-edged play on the notion of 'greening'. Most contributions to this issue line up with ecocriticism, as both a form of analysis and critique of texts (e.g., Morgan),*

Brazilian Journal of Environmental Education, volume 3, 2008, which makes strong use of these terms in exploring poststructuralist, psychoanalytic and vitalist theories for environmental education).[4]

Thus, if we proceed with this as some kind of budding 'momentum', given that such terms and their discourses have haunted Deleuze's and Guattari's work (e.g., Guattari 1989/2000), and find their way into those that Noel Gough (2006) amongst others has drawn on to inform a variety of 'post-…' studies in environmental education (less 'usual suspects' are included in Hardy 2002, 2006) – it may be timely to ask more serious questions about how reality is made necessary to our understandings and expectations of environmental education. Is it, in fact, regarded as a 'necessary fiction' in some quarters or instantiations of the field, as in when we consider a revitalized or reimagined role for children's literature and illustration in environmental education? Or, given contemporary debates such as the disputes about the social construction and mediation of climate change data, would these not suggest significant and wider warrant for re-examining our assumptions about the reality necessary to environmental education? In such cases, after or alongside Gough, Hardy and others, we might start by revisiting the logics and underpinnings that suppose environmental education must always have to represent 'Reality' – which, whose, on what terms, etc., are often deemed to be obvious starting questions (see Russell 2005; Russell and Dillon 2010, on how 'scientific' environmental education might (well/need to) be)?

To move closer to a Deleuzian project, this would require considering which figurations of *truth, reality, objectivity* and *subjectivity* are to hand in environmental education theory and practice, or for that matter, which prefigurations or configurations, if we were to (re)inflect it with strains of Ricoeur's work on narrative, in

stirring children's imagination conjuring up a world of endless possibilities and then leaving young readers pleasantly sleepy. Today's versions, sounding the alarm over our shrinking hopes and resources, may leave them exhausted.

The ecologically imaginative 'magic' and 'spell' (Abram 1996) that Sobel (1996, 2005, 2008) and Louv (2005), among others (see Bowers 1993, 1997; Gruenewald 2003), have claimed is lost in environmental education is arguably overstating the case given these and wider 'findings'. Yet, it might well serve to confirm another source of fear, or denial, in that such generalizations devalue children's everyday

assessment (e.g., Hug) and socio-cultural commentary (e.g., Wason-Ellam) for the messages they convey and, therefore, as a means of ethical and political commentary about the human sources of the environmentally problematic human condition as it is textually constructed in the literature and which might be used therefore to develop a sense of agency (e.g., Bigger and Webb). Sloane's contribution further opens up for inspection how we might aesthetically and politically consider the 'message' aimed to be conveyed by the role or place of the text and, presumably, the visual image. Ecocriticism, as it might be reimagined in children's ecoliteracy development will deal with the textual, literary and visual conceptions and constructions of, for instance, environmental racism that are indicated already in this collection and are informed by a range of critical approaches and perspectives, for example, poststructural ecofeminism, postcolonialism and feminism.

environmental education research (cf. Bigger and Webb 2010). Indeed, which analytical difference/s – fundamental to superficial – emerge, if we consider working on reality with children's literature, empirical datasets, experiential learning, etc., or some such blend of their 'material' in environmental education? Thus, we might find we can use this brief 'dérive' as a spur to a meta-question, *how has an environmental education become what it is such that people claim it and recognize it to be really so in their everyday life and practices*? Is it through the stories and realities their environmental education mobilizes, avails or contests? Through the 'materiality' it is argued to portend? Through the unconscious, abstracted or other such dimensions that are excluded? Through the reappreciations and confrontations of its totality and contexts – such as the interiors and outsides of environmental education, their dynamics and constitution? Arguably a Barthian-inspired reading of such matters in relation to Alun Morgan's interests in the *Lord of the Rings* would take this as an impetus to explore how a myth says what its says in the 'everyday' of environmental education and of its participants, including how this myth's inflexions distort and transform one's reality through its Middle-earth 'naturalizations'.[5]

Returning more directly to the thematics of the special issue, a clear implication of such possibilities and questions is to open up (once more) the matter of whether we presuppose language and experience are uniformly transparent (rather than opaque, differentiated ...) or arguably not yet fully understood or known in relation to their referents for this field (e.g., Stables 2004, 2006, 2007). Another might be to ask, whether the truth of literature as an art in environmental education should be predicated on verisimilitude rather than some other criteria (cf. Abram 1996) such as the lived experiences. They invoke a sense of hopelessness when vision, alongside imagination and hope, are needed, mixed in with a bolder approach to risk-making and taking. As David Hicks (1998, 174) states (citing Richardson 1996), we need:

> Stories – myths and folktales as well as true accounts – to help us hold the beginnings, middles and ends of our lives together. Without them we shall not have hope: yes, to lose stories is to lose hope, but conversely to construct and cherish stories is to maintain hope.

Not quite did they/we live happily ever after

Buell's (2005) non-closured take on the past, present and future of 'environmental criticism' and the role of literary imagination addresses a wide range of the above interests that, in sum, reflect an 'environmental turn' and opening in literary and cultural studies. Buell asserts that the notion of environmental criticism better conveys the hybridity and heterogenous foci of this turn as it has captured the diverse interests making up the interdisciplinary study of literature and environmental studies. He consistently links environmental criticism to the arts and the imagination. Buell traces the emergence of 'first wave' ecocriticism in the early 1990s and extracts or synthesizes three distinctive concerns of the turn as subsequent waves continue to the present and, undoubtedly, the future of the literary imagination. His three

irreal or even the 'sublime'? In such a vein, it might even be argued that a theory of environmental education in 'full flower' should be capable of opening up ways to changing the field's thinking and capacities and their dimensions, including their regularities of actions (and hence the field's techniques and technologies). Doing so, it appears, would require ensuring a fuller range and quality of contributions are appraised when adjudicating the contributions that experiences of environmental education might make to social–ecological life, in that inquiries would require attention to a wider range of factors, concerns and priorities that have demonstrable traction within and across the spheres of 'imagination, symbol, and real'.

Yet it would also appear that such provocations are only comprehensible and actionable if we are prepared to discuss the various strategies and tactics we use to 'sail close(r)' to reality in environmental education. To secure ontological purchase here might well require a moving on from some realities, so to speak, breaking their chains, binds, and hold … seeking out the 'grounds' and conditions for new leases of life, for generative (and not just performative gestures at) theory and theorizing in the field. We can recognize that the goal of much work under the banner of decolonization in environmental education has been an attempt to do just that, as exemplified in a range of contributions to this collection about its possible role and place in working with children's literature. The decolonizer's aims are historically and contextually attentive: to dismantle the assumptions and apparatus that prevent an indigenous people speaking for itself. For environmental educators, it amounts to a plea to refuse and resist colonized peoples being spoken for and represented by a more powerful hegemonic Other that proceeds as if that other is more rational, reasonable and

Ecology of hope

Collectively, the articles in the special issue have featured teachers', parents', researchers' and children's voices, to varying extents. Yet, often reflected in these voices are stories of hope, their challenges, and not simply their achievement. In particular, Bai et al. have reflected on their collective experience as teachers, researchers, parents and children. They identify *biophilia* as fundamental to an environmental education and, in so doing, attempt to unravel the complex relationship between *biophilia* and *bibliophilia* through a process of indwelling. This resonates with Bigger and Webb's article which explored the

concerns are glimpsed, partially, in the various contributions to this collection. The first abiding concern of environmental criticism is its investment in the literature with issues of environmental imaging and representation. Second, its interest in the reconceiving of 'place' as a fundamental dimension of art and lived experience. Third, its strong ethical and/or political commitment.

Titled 'environmental criticism's future', Buell's (2005) final chapter provides a cue for this ends-in-view piece, noting Buell wanted to open that future up for discussion rather than close it down. In his preceding chapter on the ethics and politics of environmental criticism, Buell observed the most discernible trend in North American environmental criticism was towards environmental justice but from within a shift to a sociocentric perspective.[2] Elements of this trend to justice can be found in Wason-Ellam (2010), Korteweg, Gonzalez, and Guillet (2010) and Morgan (2010). Any hint

enlightened than those silenced by the processes and outcomes of colonization. On the one hand, removing the 'coordinates' that allow for superiority to be presumed, and on the other, challenging the biases that are implicit in what passes as accepted wisdom and the essential truths and realities of environmental education, are all part and parcel of achieving such decolonization, as Korteweg, Gonzalez and Guillet argue in their article.[6]

Likewise, those proceeding to argue that ideas in science about nature are not somehow automatically 'objective' – in fact, the stories science tells are often those it wants to tell itself, as Donna Haraway (1994) forcefully puts it – serves to articulate the claim that story-telling about nature in a science-based environmental education may be such that it positions nature in ways that do harm: to the constituents of ecology and culture, our mental furniture as well as our experiences of embodiment, and their interrelations given our immediate context for discussion (cf. Hug 2010; Payne 2010b). Nature as (always?) the abstracted, irreal, untamed other in feminine guise; the metaphorically realist/material comforting Mother Earth; the inscrutable object that must ceaselessly be investigated to yield its secrets and essence; the text to be read in the code of mathematics and biomedicine; and so forth, have been widely critiqued in feminist and post-informed scholarship (see Garrard 2004 for an engaging survey). Certainly, the oppressions environmental educators and learners may confront in working with literature may not simply be those that relate to colonization but also extend to questions of gender, age, ableness, sexualities, ethnicity and cultural predominances (cf. Garrard 2010). As Hug illustrates, with environmental education being so often predicated on or/and subtended by Western-based notions of science role that teachers and parents play in encouraging deep and critical discussion about environment and place with children via literature. Central to these articles and others in the special issue (Burke and Cutter-Mackenzie, Hug, Korteweg, Gonzalez, and Guillet, Payne, Wason-Ellam) is a paramount focus on 'the local'. In other words, stories of hope are *placed* ecologically, as Wason-Ellam demonstrates in her account of a Year 3 teacher engaging her prairie class with the picture book, 'If you're not from the Prairie' (Boughard and Ripplinger 1993).

Wason-Ellam has also emphasized that this apparently nostalgic text captures a prairie or rural lifestyle which is all too often characterized (and

that this trend is generalizable or transferable must be treated cautiously though, noting the various cultural and regional views about nature, the national differences in which literary histories are constructed and traditions exist, as also with children's cultures and, for the immediate critical purposes here, reconceptualized approaches in education to 'ecoliteracy', as well as the availability and accessibility in the academy of resource bases supporting, or denying, environmental criticism and environmental education research.

Buell's (2005, 128) 'futures' identify four basic challenges that are paraphrased below and partially contextualized via this special issue in opening up the possibilities for environmental education research, children's literature and environmental education. First, the challenge of organization. This collection is a first for the field in that it thematically draws our attention to children's literature but

and its stories about nature, the acts of appraising and then tackling the tropes and narratives articulated in environmental (science) learning and texts may well become points of departure for many educators, but we would argue they may also lead to other queries: concerning the symbolic and imaginative powers and projects of the field's groundings, discourses and narrativizations, including how these might be taken up and challenged by teachers and teacher educators in the experiences they frame and encourage (see Burke and Cutter-Mackenzie 2010).

For Korteweg, Gonzalez and Guillet (2010), doing such work entails a difficult but necessary process of decolonizing our narratives and the realities they speak of or to, including those associated with using and experiencing children's literature in environmental education. As Elsie Cloete (2011) argues in *Environmental Education Research*, the very construction and emplacement of historic English terms like 'animal', 'bush' and 'game' in conservation institutions and practices in Southern Africa has inscribed much of the environmental education there with a set of theoretical and ideological assumptions that have profound political, pedagogical and ontological implications for the status of local, traditional and indigenous knowledge and experience in that region (see also Shava et al. 2010). Scholarship though is but one avenue, activism another. How (else) might these be furthered or reconceived in the research field?

If we consider the production of this collection, the first draft of Wason-Ellam's article drew on the notion of creating 'a pictorial atlas of the world'. The children in her study are from different backgrounds and work with a diverse set of expectations and articulations that frame locally based knowledge and ways of knowing; in this

thus dismissed) as simple. The book jolts such assumptions, deeply focusing on the primordial power and cycles of nature – the elementals of wind, the sky, the snow, the sun. It affirms the evocative strength and somaesthetic significance of embodied meaning-making (Shusterman 2008) of a locally based curriculum in which carefully considered and emplaced ecopedagogies might flourish, all the while governments (worldwide) (for example, UNESCO 2004) push a globalized curriculum that is largely placeless and perhaps even baseless (in as much as its ability to produce/prepare an ecoliterate population).

in so doing is partially attentive to the earlier environmental education research literature mentioned in the introduction above that has consistently but eclectically over the past decade or so focused on children, learning, significant experiences, voice, narrative, story, ways of knowing/thinking and pedagogy. This special issue may inspire further research along the lines of, or otherwise to, the limited number of contributions appearing here, but extend to reviews that bring that existing eclecticism into a more useful frame of understanding about children's ecoliteracy and its formative processes and developments through the idea of ecopedagogy.

Second, Buell (2005) identifies the challenge of professional legitimation. While children's literature has always enjoyed a reasonable status in, for example, pre-service teacher education in Australia (from where two of us usually write), research

instance, to foreground those from Indigenous, scientific, artistic, and migrant communities. While the title and focus of Wason-Ellam's paper has shifted considerably during the preparation of this collection, we might also note that in Michel Serres' stimulating work (2006) on the philosophy and history of science and on the significance of narrative to both, he too has discussed the atlas as metaphoric, arguing that the communication it embodies and facilitates may enable a 'voyaging' that renders purported or real boundaries quite permeable.

Serres has made similar observations about the Harlequin and the angel as metaphors to speak of an ir/reality that is not universally or continuously experienced. In the particular case of an atlas though, as one creates horizontal connections between North and South, local and global, we can readily appreciate how utterly diverse spatially distributed elements might be brought together in 'non-hierarchical' structures and relations on the pages of a book. In so doing, the atlas (via our workings with its 'pictures' and 'words') can help displace a sense of isolation, marginality or absolute Otherness.[7] Likewise, translating, telling and hearing stories from one language to another's can bring diverse cultures face to face, be that on paper or aurally: both modes offer means of travelling across or between different domains, planes and even realities (a set of terms more widely discussed in Deleuze and Guattari 1980/2004; cf. Gough 2006; Law and Mol 2008). Thus, it is with these idea(l)s and practices as priorities for narrative-informed approaches, accompanied by an eschewing of assumptions of an essentially hermetic or homogeneous field of experience (in life or inquiry), that we might be enabled to continue to explore questions not just of the 'other and otherness' of a field but of the 'inter' in our understandings and analysis of the ir/realities

Yet at the same time that Hicks (1991), among others, was stating that global problems were too big for little kids, teachers and children were also being described as ecological illiterates or ecological yahoos (Cutter-Mackenzie and Smith 2003; Orr 1992, 1994). David Orr (1992, 85–6) charged:

> **Not only are we failing to teach the basics about the earth and how it works, but we are in fact teaching a large amount of stuff that is simply wrong. By failing to include ecological perspectives in any number of subjects, students are taught that ecology is unimportant for history, politics, economics, society, and so forth. And**

about its environmental qualities and characteristics is rare. Indeed, we were very pleased with the number of abstracts we received following the call for papers. Over half were from researchers not working exclusively in environmental education research but from other disciplinary bases such as literature and sciences but operating through an interdisciplinary approach to research. We do, therefore, feel a little more confident about the future nexus of environmental criticism and children's literature as they are developed in educational directions from both within and outwith environmental education research.

Third, the challenge of defining distinctive models of critical inquiry. Here, we encouraged an autoethnographic approach for our contributing authors so that an embodied cultural story about story/telling/children's literature could be (re)told with different emphases on the aesthetic, ethical and political. The methodological result

of experiencing children's literature about place and environment and their status in this field – be that through their 'intertextuality', 'intersubjectivity', 'interpellation' or 'interpretation'.

Moreover, mindful of Sloane's interests too, we might also note that Serres (2006) has made great play of the idea that any message (signal) is accompanied by noise (interference). The 'resistance' that the notion of noise in a system invokes can invite a moment of reflection; in this case, no matter what the 'purity' of the message, noise is transported too and does that also communicate? Is it simply static, the chaotic, non-knowledge, and thus should be excluded from our considerations? (Sloane's work would suggest this is the prevailing view in many 'modernist'-based approaches to children's literature in environmental education.) Or is noise something parasitic (its French cognate) on the system – albeit that which cannot be eliminated for if so, the system would cease to function? (Again, we might recall Sloane invites us to consider the role of 'white space' in Agamben's work, to a text, to our embodied selves and to their potentialities.) Might the notion of interference require further consideration of the deep structures, chance effects and openness of our systems of knowing, learning and being in this field (cf. Hardy 1998, on 'chaos' in environmental education – in essence, that which speaks of the 'pure multiplicity behind things')?

For Serres, the very vitality and viability of the scientific enterprise depends on the degree to which it is open to its other – not as if it were its nemesis in this case but a catalyst – spurring a 'voyaging further' into what may strike the voyager (child or adult or someone/where in between), as turbulent, unexpected or unexplained. Undeniably, given that the sciences of tomorrow don't automatically have to proceed in the

through television they learn the earth is theirs for the taking. The result is a generation of ecological yahoos ... as ecological illiterates they will have roughly the same success as one trying to balance a checkbook without knowing arithmetic.

There is an obvious tension here. On the one hand, environmental education (in schools) is labelled as being developmentally inappropriate and abstract (Hick 1991; Sobel 2008). On the other, it is described as grossly inadequate with respect to what is taught (Cutter-Mackenzie and Smith 2003; Orr 1992). So

here is mixed, although a number of these autoethnographies have been 'innovative' in both process and content. As we have done in the first layer of this Endpiece about the importance of narrative, there remains a great deal of original work to be undertaken here when we remind ourselves that the convergent notions of environmental criticism and imagination being expounded above, riskily, may or may not be aesthetically, ethically and politically appropriate or adequate to the role and place of children's literature, environmental education, ecoliteracy and, therefore, conventional approaches to environmental education research.

Fourth, the challenge of establishing the legitimacy of such critical inquiries beyond the academy. We welcome the increased presence in the popular media of the 'environmental crisis' but note how those apocalyptic adult versions of fear can diminish hope, create despair, stultify risk and increase a sense of powerlessness. From the

same ways as the sciences of the past – particularly when changes in the human and social sciences and to the nature and experience of life all stand to destabilize and outdate the understandings and practices of today and yesteryear – the possibility of literary narratives as both a comparative vehicle for comprehending the shifting horizons for experience and identities and as a means to bridging the gaps between lives lived, say, in the 'First World' as compared to those with 'Third World' conditions or continuities, has gained considerable import in some circles.[8]

In this regard, Dobrin's attention to the technologies of the First World, to the screen and its effects on our 'green eyes', and hence more broadly, to our embodied experience of information technology and the technologies of vision in a globalized world, might equally raise an important question about the 'prosthetics' and 'technics' of environmental education too (cf. Lotz-Sisitka 2010). As Payne (2003b, 2005) has previously argued, the increasing dominance of technology in mediating the realities of our experience of time and space has often gone unappreciated in our theorizing of environmental education. Outside the field, we might also note that Paul Virilio (1995) ('the chronicler of teletopia' – Conley 1999, 201) is but one of many who have attempted to theorize the effects of the emergence of communication at the 'speed of light', the increasing dominance of virtual reality alongside the 'disappearance' of materiality, of identities and of times and places as a definite space to be, and thus of perception as contact with a material reality, including that of or related to the body (see Thrift 2004; cf. Dobrin 2010).

Given all this, a postphenomenological inquiry of screen-based activities with children's literature as a means for achieving an environmental education might in fact which is it – be it then, now, or into the future? Rather than give a categorical response, this collection suggests an 'other' in-between or third space for consideration; the bodily role of the visual and the head of the textual within the exchange or tension between ecological being, hope and literacy. In this kernel of in-between we find signs of an aesthetics, somaesthetics and/or ecoaesthetics that is rarely or overtly considered in the theories, evidencing or appraising of environmental education in this context, or for that matter, the framings of research more widely about children's literature.

inside of environmental education research, we need to work hard with the public, with authors/artists/poets/musicians/dancers/software designers/ ... and so on, to provoke imaginative and constructively positive or possible responses to the otherwise debilitating crisis of fear and danger that this next generation will inherit and have the responsibility to 'lead' a way ecocritically and ecohopefully through and beyond.

On the basis of this special issue then, what or where next? We offer some suggestions for discussion, debate and engaged research development, noting the two broader intentions of the need for environmental education research to continue earlier conversations and build credible bodies of knowledge while, at the same time, reflexively forging a more comprehensive theorizing of an aesthetics, ethics and politics of environmental education that informs and is informed by numerous 'ecos' – pedagogy, literacy, learning, experiences and so on:

seek to unwrap whether priority is given to position over movement, or to reality over irreality (or vice versa in either case), alongside their relative merits and justification. Indeed, perhaps such virtualities and virtues, so to speak, occur in oscillation (flagging up the possibilities of a curriculum conceived as a non-linear course and hence *i-currere,* rather than simply an inchoate assemblage of events or activities?). Yet if we consider examples of intertextuality and its complex role in the negotiation of a series of interventions presented and mediated largely by the educator's 'technologies of perception', must we not also consider their horizons, repetitions and logic: for example, to their value as an effective, short as well longer term, or life long, environmental education (cf. Cooper 2002)? Indeed, when Lyotard can observe that an experience of the world is never entirely captured by any one reading of the world (the world as represented), questions of the inter- and representation and 'representationalness' become crucial to understanding and critiquing our instances of experiencing and weaving of time–space and thus to their wider analysis, including pedagogically (cf. our opening quotations to each layer, including from Bruner). Might, for example, the rhythm of environmental education now be too accelerated, and is a slow pedagogy the counterpoint (e.g., Payne and Wattchow 2009)? Or should it be something other to augment the differentiation and proliferation of a multiplicity of forms and logics that are arguably working their way into or through this field (see, for example, McKenzie et al. 2009)? Moreover, when the old tyrannies of distance are seen to give way to tyrannies of real time, or when 'convergences' always seem to trump 'divergences' in our appreciation of what is valued in the field, arguably it isn't long before either an 'immobility' or 'sedentariness' risks becoming the primary phenomenological marker of the field's

As Dobrin points out, many children now operate in a screen and networked culture where 'visual rhetorics are the environments in which texts for the child subject, texts about the child subject, texts about texts-for-the-child-subject, and the child subject now function'. In practice, Burke and Cutter-Mackenzie reveal possible ways in which visual literacy and ecoliteracy, as reconceived through an immersive/experiential investigation of children's picture books, can be used as a pathway to active forms of community participation. Korteweg, Gonzalez and Guillet open up further imaginative possibilities in decolonizing environmental education through a visual immersion in indigenous children's literature. Payne,

(1) *How are children (which, where, all?) positioned in the possible/actual uses of children's literature as we have aimed to open up for critical deliberation?*

(2) *Relatedly, whose/which childhoods have been and need to be considered in deliberating about the 'nature' of intergenerational ethics and, therefore, the role and place of children's literature as has been broadly opened up in relation to the undertheorized notion of ecoliteracy? Equally, whose voices thus far, and which voices of children in future? Whose experiences, which experiences? Whose environmentalism? Which environmentalisms? Which and whose framings of childhood? Indeed, in terms of 'literatures' – what of graphical novels, comic forms, Web 2.0, …?*

(3) *How do approaches to children's literature (de/re)value children's, teachers' and parents' everyday lived experiences, and particularly those that may or*

and its members' activities, be that in 'its' or 'their' or 'our' habits of thought, modes of action and practice, or relation to other fields.

It is in such contexts that Nigel Thrift (2007) has argued (albeit with some irony) for a place and space for a non-representational form of and approach to theory and theorizing, given that people are at risk of becoming increasingly indifferent to that which is immediately around them. Of course, Thrift's contention about re-engaging the horizon and experience of the local is not new: embodied practices are often seen to offer alternative sites of engagement. But the charge indicated here and also in, for example, the spatial turn is for a renewed focus that helps move the human and social sciences away from and beyond a narrow preoccupation with linguistic interactions. Thrift's work can be used to re-articulate our questions of involvement, participation and engagement, as ones that pertain to embodied actors and most pertinently, to somaesthetics, variously situated in socio-technico-materially configured spaces and places. And thus in this regard, it may well be that an ecologically oriented form of the culturally disposed autoethnographic approach offers a way of substantiating a commitment to resituating such engaged and to-be-engaged subjects in a spatially, socially, materially, technically, emotionally, ethically, politically, aesthetically 'thicker' world.

Thrift's concerns can also be read as part of the 'spatial turn' (Pugh 2009) now informing debates about the broader politics of democracy of the globalized, extended social relations and, inevitably, abstracted stories we may tell and read about, for example, climate change, global human rights, fair trade, postcolonialism, genetically modified foods and indigenous peoples, amongst others, some of which have attracted

Morgan and Sloane make known further layers identifying an ecopedagogy of imagination, a mythopoetic imagination (of the outdoor/natural environment) and the role of human potentiality in environmental education, respectively. This third place into which children's eco-literature partially and potentially fits is not without risks and challenges though, as environmental educators work in a transdisciplinary context in the attempt to provoke hope-filled imaginations, thoughts and actions in, of, or for the environment/nature and their socio-cultural ecologies.

may not be deemed more or less 'ecological' or 'researchable', be that in their approach or the literature under consideration?

(4) *What kinds of imagination – ecological, social, mythopoetic, moral, radical, … – are being engaged here? To which ends, and with which more worthy, valuable and useful ends-in-view? For example, might they (pedagogy, material, interactions) be about instilling notions of hope(lessness) and risk(lessness) or fear(lessness), or something other?*

(5) *How (else) are children themselves constructors, producers and authors/ artists as distinct from recipients, consumers and spectators of children's literature?*

(6) *Is there a balance to be struck between fostering* biophilia *and* bibliophilia? *[when, where, and what are the openings here?]*

the interest of contributors to this special issue. Pugh's concerns also relate methodologically and critically to the point made earlier in our second layer of interpretation and commentary where we employed Buell's (2005) encouragement for environmental criticism to address the pressing need to connect professional legitimation to new modes of critical inquiry and, in doing so, extend the reach of environmental criticism beyond the academy. Pugh (2009, 580) asks us to examine how the latest spatial turn in human geography positions us in rethinking our politics and accounts of democracy in ontologically abstracting globalizing conditions. Indeed, what narratives and stories might now be considered in dealing with, for example, the intergenerational stories we might tell our children about climate change, genetically modified food, indigenous rights and so on? Pugh pushes the methodological implications of the spatial turn into six sensitizing themes, all of which have considerable bearing on the way we frame, for example, the ecocomposition aspects of children's literature or art. Or, for that matter, how we might think about a critical pedagogy of place whose own 'story' has become more conspicuous over recent years in environmental education discourse. For the record, Pugh's themes include: the denaturalization of space, the forging of ethical commitment, the question of representation and participation, the remaking of political identities in a geographically connected way, the rise of a new form of materialism, and the politics of claims made on space.

While much of this increasingly 'processual' focus might be interpreted in this field as making the case for a more-than- rather than non-representational form of inquiry (see also Whatmore 2002), the main point we derive from this is that such a focus and its corresponding circumstances help highlight the attention we give to understanding

Ecology of risk

Often in contrast to the rhetoric of hope, risk has become a prominent concept in public discourse about the environmental predicament that we and future generations are assumed or expected to now confront (e.g., Bauman 2006; Beck 1995). Alongside the challenges of its associated anxieties and discontents, risk underscores the vigour with which intergenerational ethics need pursuing in families, schools, and other primary socializers and cultural institutions, including in the ways in which literature and ecoliteracy can be engaged and reimagined. The contributors to this collection have been bold in searching for valuable ways to capture the imaginations of the next generation of adults and deal with such

(7) *Are these children's literature approaches best imagined as a form of places (real, irreal, virtual and/or imagined) based education? Even in screen- and network-based cultures? Who is included and excluded as a result? Or is a global imaginary pressing hard on the locally placed? How can place exist in a globalizing or virtualizing 'community'?*

(8) *Is the now popularized schooling notion of ecoliteracy a limiting or limited concept, noting 'out there' exists ecorhetoric, ecocomposition, ecopoetics, ecodrama, ecocriticism, environmental criticism and elactracy (but often defaulting to adult voices)?*

(9) *Might a research focus on text/image – interactions/contextualizations be too constrained, given the above?*

and appreciating our own preferences and their production, shaping and disruption. In effect, with these no longer being 'indexed' to the exposure, intimacy and unpredictability engendered by co-proximity to places and their various real (and irreal) presences, such a shift would suggest our inquiries might be better configured by questions that explore the immediacy, control and de-centring of presence and presentation (and quite often mediated by electronic technology), and thus, for environmental education and its research, whether what these are becoming increasingly caught up with (or by) is that which is present(ed) to us from or at a (considerable) distance.

As conditions for and in environmental educators' engagements with children's literature change then, we might do well to ask, has and does experience of the visible and tangible via embodied understandings too, with literature or otherwise? Whether that is in work in the outdoors, for example, as children's stories and art might be experienced there irreally; or equally, in their giving way to experiences cast as 'realist' and largely classroom based, via book or screen-based learning? And if we were to explore where such interests might lead, then perhaps we should consider quite seriously if a forsaking of fieldwork and its ilk are likely: book and screen-based experiences of the outdoors appear more available and amenable to our pedagogical ends, yet must this inevitably take the place of direct perception and experiential learning (Payne 2003a), and to what effects (cf. Fox 2008; Roberts 2008)?

These conjectures remain speculative. And of course to some, they may suggest that the field's moorings have began to slip (once more) as has its sense of proportion and we are entering (once again?) unfamiliar disputable territories. Yet, in bringing this layer to an end, and noting her reliance on Agamben's work, we note that Sloane's contribution would appear to militate against such interpretations. Sloane deliberately

matters. Notwithstanding the limitations of any special issue, each author in their different ways – academic, teacher, parent, activist – has raised important issues and insightful questions into what, at first glance for educators, might conveniently be gathered under the concept of an 'ecoliteracy'.

However, only locating children's literature within the push for an extended form of ecoliteracy and an expanded imagination takes on a purposive, perhaps instrumental, perspective about the relationship of literature, education and the uncertainty and fear associated with environmental issues. So perhaps we should immediately qualify and extend this less literally and more aesthetically, even politically, into reflections on the environmental imaginary it articulates, as well

(10) What is represented and legitimized in these assumptions and approaches to researching children's literature? What hasn't been conceded, acknowledged, said, recognized?

Given our editorial license in this end piece and those hopes for the future, shared and inspired not only by those represented in this special issue but by many other scholars and practitioners, we note there is some conceptually innovative work bubbling up throughout this collection that calls for some additional teasing out and that constitutes yet another formal line of inquiry beyond the sampling of possible research directions envisaged above. One caveat. In working through the realities depicted in

encourages us to tap into currents of theorizing that focus on feelings of uncertainty and anxiety, including on some of the difficulties of speaking and writing about lived experiences which are barely translatable into symbolic form (and not simply equivalent to the sublime). In this scenario, this is never a trivial or esoteric matter; silence is not an escape from the responsibility to address issues concerning the enigmatic and intractable problems of any field of inquiry, including this one. For Agamben (2002), and thus agin Kant, it has involved investigations about what is actually 'sayable' in and through literature given the embodied experience of the Holocaust. Agamben's burden in *Remnants of Auschwitz: The witness and the archive* is to examine how the embodied practice of bearing witness and the notion of testimony are made possible when confronted with the 'unspeakable', given monstrous or horrific events. His inquiries lead him to conclude that 'the authority of the witness consists in his capacity to speak solely in the name of an incapacity to speak – that is, in his or her being a subject' (158).[9]

In Sloane's contribution, and a relocation of these arguments to the sphere of nature and to 'a body without its own voice', it is never simply a question of investigating the words or the layout of the page (including its white spaces) so as to understand the significances and 'subjectivities' a children's book is charged with conveying, or for that matter, what it witnesses to or testifies about as (part of) an environmental education. Just as a sigh or touch between lovers (a subjectivity that is equally un-universalizable) may seek to bodily convey a deep longing or even a moment of inarticulateness or an otherwise ineffable joy, etc., researching lived experiences of children's literature invites close attention to the cycles and disruptions of contextualizations and decontextualizations or recontextualizations. Indeed, the natured and de-natured representations and responses of authors and readers with/in the texts, regarding that which it is deemed possible to include, and what it has

as pedagogically, into how that is nurtured directly with children and revealed in research. At risk, but worth restating, is that enduring reminder to 'let children be children' and resist, for a slow while, the temptation of adults, teachers and researchers to download fast on children their fears and anxieties, aspirations and expectations. Stories, reading, play, music, art and drama should also intrinsically cater for or promote joy, pleasure, imagination, escape and other non-worldly dimensions of childhood experience.

Are there yet other ways in which the story of children's literature can combine risk, critique and hope, and a way forward, as Dobrin's contribution expects? Wason-Elam can be read as a counterpoint. To be sure, solely locating

much environmental education research, despite interest or intrigue with the imaginary, we openly concede that the undertheorized imaginary of an aesthetics in environmental education and its research might occupy a relatively limited pathway of hope and risk for the future. Indeed, children's literature might occupy a somewhat special place, or space, within the broader ambit of environmental education. If so, perhaps our other layer in the Endpiece does well to dwell for more than a brief moment on what we think are some of the assumptions made about realities and irrealities as they emerge from this collection. We feel that the irreal as a different line of inquiry also has a special place, and that children's literature and ecoliteracy, understood, conceived and contextualized more broadly, can heighten how the currently

become necessary to leave out, are matters that return us to questions about the technics of production and imagination and, indeed, the technics of environmental education (Payne 2003b).

The brute fact of, on the one hand, the multifarious ecologies, and on the other, (constrained) possibilities of reading that are viable, Sloane reminds us, also serve to highlight how environmental education and its research may risk be(com)ing locked into repetitive cycles of inquiry – in effect, closed loops of practice, theory and research where the premises of 'analysis' are such that they overly constrain and foretell the outcomes possible. We regard Sloane's unique contribution via this collection as a plea for a catharsis of sorts and continued coming-to-terms with the problematics and ambiguities that such approaches to practice and research and understanding both exemplify. Thus, rather than practices or researches continuing as a symptom of conventional framings, with their concomitant problematics and ambiguities – a confirmation rather a possible transcending of them – Sloane lays claim to opening up the very filters and filtering of the field and its research priorities to critique and transformation.

Her resolution on this point offers a voice to 'murmurings' that would suggest environmental education and its research shouldn't be regarded as irretrievably Kafkaesque, nihilistic, or without any particular end, even though no end may be specified or would appear to be forthcoming. Thus, while the (absurdist) possibility of profound failure in the field has to be entertained (perhaps its Godot imaginary?), and apparent lacks of progress on a range of fronts may well lead to despair in and anxiety about environmental education and its operations, support, barriers, etc., these 'states' of 'being' are not actually fundamentally corrosive of the underpinnings to the field's enterprises. Yet their very likelihood and actuality in people's experience of this field suggest that a 'defamiliarization' and 'deterritorization' might well be required, to children's literature in the push for ecoliteracy is somewhat risky, as well might be an uncritical acceptance of the rush of the new media and easy flexibility of a postmodern environmental education. But in terms of how the field of environmental education and its research might respond in a coherent, theoretically informed and carefully considered manner, there are other 'harder to reach varieties' (Reid and Scott 2006) of theory and discourse, practice and inquiry, that might provide new vantage points from which those risky stories of expanded hope, and constructive criticisms, can be nurtured in children's literature and its 'place' in responding to environmental fear and anxiety, as suggested in our other layers.

irreal can be part of the imaginary of what might be the real, particularly in terms of the possibility of an intergenerational ethics and politics through environmental education.

change the nature of our perception of the experience of environmental education and its research significantly, if not immediately or even somewhat imperceptibly for some of its more 'avant garde' members (let alone 'acolytes'). In other words, the challenge is not to consciously regard environmental education and its research as already finally constituted and unified, but temporarily 'locked' into times and places that remain subject to change, bidden and unbidden – where the keys to their unlocking may actually be closer to hand than previously thought.

Thus, as with Agamben and company, and from Dobrin through to Sloane, we suggest that the focus in researching the experience of children's literature could well undergo a profound, risky, hopeful and structurally legitimizing shift as an important generator of human understanding, meaning-making and ways of knowing and knowledge producer in this field on inquiry. In this case, from being cocooned in relation to exploring and explicating the meanings of the stories in the first instance, towards engaging how (these) stories about nature/culture can be ecologically told in the first place, to the role of literature in narrative imagination and ethical and political questions, and thus, to matters of the potentialities that experiences of children's literature inflect and afford in and through an environmental education.[10] And it is in this very engaging and articulating of this struggle for a language of inquiry – of being able to be(come) a witness to life, including one's own and its groundings and ends in relation to the socio-ecological – that has become quite the matter at stake over the course of this special issue on experiencing environment and place through children's literature, let alone in its various probings of the conditions of possibility for an effective, holistic, multitextualized environmental education.

Notes

1. For example, Barratt Hacking and Barratt (2007) note that at an international conference held in 2005 called 'Childhood', devoted to examining their role in transforming societies, only a 'limited number' of the 700 papers explored environmental perspectives. In extracting some lessons from the articles published in that special issue of *Environmental Education Research*, namely children as environmental stakeholders, researching their environmental learning, including agency and restrictions on learning, and further directions for childhood environment research, there are numerous positive and important suggestions that pertain to questions of marginalization and restorative justice, participatory approaches that give voice to children, intergenerationality of interest and power, and the existential (and phenomenological) significance of everyday, local environments. Methodological adjustments and new directions are also recommended. Children's literature is not mentioned though, and ecoliteracy, in the sense anticipated by literature, is implied only.

2. According to Buell (2005, 113) the challenge for environmental justice revisionism will be to fill the ecocriticism gap of explaining '… how nature matters for those readers, critics, teachers, and students for whom environmental concern does not mean nature preservation first and foremost and for whom nature writing, nature poetry, and wilderness narrative do not seem the most compelling forms of environmental imagination, then the movement may fission and wane'.

3. Somewhat akin to the surrealist movement in Art, and exemplified by Salvador Dali's *The persistence of memory*, commonly referred to as the 'melting clocks', we bear witness to the time of the landscape being partially deconstructed via Dali's paranoia-critical method. Ants and flies feed on the disintegration of the rotting carcass of 'modern time', measured by and symbolized through numerically quantified clocks.

4. Indeed, while it may surprise some readers that advocates of poststructural analysis in environmental education haven't (quite? yet?) taken the increasingly familiar route to this troika in such work – to explications of Jacques Lacan's psychoanalytic theory perhaps via Slavoj Zizek's post-Marxist commentaries or Julia Kristeva's inquiries about language, the subject and semiotics, is perhaps putting it (too) crudely – it does appear to have been on the horizon for some time (cf. early work by Conley 1997).

5. This is rather than to privilege a direct focus on what it might hide in the classroom, as in an ideologically driven critique. Interestingly perhaps, Alain Badiou (2003, 4) has defined a fable as 'that part of a narrative that, so far as we are concerned, fails to touch on any Real, unless it be by virtue of that invisible and indirectly accessible residue sticking to every obvious imaginary'.

6. There is a considerable hill to climb here. What counts and is experienced as restrictive forms of thought and action imposed on people by the social conditions, of say, capitalist globalized societies, can be easily contested and thus derailed in disputes about notions of false consciousness, the credibility of Marxist and Marxian analysis, etc.; while an identity (colonized or not to different degrees and hybridities), being a fundamental attachment for the subject, cannot simply be thrown off at will. Indeed, identifying it is not reducible to claims of an identity, as if the claim were identical and identifiable with what is labelled or assumed as the identity, or if simply speaking otherwise in the face of irreducibility can erase difference. As noted in the Editorial, MacIntyre, Ricoeur and Gare, each lay claim to identity requiring narrative competence – accounts of ourselves are intersubjective and interlocutory, and thus never fully or solely subject to the control of an individual alone.

7. Cf. Aleksandra Mir's 'Switzerland and Other Islands', exhibited at Kunsthaus Zurich, August–September 2006. This series of political, geographical and mythological drawings on the subject of islands includes *Insula Svizzera*, which reimagines Switzerland's landlocked borders as a coastline, while the *Unexplored Islands* series uses a range of frames and objects to resituate family political boundaries as those yet to be explored or integrated with existing atlases. http://www.aleksandramir.info/projects/switzerland/switzerland.html.

8. The Harlequin, lest we forget, stands in the place of the chaos of life and has been a commonplace in historic European children's literature. According to Lechte (2008, 347), this 'hybrid, hermaphrodite, mongrel figure, a mixture of diverse elements' and 'a challenge to homogeneity', with the Harlequin, when one costume is removed, another is underneath to take the former's place. Equally, the Harlequin's presence and story-telling can be used to

bear witness to the tragedy and absurdities of our stories and times, revealing, challenging and redistributing knowledges that might otherwise escape attention or reflection.

9. This is a markedly different conclusion to that of Theodor Adorno. Given this, and following Sloane's lead, an 'eco'-informed engagement with John Boyne's 2006 children's novel, *The boy in the striped pajamas*, presents a potentially rich and compelling scenario to explore the intersections of its aesthetic, ethical and political dimensions, responsibilities and limitations, given the im/possible and forbidden childhood friendship Boyne portrays on either side of a camp fence.

10. If it is said, 'every tool is a weapon – if you hold it right' (Ani DiFranco), is a stone or stick a weapon if you throw it (right)? More pointedly and abstractly, it is said, representations remain objectifications because they articulate an external position. So, in one view, children's storybooks, mythic tales, etc., as objects, are, by their very nature, quite literally a 'frozen' relation that immobilizes and condenses meanings, concepts and possibilities. Equally, in themselves they do not avail the interiority to a meaning or self in time engaging with 'the ways things are' or one's or another's life as lived. But in throwing a stone, or in 'teaching a stone to talk', as Annie Dillard would have it, they can present openings to many things: they may afford transformative interdictions, even when – perhaps, better when – their genre isn't intentionally transgressive but rather 'conservative'. To understand how this may be so, autoethnographic approaches are arguably well suited to the exploration and examination of these claims, in that these approaches foreground inquiries as to whether the reader is awake to possibility, regards a text as provisional and not closed or incontestable, or, as Burke and Mackenzie (2010) have suggested, can demonstrate they are ecoliterally competent to make good use of all that in, as and through an environmental education worthy of the name.

References

Abram, D. 1996. *The spell of the sensuous: Perception and language in a more-than-human world.* New York: Vintage.

Agamben, G. 2002. *Remnants of Auschwitz: The witness and the archive.* Trans. D. Heller-Roazen. New York: Zone Books.

Badiou, A. 2003. *Saint Paul: The foundations of universalism.* Trans. R. Brassier. Stanford, CA: Stanford University Press.

Bai, H., D. Elza, P. Kovacs, and S. Romanycia. 2010. Re-searching and re-storying the complex and complicated relationship of *biophilia* and *bibliophilia*. *Environmental Education Research* 16, nos. 3–4: 351–65.

Ballantyne, R., S. Connell, and J. Fien. 1998. Students as catalysts of environment change: A framework for researching intergenerational influence through environmental education. *Environmental Education Research* 4, no. 3: 413–27.

Ballantyne, R., J. Fien, and J. Packer. 2001. School environmental education programme impacts upon student and family learning: A case study analysis. *Environmental Education Research* 7, no. 1: 23–37.

Barrett, M.J. 2008. Participatory pedagogy in environmental education: Reproduction or disruption? In *Participation and learning: Perspectives on education and the environment, sustainability and health*, ed. A. Reid, B.B. Jensen, J. Nikel, and V. Simovska, 212–24. Dordrecht: Springer.

Barratt Hacking, E., and R. Barratt, eds. 2007. Special issue: Childhood and environment. *Environmental Education Research* 14, no. 4: 419–54.

Barratt Hacking, E., A. Cutter-Mackenzie, and R. Barratt. 2012. The challenge of undertaking environmental education research involving children: Framing a future research agenda. In *The handbook of research on environmental education*, ed. R. Stevenson, A. Wals, M. Brody, and J. Dillon. Washington, DC: American Educational Research Association.

Bate, J. 2000. *The song of the earth.* London: Picador.

Bauman, Z. 2006. *Liquid fear.* Cambridge: Polity Press.

Beck, U. 1995. *Ecological politics in an age of risk.* Cambridge: Polity Press.

Bigger, S., and J. Webb. 2010. Developing environmental agency and engagement through young people's fiction. *Environmental Education Research* 16, nos. 3–4: 401–14.

Boughard, D., and H. Ripplinger. 1993. *If you're not from the prairie.* Vancouver: Raincoat Books.

Bowerbank, S. 1999. Nature writing as self-technology. In *Discourses of the environment*, ed. E. Darier, 163–78. Malden, MA: Blackwell.

Bowers, C.A. 1993. *Education, cultural myths, and the ecological crisis: Towards deep changes.* Albany: State University of New York Press.

Bowers, C.A. 1997. *The culture of denial: Why the environmental movement needs a strategy for reforming universities and public schools.* Albany: State University of New York Press.

Brady, E. 2003. *Aesthetics of the natural environment.* Edinburgh: Edinburgh University Press.

Bruner, J. 1990. *Acts of meaning.* Cambridge, MA: Harvard University Press.

Bruner, J. 2002. *Making stories: Law, literature, life.* Cambridge, MA: Harvard University Press.

Buell, L. 1995. *The environmental imagination: Thoreau, nature writing, and the formation of American culture.* Cambridge, MA: Belknap Press.

Buell, L. 2001. *Writing for an endangered world: Literature, culture, and environment in the U.S. and Beyond.* Cambridge, MA: Harvard University Press.

Buell, L. 2005. *The future of environmental criticism: Environmental crisis and literary imagination.* Malden, MA: Blackwell.

Burke, G., and A. Cutter-Mackenzie. 2010. What's there, what if, what then, and what can we do? An immersive and embodied experience of environment and place through children's literature. *Environmental Education Research* 16, nos. 3–4: 311–30.

Chawla, L. 2002. *Growing up in an urbanizing world.* Paris: UNESCO Publishing.

Cheney, J. 2002. The moral epistemology of first nations stories. *Canadian Journal of Environmental Education* 7, no. 2: 88–100.

Chua, J. 2009. No kidding, one in three children fear earth apocalypse. http://www.treehugger.com/files/2009/04/kids-worry-about-environment.php.

Cloete, E. 2011. Going to the bush: Language, power and the conserved environment in southern Africa. *Environmental Education Research* 17, no. 1: 35–51.

Conley, V.A. 1997. *Ecopolitics: The environment in poststructuralist thought.* London/New York: Routledge.

Conley, V.A. 1999. The passenger: Paul Virilio and feminism. *Theory, Culture & Society* 16, nos. 5–6: 201–14.

Cooper, S. 2002. *Technoculture and critical theory: In the service of the machine?* London/New York: Routledge.

Cutter-Mackenzie, A., and R. Smith. 2003. Ecological literacy: The 'missing paradigm' in environmental education (part 1). *Environmental Education Research* 9, no. 4: 497–524.

de Certeau, M. 1984. *The practice of everyday life.* Trans. S. Randall. Berkeley: University of California Press.

Deleuze, G., and F. Guattari. 1980/2004. *A thousand plateaus.* Trans. B. Massumi. London/New York: Continuum.

Dillon, J. 2003. On learners and learning in environmental education: Missing theories, ignored communities. *Environmental Education Research* 9, no. 2: 215–26.

Dobrin, S. 2010. Through green eyes: Complex visual culture and post-literacy. *Environmental Education Research* 16, nos. 3–4: 265–78.

Dobson, S., and K. Kidd. 2004. *Wild things: Children's culture and ecocriticism.* Detroit, MI: Wayne State University Press.

Dunlop, R. 2002. In search of tawny grammar: Poetics, landscape and embodied ways of knowing. *Canadian Journal of Environmental Education* 7, no. 2: 23–37.

Dunlop, R. 2009. 'Primer: Curriculum for the New Republic.' In *Fields of green: Restorying culture, environment, and education*, ed. M. McKenzie, P. Hart, B. Jickling, and H. Bai, 11–64. Cresskill, NJ: Hampton Press.

Fielding, M. 2004. Transformative approaches to student voice: Theoretical underpinnings, recalcitrant realities. *British Educational Research Journal* 30, no. 2: 295–311.

Fox, K. 2008. Rethinking experience: What do we mean by this word 'experience'? *Journal of Experiential Education* 31, no. 1: 36–54.

Garrard, G. 2004. *Ecocriticism.* New York: Routledge.

Garrard, G. 2010. Problems and prospects in ecocritical pedagogy. *Environmental Education Research* 16, no. 2: 233–45.

Glotfelty, C., and H. Fromm, eds. 1996. *The ecocriticism reader: Landmarks in literary ecology.* Athens/London: University of Georgia.

Gough, N. 2006. Rhizosemiotic play and the generativity of fiction. *Complicity: An International Journal of Complexity and Education* 3, no. 1: 119–24.

Gray-MacDonald, J., and D. Selby, eds. 2008. *Green frontiers: Environmental educators dancing away from mechanism.* Rotterdam: Sense Publishers.

Greene, M. 2000. *Releasing the imagination: Essays on education, the arts, and social change.* San Francisco: Jossey-Bass.

Gruenewald, D. 2003. The best of both worlds: A critical pedagogy of place. *Educational Researcher* 32, no. 4: 3–12.

Guattari, F. 1989/2000. *The three ecologies.* Trans. I. Pindar and P. Sutton. London: The Athlone Press.

Haraway, D. 1994. A game of cat's cradle: Science studies, feminist theory, cultural studies. *Configurations* 2, no. 1: 59–71.

Hardy, J. 1998. Chaos in environmental education. *Environmental Education Research* 5, no. 2: 125–42.

Hardy, J. 2002. Levinas and environmental education. *Educational Philosophy and Theory* 34, no. 4: 459–76.

Hardy, J. 2006. 'In the neighbourhood of': Dialogic uncertainties and the rise of new subject positions in environmental education. *Mind, Culture, and Activity* 13, no. 3: 257–74.

Hardy, J. 2008. Neoliberalism and environmental education. *The International Journal of the Humanities* 6, no. 7: 7–13.

Hart, P. 2002. Narrative, knowing and emerging methodologies in environmental education research: Issues of quality. *Canadian Journal of Environmental Education* 7, no. 2: 140–65.

Hart, P. 2003. Reflections on reviewing educational research: (Re)searching for value in environmental education. *Environmental Education Research* 9, no. 2: 241–56.

Hart, P. 2005. Transitions in thought and practice: Links, divergences and contradictions in post-critical inquiry. *Environmental Education Research* 11, no. 4: 391–400.

Hart, P. 2008. What comes before participation? Searching for meaning in teachers' constructions of participatory learning in environmental education. In *Participation and learning: Perspectives on education and the environment, health and sustainability*, ed. A. Reid, B.B. Jensen, J. Nikel, and V. Simovska, 197–211. Dordrecht: Springer.

Hicks, D. 1998. Stories of hope: A response to the 'psychology of despair'. *Environmental Education Research* 4, no. 2: 165–76.

Hicks, S. 1991. Global problems are too big for little kids. *The Wall Street Journal* CXXVII, no. 74: A20.

Huebner, D. 1999. *The Lure of the transcendent: Collected essays.* Ed. V. Hillis and collected and introduced by W.F. Pinar. Mahwah, NJ: Lawrence Erlbaum.

Hug, J.W. 2010. Exploring instructional strategies to develop prospective elementary teachers' children's literature book evaluation skills for science, ecology and environmental education. *Environmental Education Research* 16, nos. 3–4: 367–82.

Jickling, B., et al. 2002. What stories shall we tell? *Canadian Journal of Environmental Education* 7, no. 2: 282–93.

Kant, I. 1790/1987. *The critique of judgement.* Trans. W.S. Pluhar. Indianapolis, IN: Hackett.

Kellett, K. 2005. *How to develop children as researchers.* Thousand Oaks, CA: Paul Chapman Publishing.

Killingsworth, M.J. 2005. From ER to ecocomposition and ecopoetics: Finding a place for professional communication. *Technical Communication Quarterly* 14, no. 4: 359–73.

Korteweg, L., I. Gonzalez, and J. Guillet. 2010. The stories are the people and the land: Three educators respond to environmental teachings in Indigenous children's literature. *Environmental Education Research* 16, nos. 3–4: 331–50.

Law, J., and A. Mol. 2008. Globalisation in practice: On the politics of boiling pigswill. *Geoforum* 39, no. 1: 133–43.

Lechte, J. 2008. *Fifty key contemporary thinkers: From structuralism to post-humanism.* 2nd ed. New York: Routledge.

Lotz-Sisitka, H. 2010. Changing social imaginaries, multiplicities, and 'one sole world': Reading Scandinavian environmental and sustainability education research papers with Badiou and Taylor at hand. *Environmental Education Research* 16, no. 1: 133–42.

Louv, R. 2005. *Last child in the woods: Saving our children from nature deficit disorder.* Chapel Hill, NC: Algonquin Books.

McKenzie, M. 2005. The 'post-post period' and environmental education research. *Environmental Education Research* 11, no. 4: 401–12.

McKenzie, M., P. Hart, H. Bai, and B. Jickling, eds. 2009. *Fields of green: Restorying culture, environment and education.* Cresskill, NJ: Hampton.

Merchant, C. 1995. Reinventing Eden: Western culture as a recovery narrative. In *Uncommon ground: Rethinking the human place in nature*, ed. W. Cronon, 132–59. New York: W.W. Norton.

Morgan, A. 2010. *The Lord of the Rings* – a *mythos* applicable in unsustainable times? *Environmental Education Research* 16, nos. 3–4: 383–99.

Muris, P., H. Merckelbach, C. Meesters, and P. Van Lier. 1997. What do children fear most often? *Journal of Behavior Therapy and Experimental Psychiatry* 28, no. 4: 263–7.

Ollendick, T., and B. Yang. 1996. Fears in American, Australian, Chinese, and Nigerian children and adolescents: A cross-cultural study. *Journal of Child Psychology and Psychiatry* 37, no. 2: 213–20.

Orr, D.W. 1992. *Ecological literacy: Education and the transition to a postmodern world.* Albany: State University of New York.

Orr, D.W. 1994. *Earth in mind: On education, environment, and the human prospect.* Washington, DC: Island Press.

O'Sullivan, E. 2002. What kind of education should you experience at a university. *Canadian Journal of Environmental Education* 7, no. 2: 54–72.

Pagano, J. 1991. Moral fictions: The dilemma of theory and practice. In *Stories lives tell: Narrative and dialogue in education*, ed. C. Witherell and N. Noddings, 234–56. New York: Teachers College Press.

Payne, P. 2003a. Postphenomenological enquiry and living the environmental condition. *Canadian Journal of Environmental Education* 8: 11–37.

Payne, P. 2003b. The technics of environmental education. *Environmental Education Research* 9, no. 4: 525–41.

Payne, P. 2005. Lifeworld and textualism: Reassembling the researcher/ed and 'others'. *Environmental Education Research* 11, no. 4: 413–31.

Payne, P. 2010a. Moral spaces, the struggle for an intergenerational environmental ethics and the social ecology of families: An 'other' form of environmental education. *Environmental Education Research* 16, no. 2: 209–31.

Payne, P. 2010b. Remarkable-tracking, experiential education of the ecological imagination. *Environmental Education Research* 16, nos. 3–4: 295–310.

Payne, P., and B. Wattchow. 2009. Phenomenological deconstruction, slow pedagogy, and the corporeal turn in wild environmental/outdoor education. *Canadian Journal of Environmental Education* 14, no. 1: 15–32.

Peters, M., and R. Irwin. 2002. Earthsongs: Ecopoetics, Heidegger and dwelling. *The Trumpeter* 18, no.1: 1–17.

Pugh, J. 2009. What are the consequences of the 'spatial turn' for how we understand politics today? A proposed research agenda [The Spaces of Democracy and the Democracy of Space network]. *Progress in Human Geography* 33, no. 5: 579–86.

Reid, A. 2003. Sensing environmental education. *Canadian Journal of Environmental Education* 8: 9–30.

Reid, A. 2009. Environmental education research: Will the ends outstrip the means? *Environmental Education Research* 15, no. 2: 129–53.

Reid, A., and W. Scott. 2006. Researching education and the environment: Retrospect and prospect. *Environmental Education Research* 12, nos. 3–4: 571–87.

Rickinson, M. 2001. Special issue: Learners and learning in environmental education; a critical review of the evidence. *Environmental Education Research* 7, no. 2: 208–317.

Rickinson, M., C. Lundholm, and N. Hopwood. 2010. *Environmental learning: Insights from research into the student experience.* Dordrecht: Springer.

Rifkin, J. 1991. *Biosphere politics: A new consciousness for a new century.* New York: Crown Publishers.

Roberts, J. 2008. From experience to neo-experiential education: Variations on a theme. *Journal of Experiential Education* 31, no. 1: 19–35.

Robottom, I., and P. Hart. 1993. *Research in environmental education: Engaging the debate.* Geelong, Australia: Deakin University Press.

Russell, C. 2005. 'Whoever does not write is written': The role of 'nature' in post-post approaches to environmental education research. *Environmental Education Research* 11, no. 4: 433–43.

Russell, C., and J. Dillon. 2010. Environmental education and STEM education: New times, new alliances? *Canadian Journal of Science, Mathematics and Technology Education* 10, no. 1: 1–12.

Salcuni, S., D. Di Riso, C. Mazzeschi, and A. Lis. 2009. Children's fears: A survey of Italian children ages 6 to 10 years. *Psychological Reports* 104, no. 3: 971–88.

Serres, M. 2006. *Récits d'humanism.* Paris: Pommier.

Shava, S., M.E. Krasny, K.G. Tidball, and C. Zazu. 2010. Agricultural knowledge in urban and resettled communities: Applications to social-ecological resilience and environmental education. *Environmental Education Research* 16, nos. 5–6: 575–89.

Shusterman, R. 2008. *Body consciousness. A philosophy of mindfulness and somaesthetics.* Cambridge: Cambridge University Press.

Sloane, A. 2010. Reading *The Lorax,* orienting in potentiality. *Environmental Education Research* 16, nos. 3–4: 415–28.

Sobel, D. 1996. *Beyond ecophobia: Reclaiming the heart in nature education.* Great Barrington, MA: The Orion Society and The Myrin Institute.

Sobel, D. 2005. *Place-based education: Connecting classrooms & communities.* Great Barrington, MA: The Orion Society.

Sobel, D. 2008. *Childhood and nature: Design principles for educators.* Portland, ME: Stenhouse Publishers.

Stables, A. 2004. Responsibility beyond rationality: The case for rhizomatic consequentialism. *International Journal of Children's Spirituality* 9, no. 2: 219–26.

Stables, A. 2006. On teaching and learning the book of the world. In *Ecodidactic perspectives in English language, literatures and cultures,* ed. S. Mayer and G. Wilson, 145–62. Trier: WVT.

Stables, A. 2007. Is nature immaterial? The possibility of environmental education without an environment. *Canadian Journal of Environmental Education* 12: 55–67.

Thrift, N. 2004. Driving in the city. *Theory Culture & Society* 21, nos. 4–5: 41–59.

Thrift, N. 2007. *Non-representational theory: Space, politics, affect.* London: Routledge.

UNESCO. 2004. *United Nations Decade of Education for Sustainable Development 2005–2014.* Paris: UNESCO.

Wason-Ellam, L. 2010. Children's literature as a springboard to place-based embodied learning. *Environmental Education Research* 16, nos. 3–4: 279–94.

Whatmore, S. 2002. *Hybrid geographies: Natures cultures spaces.* London: Sage.

Virilio, P. 1995. *The art of the motor.* Minneapolis: University of Minnesota Press.

Young, R., and J. Saver. 2001. The neurology of narrative. *Substance* 30, nos. 1–2: 72–84.

Index

Page numbers in **Bold** represent figures.

a/r/t-e-ographic 99; renderings **99**
a/r/tography 96
Aboriginal: cultures 78; epistemology 76; families 64, 67; knowledge 91; participation 65; values 81;
Abram, David 36, 44–5; *Spell of the sensuous* 7, 56
academic legitimacy 18
accelerated learning 54
acculturation: ecocriticism 18
accuracy 123; literature 121
acting: theorizing 179
active citizenship 141
adaptations 122
adult colonization 18
adult perspective: creating ecological change **107**
aesthetic education 53
aesthetics 10, 180, 197
After Virtue (MacIntyre) 5
Agamben, G. 9, 163–7, 195, 200, 203; *Remnants of Auschwitz: The witness and the archive* 201
Alfred, Tainaike 81
alienation 60
Alps 148
American ecocriticism 186
American Library Association 121
Anderson, M.V. 124
Animal heroes (Seton) 135
animals 30
Anishinaabek territory 77
Annishnaabe people 87, 89
Anstey, M. 103
anthropocentrism 30, 169
anthropomorphism 8; children's literature 124–6; stereotypes 124
anti-heroes 140
apocalypse 146
Ardoin, N. 164
Aristotle 165, 166, 167
Armageddon (film) 20
Armstrong, K. 150, 151

artefacts: visual texts 14
artful pedagogies 7, 98
artist: narrator 185; role 98
associational complexities 82
Atkinson, T.S. 121
Attention Deficit Disorder 16
Aurora Borealis 86
Australia 7, 43; ecology 95
authentic experiences 95
autism 28
auto dilemma: research methods 118–19
auto-ethnography 3, 6, 8, 44, 55, 56, 60, 62–4, 69, 81, 97, 104, 116, 118, 126, 133, 178, 198; environmental educators 77–8; investigation 102; journaling 77
autodidacticism 146
Avatar (film) 20

Bai, H. 8, 27, 28, 192
Baker, J.: *Home* 62; *Window* 7, 62, 95–7, 104, 112
Bakhtin, M. 67, 139
Bamford, A. 101
Bannatyne-Cugnet, J.: *Prairie alphabet* 67; *Prairie year* 67
Barclay, J.: *How cold was it?* 67
Barratt Hacking, E. 132, 178
Barratt, R. 132, 178
Basho, Matsuo 95
Bateman, R. 34
Bateson, M.C. 65, 69
Battiste, M. 89, 91
Baylor, B.: *Everyone needs a rock* 120
Bear Gully 50
Beck, Ulrich 2
behaviour-change research 164
Benjamin, Water 37
Beowulf 46
Bergthaller, H. 169
Berry, Thomas 182
Bettelheim, B.: *The uses of enchantment* 31, 32
Bigger, Stephen 19, 133, 141, 192

Bildungsroman 151
biological existence 171
biophilia 8, 138
biophilia and *bibliophilia* 199; becoming the
    moon 35–7; forest of colours 35; inclusion
    37–9; on the lap 29–32; our story 27–9;
    parenting 28; pointing to the moon 32–5
biophobia 30, 185
BioScience 20
Birmingham 148, 152, 153
Black Country 153
Blanchet-Cohen, N. 132
Bombadil, Tom 156
Booth, D.: *The Dust Bowl* 68
Bouchard, D.: *The elders are watching* 63; *If
    you are not from the prairies* 65, 66
Bourriaud, N.: co-existence criterion 99
Bowers, C.A. 59, 64
Bradford, C. 79
*Brazilian Journal of Environmental
    Education* 189
Brett, M.G. 134
Breunig, M. 132
Bringhurst, R. 79, 80
Bruner, Jerome 177–8
Buell, Lawrence 6, 14–15, 188, 191–4, 199
Bull, G. 103
Bunting, E.: *Secret place* 121
Bunyip at Berkeley's Creek (Wagner) 47
Burbules, N.C. 97, 111
Burke, G. 7, 8, 19, 106, 198

Caldicott Award 122
Campbell, L.M. 121
Canada 7; history 81; society 81
Cannock Chase 148
capitalism 171
Caribou song (Highway) 85, 86
caring 62
Carson, Rachel 163
catalyst story 65
Catholicism 157
cautionary tales 32
celebrity 23
change research 164
Charlie and Lola (Child) 3
Cheney, Jim 180
child: and reader 173–4; subject 15, 16
Child, Lauren: *Charlie and Lola* 3; *What
    planet are you from Clarice Bean?* 3–4
childhood 67; experience 179, 202;
    subjectivity 18; western 15
childish 151
children: relationship with the
    environment 20
children's literature: anthropomorphism 124–
    6; book quality considerations 130; realities

of environmental education 182; science
    teaching methods, and 116, 117, 120, 121,
    126; visual rhetoric 15–18
children's texts: early 18
child's perspective: ecological change **108,
    109, 110**
Christianity 171
Chronicles of ancient darkness (Paver) 137
Cinderella 31
circulation 18, 20, 22, 23: cultural 17; hyper-
    14, 18; information 16, 17; textual 21;
    visual 18
citizen-consumers 2
citizenship 2, 141; education for 132
Civil Rights 146
civilization 34
Cleaver, E.: and Toye, W. 79
climate change 45, 198, 199
Cloete, Elsie 193
co-existence criterion: Bourriaud 99
collaboration 170
collective memory 54
colonization 78, 90
colonized beliefs 8
colonized education 77
commodity consumption 59
communication 17
communion 182
community 60, 68, 140, 171; action
    projects 111
complex ecology 19; environmental
    criticism 18–22
consciousness 178
constructed 170
contemporary fiction for young people 137–9
cooperation 141
copyright date 123
creating ecological change: adult
    perspective **107**
Creationism 148, 157
Creator 84, 86, 86–7
Cree peoples 85, 87
Crick, Bernard 132
Crisis: reciprocal 170, 172, 173
critical readers 140
critical reflection 178
critique criteria 119
cultural annihilation: Indigenous history 77
cultural commons: sustainable traditions 76
cultural communication 61
cultural identity 78
cultural resistance 89
cultural responsiveness 65
cultural understandings: educator 89
culturally responsive teaching 89
culture 180; nature 119
curriculum 64, 184, 194

Curry, P. 147
Cutter-Mackenzie, A. 7, 8, 19, 198
cyborgs 6, 21, 59

Dante's Peak (film) 20
darkness 30
Davis, J. 132
The Day After Tomorrow (film) 20
de Cosson, A. 99, 100, 103
Deakin University 46, 49
Debes, J.: visual literacy 100
decision making 115
Declaration on the Rights of Indigenous
    Peoples: United Nations 79
decoding 101
decolonization 76, 77, 90, 191; environmental
    education 88–90; methods of focal
    practices 82–4
decolonizing education 91
decolonizing environmental education 80–1
decolonizing journeys 83
decolonizing narratives 193
decomposition 120
deep ecology 186
Deep Impact (film) 20
deep reading 134
defamiliarization 202
Deines, Brian 85, 87
Deleuze, G. 165, 189
Denzin, N.K. 118
Dewey, John 9, 47, 50, 60–1, 62, 141;
    experience and democracy 134; philosophy
    134; primary of experience 131
Dickerson, M. 147, 151, 156–8
differentiated communion 182
dilemmas 32
discovery 67
Discovery camp 50–2
Discovery Channel 20
discrimination 78
Discworld (Pratchett) 150
disease 45
disempowered 183
disenfranchised 183
Disney 60
displacement 59
divergences 197
diversity 75
Dobrin, S.I. 186–9, 196, 198, 202, 203;
    *Through green eyes: complex visual culture
    and post-literacy* 5–6
Donovan, C.A. 121
double transmissibility 166
Dr Seuss *see* Geisel, Theodor Seuss
Dragonfly kites (Highway) 86, 87, 89
Duane, D. 155

Dunlop, Rishma: *Primer: Curriculum for
    the New Republic* 180
The Dust Bowl (Booth) 68

earth warriors 183
eco-biographies 96
eco-cultural relations 2
eco-experience 188
eco-identity 2
eco-journals 104
eco-justice 63
eco-literacy 96, 101; syllabus *101*
eco-literacy strategies: visual literacy 102
ecoaesthetics 6, 180
ecoart 183
ecocomposition 182, 185, 188, 199
ecocosmopolitan 2, 4
ecocriticism 1, 14, 48, 182–3, 185, 188;
    acculturation 18; ecology of 18;
    first wave 191
ecodrama 183, 200
ecofeminism 146, 190
ecoliteracy 7, 44, 179; visual literacy 111
ecological being and becoming 179
ecological change: adult perspective **107**;
    child's perspective **108**, **109**, **110**
ecological illiteracy 171, 195
ecological literacy syllabus 101
ecology: of fear 182; of hope 192; of risk 200,
    see also complex ecology
economic collapse 45
ecopedagogy 179, 184, 194; of imagination
    43–5, 48, 53–6, 199
ecopoetics 182, 185, 188
ecosystem knowledge 117
The Edge (film) 20
education 35; conventional 29
educational research literature 118
educational value 150
educator: cultural understandings 89
Edwards, G. 79
Eggerton, S. 121
elders 84
The elders are watching (Bouchard) 63
electracy 17
Ellsworth, E. 65
Elvish 148
Elza, Daniela 27; *if bachelard were
    in verse II* 39
Elza, Mina 27; *Forest of colours* 35
embodied learning 7, 68
enculturation 18
engaged 170
Englishness 136
Enlightenment 150
environment and place 99, 111–12; active
    participation 104; contextualizing 95–7;

detective work 103; ecological change 106–10; imaginative and relational interpretations 103; immersion and embodiment 97–8; notions of agency 110–11; opening minds to change 104; provocations and gaps 111; toward an a/r/t-e-ographic approach 98–100; visual-eco-literacies 100–2, 103
environmental activism 9
environmental agency and engagement: introduction 131–2; methodology 133–4
environmental children's literature: evaluating 121–2; prospective teachers 119–21
environmental crisis 16, 91, 185, 196
environmental criticism 44, 56, 182, 191; complex ecology 18–22
environmental developmental appropriateness 118
environmental education 3, 35, 36, 46–7, 116, 117; children's literature 126, 182; decolonization 88–90; ecocritical approach 146–8; Indigenous view 87; international policies 171; poetry-making and storytelling and 38; shifting understandings 83; teaching of 117
environmental education research 118
Environmental Education Research 171, 193
environmental educators: auto-ethnographic positioning 77–8
environmental imagination 44
environmental inheritance 77
environmental responsibility 132, 139
environmental rhetoric 182, 186, 188
environmental tropes 146
environmentalism 5; literature 182
environmentalists 7, 111
equal opportunity 64
Erasmus, George 90
ethico-political dimension 180
ethics 10, 164, 173
ethnographic reflexivity 133
Eurocentric literature 79
evaluating environmental children's literature 121–2
Evans, J. 147, 151, 156–8
Evernden, Neil 34
Everyone needs a rock (Baylor) 120
evil 31
evocative ethnography 118
experiences 97
experiential education 50
Experiential Environmental Education 95
experiential learning 200; program 50
extinction 30

fair trade 198
fairy tales 151; nature 29

family dynamics 179
fantasy 9, 149, 150–1
Far forest (Young) 154
fear 203; children's 183; ecology of 182; nature 30
fiction: education and experience of place 132–3
fieldwork 200
film 20
fire 175
Firedancers (Waboose) 86, 88
First Nations 135
First Nations peoples 77
first order dividing and abandoning 169–70
First World 196
focal practice 82–4
folklore 53
folktales 79, 191
forest of colours (Elza) 35
forests 30
Fort William First Nation 81
Foucault, M. 9, 163, 165, 167
Frankston community 96
Fredericks, A.D.: *Near one cattail* 121
free choice 146, 148
freedom 87
Freire, P. 64, 68
Fromm, Erich 138
Futurism 136

Gandalf 157
Garden of Eden 138
Gare, Arran 5
Garrard, Greg 185
Geelong 52
Geisel, Theodor Seuss: *The Lorax* 9, 163–75
globalization 6, 59
gnome stories: Bear Gully **51**
gnome tracking festival 47
gnomes 6, 7; storytelling 43–6; Teresa and eight hairy Peruvian **44**; vindictive marram-grass gnomes **48**
Gonzalez, I. 7, 77–8, 192, 193, 198
good enough 118
Good Stewardship 157
Graham, M.A. 60
Grahame, Kenneth 9, 136, 137, 139, 140, 141; *Wind in the Willows* 30, 135
Great Bridgeford 148
Great Haywood 154
greed 172
green: etymology 13; metaphor 13–14
Green Belt legislation 137
green eyes 186
Green, Peter 136
Green, Teresa 43, 48, **49**
Greene, Maxine 65, 70, 186

Greenfield, Baroness Susan 16, 17
Greenwood, David 7
Grimm's *Fairy Tales* 29
Gruenewald, D.A. 60, 64, 67, 68
Guattari, F. 189
Guillet, J. 7, 78, 192, 193, 198
guilt 172, 173
Guttenberg printing press 16

Haberman, M. 64
Haig-Brown, C. 63
Halflings 155
hands-on activities 123
Hans Christian Anderson Award for
    Children's Literature 49
Hansel and Gretel 32
Haraway, Donna 192
Hart, P. 28, 37, 111, 116, 164, 178–80;
    research methods quality criteria 119
Heimlich, J. 164
Henderson, A.J.Z. 124
hermeneutics 9, 134
heroic resister 9, 139, 140, 141
Hicks, David 182, 191
Hicks, Stephen 183, 186, 195
Highnoon (Romanycia) **38**
Highway, Tomson 86, 87; *Caribou song* 85,
    86; *Dragonfly kites* 86, 87; *Songs of the
    north wind* 85, 86, 89
His dark materials (Pullman) 138
historicity 63
The Hobbit (Tolkien) 149
hobbits 155
holistic philosophy 28
holocaust narratives 119
Home (Baker) 62
hope: ecology of 192
How cold was it? (Barclay) 67
Huber, L. 121
Hug, J.W. 8, 192
Hughes, S.A. 118
human actions: natural health 124
human community: natural community 172
human domination 30
human emancipation 140
human existence 173
human experience 55; mythic dimension 151;
    narrative 178
human potential 166, 171
human qualities 125
human rights 198; violations 79
human values 125
human violence 168; natural life 163
human-environment relationship 119
humanity 150
humour 90
Hundal, N.: *Prairie summer* 66

Hunt, P. 131, 155
Hunter, P. 76
Hurricane Katrina (2005) 20
Hussein, Saddam 183
Husserl, E. 134

if bachelard were in verse II (Elza) 39
If you are not from the prairies
    (Bouchard) 65, 66
Illich, I. 132
imagery 185
imagination 30, 36, 199; downside to 55;
    ecopedagogies of 56; educational research
    45; meaning making 19
imaginations 188
Imagined Community 152
immersion 183; attributes 111
immersive investigation: picture books 111
immersive pedagogical experience 97
immersive picture book investigations **99**;
    visual and eco literacies **102**
immobility 197
Indented Head 47
Indian Ocean tsunami (2004) 20
indigenous children's literature 7, 80–1, 90–1;
    decolonizing environmental education 80–
    1; introduction 75–7
indigenous cultures: representing and
    misrepresenting 78–80
indigenous history: cultural annihilation 77
indigenous knowledge 91
indigenous language: role of 89
indigenous peoples 198, *see also*
    Aboriginal
indigenous rights 199
individualization 2
indwelling experience 8, 36–7
inequality 63
inexperience 15
information 37
information exchange: hyper-circulatory 18
information technology 16
Ingpen, Robert 43, 45–53, **49**, 56, 187; chancy
    encounters with 46–8; *Voyage of the
    poppykettle* 7, 47, 51
insightfulness 184
instrumentalism 29
intergenerational ethics 10, 179, 198, 200, 203
intergenerational learning 88, 179
interiority 182
interpretation 101; to production 22–4
intersubjectivity 132
inventors 111
irony 90
irreal 48, 183
Irwin, R.L. 99, 100, 103
isolation 60

Jack and the Beanstalk 29, 32
Jackson, Peter 145, 148
justice 140

Kant, Immanuel 201; *The critique
    of judgement* 187
Kelly, W.: *Pogo* 163
Kidd, Kenneth B. 19
knowing 51
Korteweg, L. 7, 192, 193, 198
Kovacs, Peter 28
Kress, Gunther 17, 19
Kriesberg, D. 96
Kruger, L. 60

La Trobe, Charles 47
Ladies Home Journal 135
land: based stories 91; ceremonies 78;
    creatures of 84–6; language of 87–8;
    relationship to land 80; understandings
    of 76
landscape 61
language: endangered 79; Indigenous 89;
    power of 33
language-as-speech 17
language-as-writing 17
*Last child in the woods: Saving our children
    from nature-deficit disorder* (Louv) 21
learners: risk takers 64
learning 35; immersive 97; intergenerational
    88, 179; positive 179
learning communities 6, 62
Leopold, Aldo 34
Levenson, G.: *Pumpkin circle* 120
Lewis, C.S.: *Narnia* books 30
lifelong learning 151
Lima 43
Limeburner's Point 47, 52
Lincoln, Y.S. 118
literacy 17
literariness 82
literary imagination: future of 191
literature: environmentalism 182; meaning 37;
    play 22; selection strategy 122
literay communication 61
Little Red Riding Hood 32
Lives of the hunted (Seton) 135
local environment 60
logging 29
logos 150
The Lorax (Seuss) 9; child and reader 173–4;
    existence in the second order 171–2; first
    order dividing and abandoning 169–70;
    introduction 163–5; lifted and taken away
    169–74; matter of critique 175; method
    165–8; reading with potential not to
    transmit 168–9; responsibility 172–3;

second order dividing and abandoning
    170–1; *The Street of the Lifted Lorax*
    168–9; white space 174–5
The Lord of the Rings (Tolkien) 8, 187;
    conclusion 158–9; ecocritical approach
    146–8; formative years 152–5; introduction
    145–6; lifelong educational potential 149–
    52; places, people and environmental ethic
    155–8; this reader and writer 148–9
Louv, Richard 190; *Last child in the woods:
    Saving our children from nature-deficit
    disorder* 21
Lundin, A. 66

machine: cult of 136
MacIntyre, A.: *After Virtue* 5
McKenzie, M. 60, 132
Macmurray, John 9, 141
map-making 121
Martel, Yann 27
Martin, D.J. 121
materialism 199
materiality 190, 196
Matusevich, M.N. 121
Mayor-Cox, Sarah 50
Mazer, A.: *Salamander room* 120
meaning: collective elaboration 99; literature
    37; making 19, 51, 67, 179, 203
Meir, D. 67
memories: childhood 55
memory 54, 96
memory work 1
Metis 81; history 79
middle class 15–16
misconceptions 121
misinformation 121
misrepresentation 78–80
modernity 30, 150
Mohawks 81
Molly goes hiking (Radlauer) 120
momentum 189
Monarch (Seton) 135
moral lessons 31
moral purpose 139
Morgan, A. 8, 9, 145, 190, 192, 199
Morning on the lake (Waboose) 63, 84, 86
Moseley 148
Mother Earth 62, 68, 192
multi-lingual classroom 65
multiculturalism 7, 81
municipal communalism 156
Myhill, D. 147, 152
myth 53, 150
mythic dimension: human experience 151
mythopoetic imagination 9, 150
mythos 150
myths 191

naming 33
Narnia books (Lewis) 30
narrative 70; human experience 178; power of 37; sensibility 178
narrator: artist 185
National Geographic Channel 20
National Science Teachers Association (USA) 121
natural 18
natural community: human community 172
natural disaster 20
natural health: human actions 124
natural life: human violence 163
Natural Resource Ecology Laboratory 19
nature: affinity for 119; becoming one with 34; culture 119; fairytales 29; fearless relationships 87; first engagements 1; journaling 121; modern perceptions of 33
The Nature Channel 20
Near one cattail (Fredericks) 121
network mechanisms 23
network theory 14
networked societies 24
networked technologies 18
networks 16
new landscapes: picture storybooks 61–2
Nielsen, Thomas 55, 56
Nieto, S. 69
No Child Left Behind Act 117
Nodelman, Perry 61
nostalgia 1, 149

objectivity 189
obligation 173
octopuses 123
Odum, E.P. 20
Ojibwe 87
online children 23
oral art 44
oral storytelling 45
orality 17
Orr, David W. 30, 34, 101–4, 195
O'Sullivan, Ed 183
outcomes 54
outdoor experiences 119
outdoor learning 200
outside research 123
Owen, Robert 141
Owl Moon (Yolen) 120, 122

Pagano, J. 179
Panikkar, Raimondo 28
parenting: biophilia and bibliophilia 28; fear based 85; Indigenous 85; memories 1
parents: as teachers 29
past 175
pastoral 146

Patten, Bernard C. 19
Paver, Michelle 9, 137, 138, 139, 140; *Chronicles of ancient darkness* 137; *Wolf brother* 137
Payne, P.G. 6–8, 19, 187, 188, 198; irreals 183; problematization 134; technoscape 59, 196
pedagogical issues: opening reflections 117–18
pedagogical kinships 132
pedagogical puzzle 115–17, 127
pedagogy: actualizing 171; of place 65–8; of poverty 6, 64; remarkable 53–5
peer culture 9
Peet, Bill: *Wump world* 47
perceptual horizons 76, 83
performance 56
Peruvian gnomes *see* gnomes
phenomenology 134
philosophy 134, 165
phonetic alphabet 44–5
picture books 18, 75–7, 83; children's, decolonizing environmental education through 88–90; indigenous 79–82, 84, 86, 87;
picture storybooks: new landscapes 61–2
place 155; environment 99; fiction and education 132–3; pedagogy 65–8; teaching 3; undifferentiated space 99
place attachment 152
place identity 152
place literature 181
place-based embodied learning: autoethnographic study 62–4; introduction 59–61; lessons learned 69–71; neighbourhood 64–5; ongoing conversations 68–9; pedagogy of place 65–8
place-based learning 132; primary value of 69
place-based pedagogy 6
placelessness 153
placeness 18
planet savers 183
plant life cycles 120
Plato 165, 166, 167
play: literature 22
Playstation 65
poetic consciousness 36
poetry 36, 37
poetry-making 8
Pogo (Kelly) 163
pollution 146
polyphonic forms 76
Poppykettle festival 52
post-humanist theory 21
postcolonialism 190, 198
Potter, Beatrix 30
power paths 111
powerlessness 196

Prairie alphabet (Bannatyne-Cugnet) 67
Prairie summer (Hundal) 66
Prairie year (Bannatyne-Cugnet) 67
Pratchett, Terry 150, 155
Pratt-Serafini, K.J.: *Salamander rain: A lake and pond journal* 121
Primer: Curriculum for the New Republic (Dunlop) 180
progress 140–1
prospective teachers: environmental children's literature 119–21
Pugh, J. 199
Pullman, Philip 9, 138–41; *His dark materials* 138
Pumpkin circle (Levenson) 120

quality considerations: children's literature 130
Queen Victoria's jubilee 152

racism 89
Radlauer, R.S.: *Molly goes hiking* 120
Räthzel, N. 133
rationality 184
re-inhabitation 76
read-aloud strategies 119
reader: and child 173–4
reader response: as design 81–2
reading 134
real-world learning 60
reality 183, 189
realm 155
reconciliation 81
Rediscovery 50
regional identity 152
relations 86–7
remarkability 185
remarkable: slow discovery of 50–3
Remnants of Auschwitz: The witness and the archive (Agamben) 201
research methods: auto dilemma 118–19
researchers 179; role 98
respect 173
responsibility 172–3
Rice, D.C. 121
Rickinson, M. 178
Ricoeur, Paul 5, 9, 132, 134
Rifkin, Jeremy 182
risk: ecology of 200
risk takers: learners 64
rivers 63–4
rocks 120
romantic identification 152
romanticism 31
romanticized Indigenous people 79
Romanycia, Serenna 27, 32; *Highnoon* **38**; *Unity* **31**

Rushdie, S. 5

sagas 9
Salamander rain: A lake and pond journal (Pratt-Serafini) 121
Salamander room (Mazer) 120
Saltman, J. 79
Santa Claus 52
Sarehole Mill 153
Saruman 156
Saul, J.R. 79, 81
Saver, J. 178–9
scholarship 193
Schusler, T.M. 132
science: western notions of 192
science fact memorization 120
science teacher educator 118
science teaching methods and children's literature 116, 117, 120, 121, 126
scientific accuracy 8, 121, 123
Scott, W. 132
Scottish Wildlife Trust 141
The Scouring of the Shire (Tolkien) 153
scouts 135
screen based learning 200
screen cultures 16, 24
second order: existence 171–2
second order dividing and abandoning 170–1
Secret place (Bunting) 121
selection strategy: literature 122
self-conscious awareness 98
self-determination 90
self-education 146
self-identity 33
self-learning 148
self-reflexivity 77
self-scaffold 67
selfhood 177
Sendak, Maurice: *Where the wild things are* 47
September 11th terrorist attacks 20
Serres, Michel 194, 195
Seton, Ernest Thompson 9, 135, 139, 140, 141; *Animal heroes* 135; *Lives of the hunted* 135; *Monarch* 135; *Two little savages* 135; *Wild animals I have known* 135
Seuss *see* Geisel, Theodor Seuss
sexism 29
shape-shift 76, 90
Shark week (television show) 21
Sharpe, E. 132
Sidman, J.: *Song of the waterboatman* 121
Sky Sisters (Waboose) 86
Sleeping Beauty 29, 32
Sloane, Amy 8–9, 19, 181, 190, 195, 199–203
slow food 51
Smith, G. 69

Smolkin, L.B. 121
Snow White 32
Sobel, D. 118, 187, 188, 189, 190
social constructivism 61, 70
social cyborgs *see* cyborgs
social injustices 171
social networks 59
social-ecological frameworks 95
socio-cultural interpretation 75
solar system 125
Somme 154
Song of the waterboatman (Sidman) 121
Songs of the north wind (Highway) 85
space: denaturalization 199
spatial turn 198
species identification 120
speculative fiction 9
Spell of the sensuous (Abram) 7, 56
Spinggay, S. 97
spring 68
Squire, S. 61
standpoints 82
Steiner classrooms 55
Steiner, Rudolf 55
Steinhauer, Evelyn 88
stereotypes: anthropomorphism 124
stereotyping 89
Stone Age people 137
storied space 134
stories 191; theories 180; transformative
   power 5
story-sharing 83
storytelling 8, 37; gnome 43–6, 50, 53; poetry
   and 36, 37, 38; teaching 34
Strong-Wilson, T. 76
student responses: children's literature 122–4
Sturdavant, D.W. 101
sub-creation 9
subjectivity 189; childhood 18
sublime 187, 191
Sumara, D. 82
superstition 53
sustainability 63
sustainable traditions: cultural commons 76
systems ecology 20

teacher education 115–27
teacher thinking 122
teachers: role 98
teaching: behaviours 164; culturally
   responsive 89; environment 3; place 3;
   transmitting 9
technologies of perception 197
technoscape 59
technospace 6
television 20
Telling Our Stories (conference) 180

territory issues 76
text matching 122
texting 23
textual interpretation: textual production 15
The critique of judgement (Kant) 187
Third World 196
third-space 65
Thrift, Nigel 198
*Through green eyes: complex visual culture
   and post-literacy* (Dobrin) 5–6
Tolkien, J.R.R. 8, 145–59, 187; *The Hobbit*
   149; *The Scouring of the Shire* 153, *see
   also* The Lord of the Rings
touchstones 76, 82
Toye, W.: and Cleaver, E. 79
transmission 163–75; conception of 164
transmitting: teaching 9
tropical rainforests 118
truth 189
Tuan, Y. 99
Twister (film) 20
Two little savages (Seton) 135

Ulmer, Gregory 17
undifferentiated space 99
United Nations: Declaration on the Rights
   of Indigenous Peoples 79
Unity (Romanycia) **31**
unselfed world 36
urban children 70
urbanization 137; effects on children 33;
   threat of 135
The uses of enchantment (Bettelheim) 31, 32
Uzzell, D. 133

van Dyne, George 19
Verde, Teresa *see* Green, Teresa
video game 65
Vietnam 146
violence 29
Virilio, Paul 196
vision-competencies 100
visual 197
visual and eco literacies: immersive picture
   book investigations **102**
visual literacy 96, 100; Debes 100; definition
   100; eco-literacy strategies 102;
   ecoliteracy 111
visual representations 185
visual texts 6; artefacts 14
vocabulary memorization 122
Volcano (film) 20
Voyage of the poppykettle (Ingpen) 7, 47, 51
voyaging 194

Waboose, J.B. 87, 89; *Firedancers* 86, 88;
   Morning on the lake 63, 84; *Sky Sisters* 86

Wagner, Jenny: *Bunyip at Berkeley's Creek* 47
Wall Street Journal 183
war 45
Wason-Ellam, L. 6–8, 192–4, 202
water quality monitoring 121
Webb, Jean 19, 133, 192
Wells, G. 70
Welsh 148
westernized children 6, 15, 16, 17
Weston, A. 132
What planet are you from Clarice Bean? (Child) 3–4
When dinosaurs walked (stage show) 21
Where the wild things are (Sendak) 47
Wiesel, Elie 119
Wild animals I have known (Seton) 135
wilderness 146; benign 85
wildness 35
Wind in the Willows (Grahame) 30

Window (Baker) 7, 62, 95–7, 104, **105**, 112; ecological change 106–10; responding to 105–6
witness: authority 201
Wolf brother (Paver) 137
wolves: Big Bad 29
woodcraft 135
Worcestershire 148
words-only narrative 82
Wump world (Peet) 47

Yellowstone National Park 123
Yolen, J.: *Owl Moon* 120, 122
Young, Francis Brett: *Far forest* 154
Young, R. 178–9
youth agency 132

Zimbardo, P. 139, 141
Zoo Tycoon (video game) 20
Zwicky, Jan 35, 36

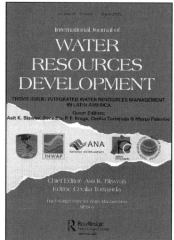